About the Author

Donovan L. Hofsommer was born in Fort Dodge, Iowa. He received his B.A. and M.A. from the University of Northern Iowa and a Ph.D. from Oklahoma State University.

Don Hofsommer has had a long standing interest in railroad history and has authored numerous articles and book reviews on the subject. He is currently doing research for a book on the history of Iowa railroads and one on a Texas railroad, The Quanah, Acme & Pacific.

The author now makes his home in Plainview, Texas, where he is an associate professor of history at Wayland College.

KATY Northwest

KATY Northwest

The Story of a Branch Line Railroad

By

Donovan L. Hofsommer

Foreword

By

John W. Barriger

PRUETT **P** *PUBLISHING COMPANY*
Boulder, Colorado

L.C. No. 76-1442
ISBN: 0-87108-086-9

First Edition

1 2 3 4 5 6 7 8 9

Printed in the United States of America

For

LELAND L. SAGE

ROBERT C. VOIGHT

ODIE B. FAULK

. . . who had faith

"When the iron rail network was built to completion in the half-century before World War I, the nation needed nearly every railroad that was constructed. Every little valley could afford a branch line. In a day when the farm wagon was the main mode of transport closely spaced lines with depots located every few miles made real sense." John F. Stover, *The Life and Decline of the American Railroad* (New York: Oxford University Press, 1970), pp. 239-240.

Contents

Foreword

The public attention now focused on the railroad problem by reason of the bankruptcies of the Penn Central and other eastern lines, along with the sudden redirection of traffic back to the rails resulting from the energy crisis, has brought light traffic railroad branch lines into the center of a national controversy.

Several railroad managements have emphasized the debilitating effects of what they refer to as "parasitical mileage." They contend that this mileage drains strength from the main body and thereby materially contributes to the anemia of the entire railroad industry. They further contend that this anemia must be eliminated lest dire consequences result. On the other hand, small communities served only by such routes have organized, militantly, for their preservation, insisting such trackage will reduce their communities to ghost towns.

The railroad to which Professor Donovan Hofsommer's study is devoted was developed between 1906-1912 as the Wichita Falls & Northwestern Railroad Company by two Wichita Falls, Texas businessmen—J. A. Kemp and Frank Kell. The WF&NW, linking Wichita Falls with Forgan, Oklahoma, was ultimately sold to the Missouri, Kansas & Texas Railway—predecessor to the Missouri-Kansas-Texas Railway—and became its Northwestern District. The Beaver, Meade & Englewood Railroad, from Beaver to Forgan and on to a western terminus at Keyes was a corollary to the Northwestern in the Oklahoma Panhandle. It was completed in the depression year of 1931 by Jacob A. Achenbach, a promoter from a small town in Kansas. Katy acquired the BM&E in that same year after a bitter contest with the Chicago, Rock Island & Pacific.

The vicissitudes of this rail network parallels the history of most small railroads operating in the nation's interior and similarly reflect the general traditions of the trunk carrier's branch line systems in the same region. The author has used the WF&NW, Katy's Northwestern District, and the BM&E as a collective model in order to portray the usual financial and corporate birthpains, the struggles of construction, the trials and disappointments incident to the development of traffic, the occasional hours of success and triumph and then the lapse into poverty and old age, characterized by continuously declining traffic caused by the diversion of tonnage to state and nationally supported systems of highways and super-highways.

On Katy's Northwestern District, declining fortunes due to declining traffic which forced curtailment of service, were first evidenced by the discontinuance of passenger trains and then by the continually reduced frequency of, and the decreased length of freight trains—moving at slower and slower speeds. Maintenance then was deferred, partly because of reduced requirements and partly because of Katy's failing circumstances. Predictably, abandonment of the mileage between Altus and Keyes, Oklahoma came in 1973. It should be noted that this was the longest single branch line abandonment ever authorized by the Interstate Commerce Commission. Only complete railroad abandonments such as that of the Fort Smith & Western and the New York, Ontario & Western involved more mileage.

Dr. Hofsommer's historical narrative is of particular interest to me because when I arrived at Katy headquarters in mid-March of 1965 as its newly appointed president, one of the principal questions pending was whether to proceed with the previous adminstration's application for abandonment of this mileage, or defer such action. Due partly to the very glowing outlook for a bumper wheat crop that year and the importunings of both public officials and the on-line shipping public generally, I ordered the abandonment petitions withdrawn. I had truly hoped—and for a while I firmly believed—that the M-K-T might be able to save this mileage. Nevertheless, the losses on the BM&E and on the Northwestern District (except for the 76-mile portion between Wichita Falls and Altus) continued to pile up. Thus the abandonment applications were reinstated with the I.C.C. and hearings were begun late in 1969. I was Katy's lead-off witness.

The rest is history and the subsequent events —and the preceding ones too—are so well told by Dr. Hofsommer that it would be merely an ineffective preview for me to endeavor to elaborate upon them. As a case study, *Katy Northwest* will be of interest to scholars who are concerned with the economic, social, and political ramifications involved in the current and future status of all light traffic railroad branch lines. It will likewise appeal to readers who have a particular interest in the history of the Great Plains. Additionally, this volume will be warmly received by rail buffs and by loyal friends of the Katy. In sum, the author has skillfully written an affectionate but evenhanded history of Katy's Northwestern District—a typical branch line railroad of the Great Plains. Correspondingly, the book deserves national and not just local attention.

John W. Barriger
Special Assistant
Federal Railroad Administration
Washington, D. C.

Introduction

Between 1900 and 1910, the United States witnessed a veritable explosion of railroad lines. This expansion represented the construction of few major trunk operations; the railroad companies were merely fleshing out their trade areas with branch lines and feeder routes. Not surprisingly, much of this growth occurred in the more recently settled areas of the Great Plains. This pattern was evident in microcosm within the Territory (later the State) of Oklahoma. In 1900, only 828 miles of road were operated in the Territory; ten years later, statehood had been obtained, and the mileage had risen dramatically to 5,980. Few of these new construction projects took the form of main routes; they were auxiliary lines and branches. One of these, the Missouri-Kansas-Texas Railroad's Northwestern District and its wholly owned Beaver, Meade & Englewood Railroad, is typical.

In the early twentieth century, a number of enterprising businessmen from Wichita Falls, Texas, sponsored the construction of numerous short line railroads extending from Wichita Falls like spokes from the hub of a wheel. Judge R. E. Huff of that city was fond of saying that only one railroad had been built into Wichita Falls; the others were built out of it. Most important of these several lines was the Wichita Falls & Northwestern Railway, an organization headed by Joseph A. Kemp and Frank Kell. Initially, the WF&NW was chartered to build from Wichita Falls through Oklahoma to Englewood, Kansas. There were no transcontinental or truck line aspirations then, nor were there ever. The line was designed to foster the commercial development of Wichita Falls and to make a profit for its owners. Indeed, the twin goals of urban economic imperialism and pursuit of private profit were central to the inception of all Kemp and Kell roads.

In 1907, the waters of the Red River were bridged near Devol, Oklahoma, but the WF&NW did not persevere toward the original goal of next season, track gangs passed Woodward but did not persevere toward the orginal goal of Englewood, Kansas. Instead, survey stakes beckoned the laborers into the Oklahoma Panhandle. The new townsite of Forgan was reached in 1912; Beaver City, six miles south, was bypassed. Elsewhere, the owners of the WF&NW constructed an important feeder route from Altus, Oklahoma, to Wellington, in the Texas panhandle.

Before World War I, the Wichita Falls & Northwestern passed to the control of the Missouri, Kansas & Texas Railway, the properties to be purchased fully by the Katy several years later. Meanwhile, citizens of Beaver City labored to save their village from extinction by building a railroad to connect with the WF&NW at Forgan. They hoped that the Beaver, Meade & Englewood, as the short line was christened, eventually would link Beaver City not only with the WF&NW at Forgan, but also with the Atchison, Topeka & Santa Fe at Englewood, Kansas, or the Chicago, Rock Island & Pacific at Meade, Kansas. Either connection would have forged direct communication with Kansas City and Chicago. Surveys were made, but the road never was extended to the northeast. Rather the BM&E eventually sought eastern connections by building west—tapping the Rock Island at Hooker. Finally, in the unlikely year of 1931, the rails reached their ultimate terminus at Keyes, 105 miles west of Beaver. By this time, agricultural production in the panhandle had grown significantly, and the BM&E was coveted by both the M-K-T and the Rock Island. After an intriguing legal skirmish, the BM&E was acquired by the Katy in 1931.

Although both the WF&NW and the BM&E were built and initially operated as independent carriers, both, for most of their respective lives, were work-horse branch lines whose primary function was to haul the agricultural commerce—especially wheat—of northern Texas and western Oklahoma. In its early days, one portion of the lines was flush with oil traffic, but the boom quickly passed. Later, liquid petroleum gas was handled from various stations, but that traffic, too, eventually vanished.

Through most of the twentieth century, the Katy was in poor financial condition, and as traffic on the Northwestern District became increasingly seasonal, Katy management grew reluctant to authorize adequate maintenance. This soon resulted in lower train speeds and in higher operating expenses. Although agricultural traffic remained high, the physical condition of the railroad finally became so deteriorated that by 1969 the M-K-T sought to divest itself of the 331-mile operation north of Altus, Oklahoma; the Wellington Branch had been abandoned and sold even earlier. Due to the magnitude and complexity of the 1969 application, the Interstate Commerce Commission spent a protracted period of time studying the ramifications of the request. It finally granted permission to abandon the Altus-Forgan portion of Katy's N o r t h w e s t e r n District and all of the BM&E as of August 30, 1972. Meanwhile, the State of Oklahoma sought to acquire this entire 331-mile route in order to guarantee continued common carrier rail service to an area already poor in transportation services. In this effort, the state government of Oklahoma was unsuccessful. As a result, in 1973 the entire mileage north of Wichita Falls, Texas, was classified under three categories. Part of it was still employed by the M-K-T as a branch line; parts of it were owned and operated by independent short line railroads; and parts of it were abandoned and dismantled. Thus the conception, the existence, the partial abandonment, the recent attempt by a state agency to acquire much of it, and even the current and future utilization of it—in part as a branch line railroad and in part as independent short line railroads—all combine to make this operation representative of the heritage of every branch line railroad on the Great Plains.

No important study ever has been made of branch line railroad operations on the Great Plains, and little has been done on branch line railroading anywhere. The author therefore hopes that this investigation will contribute to a better understanding of the impact which branch line or feeder railroads have made on the area which they served. Additionally, he hopes that a clearer pattern will emerge regarding the importance of such secondary lines to the companies which owned and operated them. The history of Kemp and Kell's Wichita Falls & Northwestern serves to illustrate an energetic policy of urban economic imperialism which those Wichita Falls promoters skillfully implemented. On the other hand, the case of the BM&E demonstrates both a successful local campaign to provide needed transportation services and a successful rally against an urban assassination plot which was conceived by Frank Kell. The interesting history of the Wellington Branch's successor, the Hollis & Eastern Railroad, surely is a harbinger of things to come. So, too, is the Oklahoma Railroad Maintenance Authority, the agency which in this instance unsuccessfully sought to acquire the Katy and BM&E trackage from Altus to Keyes. Virtually all railroad companies are engaged in a race to divest themselves of what they call marginal branches, and most levels of government are finally awakening to the important ramifications of such developments. Each of these important elements have been included in this investigation. But above all, this is the story of an obscure but important branch line operation.

Because of the patchwork history of the lines in question, and due to quirks in the corporate law of Texas, this study is somewhat complex. The problem is compounded by the fact that after the WF&NW became part of the M-K-T, few independent records were made—and even fewer remain extant. The latter difficulty is not unique to this project; it is an inherent handicap in the investigation of any branch line road. Fortunately, however, the author received unusually helpful support from a variety of sources which hopefully will make the work more valuable and readable.

Indeed, without the aid of numerous individuals and institutions, the project could never have reached fruition. It has been the author's good fortune to have found librarians and archivists who consistently exhibited interest in the project and a willingness to share their knowledge of the holdings of their repositories. Among those who generously extended personal help were Rodger D. Bridges, Director of Research, Illinois State Historical Society, Springfield; Mrs. Helen M. Rowland, Reference Librarian, Economics and Finance Department, Association of American

Railroads, Washington D.C.; Brigitte Lingk and Diane Brown, Reference Librarians, Hill Reference Library, St. Paul, Minnesota; Lorna M. Daniels, Reference Librarian, Baker Library, Harvard University, Cambridge; Vicki D. Withers, Reference Librarian, Oklahoma State University, Stillwater; and Everett L. DeGolyer, Jr. of the DeGolyer Foundation Library, Dallas. The author also thanks the staffs of the University of Oklahoma Library, the Oklahoma Historical Society Library, Newberry Library, Library of Congress, National Archives, and the Kansas State Historical Society Library.

Business records make up much of the documentation of this study, and several corporations opened their archives to the author without restriction and with hospitality. Jerry Neilson and John L. Rodda, officials of the Republic Gypsum Company, provided the minute books for the Hollis & Eastern and other corporate records dealing with that line. The entire legal file relating to the Rock Island's attempt to purchase the BM&E was made available through the kindness of Thomas I. Megan, General Counsel for that company. On the Katy and on the BM&E, every employee from the lowest to the highest gave support to this investigation. President Reginald N. Whitman and former President John W. Barriger both provided personal assistance and encouragement. Other members of Katy's official family who were equally helpful include: Karl P. Ziebarth, Vice President; Frank Heiling, Vive President-Sales; Fred R. Carroll, Manager of Personnel; John H. Hughes, Chief Engineer; and William D. Dennis, Sales Manager, Wichita Falls. Several Katy officials eventually became infected by an interest in this work and went far beyond the "call of duty" in making materials available and otherwise assisting the author. As a result, he owes a special debt to William A. Thie, General Counsel, whose assistance and critical comments have been especially valued; Vernon E. Smith, Valuation Engineer, who left no stone unturned in that department; and Albert Dowdy and Leon H. Sapp, Trainmasters, whose friendly interest and assistance were constant.

Others who unhesitatingly supplied information were Mrs. Leota Hodges, representing the Beaver County Historical Society; Mrs. George Risen, who once was agent for the CRI&P at Baker; Veldo H. Brewer, contractor of Holdenville, Oklahoma, who purchased the land, bridges, and buildings, between Altus and Keyes in 1973, and then developed a historical interest in the line to match his earlier economic interest; Jack W. Kelly, Assistant Valuation Engineer (System) for the AT&SF at Topeka, who made available all records regarding Santa Fe's early strategy for the area in and around the Oklahoma Panhandle; Professors Forrest D. Monahan, Jr., of Midwestern University and Richard C. Overton of Western Ontario University, both of whom expressed great interest in the project and offered valuable advice and encouragement; on-line newspaper writers who published notices of the author's study; and the many current and previous patrons, employees, and residents of the region served by these lines who contributed in one way or another.

Finally, the author is grateful to his wife, whose tolerance knows no bounds; to Ann Smith, typist *extraordinaire;* to Professors LeRoy H. Fischer, H. James Henderson, Norbert R. Mahnken, and C.A.L. Rich of Oklahoma State University, all of whom offered constructive suggestions; and most of all, to Dr. Odie B. Faulk who has always given the author a "clear track and a high green signal." To all of the above, and to those whom he has inadvertently overlooked, the author is indebted. For errors of fact and infelicities of style which remain, he alone is responsible.

Donovan L. Hofsommer
Plainview, Texas
January, 1976

Farewell to Cow Country

"The line on which your railroad is built controls the trade of the upper Red River Valley, and the Panhandle of Texas, the finest agricultural and grazing portion of the state." President J. M. Eddy to the Stockholders of the Fort Worth & Denver City Railway, 1882.*

On September 26, 1882, a number of early risers made their ways to the right-of-way recently constructed by the Fort Worth & Denver City Railway. They milled around, exchanged small talk, and speculated about the impact of the new railroad. As the sun rose higher in the Texas sky, the number of people mingling along the FW&DC track rose to several hundred. Suddenly they were startled by the as yet unfamiliar report of a steam whistle. Many began to shout and to point down the track where the oncoming train was no more than a mere speck on the horizon. Soon, however, the train was upon them, and the proud engineer leaned far from his cab window to wave at the exuberant admirers. As the cars ground to a noisy halt, the capacity crowd on board struggled to detrain. The mood was euphoric. There was laughter, backslapping, and handclasping. In time, the crowd dispersed, promising to assemble again on the morrow, September 27, for the purpose of participating in a "grand public sale" designed to form the real nucleus of Wichita Falls.[1]

The Fort Worth & Denver City Railway Company had been granted a charter by the State of Texas on May 26, 1873. It had been conceived as an interregional project, to link the cities of its corporate namesake. Events, however, conspired against the early completion of this task; it was not until November 27, 1881, that grading first began near Fort Worth. The tracks reached Henrietta in July 1882, and on September 21 of that year the FW&DC accepted from the construction company the last ten miles of track into Wichita Falls. Grenville M. Dodge, who had gained fame in the Civil War and in the building of the Union Pacific, was closely linked with the FW&DC and was the moving force behind the firm which held The Denver Road's construction contracts. Moreover, it was Dodge who procured land for townsites along the new railroad. He and his son-in-law, R. E. Montgomery, subsequently formed the Texas Townsite Company to hold and then dispose of lands such as those at Wichita Falls. Thus the railroad did not directly participate in the promotion at Wichita Falls except to authorize the special train from Fort Worth and to guarantee reduced rates for those making the trip. During the sale on September 27, average lots sold for between $200 and $500, although one choice business location brought more than $1,000. Cash was demanded for sales of less than $100, but "terms" were arranged for the more expensive acquisitions.[2]

Wichita County had been formed as early as 1858 but was not permanently organized until shortly before the arrival of the railroad. At the census of 1880, the population was only 433, and the stock raisers who inhabited the county attempted only a minimum of agriculture. There was a post office at Wichita Falls before the coming of the rails, but it served only a miniscule

*Cited in Richard C. Overton, *Gulf to Rockies: The Heritage of the Fort Worth and Denver—Colorado and Southern Railways, 1861-1898* (Austin: University of Texas Press, 1953), p. 107.

number of patrons. By 1890, however, the census revealed that 4,831 people claimed residence in the county, and old-timers considered that the area was thickly populated. The arrival of the FW&DC marked the end of the frontier days for "Cow Country," as North Texas long had been labeled. The unique epoch of the cowboy and the open range began to decline rapidly thereafter.[3]

Rather than pushing on from Wichita Falls with expected construction, the management of the FW&DC instead chose first to consolidate its gains and to put the modest railroad on a healthy basis. There were other reasons, too, why the Denver Road continued its end-of-track at Wichita Falls. There had been a distressing absence of construction activity on the northern end of the line, and the Texas company considered it wise to refrain from further expansion until its Colorado counterpart, the Denver & New Orleans, showed good faith. The FW&DC management reasoned, moreover, that the road could control the lucrative livestock traffic emanating from the Texas Panhandle without immediately extending the line beyond Wichita Falls. Finally, it was believed that Wichita Falls would naturally drain the surrounding area—Seymour, Vernon, and even Fort Sill—and thus gather "to itself a considerable and growing trade which had previously found its way to market via Fort Dodge, Kansas, the long established shipping point" on the Atchison, Topeka and Santa Fe Railroad. Meanwhile, the construction of businesses and homes in Wichita Falls followed closely after the townsite sale. The community was flush with optimism. The forecasts made by the FW&DC management proved to be accurate, for commercial activity soon abounded. Wichita Falls willingly waxed fat as the FW&DC's railhead. Yet the town's long-range status was not assured, as news from the Denver Road's office soon revealed.[4]

The unexpectedly rapid growth of population in the area northwest of Wichita Falls made it apparent that an extension to Vernon, 50 miles distant, was necessary to assure that the Panhandle business, which was rapidly becoming available, would pass to the FW&DC. Thus on February 3, 1885, grading began; within a few months, the road had been advanced 34 miles to Harrold. The railroad entered Vernon on October 16, 1886, but construction crews continued onward until they reached Quanah on February 1, 1887. Concomitantly, the FW&DC's Colorado counterpart was energized, and, while the Texas company was building toward the northwest, the Colorado firm pressed on toward the southeast. Finally, on March 14, 1888, the last spike was driven on the long-hoped-for Gulf-to-Rockies route; Denver and Fort Worth were linked by rails at last. The expected and traditional celebrations were held at the terminal ends of the line; but for the city of Wichita Falls, it also was a time for reflection and contemplation. Gone was the excitement of its railhead days, and Wichita Falls seemed ill equipped to compete with other aspiring communities. Nearby Henrietta, about 18 miles to the southeast, was strategically located at the west edge of the tangled forest known as the Cross Timbers. Wichita Falls, on the other hand, was in the heart of a huge prairie pasture. Additionally, Henrietta had the service of two railroads—the same FW&DC route which passed through Wichita Falls and, since 1887, the Missouri, Kansas & Texas Railway's branch from Gainesville. Henrietta thus had every reason to believe that it was destined to become the metropolis of the great north-central plains. But Wichita Falls had Joseph A. Kemp—and Henrietta did not.[5]

Joseph A. Kemp: The Energizer

"That a city may become great in its facilities and commercial service to a large scope of the country all through the vitalizing energy of one man is the conspicuous fact in the career of Joseph A. Kemp of Wichita Falls."*

By 1890, Wichita County's population had increased to 4,831; of these Wichita Falls claimed 1,987 as residents. Yet Wichita Falls had been considerably demoralized when the Fort Worth & Denver City Railway pushed on to the northwest. Its days as an important railhead were but memories, and it appeared that the once promising village would slip into obscurity. To be sure, it was hard pressed to retain its position as the seat of Wichita County.[1]

Nevertheless, in 1890, the first of many branch line railroads was thrust outward from Wichita Falls into the surrounding areas. On February 8, 1890, Colonel Morgan Jones, Grenville M. Dodge, and others incorporated the Wichita Valley Railway to link Seymour with Wichita Falls. The line was later extended through Stamford to Abilene (it is presently operated by the Fort Worth & Denver Railway). The presence of the Wichita Valley Railway was useful to Wichita Falls but was not sufficient to lift the village from its doldrums. Fortunately for the community, one of its earliest citizens, Joseph A. Kemp, was quite unwilling to accept the *status quo*. In fact, it was Kemp who initiated the additional railroad enterprises which eventually lifted Wichita Falls from lethargy.[2]

Joseph Alexander Kemp was born at Clifton, Texas, on July 31, 1861; he was the first child of William T. and Emma F. Kemp. He graduated from Clifton High School at the age

of 17 and immediately undertook his first independent business venture by opening a mercantile store at Clifton. Then, in 1883, he moved to Wichita Falls, which he considered to be a frontier town of promise. His first enterprise in the new community was a modest retail firm which readily prospered on the heavy ranch trade. He sold out in 1887; but three years later, he established the J. A. Kemp Wholesale Grocery Company. Soon the new firm was doing a business of more than one million dollars per year, and branch stores were established in several other parts of western Texas. In 1903, Kemp sold his controlling interest in the business but continued in its management. Earlier, in 1890, Kemp had helped to organize the City National Bank of Wichita Falls and eventually became its president. He was active in numerous railroad ventures from 1894 until his death in 1930, and, additionally, was involved in countless other important commercial activities. A major boulevard in Wichita Falls bears his name, as did one of the early hotels. He was especially interested in water conservation and considered the creation of Lake Kemp, its diversion dam and irrigation project, as his greatest achievement. At one time, he undoubtedly was the richest man in Wichita Falls. It was small wonder, then, that at his passing the entire front page of the *Wichita Falls Record-News* carried his obituary under huge headlines reading "J. A. Kemp is Dead."[3]

*Frank W. Johnson, *A History of Texas and Texans*. Five volumes. Edited by Eugene C. Barker with the assistance of Ernest W. Winkler (Chicago: The American Historical Society, 1914), IV, p. 1964.

Joseph A. Kemp, circa 1927 *Author's collection*

By the early 1890s, Kemp was convinced that the key to Wichita Falls' growth and development was the acquisition of additional railroad outlets. The FW&DC had given life to the community, and the Seymour line had added to its health. Yet, as Kemp saw it, railroad competition and additional routings were absolutely necessary if Wichita Falls desired to be other than a moderately important way-station town. The Missouri, Kansas & Texas Railway was close by at Henrietta, and it offered the most immediate and plausible hope. Thus during the hard times of 1893-1894, Kemp constantly entreated the management of the MK&T to construct an extension of its line from Henrietta to Wichita Falls. The Katy, however, was loath to invest in a new route which would necessitate construction between two points already served by an existing line—in this case, the FW&DC. Considering this fact and noting the economic climate of the times, MK&T management determined that the venture was too risky.[4]

However, the Katy management did not entirely close the door to the prospect of reaching Wichita Falls. President Henry C. Rouse promised Kemp that the MK&T would gladly lease and operate a line of road between the two points if Kemp could arrange to build it. The Panic of '93 notwithstanding, Kemp accepted the challenge. Together with R. E. Huff of Wichita Falls and one M. Lasker of Galveston, Kemp applied for and received on April 18, 1894 a charter to incorporate the Wichita Falls Railway, designed to link Henrietta and Wichita Falls. Soon thereafter, the incorporators addressed themselves to the task of raising cash from local businessmen; Kemp alone brought in most of it.[5]

The Fort Worth & Denver City, already serving both Henrietta and Wichita Falls by way of its main line, viewed Kemp's railroad venture with a jaundiced eye. The management of the Denver Road eventually proposed that "the Katy use FtW&DC trackage to Wichita Falls rather than duplicate existing railroad." But the suggestion came too late; on June 12, 1894, Kemp signed an agreement with the Katy. He considered that the new railroad would gross approximately $180,000 per year by diverting at least one-half of the Denver Road's Wichita Falls traffic. In view of the fact that the FW&DC had literally put Wichita Falls on the map, officials of that road understandably felt betrayed.[6]

In the fall of 1894, the extension between Wichita Falls and Henrietta was completed; and by the following May, it was being operated by the MK&T under a long-term lease agreement which called for a division of the gross earnings. This contract resulted, in the course of a comparatively short time, in a condition so favorable to the stockholders of the Wichita Falls Railway that the road acquired the reputation of paying the "largest dividends of any railroad in the United States." Indeed, while making handsome profits for its investors, the new road also favored Wichita Falls with a direct line to Kansas City, St. Louis, and to the cities of the East and Northeast via these gateways. With two trunk roads and one branch line, Wichita Falls could look forward to the twentieth century with confidence.[7]

Frank Kell, circa 1930. *Jane Kell Putty collection*

Enter Frank Kell

"It would be difficult to find a citizen whose business life has been more intimately associated with the growth and development of the grain and milling business of Texas than Frank Kell."*

During the first decade of the twentieth century, additional branch line railroads were built from Wichita Falls into the surrounding trade areas. Eventually, there were so many of these lines that they resembled spokes leading from the hub of a wheel. The Wichita Valley Railway, mentioned above, extended from Wichita Falls to the southwest; it was operated by Colonel Morgan Jones and Grenville M. Dodge. In 1903, Jones and others secured a charter to build another branch road from the capital of Wichita County. This organization, christened the Wichita Falls and Oklahoma Railway Company, was authorized to build to Byers, an aspiring community 22 miles to the northeast. The road traversed the area that later became the famous Petrolia gas district. The new company was placed in service on June 24, 1904, and was eventually lengthened to form a connection with the Chicago, Rock Island & Pacific at Waurika, across the Red River in Oklahoma. The Wichita Valley and the Wichita Falls & Oklahoma companies were independent entities which served to promote the urban economic imperialism of Wichita Falls. Yet they were also closely tied to the Fort Worth & Denver City which had, on December 19, 1898, passed to the control of the Colorado & Southern Railway. The C&S, in turn, purchased the Wichita Valley and the Wichita Falls & Oklahoma firms during the summer of 1906. In essence, then, these roads became feeder lines for the FW&DC.[1]

Meanwhile, by 1900, the population of Wichita County had grown to 5,086; that of Wichita Falls increased to 2,480. These figures indicated little growth over the previous decade and were hardly encouraging to local boosters. Nevertheless, Joseph Kemp convinced Frank Kell, his boyhood friend and brother-in-law, that the area around Wichita Falls had more to offer than any other area of the state.[2]

Frank Kell was born at Clifton, Texas, on December 2, 1859, the third child in a family of 16. He attended a private school, and after graduation he entered the mercantile business. In 1885, he married Kemp's sister Lula. Kell gave up his earlier employment and spent six months as a traveling salesman before entering the milling business at Clifton. In 1888, the area around Wichita Falls produced its first important grain crop, and Kell participated in the purchase thereof. In June of 1897, he moved to Wichita Falls, and, although nearly without capital himself, he had the backing of important friends who encouraged his expansion in the grain and milling business. Shortly after arriving in Wichita Falls, Kell—with the assistance of J. A. Kemp and M. Lasker—purchased the Wichita Valley Milling Company. Four years later, this property was destroyed by fire. In a few years, however, a new plant with a capacity double that of its predecessor was in operation. Kell subsequently became

*Frank W. Johnson, *A History of Texas and Texans*. Five volumes. Edited by Eugene C. Barker with the assistance of Ernest W. Winkler (Chicago: The American Historical Society, 1914), V, p. 2193.

sole owner of this company and expanded his holdings in many others. At one time, he was either the sole owner or in stock control of nine substantial milling units and over 100 country elevators in the Southwest. Kell sold most of these properties in 1929 to General Mills, Incorporated, of Minneapolis. Although also active in the construction and operation of numerous railroads, he always considered his vocation to be the grain and milling business. At his death on September 17, 1941, the 81-year-old Kell was president of one railroad and board chairman of another, president of seven other companies, vice president of two companies, and a director of the Fort Worth & Denver City Railway.[3]

Almost from the beginning of Kell's tenure in Wichita Falls, he had difficulty in obtaining sufficient quantities of grain to make his milling concerns constantly profitable. The most difficult problem was what he labeled the "freight rate handicap." The situation was so grave in 1902 that his mills were nearly closed. The vast majority of Texas wheat was grown in the Panhandle and flowed naturally to market at Amarillo. Kell acquired as much Texas wheat as he could, but the available supply was inadequate for his needs, and he was forced to look to Kansas for additional supplies. The Wichita Falls miller purchased wheat in that state, paid the freight on it to Wichita Falls, milled it, and then paid the freight on the flour to its final destination. Yet the rates on wheat from Kansas to Wichita Falls and on flour from Wichita Falls to destination were higher than the milling in transit (MIT) rates given to millers outside of the Southwest. Thus Kell filed a claim against the railroad (the Katy, undoubtedly) and was repaid freight charges to the extent of equalizing the tariffs. Officials of another carrier eventually found out about his "home-made" rate-making arrangement and charged that such practices were illegal under the laws of the Interstate Commerce Commission. In 1906, Kell took his case to the regulatory agency. He argued that milling in transit rates granted by numerous railroads favored the farmers and millers of the states to the north and east of Texas and Oklahoma Territory. The I.C.C. agreed that rates on wheat and flour from Missouri River points to Arkansas and Louisiana were considerably less than those offered by railroads in Indian Territory and North Texas. In time Kell was suc-

cessful in forcing changes in the milling in transit and storage in transit (SIT) rates which allowed millers in Texas and elsewhere in the Southwest to make a profit. This victory guaranteed a regular flow of wheat to his mills from distant points to the north. When drought years burdened the crop in the Texas Panhandle, Kell kept his mills busy grinding wheat grown in far-off Kansas. On another front, Kell successfully labored for profitable rates on grain and flour being moved to Galveston for export.[4]

Joseph Kemp, too, was distressed by what he considered to be discrimination in rate making. In April, 1902, he complained to the Railroad Commission of Texas and to the Interstate Commerce Commission about excessive rates on sugar in carload lots from New Orleans to points in Texas, New Mexico, and Oklahoma Territory. In the first years of the twentieth century, Kemp and Kell considered means by which they could alter rates and thereby make their businesses more profitable. Yet they were not mere money grubbers. Rather, they were seeking to assist themselves and their adopted home town as well. They were becoming first-rate practitioners of enlightened self-interest. What was good for them was good for Wichita Falls; what was good for Wichita Falls was good for them. By 1905, they determined that the surest way to assist themselves and to expand the commercial importance of Wichita Falls was not to rely on the institution of acceptable rates—although that was important —but to design and construct additional lines of railroad which would make tributary ever larger portions of the surrounding area. The construction of steel trails across the plains was the perfect medium to promote the designs of Wichita Falls' urban economic imperialism; Joseph A. Kemp and Frank Kell were the chief engineers. Indeed, together they were so dynamic that observers coined a locally popular success formula: "Think like Kemp and work like Kell."[5]

The Kemp and Kell Roads

"In 1894 Wichita Falls was merely one of many small cities of Texas. Its start upward was due largely to the courage, enterprise and resourcefulness of two of her pioneer citizens, J. A. Kemp and Frank Kell."*

Frank Kell needed additional and steady supplies of grain for his mills. It was unreasonable to rely alone on the growing areas of the Texas Panhandle. These factors, more than others, explain Kell's entrance into the railroad business. Earlier, in 1893, Joseph A. Kemp had tried to convince his brother-in-law to join in the creation of the Wichita Falls Railway, but Kell was burdened then with obligations in the grain business and also was distressed by the contemporary economic dislocation. However, in 1905, Kell was willing to and did acquire M. Lasker's interest in that railway; in doing so, he created the first of the Kemp and Kell lines. Together they became the sole owners of the Wichita Falls Railway.[1]

By 1905, railroads extended in every direction from Wichita Falls—with but two exceptions. The Denver Road ran through Wichita Falls from the southeast to the northwest, the Wichita Falls & Oklahoma stretched out to the northeast, the Wichita Falls Railway served the east, and the Wichita Valley controlled the area to the southwest. Only the areas to the north and to the south remained unclaimed by railroads which passed through or radiated from Wichita Falls. Kemp and Kell moved to close off both areas in 1906 and 1907.

The Wichita Falls & Northwestern Railway Company of Texas (WF&NW of T, but nominally referred to hereafter as WF&NW or Northwestern), as the second Kemp and Kell road was labeled, was chartered on September 26, 1906, and implied no interstate aspirations. However, nine days later, on October 5, another Kemp and Kell road, the Wichita Falls & Northwestern Company (WF&NW or Northwestern) was incorporated under the general laws of Oklahoma Territory. The Texas firm was authorized to construct a line of road from Wichita Falls to the Red River, a distance of 17.1 miles. The Oklahoma firm, on the other hand, was given permission to build a railroad "from the southern border of Oklahoma on the Red River southwest of Lawton, Oklahoma, to a point in Kansas near Englewood . . . passing through or near the city of Altus," about 375 miles. The Texas company was capitalized at only $20,000, but the Oklahoma firm was capitalized at one million dollars. The charter for the Oklahoma road was drawn at a meeting in Altus on September 20 and was attended by Kemp, Kell, and R. E. Huff of Wichita Falls, and J. A. Henry, C. C. Hightower, John A. Chenoweth, and William Hossack, all of Altus. The incorporators considered that the road could be built at the rate of $15,000 per mile, or for a total cost of $5,625,000. The stock was taken by Kemp, Kell, and Huff; the four Oklahomans on the board received only a single director's share each. Even though the WF&NW claimed Altus as its principal place of business, and although the company was chartered in Oklahoma and its directors were mostly from Oklahoma, the road—like its Texas counterpart—was clearly a Kemp and Kell line with headquarters at Wichita Falls.[2]

*S. G. Reed, *A History of the Texas Railroads and of Transportation Conditions Under Spain and Mexico and the Republic and the State* (Houston: The St. Clair Publishing Co., 1941), p. 390.

9

In 1915, J. A. Kemp (left) and Frank Kell (rnght) posed for an unknown photographer in the railroad offices at Wichita Falls. *Author's collection*

S. Burke Burnett sold 16,997 acres of land to a syndicate of Wichita Falls businessmen headed by Kemp and Kell. *Author's collection*

Kemp and Kell had declared themselves to an extremely ambitious plan, if only on paper. Frank Kell knew only too well that there was no direct route between the Kansas wheat fields and his mills. The proposed WF&NW lines would forge such a link. Moreover, Oklahoma Territory was rapidly being settled, and many of the counties through which the new road was projected promised to become fine wheat-growing areas. All of which augured well for Kell's mills. Joseph Kemp likewise saw potential in the new lines. The railroad company itself would increase employment in Wichita Falls and simultaneously would act as an umbilical cord tying outlying areas, new townsites, and new businesses to the commercial and banking houses of Wichita Falls. All of which augured well for the Kemp enterprises. Additionally there was money to be made by the mere operation of the railroad. To be sure, the returns from the Wichita Falls Railway, long leased to the MK&T, were especially lucrative. In fact, the large earnings of this road made it possible to call the small issue of first mortgage bonds then outstanding and create a large new mortgage. These new bonds were then sold in order to obtain funds for the new construction.[3]

However, their hope in 1906, to reach Englewood, Kansas, was no more than a long-range desire. Probably Kemp and Kell really did not expect, in that year at least, to push their railroad much beyond the Red River. On the other hand, the promoters clearly wished to tap the area in Texas above Wichita Falls. Moreover, they wanted to penetrate the potentially rich grain and cattle markets of the Big Pasture, an area across the Red River in Oklahoma Territory.

Much of the land between Wichita Falls and the Red River belonged to a remarkable rancher named S. Burke Burnett. Burnett was born in Missouri on January 1, 1849; but prior to the Civil War, his parents moved the family to Denton Creek in northeast Texas. As a very young man, Burnett became involved in the cattle business; in 1876, he purchased the 6666 Ranch, some 15 miles from present-day Wichita Falls. The drought of 1881, which reduced West Texas to an arid state, pushed the 6666 cattle to the Red River. Burnett, Dan Waggoner, and others then leased large tracts of land beyond the river in an area of the Kiowa-Comanche Reservation known by the Indians as the Big Pasture. By 1895, the

6666 Ranch embraced 35,000 acres of owned and leased lands. Burnett's livestock holdings included 25,000 head of Durham and Hereford cattle and 2,000 head of horses and mules.[4]

At the turn of the century, the federal government ordered the cattlemen to vacate their leases in the Kiowa-Comanche Preserve. This was done preparatory to the opening of the area for homesteading. Burnett went to Washington in 1901 to confer with President Theodore Roosevelt about the matter. As a result, the government's position was modified, but it merely postponed the inevitable. In 1905, the Secretary of the Interior notified cattlemen that the Indian land would be leased in 160 acre tracts. President Roosevelt again intervened, however, and the ranchers were granted an interim period to make adjustments. Nevertheless, the Secretary of the Interior announced, and President Roosevelt acknowledged, that the land would be sold by public sale on December 6, 1906. Thus, the Big Pasture was emptied of 6666 cattle—the invasion of the plow was at hand. At the same time Burnett sold that part of his ranch which fronted the Red River, some 16,997 acres; the sale price was $289,000. The land was purchased by a syndicate of Wichita Falls entrepreneurs of whom Joseph A. Kemp and Frank Kell were the principal members.[5]

Kemp and Kell subsequently formed the Red River Land Company, cut up the former ranch land into 160-acre parcels, and sold these tracts to eager farmers. Burnett had been paid approximately $18 per acre, but the Red River Land Company sold the same lands for from $35 to $65 per acre. One J. G. Donaghey of Kansas City was retained for the dual purposes of marketing the lands and forming a townsite company. Donaghey later counseled Kemp and Kell to retain mineral rights, but strangely this advice was rejected.[6]

Even before the parceling out of Burke Burnett's former 17,000 acres of grassland, a small community had sandwiched itself between the two principle portions of the 6666 Ranch. For nearly 30 years before the coming of the railroad, a rural store owned by J. G. Hardin held forth a short distance south of what later became the municipality of Burkburnett. Meanwhile, cowboys from the 6666 Ranch made fun of the farmers who lived around Hardin's store by calling these residents "nesters." The community was officially known as "Gilbert" but was better known locally as "Nesterville."[7]

Residents of the Gilbert vicinity subscribed to a bonus for the purpose of assisting in the construction of the Wichita Falls & Northwestern. J. G. Hardin, owner of the store at Gilbert and a prominent landowner, reportedly contributed as much as $1,000 to the project. However, he failed miserably if his goal was to induce the construction of the railroad via Gilbert. Kemp and Kell had other plans, and they scrupulously avoided Gilbert (or Nesterville), which for their purposes was already too thickly settled. In sum, no money could be made by selling townsite property and farm lands in and around Gilbert.[8]

The first farm on the former 6666 Ranch was purchased from the Red River Land Company in 1906 by F. R. Knauth. The railroad was not yet in service, but when the Knauth immigrant car arrived in Wichita Falls, a WF&NW work train took it to a location near the new farmstead and unceremoniously shoved it off on the ground until it was unloaded. Before the end of the 1906 construction season, WF&NW rails reached the banks of the Red River. However, the track between Wichita Falls and Burkburnett was not put into full revenue service until April 8, 1907.[9]

The Red River Valley Townsite Company, headed by Frank Kell, owned 2,000 acres of the former 6666 Ranch and planned to locate and plat a new townsite a few miles south of the Red River—naturally, on the newly constructed line of the WF&NW. Burnett told Kell that he wanted the town named after him, inasmuch as it would be located on what formerly had been his land. Kell agreed and submitted the name "Burk," but the Post Office Department objected since there already was a town named Burke in Texas. "Burnettsville" and "Burke Burnett" were also suggested, but the Post Office preferred "Gilbert." Finally, President Roosevelt, who had met Burnett in Washington during 1901 and who had hunted on portions of the 6666 Ranch during 1904, convinced postal authorities that it would be wise to accept the town name of "Burkburnett."[10]

On June 1, 1907, the *Wichita Falls Daily Times* gleefully announced that the opening of the new town of Burkburnett would be held the following Thursday. The townsite company offered 600 lots for sale by auction. Not surprisingly, the railroad offered to operate a free special train to carry interested speculators, settlers, and observers to the new townsite location for the event. Five days later, on June 6, the *Daily Times* reported that there had been over 300 passengers on the train, "including 16 women." For the auction of the lots, the townsite company brought in a "high-hatted stentorian from St. Louis." Burke Burnett, as expected, purchased the first two lots offered, at $585 each. He announced that he would build a two-story brick hotel on these properties, but he never made good on that promise. Lots were sold at an average of one per minute. Sales prices for downtown parcels ranged from $275 to $585, while residential offerings brought from $60 to $250. The townsite promoters thoughtfully provided a barrel of whisky for the crowd; this act of civility resulted in the alleviation of parched throats, the cultivation of camaraderie, and the proper introduction of civilization to the grassland wilderness. Additional excitement was created when a bewildered rattlesnake interrupted the proceedings with his unwanted presence. The day proved to be successful for all parties except the rattlesnake, which was promptly dispatched, and rapid growth followed. By September, the editor of Burkburnett's newly founded 6666 *Star* optimistically predicted that the town, as "queen city of the Red River Valley," was soon destined to be a city of 1,000 people "if it kept growing at the present rate."[11]

Meanwhile, Kemp and Kell moved to close off the southern approaches to Wichita Falls by incorporating, on June 1, 1907, the Wichita Falls & Southern Railway Company. This line was initially constructed from Wichita Falls to Newcastle and subsequently lengthened through Graham to Breckenridge. The first train reached Archer City, 26 miles from Wichita Falls, on December 21, 1907, and rails reached the coal fields near Newcastle the following year.[12]

The Wichita Falls & Northwestern of Texas acquired over 70 acres of donated land, and it paid out nearly $42,000 for additional land necessary for its construction and operation. It owned only the trackage from its yard, north of the downtown passenger station in Wichita Falls, to the Red River. The road was built by the Texas &

Locomotives of the Wichita Falls & Southern Railway periodically labored on other Kemp and Kell lines, and locomotives of all roads making up the Wichita Falls Route labored in the yards at Wichita Falls. This view is typical. In the background, note the cars of coal loaded at Newcastle, Texas—on the WF&S. *Eugene R. Dowdy collection*

Oklahoma Construction Company, an affiliate of the railroad. Indeed, the construction company was owned by Kemp and Kell. The railroad paid over its entire capital stock of $20,000 and all of its $250,000 first mortgage five percent bonds to the Texas & Oklahoma Construction Company for the construction of the line. In essence, then, Kemp and Kell owned the road outright.[13]

The railroad immediately spurred economic expansion in the area between Wichita Falls and the Red River. Corn at this time was a major cash crop in the area, and it flowed to market via the new rails. Cotton production was increased in the area, and soon G. W. Wigham of Wichita Falls opened a string of gins, one of which was located at Burkburnett.[14]

The Red River provided a significant obstacle to the railroad's entrance into the Big Pasture. The fact that salt cedar and cottonwood trees grew far into its bed belied the reality of almost yearly floods. Then the ordinarily docile flow of water changed to a raging torrent which spread through the natural valley of the stream. Engineers of the WF&NW thus had to design and construct an extremely lengthy and expensive

single-deck pile trestle to bridge the wide, usually dry stream bed. As bridgemen labored to finish the structure during the winter of 1906-1907, graders made cuts and fills along a line of engineer's stakes which led away from the Red River and into the Big Pasture. The 14.09 miles between Burkburnett and Kell, a new townsite in the Big Pasture, was opened to service on June 10. Then there was trouble.[15]

As noted earlier, the Big Pasture was formally opened, and its land sold—for an average of $6 per acre—on December 6, 1906. At that time the government authorized a scattering of new town-sites, among which were Randlett, Quanah, Ahpeatone, and Eschiti. The first townsite was named for the Secretary of the Interior; the latter three were named after prominent Indians. Totally absent from the list of authorized townsite names was that of Kell.[16]

On October 6, 1906, Joseph A. Kemp had advised the Office of Indian Affairs that the WF&NW intended to petition the courts of Oklahoma Territory for permission to condemn a 100-foot right-of-way through the Kiowa, Comanche, and Apache reservation in Comanche County,

13

Oklahoma Territory. Kemp wrote that the new road might extend for a distance of 26 miles through the Indian lands. Permission was secured as a matter of course, although the railroad was restricted under the laws of the Enid-Anadarko Act which had been passed in 1902. In essence, the WF&NW was allowed to do no more than condemn a right-of-way, build a railroad, and install telephone and telegraph lines.[17]

A representative of the Office of Indian Affairs was surprised, then, to discover on April 13, 1907, that a number of unauthorized frame buildings had been constructed in the Big Pasture area on lands which had recently been acquired by one John Walter Field. The Washington office was advised that the occupants of these buildings were actually merchants, offering their goods and wares for sale at "railroad prices." Further investigation revealed that Field had paid $4,400 for the land, which proved to be the intersection of the soon-to-be-built WF&NW and a proposed branch of the Rock Island Lines. Government agents were dispatched to the area, and the residents of the bogus town were advised to seek property at nearby Eschiti in a forth coming townlot sale. The government agents received promises of co-operation. The sale of lots at Eschiti took place shortly as scheduled, and all lots offered were sold. However, the residents of the bogus town reneged on their promises and then took a new tack. They made an effort to establish a new townsite, labeled Kell, a short distance from the place originally chosen but on lands claimed by the WF&NW. Agent J. P. Blackmon of the Kiowa Agency telegraphed the Washington office on June 15 warning that organizers of Kell were "making an effort to demoralize purchasers of lots in Government townsite [Eschiti] and effect its abandonment." Officials in the General Land Office and in the Office of Indian Affairs were quick to realize that if the railroad townsites were allowed to survive, "many purchasers of lots in the Government townsite would decline to pay the remaining 75% of the purchase price, which would result in a considerable loss to the Indians." By June 20, Agent Blackmon learned that the Kell townsite was being platted and that lots were being offered for sale. Blackmon thereupon sought the aid of the United States Attorney for Oklahoma.[18]

The U.S. District Attorney at Guthrie, John Embry, assured J. P. Blackmon on June 24 that the WF&NW had received only a right-of-way grant through Indian lands. Failure by the railroad to adhere to the provisions of the Enid-Anadarko Act, said Embry, would permit the government to demand the reversion of the lands to the appropriate Indian tribes. Embry also advised Blackmon to post notices at Kell announcing that legal action would be brought to recover the lots from purchasers. On the same date, Blackmon asked for an injunction against the WF&NW. In far-off Washington, government officials studied the map filed by the railroad with the Indian Affairs Office in 1906. The map confirmed that the WF&NW had not proposed any townsite at the time of its filing. On July 9, Phillip Taylor and 104 other Eschiti property owners sent a strongly worded petition to President Theodore Roosevelt reminding him that Eschiti was the site where he and his party had camped during the 1904 wolf hunt which had been hosted by S. Burke Burnett. Taylor told the President that the property owners had been promised by the government that it would "keep the railroad from establishing a rival town in close proximity to and in rivalry with the site of Eschiti." They expressed a fear that government intransigence and bad faith would result in the "most gigantic piece of humbug and flimflamming that has ever been executed in this western country." What Taylor and the others demanded from the President and the government was, in their words, a "Square Deal."[19]

On the day that Phillip Taylor forwarded this petition and letter to President Roosevelt, the U.S. Attorney for Oklahoma obtained from the District Court at Lawton a temporary injunction against the railroad restraining it from surveying the townsite tract and from selling for townsite purposes the lands which had been secured for railroad use. U.S. Attorney Embry had earlier advised Blackmon that railroad officials and employees would be allowed to reside on the right-of-way during the actual construction of the railroad. While there, however, they would be subject to rules and regulations under the Indian Intercourse Laws.[20]

Meanwhile, the town of Kell was "developing rapidly," and on July 17 U.S. Attorney Embry received a temporary injunction against 46 persons who were, in his view, attempting to establish the town in opposition to the authorized town of Eschiti. Within this list of 46 persons were lumber yard operators, a barber, and even one member of the WF&NW board of directors. Five days later, Embry revealed that the railway had condemned certain lands belonging to John W. Fields, and referees had later awarded him $1,200 for these properties. The railway then had attempted to induce officers of the U.S. Land Office in Lawton to accept the money, but the Land Office officials rightly refused. In these condemnation proceedings, Embry pointed out, the railway had failed to make the Kiowa, Comanche, and Apache Indians parties, to give their chiefs notice, or to file the plats and maps as required by law. Embry even suspected that Fields was actually the locating engineer for the WF&NW. The temporary injunction issued on July 17 against those who were residing and doing business at Kell was challenged; but by mid-August, these citizens were ordered to vacate the bogus town. The federal judge who heard the case agreed that the town lots were sold illegally in violation of the Enid-Anadarko Act of 1902.[21]

The other temporary injunction against the WF&NW was assigned to the September docket of the District Court at Lawton. The case dragged on for several months, but in reality it had been decided in August when the injunction against the residents of Kell had been affirmed. During this time, Frank Kell solicited the assistance of his friend, Burke Burnett, who, it developed, had once helped Quanah Parker, the famous Comanche chief, and Parker considered the Texas rancher to be "a great friend." As a result, he met with Burnett and Kell and used his influence to facilitate a compromise. Late in the following year (1908), the WF&NW paid damages in the amount of $2,340.75 but retained its right-of-way through the Indian lands. The townsite of Kell, nevertheless, passed into history. Heralded by bold black type in the WF&NW time tables of late 1907 and 1908, the name Kell entirely disappeared from station listings before Christmas, 1908. Several years later, an inconspicuous passing track named Kell was placed in service at mile post 46.0 between Hollister and Frederick, more than 18 miles from the original townsite. Interestingly, the Post Office Department changed the name of Eschiti to Grandfield on January 21,

1909, and by then WF&NW had altered its survey to serve this "new" town.[22]

While the fate of Kell townsite was being determined, construction crews were building a railroad grade that pointed toward the northwest. In May, Kemp and Kell resorted to a form of blackmail that was traditional among western railroad developers. Soon after they had pushed rails into Oklahoma Territory, WF&NW promoters let it be known that their immediate goal was a junction with the St. Louis & San Francisco Railroad (SL&SF or Frisco) at or near Frederick. A connection with the Frisco offered numerous advantages, not the least of which was the creation of a rational means of transporting grain from the northern wheat belt to the Kell mills of Wichita Falls. On May 17, 1907, Kemp and Kell announced that they had secured sufficient rails to push their line to one of two possible junctions with the SL&SF—at Frederick or five miles south of that community. The latter option implied the creation of a new town which was bound to prosper as the junction of two railroads. Citizens of Frederick immediately saw the wisdom of courting the Wichita Falls company; ten days later, it was announced that right-of-way lands, a depot site, and a $30,000 bonus would be offered as inducement to secure the WF&NW. Such generosity moved Kemp and Kell to order company surveyors to locate the line from the Kell townsite to Frederick.[23]

The first WF&NW train reached Frederick on November 9, 1907. A week later, on November 16, an enthusiastic delegation of people from Wichita Falls and from the Big Pasture country boarded a special two-car train bound for Frederick. A cheering crowd of perhaps 1,000 people met the train when it arrived at 11:30 a.m. The town was in a festive mood and, as the visitors detrained, a "crack military band" from Snyder played a patriotic air which was accented by the unsolicited thunder of numerous but unmusical anvils. The news that President Roosevelt had signed the Oklahoma statehood bill into law had reached Frederick about two hours earlier. Thus there were two reasons to celebrate. Under the direction of R. S. Houssels, master of ceremonies, the last-spike ceremony was begun at noon. W. A. Stinson, chairman of the local railroad committee, placed the spike, and Frank Kell drove it home. An address of welcome by Hous-

A gala celebration occurred at Frederick, Oklahoma when the WF&NW arrived there in 1907. The station, at right, was unfinished when service began. *J. P. Vander Maas collection*

sels followed. Then the crowd "cried for" Kell, who responded with words of thanks and predicted a bright future for Frederick and the new railroad. A parade followed the spike-driving ceremony, and then the new county officials were installed. Finally, at 5:30 p.m., the excursion train left for Wichita Falls. It had been a gala day—for Frederick and for the Wichita Falls & Northwestern. A reporter from the *Wichita Falls Daily Times* who covered the events at Frederick observed that the new railroad would "open a rich and splendid territory tributary in a great measure to Wichita Falls." The immediate goals of Kemp and Kell had been satisfied. By now a plethora of railroad lines issued forth from Wichita Falls and tied the outlying regions to the commercial interests of Wichita Falls. Yet the long-range goals which Kemp and Kell had for the Wichita Falls & Northwestern were not clear. If they actually aspired to a Kansas terminal for the WF&NW, it was not apparent in the closing days of 1907.[24]

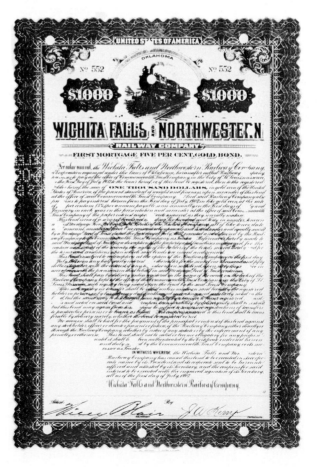

16

Truly Northwestern

"The first half of the twentieth century saw the completion of the southwestern rail network largely accomplished before 1907 except for the western part of Oklahoma, Texas, and Kansas."*

The several Kemp and Kell railroads were collectively advertised as the Wichita Falls Route. In 1908, a total of 95 miles of railroad were operated by the WF&NW, the WF&NWof T, and the Wichita Falls & Southern. Not included were the 18 miles of the Wichita Falls Railway, leased to the MK&T. All four roads, however, shared common officers and common office quarters at Wichita Falls. J. A. Kemp was President; Frank Kell served as Vice President and General Manager; and Wiley Blair (a Kell son-in-law) held dual positions as Secretary and Treasurer. M. M. Murray was appointed as Auditor, and C. L. Fontaine represented the lines as General Freight and Passenger Agent.[1]

At Frederick, the WF&NW's end-of-track was located at the southern edge of the business district. The location precluded further construction from that point, and the entire trackage arrangement there suggested that no more mileage would be added by the WF&NW. Later, when the road was continued into the Oklahoma Panhandle, Frank Kell admitted to an employee that the lengthy extension of the road had been a surprise to him. As Kell explained, the successive construction projects developed somewhat by accident. Initially, he had wanted the road to tap the area in Texas north of Wichita Falls. Then, some leading citizens of Frederick, who desired the competition which would be vouchsafed to them with a second railroad, tempted the WF&NW with a hint of financial support. Kemp and Kell then

pushed the road into the Big Pasture, collected the usual but necessary ransom from Frederick, and built the road to that point—but with the thought that it would end there. Sometime thereafter, delegations from Altus, Elk City, and even Woodward sought out the Texas railroaders and urged lengthening the Wichita Falls Route to serve their communities. These delegations, as Kell recalled, were authorized to promise donations sufficient to promote a favorable response.[2]

In any event, Frederick served as terminus for the WF&NW between the fall of 1907 and the summer of 1909. At a board of directors' meeting held on May 4, 1909, they decided to expand the road by 85 miles to Altus, Mangum, and Elk City. Accordingly the directors authorized the issuance of $2.3 million in First Mortgage Five Percent Gold Bonds to fund the necessary construction. A contract between the WF&NW and the Texas and Oklahoma Construction Company, signed on May 25, called for the railroad to deliver its par value capital stock and its par value first mortgage bonds to the hands of the construction company, itself owned by Kemp and Kell. These first mortgage bonds were secured by an absolute lien on 160 miles of road between Henrietta, through Wichita Falls to Elk City along with all terminals. Earlier, on December 20, 1908, the WF&NW, WF&NWofT, and the Wichita Falls Railway entered into a reciprocal agreement to guarantee the principal and

*Ira G. Clark, *Then Came the Railroads: The Century from Steam to Diesel in the Southwest* (Norman: University of Oklahoma Press, 1958), p. 289.

The WF&NW initiated service to Altus, capital of Jackson County, Oklahoma on December 15, 1909. *Author's collection*

In 1907, 20,000 bales of cotton had been ginned and marketed at Altus. Such potentially lucrative business was one of the inducements which lured the WF&NW to Altus. *Author's collection*

18

Cornerstone, Altus depot. *Author's photograph*

interest of each other's bonds. Then, on January 1, 1909, the WF&NW and the WF&NW of T were combined into one operating unit, but not one legal or corporate unit, under the operation of the WF&NW as the parent road. All of this served to make the bonds more secure and hence more salable.[3]

The route from Frederick to Altus necessitated little excavation, and the track essentially was thrown down on a superficial grade. Track layers raced toward Altus, and on December 15, 1909, the Northwestern began revenue service to that point. Actually, the Wichita Falls company was the third railroad to reach the capital of Jackson County, Oklahoma. The Oklahoma City & Western (a St. Louis-San Francisco predecessor) had arrived in 1903 and was followed five years later by the romantic Kansas City, Mexico & Orient.[4]

Crews of the Texas and Oklahoma Construction Company barely paused at Altus. Rather they hurried on toward Mangum, 22 miles distant. That community was accorded regular service by the Wichita Falls steam cars beginning on the first day of January, 1910. The event was mildly anticlimactic, however, for the

Chicago, Rock Island & Pacific had reached Mangum as early as 1900. Nevertheless, the residents of Mangum desired the benefits of railroad competition and alternate rail routes similar to those recently won by Frederick and Altus. Hence, Mangum was perfectly willing to accord the WF&NW a right-of-way and a bonus amounting to $105,000. A writer for *Sturm's Oklahoma Magazine* commented that "nearly every man who owned property came up and donated 8% of the assessed value of his property to secure it."[5]

Aside from the cash incentive, there were other and more important long-range reasons why Kemp and Kell chose to extend their railroad. The areas around Altus and Mangum were rapidly being homesteaded with enterprising farmers who promised to produce volume shipments of cotton, oats, corn, milo maize, and fruit. In 1907, 20,000 bales of cotton had been ginned and marketed; 54,000 bales were compressed at Altus alone. Mangum boasted six cotton gins three years later and had shipped 30,000 bales of cotton in 1909. The Texas railroaders correctly saw that there was a profit to be made by operating a railroad which tapped these rich farming areas. Moreover, construction there would correspond with the Wichita Falls plan for urban economic imperialism.[6]

The owners of the Wichita Falls Route observed that there was another vast untapped but promising trade area west of Altus. An earlier group of promoters had urged an ambitious plan which effectively would have closed off the region to additional aspirants. This group, composed entirely of Altus residents, had incorporated the Altus, Roswell & El Paso Railway Company on April 1, 1908. It was capitalized at $3 million and was designed to lay track some 400 miles in length from Altus through Jackson and Greer Counties in Oklahoma, thence in a southwesterly direction to El Paso, Texas. The project was well advertised, but like so many other "paper" railroads, it came to naught.[7]

Kemp and Kell were easily persuaded to fill this vacuum by building their own road. To this end, articles of incorporation were filed in Oklahoma City on February 10, 1910, which brought into life the Altus, Wichita Falls & Hollis Railway Company (AWF&H). This new corporation was authorized to build a road, at $16,000 per mile, westward from Altus to the border of the Texas

Panhandle. Directors of the road included Kemp, Kell, C. C. Huff of Wichita Falls, and J. A. Henry, C. C. Hightower, J. R. McMahan, and Cage Branch, all of Altus. Kemp and Kell each took 222 shares of the road's capital stock, Huff held two shares, and the others each held the traditional single director's share.[8]

The management of the new railroad entertained no romantic notions of creating a new trunk route. Instead, they merely hoped to construct a strong feeder line which would serve to drain the commerce of western Jackson County, Greer County, and Collingsworth County, Texas. In order to lengthen the branch westward into Texas from the Oklahoma line, it was necessary to incorporate yet another company. Consequently, on March 3, 1910, the Texas Secretary of State issued a charter to the Wichita Falls & Wellington Railway Company of Texas (WF& W). The Wellington company was given permission to build 15.521 miles of road from a junction with the Altus road to Wellington, the Collingsworth County seat.[9]

The directors of the Altus, Wichita Falls & Hollis and the Wichita Falls & Wellington firms —Kemp, Kell, and their associates—met in Altus on March 11, 1910, and unanimously voted to issue $900,000 WF&NW First Lien Collateral Trust Bonds earning five percent interest. These bonds were to be used in payment for the construction of the Wellington Branch, known also as the Panhandle Division. The means by which Kemp and Kell paid themselves for the construction of this line and simultaneously retained control of the railroad was as interesting as it was complicated. Earlier, on March 5, the Texas and Oklahoma Construction Company accepted $45,000 in par value stock plus $670,000 in par value bonds—all issued by the AWF&H. Then the construction company exchanged these securities for $675,000 of the WF&NW par value First Lien Collateral Trust Bonds authorized on March 11. These bonds were later sold under an agreement by the National City Bank of Chicago for $600,750 in cash. Of this amount, $568,500 was turned over to the Texas and Oklahoma Construction Company or, in reality, to Kemp and Kell. The financial machinations of the Wichita Falls & Wellington construction were equally complex but, in any event, Kemp and Kell built it, paid themselves for the construction

thereof, and owned the completed railroad. As quickly as the financing was perfected, and even before the two lines making up the Panhandle Division were constructed, they were leased to the WF&NW for sole operation.[10]

Construction crews began their labors on the Wellington Branch in the spring of 1910. The Salt Fork of the Red River just west of Altus presented an immediate problem, but while bridge gangs drove pilings, graders followed engineer's stakes which led through the villages of Victory and Duke. The Post Office Department had authorized postal facilities at Duke as early as September 11, 1890, and, in spite of the absence of rail facilities, its merchants had seemingly prospered. The Duke Townsite Company and other boosters of the ill-fated Altus, Roswell & El Paso Railway in 1908 had predicted that this village would eventually claim 3,000 inhabitants. Several months before Kemp and Kell built toward the Texas Panhandle, Duke did boast one bank, four mercantile stores, one drug store, a cotton gin, two lumber yards, two hotels, a blacksmith shop, and a tailor shop. However, as the railroad progressed toward the town, curious observers noted that carpenters were building a depot—one mile east of Duke. Emulating the habits of countless other but better known western railroad builders, Kemp and Kell proceeded to locate a new townsite within clear visibility of the original village. The tactics were similar in nature to those which had been employed at Kell, but unlike the earlier experience, the new townsite at Duke effectively strangled the existing town. Although the venture enriched the promoters, it coincidentally precipitated major antagonisms which lasted until later when an official (and literal) hatchet-burying ceremony was conducted at the main intersection in "new" Duke. Kemp and Kell were active in land promotions at the other towns between Altus and Wellington, but there were no more "Dukes" on the Panhandle Division.[11]

The Texas railroaders solicited financial bonuses and land donations on the entire line. Aids and gifts in the amount of 49.10 acres of land accrued to the Wichita Falls & Wellington, but the two roads making up the Panhandle Division undoubtedly secured sizable bounties beyond this. In any event, land was acquired by donation, secured by easement agreement, purchased outright, or condemned under right of eminent

The Oklahoma portion of the Wellington Branch was charted at the Altus, Wichita Falls & Hollis Railway and owned a few locomotives of its own. Nevertheless, AF&NW power wandered to every corner of the Wichita Falls Route, and was never restricted to the branch itself. Here proud enginemen are posing with lady friends on AWF&H #21. *Eugene R. Dowdy collection*

domain. On the Oklahoma side, "bridge monkeys" completed their work on the Salt Fork and moved west to the troublesome Sand Creek. There another long trestle was driven, and engineers wisely directed that a two-story section house be constructed nearby. When this was completed, permanent laborers were sent to live there and to keep an eye on that cantankerous stream.[12]

The 57-mile Panhandle Division was taken over from the Texas and Oklahoma Construction Company and placed in revenue service on November 1, 1910. The 41.90-mile stretch between Altus and the Texas-Oklahoma line was then deeded to the WF&NW by the Altus, Wichita Falls & Hollis Railway on August 23, 1911. During the first year of operation, daily freight and passenger service was instituted in each direction between Altus and Wellington. To facilitate the handling of the unexpectedly heavy volume of freight originating and terminating on the line, an additional weekday freight train plied the line between Altus and Hollis. In fact, the Wichita

Falls Route had expanded so rapidly that it was forced to use box cars equipped with steps as cabooses. Expansion of the railroad beyond Wellington, however, was never seriously considered. Such was not the case on the main line.[13]

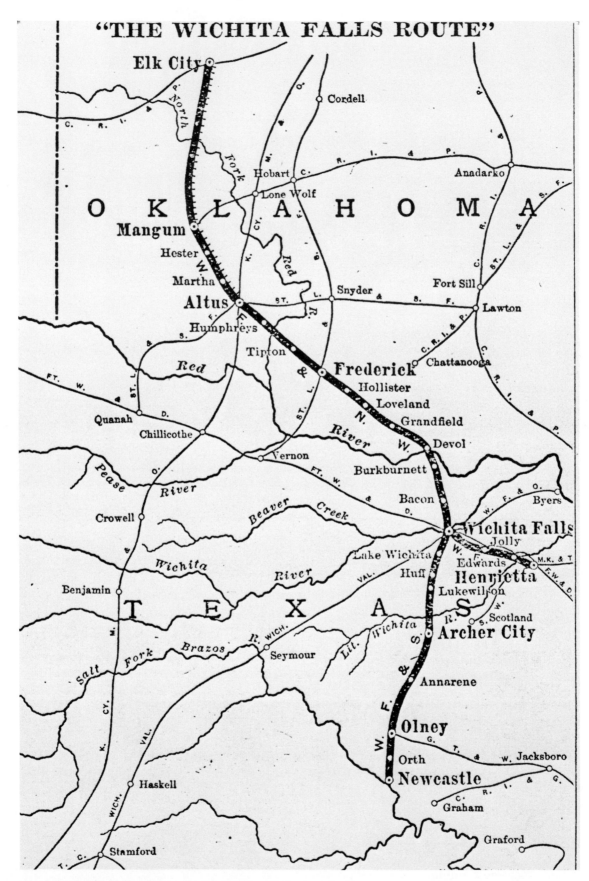

Map of the Wichita Falls Route, circa 1909. *Author's collection*

To the Panhandle . . . And Beyond?

"Forgan was the last of the purely railroad towns in Oklahoma."*

Rather than stopping for the winter of 1909-1910 at Mangum, graders on the main stem of the Wichita Falls & Northwestern pushed on toward Elk City. At the Elm Fork of the Red River north of Mangum and at the North Fork of the Red between Willow and Carter, the bridge gangs encountered difficulties which were typical in crossing the major streams of western Oklahoma. The river beds were wide and shallow, and the composition of the soils was so sandy that driving permanent piling was virtually impossible. Nevertheless, the "bridge monkeys" persevered, and eventually long timber trestles spanned both of these important streams.

Once the major bridges were installed, track gangs pushed ahead toward Elk City. Before reaching that point, however, Kemp and Kell again fostered the development of a new town designed to starve out an old one. In 1906, a religious group had organized a town-site south and west of Elk City. They named it "Beulah," after a land of rest described in Bunyon's *Pilgrim's Progress*. Six years earlier, the Post Office Department had instituted mail service to Carter, a very small community located about one mile south of Beulah. In 1909, Beulah and the original Carter effected a merger whereby the Beulah townsite survived but only by assuming the name of Carter, presumably to satisfy the Post Office Department. Residents of Carter expected to receive full rail service when the WF&NW passed through town in the spring of 1910. Nevertheless, a bitter struggle over the location of a depot developed between the residents of Carter and a

new railroad townsite located a few miles north. The new town was proudly named Kempton, and the Wichita Falls promoters expected great things for it. Their hopes were strengthened when postal service to their town was instituted on May 10, 1910. The residents of nearby Carter proved to be more resilient than had been expected, however. Much to the surprise of Kemp and Kell, residents of their new town began to pack their bags to establish new homes at Carter. When the Post Office Department discontinued mail service to Kempton on January 14, 1911, the disappointed Texans had to admit failure. The towns designed and named after them, Kell and Kempton, were equally failures. But their railroad ventures were hardly failures. Service to Elk City began on July 1, 1910.[1]

Elk City had been the announced goal of the WF&NW promoters since May, 1909, when bonds were authorized to extend the road from Frederick. Several years earlier, in 1901, the Choctaw, Oklahoma & Gulf, a predecessor of the Rock Island System, had built its east-west main line through Elk City. But by 1908, this western Oklahoma community had grown significantly, and the operators of its flour mill, cotton oil mill, four cotton gins, six lumber yards, and numerous mercantile houses all clamored for a second railroad. Delegations, usually headed by Francis E. Herring, were accordingly dispatched to confer with Kemp and Kell. They promised the necessary financial aids but, more important, they affirmed that there was a sufficient volume of business in their community to support two rail-

*Ira G. Clark, *Then Came the Railroads: The Century from Steam to Diesel in the Southwest* (Norman: University of Oklahoma Press, 1958), p. 262.

Officials of the WF&NW ordered commemorative cornerstones for several stations, including the one at Elk City, Oklahoma. *Author's photograph*

roads. Kemp and Kell were told that more than one-half million dollars in freight—including 22,000 bales of cotton, 3,200 tons of broomcorn, 300 cars of livestock, and large quantities of wheat and corn—had been shipped from Elk City in 1906 alone. Business in later years had been even better. The Texas railroaders were persuaded. Expansion of the road, they decided, would be in keeping with the general corporate goals, and it would aid the collective interests of Wichita Falls and the WF&NW—as well as those of Kemp and Kell.[2]

During the summer of 1910, Kemp and Kell cautiously commissioned the lengthening of the road to Hammon, 18 miles north of Elk City. To finance this expansion, the WF&NW issued $220,000 in first mortgage six percent, two-year notes, dated October 1, 1910. Before the coming of the WF&NW, Hammon had been the trading post of the Red Moon Indian Agency; it was located in Custer County. Frank Kell, who by mid-1910 was fully in charge of townsite development, decided that Hammon ought to be relocated on the railroad. Consequently, he purchased land which theretofore had been used by W. S. Creach as corn and alfalfa fields. The newly acquired property was quickly platted and soon "old" Hammon was removed to the railroad townsite in nearby Roger Mills County. The new town opened in June 1910; by September, it was "booming." A representative newcomer, E. B. Savage, immediately established a mercantile business. As the railroad neared the townsite, Savage did a brisk business with the grading crews

and later with the steel gangs. The coming of the railroad had lured Savage to Hammon. Its construction proved to be remunerative for him, and its subsequent operation promised a bright and profitable future for him. By Christmas, the construction was completed, and the road was placed in revenue service on January 1, 1911.[3]

The Wichita Falls & Northwestern had introduced railroad transportation to the 50-mile area between Wichita Falls and Frederick. In large measure, the WF&NW began its operation in an area that was yet a frontier. Nevertheless, later construction was more typical of that which occurred throughout the Great Plains during the 1890s and in the early years of the twentieth century. From Frederick to Altus, over the entire Panhandle Division from Altus to Wellington, and from Altus to Elk City and Hammon, the WF&NW built through a region which was largely settled and some years removed from the frontier. Such was ordinarily the case for railroads like the Northwestern—close to the frontier but rarely if ever ahead or even abreast of it.

Until it reached Frederick, the WF&NW had experienced no competition with other railroads. At Altus, on the other hand, it was the third of three carriers to arrive. The Rock Island had been in Mangum for ten years before the coming of the Wichita Falls Route, and the Rock Island also was well entrenched at Elk City when the WF&NW reached that point. After the rails had been pushed as far north as Hammon, Kemp and Kell had to do some hard thinking about the ultimate goals of their road. Should they push on to Kansas, their stated goal in 1906? Should they head for the Oklahoma Panhandle—an area virtually devoid of transportation services? Should they merely complete another short section of road to a terminus at Woodward? Or should the terminal simply remain at Hammon? These were the options. An ultimate decision, however, was not forthcoming until after Kemp and Kell had studied the economic condition of the Wichita Falls Route and had reviewed the strategy of all competitors and prospective competitors.

There long had been interest in linking central and western Oklahoma with the northwestern section and the Panhandle. In 1904, there had been rumors to the effect that an interurban line would be built through western Oklahoma on a route connecting Wichita Falls and Denver.

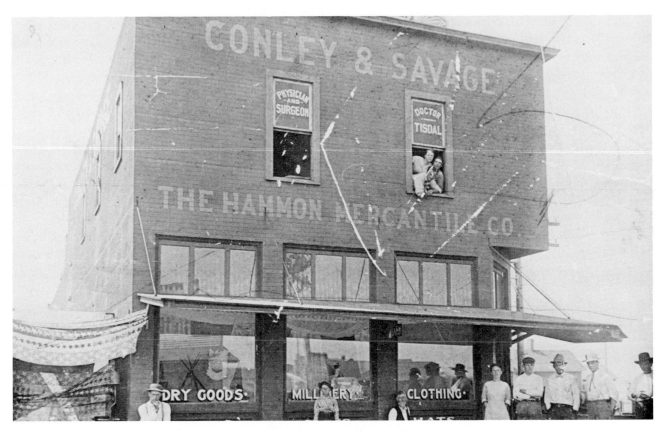

E. B. Savage established a mercantile business at Hammon, Oklahoma in 1910. With the arrival of the WF&NW his prosperity was assured. *Mrs. E. B. Savage colleciton*
W. H. Dennison's camp was located between Camargo and Vici, Oklahoma during the early spring of 1912. *Mrs. Dorothy Peters collection*

That same year, the Oklahoma & Northwestern Rail Road Company had been chartered to build a line of road in a northwesterly direction from an undefined point in Roger Mills County through the nearby counties of Day, Woodward, and Beaver, with a branch from a second undetermined point to yet another undisclosed point on the South Fork of the Red River. In 1905, a railroad from Elk City to Canadian, Texas, was also considered. A more ambitious plan was promoted by the Beaver Valley & North Western Railroad, formed on October 14, 1907. This concern was created by eager businessmen of Beaver City who optimistically hoped to build a road from Oklahoma City to La Junta, Colorado. Of course, they planned that this road would pass through their community. During 1908 and 1909, George B. Stone of Oklahoma City labored for the development of another road to link the capital of Oklahoma with Woodward. In 1911, the Oklahoma Northwestern Railway Company was devised to do that very thing. Kemp and Kell naturally were aware of both these earlier as well as contemporary plans, and they fully realized that if any one of them reached fruition, the status of their own enterprise would be severely jeopardized.[4]

As the Texas railroaders reviewed their operations for 1910, they were reminded that the Panhandle Division and that portion of the main line between Wichita Falls and Frederick served generally rich agricultural country without competition. In these areas, the WF&NW originated a large and profitable tonnage on its own lines. The several available connections at Frederick, Altus, Mangum, Elk City, and even Wichita Falls also enabled the Northwestern to become an intermediate line for a large and profitable tonnage seeking outlets to various points, including the Gulf ports. All interstate interchange traffic naturally was assured of a favorable division of rates, especially on those shipments which were originated on the WF&NW. The road was prospering. In fact, it turned an amazing profit of more than half a million dollars in the 1910 calendar year.[5]

25

Kemp and Kell finally determined that their railroads were sufficiently healthy to support additional expansion. Woodward interests offered generous financial assistance, and the area to the north and west of Hammon promised numerous opportunities for townsite development. The entire region already had been opened for settlement, and, inasmuch as it was no longer a raw frontier, Kemp and Kell correctly determined that it was ready for their railroad. Furthermore, they thought it necessary to move into northwestern Oklahoma if only to protect the flanks of the WF&NW from invasion by other railroads. To be sure, the Clinton & Oklahoma Western was already approaching Hammon from the east.[6]

At a meeting in Altus on June 15, 1911, the stockholders voted to increase the WF&NW's capital stock from one million to two million dollars. Two months later, another meeting was held at Altus. At this gathering, it was announced that the road would be extended from Hammon through Leedey, Trail, Camargo, Vici, Woodward, and Supply to a terminus at Forgan, a new railroad townsite in Beaver County. The Englewood, Kansas goal, long the stated objective of the road, was temporarily—although as it later developed, permanently—shelved. Instead of pursuing that goal, Kemp and Kell decided to turn the new line to the northwest after passing Woodward. The area west of that community to the midsection of Texas County—more than 100 miles—was totally devoid of railroad service. In effect, then, the Texas railroaders decided to exchange a guaranteed supply of grain and other interchange traffic at Englewood for a gamble that they could originate sufficient similar traffic in a virgin area. On the other hand, Kemp and Kell did not entirely dismiss the Englewood possibility.[7]

It was also decided at the August meeting to authorize $10 million in first and refunding mortgage bonds, earning five percent. Revenue from the sale of a portion of this issue was allocated for the construction of the new line. These bonds were secured by a first lien on the 150 miles of new trackage and by a second lien on all other property. The latter element was particularly important, for part of the property referred to was the long established and highly remunerative Wichita Falls Railway between Henrietta and Wichita Falls. This property alone earned $113,080.67 net for the year ending December 31, 1909. By itself, this amount almost covered the annual charges on all Northwestern System bonds for that year. New York investment dealers, such as Alfred Mestre & Company and Frederick H. Hatch & Company, consequently had little difficulty in selling the new bonds.[8]

In reality, the WF&NW issued only $3 million of these bonds, which was sufficient to pay Kemp and Kell, the building contractors, for the construction of the road from Hammon to Forgan. As early as June 30, 1911, the WF&NW entered into a contract with Kemp and Kell whereby the railroad promised to give the contractors $450,000 of its par value stock, along with $2.7 million in cash for the new construction. The cash portion was paid in accordance with this same contract. It provided that proceeds from the sale of the $3 million bond issue were to be turned over to the contractors. The money eventually was paid to Kemp and Kell on their completion of every five-mile stretch of railroad. In a succeeding agreement, dated July 12, 1911, Kemp and Kell assumed the railroad's floating debt and simultaneously took over the company's working assets.[9]

Frank Kell carried the title of Vice President and General Manager, but by 1911 he was truly the WF&NW's major-domo. The railroad was commonly referred to as the Kemp and Kell Road, but few people along the line ever saw Kemp, whereas they had frequent contact with Kell. Additionally, Kell was fully in charge of townsite development. During the summer of 1911, he dispatched an emmissary to Beaver County where, through the asistance of J. C. Strickland, 1,600 acres of land were purchased. On January 3, 1912, Kell's townsite surveyor, J. A. Innis of Woodward, platted what soon became the village of Forgan, located only six miles north and one mile west of Beaver City. Forgan, as it developed, was one of the most important of the many Kell townsites located in 1911 between Hammon and the new end-of-tracks in Beaver County.[10]

A member of the WF&NW Board of Directors, Walter E. Hocker of Elk City, was in charge of Kell's far-flung townsite operations. Hocker established a central office at Camargo, next to the First State Bank, another of his financial interests. Named by F. M. Meeks after a city of the same title in Illinois, Camargo had received postal service as early as September 16, 1892. Yet it was really nothing more than a postal station until the coming of the railroad. The land on which the actual town was ultimately located had been delivered to Peter Mason under a patent dated June 15, 1901. Mason then deeded all 160 acres, less one acre assigned to School District No. 5 of Dewey County, to Frank Kell for a consideration of $6,100. Kell, in turn, issued a power of attorney to W. E. Hocker on August 17, 1911, and stipulated that the land was to be surveyed and subdivided into lots and blocks. Hocker was further authorized to "bargain, grant, sell, and convey these parcels of property." At the same time, Kell employed J. A. Innis to survey the site; this was completed by August 31, 1911. Records indicate that prices on downtown lots ranged from $150 to $750, while residential lots sold for between $30 and $75. The development of Camargo represents similar campaigns at other new stations including Leedey, Vici, Sharon, Laverne, Ross (Rosston), Gate, Knowles, and Forgan. These several townsite developments quickly lured prospective patrons to the WF&NW trade area, and at the same time, turned a tidy profit for Frank Kell and his associates.[11]

As summer moved into fall, Kell had subcontractors working at numerous locations along the surveyed route of the new railroad. The major effort naturally was from the former end-of-tracks at Hammon, although graders were also active on both sides of Woodward and near Laverne. The Washita River north of Hammon frustrated steel gangs while bridgemen drove a lengthy timber pile trestle across that stream. Graders, too, had problems; the terrain from the valley of the Washita to Vici, a 41-mile stretch, was considerably more difficult than any encountered earlier. To be sure, extensive excavation was necessary to keep the grades under one percent.

Most of the subcontractors used outside laborers, although a few local men also were employed. One young man from Leedey, M. H. Farris, was hired by the Alley Brothers Construction Company, which had the grading assignment between Leedey and Trail. Farris' job was to act as a buyer of feed and supplies for the contractor's livestock. Mules were used almost exclusively by Alley Brothers for grading purposes, and these "hay burners" consumed large quantities of feed

each day. Local farmers sold maize, kaffir corn, and baled millet hay to Farris and to other buyers who were supplying the needs of the railroad contractors.[12]

The 18.8 miles of track between Hammon and Leedey were opened for revenue traffic about Thanksgiving, 1911. By December, graders finished the roadbed between Leedey and the South Canadian River. The railroad bypassed historic "old" Trail, a stopping place on the Western (or Dodge City) cattle trail. The "old" town soon died when its few residents moved to "new" Trail, located on the railroad about two miles northeast of the original site. Kell did little to develop Trail, apparently feeling that it was too close to his other townsite projects at Leedey and Camargo. Meanwhile, track gangs laid rails to the banks of the South Canadian River and drove the last spike at 12 o'clock noon on Christmas Day, 1911. A 16-gallon barrel of whisky, thoughtfully furnished by Construction Superintendent Hatfield, then was opened, and the nearly 100 eager laborers, many of them transient Irishmen, happily downed the welcome spirits from tin cups packed along for the occasion. A temporary wye for turning locomotives had been installed at Trail, and irregular service to that point obtained through the winter. Three months were to elapse before steel gangs again renewed their labors. During the interim, bridgemen were engaged in the Herculean task of spanning the "Wild South Canadian."[13]

Perhaps there is nothing quite so unpredictable as the winter weather of western Oklahoma. Late in the fall of 1911, Kemp and Kell, along with several subcontractors, gambled that the upcoming winter would be mild. Beginning on December 17, they were proved wrong. In Beaver County, the first storm of the season lasted for three days, and more than 24 inches of snow were whipped into huge drifts by high winds. Another storm, on February 20, 1912, was even worse. As a result, half of the cattle, hogs, and chickens in Beaver County perished. Deep snow covered the new townsite at Forgan from mid-December until early March. At construction camps strung along the line from Camargo to Forgan, the laborers and livestock suffered greatly. Most were housed in canvas tents which were typically used for mobile construction camps in those days. On January 15, another severe storm blew down the

W. H. Dennison's camp was located between Camargo and Vici Oklahoma during the early spring of 1912. *Mrs. Dorothy Peters collection*

tents at Bud Hampton's camp near Laverne. Fortunately, a local farm family came to the rescue. The contractor's livestock was herded into nearby sheds and barns, while the laborers were removed to the farmer's home by sleigh. When a son was born to the farm couple a few days later, the grateful contractor took time away from his work to care for the child.[14]

In spite of difficult weather conditions, work on the grades went forward, albeit in a halting fashion. As before, contractors on the extension from Hammon to Forgan mostly employed laborers imported from distant areas. Between Hammon and Leedey, an all-white crew did most of the work. Between the South Canadian River and Woodward, the W. H. Dennison crew was composed mostly of blacks from East Texas. Local residents were initially upset by their presence, but the blacks proved to be effective workers and eventually were grudgingly accepted. Nevertheless, they were restricted to the contractor's camps near the right-of-way. There is no evidence that blacks were used on other portions of the road. Neither is there evidence that Indians from the Red Moon Agency near Hammon ever were used

as laborers at any point on the line.[15]

On February 14, 1912, Mrs. Gertie Balfour of Camargo wrote to a relative in La Prairie, Illinois, "They have the railroad bridge very near done. Camargo still grows. Everyone thinks it will make a good big town." Mrs. Balfour was, of course, referring to the bridge over the South Canadian River just two miles south of Camargo. That structure was completed in March. In early April, when the first steam cars reached Camargo, more than 2,000 people were on hand to celebrate the arrival of the steel rails to that point. The festivities were opened by Rev. W. H. Meadows, and an address was given by Judge Harry Smith. Then came a sumptuous dinner of barbecued beef and a ball game which Camargo inappropriately lost to Leedey by the score of 13-8. Other contests included foot races, horse races, and bronc riding. The event which drew the greatest interest, however, was the drawing for a free town lot. A total of 796 people registered for this drawing, which was won by Stephen Smith.[16]

While track gangs had been laying steel on the bed leading from the South Canadian River,

28

Dennison's crew working on the grade between Vici and Camargo. *Mrs. Dorothy Peters collection*

The steel gang reached Camargo in April, 1912. Curious onlookers naturally congregated along the right-of-way. *Sue Hocker Ward collection*

The South Canadian River proved to be a formidable obstacle. The first bridge was driven during the early weeks of 1912. *Mrs. Dorothy Peters collection*

The last spike on the Hammond-Woodward section was driven during April, 1912 between Vici and Camargo. Suprisingly few observers were on hand. *Mrs. Dorothy Peters collection.*

When the first WF&NW passenger train arrived in Woodward, Oklahoma on May 9, 1912, the local citizens dressed accordingly. *Author's collection*

other gangs had been working toward them from Woodward. Within a few days of the celebration at Camargo, the last spike was driven as the rails were joined between Camargo and Vici. It was an essentially unheralded event, viewed by only a handful of observers. One of the onlookers, Walter P. Smith, recalled that the occasion nearly coincided with the sinking of the *TITANIC* (April 15). The expected mood of gaiety consequently was muffled by the knowledge of the great sea disaster. Shortly thereafter, the road was officially opened all the way to Woodward, and the first WF&NW passenger train arrived in that city on May 9. Interestingly, the train was pulled by a leased MK&T American Standard locomotive—number 24, an inspection engine.[17]

The management of the WF&NW was especially pleased to open its doors for business at Woodward. That city was then being boomed as the "Wonder City of the West" and the "Broomcorn Capital of the World." The first contention might be questioned, but in 1911, no less than 500 cars of broomcorn were shipped to market from Woodward. At the same time, Woodward claimed two weekly newspapers, one cotton gin, two creameries, an ice plant, a bottling works, four banks, four lumber yards, seventeen mercantile houses, and, perhaps most important, the largest land office in the United States. One publication asserted that the Woodward area needed only "strong men, men who dare, men of nerve and unfailing confidence in themselves and in the new country." Kemp and Kell undoubtedly felt that they met these stern requirements. Certainly they were hopeful that the presence of their railroad would serve to induce people of that caliber to settle in northwestern Oklahoma. Civic leaders of Woodward confidently expected this when they pledged financial inducements to secure the WF&NW as their second railroad. The main line of the Southern Kansas Railway, a predecessor of the Santa Fe, had reached Woodward as early as 1887; but after statehood, the town eagerly sought a direct link with the capital city. The WF&NW did not provide that, but it did facilitate a direct connection via the Rock Island at Elk City. Moreover, the new road offered commercial connections with Wichita Falls merchants and bankers, a direct link to Fort Worth, and an optimum route to the Gulf.[18]

President Kemp optimistically predicted that the entire line to Forgan would be opened for business by June 15. Earlier, he had announced that some 50 miles of grade beyond Woodward were ready for the track gangs by March 1. Interestingly, about 13 miles of right-of-way west of Woodward were acquired from local citizens who earlier had graded the route as a part of an ill-fated venture to link Woodward with Des Moines, New Mexico. The fact that this earlier venture never reached fruition probably explains why many leases given to the WF&NW in Woodward County carried a proviso which stated that the lands were to revert to the grantors if the railroad was not actually constructed within a specified period of time, usually 24 months. In the late winter and early spring of 1912, steel gangs pressed their work with vigor. Historic Fort Supply was passed in early April, and soon rails were linking Dunlap, May, and Laverne. On May 9, the construction train reached Murray, soon renamed Ross, and then Rosston, after two prominent citizens, R. H. Ross and A. R. Rallston.[19]

Whenever possible, Frank Kell used local people to assist in the acquisition of land, donations, and bonuses. In the Gate vicinity, Samuel P. Kerns was among those who solicited aid for the railroad. Somewhat earlier, a delegation from Gate had negotiated with the WF&NW regarding the ultimate location of the line. Kemp and Kell agreed to locate the road near Gate but demanded the usual *quid pro quo*. Residents of Gate agreed, and a bargain was struck.[20]

The grading contract on the survey through Gate was held by Alley Brothers of Oklahoma City. They utilized more than 150 mules as prime movers for excavators, scrapers, wagons, and plows. Most of the Alley employees were "foreigners," but a few local farmers and their draft animals were hired to make grades. Other area farmers profited by selling their excess feed to the contractors. When they were unable to reach Gate, Alley's laborers purchased their necessities from the country store at Esther, which, after the coming of the railroad, became a wheat field— as did many other country stores and early post office sites.[21]

The men who labored on the grade of the WF&NW were typical of railroad construction workers throughout the West. They worked long hours, looking forward to little other than payday and Saturday night. Consummate drinkers

Construction between Woodword and Forgan, Oklahoma progressed slowly in 1912. The construction train reached Murray, later renamed Rosston, on May 9, 1912. *Anna S. Connet collection* Middle. Mounted on a flat car owned by the Tremont & Gulf Railway, this elementary but functional pile driver drove a bridge northwest of Laverne in 1912. *The Anna S. Connet collection*. Left. A more impressive pile driver was used on this structure west of Gate, Oklahoma. *Author's collection*

These two superb views were made by an unknown photographer as the construction train worked its way west of Gate. *Mr. and Mrs. Earl Kerns collection*

and amateur poker players, they frequently squandered their wages on hard liquor and poor cards. Many exhibited "shiners" on Sunday mornings as the result of Saturday-night brawls. Local residents may have frowned on such conduct, but it undoubtedly was considered a necessary evil. Furthermore, the departure of the "foreigners" and the arrival of the steam cars would collectively usher in a new day of civility.[22]

Frank Kell spent most of his time on the grade during the summer of 1912. He received his mail "on location" and was thus kept abreast of all developments by the Wichita Falls office. By the Fourth of July, the WF&NW construction train reached Knowles and then pressed on through the rolling sand hills toward Mocane and Forgan.[23]

Kell's townsite activities on the line between Woodward and Forgan, especially between May and Forgan, were particularly successful in his view. At Rosston, Gate, Knowles, and Mocane, his new townsites forced the demise of older nearby communities. In large measure, he attempted to do the same thing at Forgan. Six miles south and one mile east of Forgan was Beaver City, the Beaver County seat. In previous years, Beaver City had been the acknowledged capital of "No Man's Land" and had hoped to become the capital city of Cimarron, a ghost state comprising all of what later became the Oklahoma Panhandle. Its citizens had long hoped for railroad service; and numerous unsuccessful projects, noted earlier, had been designed to accomplish this end. Kemp and Kell were, of course, contacted by emissaries from Beaver City who hoped to convince the managers of the Wichita Falls Route to locate their line through that community. The railroaders contended, however, that construction through the broken country between Laverne and Beaver City would render the route cost prohibitive. Additionally, a line such as this, on the south side of the Beaver River, would necessitate the construction of bridges to cross the numerous tributaries which flowed to that stream from the south. Undoubtedly, these were contributing factors in the railroad's decision to bypass Beaver City. There were more plausible reasons, however. The northern route had been surveyed earlier by another aspirant, and the WF&NW management considered it no less than shrewd strategy to close off that area to competition by building its own line

on that survey. Even so, the most compelling reason for choosing the northern option was that it afforded more opportunities for townsite development than did its southern counterpart. Thus it was finally decided that the new townsite of Forgan, a creation of Frank Kell—rather than historic Beaver City—would receive the railroad. The laws of economics would deal with Beaver City.[24]

Traditionally new townsites were named for their promoters, railroad officials, or their supporters; moreover, it was simply good politics to flatter powerful friends of such developments. In the funding of the Panhandle Division between Altus and Wellington, Kemp and Kell had been aided by James B. and David R. Forgan, Chicago bankers. As a result, the WF&NW's end-of-track in Beaver County was named for this famous banking family. The town was incorporated on January 23, 1912, but Kell's lot sale did not occur until February 15. Sales contracts drawn on that day alone netted a handsome $62,000. The local agency for the townsite was placed in the hands of W. L. Beardsley. The town grew rapidly, but it was not until September 7 that the rails finally reached Forgan. Several hundred people were drawn to the resulting country-wide celebration. A baby contest was held, and Frank Kell offered a choice town lot as the prize. Three judges evaluated between 75 and 100 babies and finally decided that Allie Riggs, daughter of the WF&NW section foreman, was the winner. That evening, a banquet was held; the chief speakers were J. C. Collins of Wichita Falls and J. W. Cullwell of Beaver City. The railroad had finally come to Beaver County. Charles M. Evans put it simply: "It was a great day in No Man's Land." A week later, on September 15, the first passenger train arrived from Woodward. By November 1, 1912, the line was fully operational.[25]

Settling and Civilizing:
The Railroad and the Filling-In Process

"I can hardly say how much the railroad meant to all of us in that vicinity. It was a way in and out of that country which gave us an opening to the outside world which we'd never had before, except by horse power which was really very slow. Now a train to Woodward opened up what really seemed the world to all of us."*

The promoters of the Wichita Falls & Northwestern hoped eventually to extend their railroad beyond Forgan. The First and Refunding Five Percent Gold Bonds which were issued by the WF&NW directors in August, 1911, provided for the funding of construction between Hammon and Forgan. However, only $3 million of the $10 million authorization was so used. Another provision of this issue allowed $3.6 million for the construction or acquisition of additional but connecting lines of railroad. In 1911, Kemp and Kell urged two new construction projects; one to some undetermined point in the Kansas wheat belt, probably Englewood, and another from Forgan to the coal fields of Colorado or New Mexico. Nothing came of either proposal, and the WF&NW never ventured beyond Forgan. There were many reasons for this.[1]

Beyond Beaver County, the population of the Oklahoma Panhandle was sparse indeed. Kemp and Kell frequently asserted that their lines were built into areas which were "unusually well settled." To build beyond Forgan would have, generally speaking, defied one of the axioms of Kemp and Kell's construction philosophy—stay close to the frontier but not in advance of it. The frontier in this instance might be defined as the area beyond that which would readily support profitable rail traffic. Additionally, the average annual rainfall in the Panhandle beyond Forgan dropped rapidly from approximately 21 inches

to less than 17 inches. Kemp and Kell had already learned that the weather on the high plains was capricious at best, and they judged that the reduced rainfall beyond Forgan was a hazard to agricultural production, hence to the profitability of any rail line serving the area. Finally, the opportunities for coal traffic from distant mines was considered insufficient to risk lengthy and expensive construction. In sum, a railroad project west of Beaver County constitued a greater gamble than those undertaken earlier.[2]

The Kansas route was similarly dismissed as being unnecessary. Nevertheless, rumors continued to circulate regarding a possible expansion of the road. In February, 1913, Frank Kell assured the Commercial Club of Sublette, Kansas, that the Northwestern was not then planning any extensions. A few months later, however, *Harlow's Weekly* announced a strong possibility that "the road from Scott City, Kansas, will soon be extended to Forgan . . . making a new railroad connection with Denver." The road referred to was part of the Atchison, Topeka & Santa Fe, built earlier as the Garden City, Gulf & Northern. The GCG&N may have entertained such ambitious plans, but Santa Fe officials saw no advantage in extending that line to Forgan. Indeed, it never reached beyond Garden City, Kansas. Finally, the capital stock of the WF&NW passed to the control of the Missouri, Kansas & Texas Railroad in 1912—and the Katy, while hoping

*Mrs. Anna S. Connet, pioneer resident of Laverne, Oklahoma, September 2, 1972, to the author.

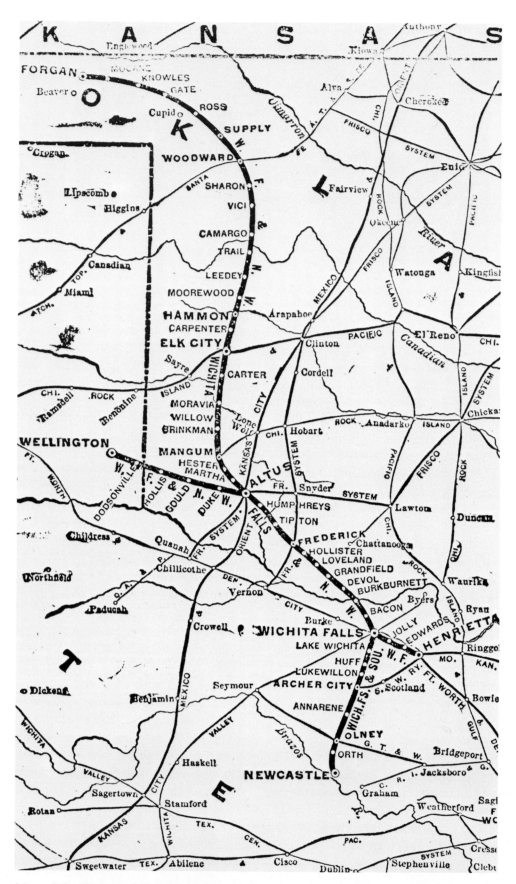

Map of the Kemp and Kell lines, circa 1912. *Author's collection*

that the road from Forgan eventually could be lengthened, fell on evil days. Throughout the period of its receivership and during its control by the United States Railroad Administration, there simply was no such opportunity. By the time Katy was in a position to consider expansion, another company, the Beaver, Meade & Englewood, had closed off the area west of Forgan and Katy's earlier thoughts of a Kansas branch had long since vanished.[3]

The civic leaders as well as the ordinary citizenry of the area through which the WF&NW built its lines assisted in the construction of the railroad by whatever means were available to them. Farmers near Leedey and Trail recalled that money was solicited from them and that it was given gladly, along with land for right-of-way. Mangum was reported to have attracted the WF&NW at a price of $105,000 plus right-of-way lands. One source indicated that Altus and Jackson County paid out $30,000 for the main line of the WF&NW and $15,000 for the Panhandle Division. When the railroad reached Gate, officials requested and received $3,000 from farmers in Beaver County. In 1912, a writer for *Harlow's Weekly* contended that towns along the WF&NW line had been "exceedingly liberal with bonuses."[4]

Unfortunately, records do not admit an exact calculation of the assistance which the railroad, its promoters, and townsite developers received. The contract between the WF&NW and Kemp and Kell for the construction of the line between Hammon and Forgan stipulated that all contributions and bonuses be deposited with the building contractors (Kemp and Kell), not with the railroad. The Interstate Commerce Commission later concluded that it was impossible to determine the amount of contributions from communities and persons along this part of the line "due to the absence of contractors records." The regulatory agency did note, however, that the WF&NW owned and used 5,068.20 acres of land in Oklahoma, of which 748.11 acres had been acquired by donation. Additionally, the Texas and Oklahoma Construction Company, Kemp and Kell's corporate puppet which built the line from the Red River to Hammon and the Panhandle Division from Altus to the Texas line, received at least $72,001.85 in cash from citizens' committees between July 1907 and August 1909.[5]

Regardless of the total amount of the assist-

ance it received, the coming of this road had a dramatic effect. Promoters who sponsored lines such as the WF&NW were loath to precede settlement. Successful builders like Kemp and Kell perceived that there was an optimum time for construction—behind the frontier but sufficiently close to profit from the "filling in process." The Northwestern lines thus arrived in the wake of organized settlement. Yet the completion of the railroad drew sizable numbers of new citizens to the area that was tributary to it. Six of the fourteen counties serviced by the WF&NW, the WF&NWof T, and the Wichita Falls & Wellington, reached their maximum population coincidentally with the arrival of the railroad or shortly thereafter. Six others peaked prior to the Dust Bowl days of the 1930s. Wichita County, Texas, leveled off in the mid-twentieth century, while Jackson County, Oklahoma, reached its maximum population in 1970.[6]

The coming of the steam car civilization meant various things to the people in the affected area. For Mrs. J. A. Moad, whose farm home near Carpenter overlooked the WF&NW tracks, the railroad meant informal but comfortable contact with the outside world. She waved her dish towel at every passing train, while her children ran excitedly down the lane to see the struggling locomotive at close range. The coming of the railroad often caused the concomitant establishment of a local weekly newspaper in the fledgling villages along its route. The first issue of the *Camargo Comet* on April 12, 1912, was coincidental with the railroad's arrival in that community. A few months earlier, Phil Hocker had moved from Elk City to Camargo in order to establish the First State Bank. One resident of that new community summed up the feelings of all when she revealed that "everyone thinks it will become a good big town." While Camargo never became a big town, it soon claimed three merchandise stores, two cafes, two hotels, two liveries, two lumber yards, a hardware store, a drug store, a bank, a butcher shop, a clothes-cleaning establishment, a pool hall, an undertaking parlor, and two elevators were under construction. In April 1912, Camargo's newspaper proudly announced that the town's "biggest problem is to keep lumber in the yards to meet the demand." In sum, clucked the editor, "It's a comer."[7]

The arrival of the railroad and the federal

The WF&NW gave life to communities such as Knowles, Oklahoma. *Hugh Parks collection*

After the arrival of the railroad in 1912, Beaver County, Oklahoma farmers increased their production. *Mrs. Leota Hodges collection*

The Floyd Nichols harvest crew took a moment from its work in the Forgan area to pose for this photograph. *Mrs. Leota Hodges collection*

government's use of passenger trains to move the mails doomed numerous county post offices. Consolidation of postal services consequently brought the swift demise of smaller towns not located on the railroad, for the railroad did tend to concentrate people in particular localities. This eventually resulted in the development of school consolidation and then in the establishment of high schools. Even at tiny Knowles, taxpayers willingly supported a high school. Though it boasted only three teachers, it had a gymnasium, "where in basketball games, the boys and girls learn sportsmanship and patriotism." Consolidated schools also encouraged literary programs, spelling bees, debates, and ciphering matches.[8]

The construction and operation of the WF&NW immediately created numerous commercial opportunities. E. B. Savage built a brick building to house his newly established mercantile business at Hammon shortly before the arrival there of the Wichita Falls Route. Later he opened a similar store at Forgan, also on the WF&NW, when the road reached that point. Frank Nichols arrived in Forgan from Milwaukee just prior to the coming of the steam cars to that community and began working in a bank. By 1929, he owned stores in Beaver, Forgan, and Keyes. W. Guy Parker of Alva, Oklahoma, heard that the railroad was building west; he applied for and received a

charter for a new bank at Knowles. Neal Briggs took a WF&NW train from Vici to Mocane where he bought a lot for a new store and another for a new home. At Gate, William E. Bishop started a dray line and hauled freight "from the depot out over the country." Meanwhile, when the railroad arrived, Fred Wells moved his store from northeast of Gate to Knowles. The initiation of rail service even provoked economic opportunities for residents some distance removed. At La Kemp, a landlocked village south of Beaver, J. D. Key had long been active as a freighter plying the trails to distant railroad towns on the Santa Fe. When the WF&NW reached Forgan, Key began freighting north to the new railroad.[9]

Perhaps residents of Beaver County appreciated the advent of railroad transportation more than the people of any other area served by the Northwestern. The region had been settled largely by people who arrived there from midwestern states by way of the railheads located at Liberal, Meade, and Englewood, all to the north in Kansas. Until the Rock Island extended its Golden State Route southwest from Liberal in 1902, there was no rail service whatsoever in No Man's Land. The citizens of Beaver County thus had to procure their necessities from outside the Oklahoma Panhandle. This meant overland trips of two to three days duration; for some, these

This busy scene was Forgan shortly after the arrival there of the steamcar civilization. Note the many farmers who have brought their broomcorn to be shipped on the WF&NW.
Mrs. Leota Hodges collection

were made as often as once or twice a month. Some farmers, like W. T. Meade, were so enthusiastic about the arrival of the Northwestern that they sold their farms and moved to Forgan.[10]

Sears & Roebuck and Montgomery Ward catalogues had long provided amusement and entertainment for citizens of No Man's Land. The availability of express service and the improved mail service, which attended the initiation of rail transportation to Forgan, encouraged catalogue sales by these and other major mail-order houses. But many of the items listed in the "dream books" could now be purchased in the stores at Forgan. Brand names such as Horse Shoe Tobacco, Lion Head Coffee, Light's Best Flour, "KC" Baking Powder, and Keen Kutter Knives soon became familiar to all Beaver County consumers.[11]

Forgan was a lively place by 1913. Because it was a railhead in a burgeoning area, commercial traffic flowed naturally to it. Two lumber yards, the Big Jo Lumber Company and the Home Lumber & Supply Company, were furnishing building materials, and already a medical doctor and a veterinarian had begun to practice there. The Forgan Trading Company offered straw hats at 15¢ each, dress shirts at 35¢ each, and "Rockford Sox" at four pairs for 25¢. C. L. Moon, proprietor of the Elk Cafe, served family-style meals at 35¢ each or $4.50 per week. Up the street, the Forgan Hotel advertised itself as "the traveling man's home and the farmer's friend." Moreover, it sent free hacks to the depot at the arrival of every train. And there was a Women's

Christian Temperance Union chapter. Civilization had truly come to the Oklahoma Panhandle.[12]

The Wichita Falls & Northwestern Railway

"It's a dirt track and a country railway."*

By the time the rails reached Forgan, the aggregate length of the Wichita Falls & Northwestern and its antecedents—the WF&NWof T, the Altus, Wichita Falls & Hollis, and the Wichita Falls and Wellington—amounted to 359.3 miles of railroad. Additionally, the WF&NW leased trackage from the Wichita Falls passenger station to its North Yard. The road passed through the North Texas Plains and the Big Pasture, skirted the Wichita Mountains, and finally reached the High Plains. Between its terminal at Wichita Falls, Texas, on the south and its northern terminal in Beaver County, Oklahoma, there was an approximately 1,500-foot rise in elevation. Within the Northwestern's trade zone, the average annual rainfall ranged from 30 inches near the Red River to less than 20 inches at Forgan. The lines of the Northwestern passed through generally open, rolling country where the top soils varied from sand to sandy loam and sandy clay. The normal annual temperatures ranged from 57 to 63 degrees. The winter average varied from 25 to 30 degrees, but the summer norm was 80 degrees. Much of the territory was then and is now devoted to farming and ranching.[1]

The general route which the road took between Wichita Falls and Altus was toward the northwest. The Wellington Branch reached the Texas border on a route which pointed almost straight west from Altus, then headed northwestward into Wellington. On the main line above Altus, the road stretched northward to Woodward. This part of the railroad became known informally as "the long-barrel." Trainmen came to call the remaining section, between Woodward and Forgan, "the top end." It ran on a northwesterly course from Woodward. Although Kemp and Kell built most of the Northwestern through flat or rolling country, there were some notably hilly areas also, such as those between Moorewood and Supply and between Knowles and Forgan. Because all major streams in the area ran at right angles to the path of the railroad, a number of expensive, long, timber trestle bridges were necessary to carry the road to its final destinations. The ruling grades were: in both directions from the South Canadian River near Camargo; northbound for ten miles in a hilly area around Gate; and southbound for nearly four miles near Forgan. The maximum grades were 1.2 percent northbound and 0.7 percent southbound.[2]

Kemp and Kell, in keeping with their usual custom, spent little money on grading and excavation. Thus the track was laid generally on low fills, in shallow cuts, and often on the natural ground. Except in rare cases, ballast other than dirt was not used. The main track on all lines was laid chiefly with new rail, two-thirds of which was 65 pound steel (per yard), and the remainder was 60 pound. Much of the rail on the Northwestern was rolled by two companies, Colorado Fuel & Iron and the Illinois Steel Company. Originally the WF&NW owned certain wires on the pole lines which had been built along the railroad right-of-way by the Pioneer Telephone & Telegraph and by the Southwest Telegraph & Telephone companies. On June 4, 1913, however, a contract was drawn whereby the Western Union

*C. P. Parks, former WF&NW and M-K-T conductor, Altus, Oklahoma, personal interview with the author, November 17, 1972.

41

Builder's photo of WF&NW #104, a dainty 4-4-0. *Avery Von Blon collection*

Company acquired these poles and wires. Joint operation and utilization by Western Union and the railroad followed thereafter. Eventually a dispatcher's phone also was installed between Wichita Falls and Altus, but Morse communication was employed on all lines of the Northwestern.[3]

Most of the depot buildings on the WF&NW were typical wood frame combination stations, but substantial station buildings were erected at Grandfield, Tipton, Altus, Elk City, Woodward, and later at Mangum. At Wichita Falls, the Northwestern shared ownership of the beautifully ornate Union Station. This fine edifice was built of brick, concrete, stone, and plaster at a cost of $100,000. It was placed in service during 1910. Its main floor contained a baggage room, mail room, smoking room, colored waiting room, general waiting room, ticket office, newsstand, kitchen, dining room, and ladies waiting room. The second floor contained offices for railroad officials. Numerals measuring 14 inches each ringed the 6'6" faces of a mechanical clock housed in the clock tower, which properly adorned one corner of the structure. Small wonder that the building was the pride of the city. Close by was the less impressive but totally functional Kemp and Kell Office Building. Its cornerstone proudly listed the current officials of the Wichita Falls Route.[4]

In 1907, the WF&NW owned two locomotives, two passenger coaches, and fifteen freight cars. Five years later, the road stabled a total of 17 engines in its roundhouses, and it owned 12 passenger and mail cars plus 600 freight cars. During its corporate lifetime, the WF&NW and allied lines owned a total of 18 locomotives, of which all save one were purchased new from the Baldwin Locomotive Company. All of these Northwestern engines had low tractive effort ratings and all had relatively short lives. The last one disappeared from the locomotive roster of the Missouri-Kansas-Texas Lines in 1932. Frequently there was more traffic on the Wichita Falls Route than could be handled by its own cars and pulled by its own locomotives. Thus Kemp and Kell had to borrow or lease power from other roads; for example, the first passenger train to Woodward on the Northwestern was actually drawn by a locomotive belonging to the MK&T.[5]

Even before the railroad had been accepted by the WF&NW from the construction company, Frank Kell allowed people to ride out from Wichita Falls on the construction trains. By mid-1907, the WF&NW System offered regular passenger service between Wichita Falls and Kell. Train No. 2 left Wichita Falls daily-except-Sunday at 6:00 a.m. and arrived at Kell, 27.6 miles distant, at 8:00 a.m.; Train No. 1 was due back in Wichita Falls at 11:45 a.m. After the road

During its corporate lifetime, the WF&NW owned a total of 18 locomotives, including this well-groomed 2-8-0. *Eugene R. Dowdy collection*

reached Frederick, two daily-except-Sunday trains provided round-trip service. This pattern continued as the road was lengthened to Hammon, although by then the trains were operated on a seven-day-a-week basis. In 1911, a daily round trip was operated over the Panhandle Division to Wellington, a service supplemented by a daily-except-Sunday "mixed" train. On January 22, 1911, daily Tourist Sleeper service was instituted from Fort Worth to Elk City via Wichita Falls and the Fort Worth & Denver City. Sleeper service was upgraded and the route lengthened on August 6, 1911, when the WF&NW announced that "Trains 3 and 4, with First Class Day Coach, Modern Chair Car and Pullman Standard Sleeper" would be operated between Hammon, Oklahoma, and Dallas, Texas, via Wichita Falls and the MK&T. However, this sleeping car service lasted but a short while. Meanwhile, passenger service was extended each time another section of track was placed in service so that by November 1, 1912, WF&NW passenger trains operated over the entire distance between Wichita Falls and Forgan. Before World War I, double daily round trip service obtained between Wichita Falls and Elk City, while a single train serviced the line above Elk City to Forgan.[6]

The Post Office Department authorized Railway Post Office service over the WF&NW between Wichita Falls and Frederick in 1909. Subsequent authorizations lengthened the RPO route almost as quickly as the railroad opened new sections of its line. Enroute distribution was also provided on the Panhandle Division as soon as that road was opened for traffic in 1910. Express service on all lines of the Northwestern was provided by the American Express Company.[7]

There were occasional special trains; for example, the railroad advertised reduced rates on a special excursion train to a ball game in Wichita Falls during 1911. This train of 18 to 20 cars began picking up passengers at Hammon, and before long the cars were overflowing. Some of these patrons missed the ball game but instead repaired to a friendly saloon. Railroad officials later were compelled to place about 50 drunks into a baggage car before the return trip began. Shortly after the train left Wichita Falls, a fight broke out in the baggage car between drunken residents of Frederick and their equally drunken neighbors from Altus. At Burkburnett, the crew stopped the train, picked up an empty box car, and herded the tipsy Frederickites into it. When the train finally reached Frederick, the box car load of inebriates was merely set out on a siding. The intoxicated Altusites, meanwhile, continued their homeward journey in the baggage car.[8]

43

The location: Hammon, Oklahoma. The date: July, 1911. On the wagon are Dr. Laird, Mrs. Laird, and Mignon Laird. Mignon sang and gave readings as the Laird troupe traveled across the country to its engagements. *Mrs. E. B. Savage collection*

Businessmen found great utility in the passenger services made available to them by the WF&NW. They could use the regularly scheduled trains to go to market in distant cities. Those who wished to go to the state capital of Oklahoma used the Northwestern as far as Frederick, Altus, Mangum, or Elk City where they changed trains for Oklahoma City. Residents of the smaller communities used the WF&NW in order to go shopping in Elk City, Woodward, Altus, and the other larger cities on the line. A Dr. Laird frequently provided "medicine shows" at Hammon and other stations on the line. Laird and his family traveled in a private car, which was placed on a siding wherever his show was booked. Mrs. Nellie Bates, a hotel owner at Hammon, sent her boys to meet every train with the idea of attracting guests for her Valley View Hotel. A merchant in the same community shipped locally purchased eggs to a Wichita Falls hotel via express. At all stations, people gathered at the depot to mail last minute letters on the RPO car. The appearance of the Postmaster with his cartload of mail heralded the imminent arrival of the "passenger."[9]

Countless cream cans were loaded aboard the baggage and express cars at stations all along the Northwestern route. At Vici, shipments billed to major creameries at Elk City and Woodward were particularly heavy on Saturdays. Liquid shipments of another kind frequently were sent to the same station, especially just before the Fourth of July and the Christmas holidays. Until the passage in 1917 of Oklahoma's "Bone Dry Law" which prohibited the receipt or even possession of intoxicating liquor transported by common carriers, the WF&NW brought large quantities of fine whisky to the thirsty of western Oklahoma. These spirits were forwarded in single glass bottles protected by cardboard containers. More than 100 such prepaid packages arrived at Vici in anticipation of the Fourth of July celebration in 1913. Most of it came from dealers in far off Wichita Falls, and was delivered by the railroad jokingly referred to as the "Whisky-taw Falls & Northwestern."[10]

Among those aboard the first passenger train into Gate were Mr. and Mrs. William Bishop and their daughter Camille. Unhappily,

Freight bill from Camargo; May 13, 1913. Note the ticket dater impression, lower left. *Author's collection*

the roadbed was not yet properly surfaced and the train swayed from side to side so violently that Camille became ill. The Northwestern's roadbed was considerably improved by the time Walter R. Smith left Vici in search of a college degree at Oklahoma A&M. He used the local road to Woodward, the AT&SF to Waynoka, the Frisco to Pawnee, and the AT&SF to Stillwater. It took 24 hours to complete the journey. Other aspiring young men boarded the cars of the Northwestern as they left home for the first time. Many were headed for the grain harvest, wherever that was. Others were merely seeking the "Big Rock Candy Mountain."[11]

Miss Zella Alkire rode the train from Woodward to Elk City, changing there to the Rock Island for a subsequent journey to Oklahoma City where she passed the state pharmacy examination. On the return trip, her fiance, Dr. Charles Rogers, met her at Woodward, and they were married before returning to Knowles on the WF&NW. Dr. Rogers frequently sent patients to the hospitals at Woodward and used the train himself when he returned to St. Louis for postgraduate work. At

Forgan, the local agent advertised the Northwestern as the "Direct Route and Connection to All Points in Texas and the Southwest." The WF&NW also featured "low round trip rates to Gulf Coast points" as well as "Summer Tourist Rates to the Northern Lakes." The company hardly needed to advertise. It carried 31,125 patrons in fiscal 1909 and 248,048 passengers in fiscal 1912.[12]

In an age before hardtop roads and motor trucks, almost every item moved from manufacturer to consumer by rail. Vast amounts of inbound freight came to all stations on the Northwestern, especially in the days after construction when the towns were "building up" and the country was "filling in." At Camargo, the operator of a general store in 1913 received a shipment that included one-half box of lemons, one-half box of oranges, and five boxes of apples. The consignment was originated by the Santa Fe at Wichita, Kansas, and given to the Northwestern at Woodward. The total transportation bill was $1.85. A month later the same merchant received 10 sacks of potatoes and one sack of cabbage from a wholesaler at Woodward. The transportation bill was

45

$1.97. Farther north, at Knowles, the depot freight room was frequently full of recently arrived goods, including hominy in five-gallon drums, bulging bags of coffee, stalks of bananas, barrels of salt fish, boxes of crackers, containers of vinegar, and bottles of liquor. Dr. Charles Rogers owned one of the few automobiles at Knowles, and all of the gasoline he used had to be shipped in by rail. Indeed, the Doctor's Model T had arrived in a WF&NW box car. The heavy volume of less-than-carload (LCL) business at Knowles gave work to three draymen who hauled freight to and from the depot.[13]

Freight in carload lots, however, provided the main income for the WF&NW. Between Wichita Falls and the Red River, large amounts of corn, wheat, and cotton were grown by area farmers. These grain commodities were handled by two elevators at Burkburnett: Hunt & Rigsby and Kell's Wichita Mill & Elevator Company. The sidings at that point were always filled with grain cars during the harvest season, and long lines of wagons waited to be unloaded at the elevators. In 1916, no less than 120 carloads of watermelons, averaging 900 melons per car, also were shipped from Burkburnett. At Leedey, rancher T. H. Farris loaded his cattle on cars of the WF&NW and billed them to Oklahoma City slaughterhouses via Elk City and the CRI&P. The same customer received commodities by the carload for use on his ranch. At the northern end of the line, livestock men were particularly pleased with the special Fort Worth-bound hog trains that were operated periodically by the Northwestern.[14]

At Hammon, a merchant received carloads of Hunter's Cream Flour as well as carloads of various brands of livestock feed. Saturday was a big day at Hammon, as it was at other stations, for on that day ranchers and farmers frequently sent their livestock to market. Saturday also was the day that farmers brought their broomcorn to town. Buyers were on hand to examine, purchase, and ship this commodity on the cars of the Wichita Falls Route. Elsewhere in 1913 a local freight train arrived in Forgan with salt for the Forgan Mercantile Company, brick and lumber for the new Forgan school building, and a registered Short Horn bull for R. B. Harrington. Shipments of wheat, broomcorn, Kaffir corn, hogs, and cattle represented the principal carload consignment at Knowles. The WF&NW business at

Camargo for the month of October, 1914, was more than $3,000 above that for the corresponding month in 1913. Carload billings at that station for October, 1914, included 12 wheat, 7 hogs, 15 broomcorn, 3 cattle, and one car of posts. The train labeled Extra 914 on August 18, 1917, represented a normally heavy Saturday livestock run on the Panhandle Division. Its consist included:

> 1—Car of cattle, Duke to Oklahoma City
> 5—Cars of cattle, Wellington to Wichita, Kansas
> 3—Cars of cattle, Hollis to Kansas City
> 1—Car of hogs, Hollis to Fort Worth
> 2—Cars of cattle, Dodsonville to Kansas City
> 1—Car of cattle, Dodsonville to Oklahoma City[15]

None of the livestock handled by Extra 914 listed above was destined for stations on the Northwestern. Cattle bound for Oklahoma City were taken to Elk City where they were given to the Rock Island. Cattle sold to packing houses in Wichita and Kansas City were delivered to the Santa Fe at Woodward, and the hogs for Fort Worth were given to the MK&T at Wichita Falls. Most of the Northwestern's freight business followed similar patterns. Shipments usually originated on foreign lines and were delivered at stations on the WF&NW or were originated at stations on the home road and delivered at foreign points. There was a low percentage of hauls that moved only between points on the WF&NW. Inbound, there were heavy interchange shipments of lumber, coal, agricultural implements, and general merchandise. The Northwestern received a high division of rates on all such cars received. Yet the real bread-and-butter revenue came from the movement of agricultural products, principally to Texas milling points and to the Gulf Coast for export. The WF&NW enjoyed a long haul on these shipments and a high division of rates as well. Happily, wheat came into its own coincidentally with the arrival of the railroad. This augured well for the future. Meanwhile, the Northwestern moved 78,521 tons of freight in 1910. By 1912, this total had risen to 318,918 tons.[16]

All of this spelled profits for the owners of the Wichita Falls & Northwestern and its allied lines. The following statistics indicate the yearly

Depot scenes at Camargo. Carload billings from that station alone totaled 38 in October, 1914. *Sue Hocker Ward collection*

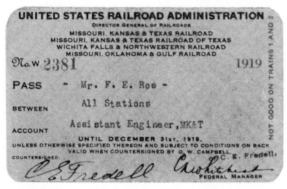

As was the custom during the passenger train era, the WF&NW issued passes to officials of other lines and to its own employees as well. *Author's collection*

net earnings for WF&NW System, less the sizable income which it received from the lease of the Wichita Falls Railway to the MK&T.

1908 - $ 55,009
1909 - $ 64,332 (reflects net earnings
of the WF&NW only)
1910 - $386,508
1911 - $382,749
1912 - $198,560

The splendid earnings record of the property resulted in equally high dividend payments: 6.619 percent on July 1, 1909; 21.40 percent on July 1, 1910; 5.50 percent on August 15, 1912; 2.00 percent on December 31, 1912; and 6.00 percent on June 30, 1913.[17]

KATY and Hard Times

"The Wichita Falls Lines occupy some of the most fertile and densely populated agricultural country in Northwest Texas and Western Oklahoma. The commercial and agricultural development of the territory contiguous to these lines is progressing rapidly."*

After the Wichita Falls & Northwestern had reached its ultimate terminus at Forgan, only three other rail lines were built into its trade area. The Rock Island pushed a branch into Grandfield during 1920, but this was short-lived; the Clinton & Oklahoma Western, a road later owned by Frank Kell, crossed the Northwestern in 1912 at Hammon Junction; the Beaver, Meade & Englewood connected Beaver with Forgan and the WF&NW in 1915. The Childress, Mangum & Oklahoma City hoped to link the cities of its corporate namesake, but it lived only in the minds of its promoters. Another road, the Kansas & Oklahoma Railway, planned to connect Liberal, Kansas, with Forgan, and in 1920 a 268-foot connection was built at Forgan. However, the K&O never arrived there, and the trackage was torn up four years later.[1]

The Kemp and Kell lines, particularly those of the WF&NW System, were profitable operations. They had been built to serve Wichita Falls —and their owners. They had done this well. There was competition for traffic, but other carriers serving the trade areas of the Wichita Falls Route were wisely employed as useful connections. Without doubt, the several lines owned by Kemp and Kell could have continued a profitable operation as independent carriers, although it is probable that their owners would have consolidated them into a single corporate as well as operating entity. However, the Wichita Falls

Route was coveted by the Missouri, Kansas & Texas Railway, a firm with which Kemp and Kell had always worked closely. Even before the Northwestern had been extended beyond Hammon, Katy officials began negotiating with the Texas railroaders for the acquisition of their operations.

The MK&T had expected expansion of its operations prior to the nation-wide economic dislocations of 1907. Yet it was not until 1910 that the Katy felt ready to undertake the acquisition of additional feeder lines. Coincidentally, a new group of investors headed by Edwin Hawley assumed control of the company in that year. Hawley first gained prominence when he facilitated the sale of the late C. P. Huntington's Southern Pacific interests to E. H. Harriman. Later he surprisingly bested Harriman in a contest to gain control of the Chicago & Alton. Hawley had earlier acquired control of the Minneapolis & St. Louis and the Iowa Central, companies which he eventually merged on January 1, 1912. He authorized considerable construction by his railroads, and at one time it was rumored that his M&StL would be extended westward to the Pacific Coast and northward to Winnipeg. Hawley continued to gather other companies under his banner. By the time he secured control of the Katy, a general geographic pattern began to emerge which suggested the creation of a gigantic system of lines stretching from the

*Missouri, Kansas & Texas Railway, *Report to the Stockholders for the Year Ending June 30, 1912,* pp. 13-14.

49

This was the Katy herald during the Hawley years. *Author's collection*

The mysterious Edwin Hawley was a banker, but also a builder—in some ways comparable to E. H. Harriman, one of his contemporaries. *Author's collection.*

Canadian border to the Gulf of Mexico and from the eastern seaboard to the Missouri River in South Dakota. Additionally, he concluded profitable traffic arrangements between his Chicago & Alton and the Kansas City Mexico & Orient, then building across Texas toward an illusive goal at Topolobampo, Mexico. Hawley was a shrewd financier and a speculative banker rather than an effective railroad owner. Nevertheless, he was also a builder, in some ways comparable to E. H. Harriman. His untimely death on February 1, 1912, ended plans for a Hawley System.[2]

Hawley's desire for expansion was mirrored by Katy's acquisition of Hetty Green's historic Texas Central in June, 1910. Early in 1911, similar negotiations were opened with Kemp and Kell. Before the year ended, the MK&T had acquired the entire capital stock of both the Wichita Falls & Northwestern and the Wichita Falls & Southern. At the time of the sale, the WF&NW itself owned the entire capital stock of the Wichita Falls Railway, the WF&NWof T, the Altus, Wichita Falls & Hollis, and the Wichita Falls & Wellington. Thus by holding the capital stock of the WF&NW (the parent company), the Katy gained an indirect control of all Kemp and Kell lines. Nevertheless, the WF&NW survived as a corporate entity and so did each of the satellites. Collectively, they were referred to by the Katy as the Wichita Falls Lines. All officials were retained for a time, and the general offices of the road were continued in the Northwestern Buildings at Wichita Falls. Early in 1913, however, Katy President C. E. Schaff succeeded Joseph A. Kemp as President of the Wichita Falls Lines, but Kemp remained in the official family as Vice President. Kell retained a similar post, while most other former Kemp and Kell officials were kept in their positions. Maps of the Katy included the Wichita Falls Lines, but these were clearly identified by their correct corporate designations. On the other hand, their earnings were included with those of the MK&T beginning in November, 1912.[3]

Previously, on August 23, 1911, the Altus, Wichita Falls & Hollis had been fully deeded to the WF&NW. This simplified the corporate structure for the parent company by consolidating all Oklahoma properties. Nevertheless, due to the unusual corporate laws of Texas, there remained no less than four separate Wichita Falls companies in that state. Early in 1913, the Missouri, Kansas

& Texas of Texas (MK&Tof T) moved to consolidate these lines and four others which Katy controlled. A law authorizing this was passed by the Texas legislature in March, but the state's Attorney General brought suit to prevent such consolidation. A settlement which was acceptable to the railroad was effected, however, on February 6, 1914. Consequently, the MK&Tof T leased for 99 years the Wichita Falls Railway, the Wichita Falls & Southern, the Wichita Falls & Wellington, and the Wichita Falls & Northwestern of Texas. The agreement was signed on April 20, 1914, and became effective 11 days later. The parent company, the WF&NW, still held the capital stock of all satellites—as well as remaining an independent company, although under the shield of the MK&T.[4]

Unfortunately the MK&T had expanded too rapidly. While it continued to pay dividends, short-term notes totaling $19 million came due. A proposal to refinance these obligations was turned down, and on September 15, 1915, the MK&T and the MK&TofT both went into receivership. Charles E. Schaff, President of both roads, was named sole receiver of each. In the following year, the Katy had a net earnings deficit of $1,134,634 on total operating revenues exceeding $36.7 million. The situation worsened in spite of war traffic. During 1919, Katy had a total operating revenue of nearly $62 million, but its net operating deficit for that year climbed to $5,162,634.[5]

As early as May, 1914, Joseph Kemp found it necessary to reassure nervous holders and potential purchasers of the WF&NW bonds. Kemp acknowledged that there already had been some severe criticism of the MK&T but concluded that whatever happened to the Katy, the Northwestern "could always be sold under the hammer for more than its mortgage debt." A year later, Kemp maintained that "the Wichita Falls & Northwestern as an independent property is as good as there is in the Southwest." Nevertheless, when the Katy went under, the holders of WF&NW bonds were understandably worried. One New York investment firm, Knaught, Nachod & Kuhne, made a thorough study of the WF&NW's condition. The firm was unable to complete an accurate audit of the Northwestern's earnings, however, since the Katy did not keep these records separate. The brokerage firm re-called, though, that prior to the acquisition of its capital stock by the MK&T, the Northwestern "earned a very handsome margin over its fixed charges." It concluded, nevertheless, that the individual portions covered by the first mortgage liens could not stand by themselves if Katy defaulted on the interest payments for the several bond issues. On the other hand, the WF&NW together with its satellites as a single unit, was considered equally valuable to investors as a fully independent company or as a part of the Katy System. The thrust of the report was, then, that corporate association with the Katy was not crucial to the ultimate health of the WF&NW. The report also quoted Joseph Kemp to the effect that other carriers, including the prosperous Atchison, Topeka & Santa Fe, had been eager to purchase the WF&NW before stock control of the line had been acquired by the MK&T.[6]

Worried bondholders of all series eventually formed protective committees. Those holding the First and Refunding Mortgage Gold Bonds, issued to fund the construction of the Northwestern between Hammon and Forgan, were especially distressed. Elisha Walker of New York, who headed the committee protecting holders of those bonds, charged that the MK&T was not allowing the WF&NW the tonnage rate to which it was entitled. The MK&T maintained, on the other hand, that the Northwestern, like Katy itself, was not making a profit. Walker retorted that Katy's figures did not represent the earnings capacity of the road. If totally divorced from the MK&T, Walker argued, the road would make a better showing. Presumably J. A. Kemp agreed, for he also was a member of the Walker committee. In the meantime, the MK&T continued to pay interest on the Northwestern bonds.[7]

That changed soon enough. The interest on the First and Refunding Gold Bonds and the Panhandle Division First Lien Collateral Trust Gold Bonds, both due July 1, 1917, was not paid. Earlier, on May 31, C. E. Schaff, former President of the Katy and then its receiver, was appointed receiver of the WF&NW. This was the result of an application filed by himself in the United States District Court at Guthrie, Oklahoma. Schaff had advised the court that the Northwestern was unable, under independent operation, to earn its fixed charges. This receivership, fumed Elisha Walker, was created without

In 1923, the Katy built a new freight house and office building at Wichita Falls, hard by Union Station. *M-K-T collection*

consultation with the bondholders which he represented. Walker, Kemp, and the rest of the committee considered that its continuance was prejudicial to their interests. F. F. Armstrong, an attorney for William Salomon & Company of New York claimed that the receivership "obviously" represented the interests of the stockholders and not the bondholders.[8]

The Katy paid no interest on any of the three WF&NW bond issues after January 1, 1918. The hopes of those who wanted to reinstate the Northwestern as a fully independent carrier were lost in the wreck of the MK&T. It was claimed by Katy that the Northwestern had a minor net deficit in 1916, but that it sustained a loss of nearly one-half million dollars in 1917. The absence of data now prevents an accurate appraisal of Katy's claims or, conversely, the claims of the protective committee. However, many bondholders of that day found it difficult to imagine how the line, which had been a profitable operation since its inception—and had a total income of more than one-half million dollars in 1913—could sustain such heavy losses in 1917 and, as was claimed, in 1918, too.[9]

In any event, significant readjustments were temporarily shelved when President Woodrow Wilson, by proclamation of December 26, 1917, brought the railroads of the country under federal control. The wartime traffic did not heal Katy's wounds, but the increased business and the protection made possible by the receivership allowed the road to rehabilitate and generally improve the property. Even before the federal government returned the MK&T to the receiver, on February 29, 1920, its reorganization committee announced that certain feeder lines would be pared away from the Katy System. One of these, the Wichita Falls & Southern, was purchased from the receiver by Kemp and Kell, its former owners, on March 1, 1920.[10]

A plan for the reorganization and sale of the Katy, dated November 1, 1921, was formulated on behalf of those who owned MK&T securities. This plan, which was subsequently adopted, provided for a considerably reduced capitalization and a similar diminution of fixed charges. Thus a new company, the Missouri-Kansas-Texas Railroad, was created on July 6, 1922. Under the new corporation, the old MK&T was completely reorganized effective April 1, 1923. Holders of all WF&NW bonds were given various issues of new M-K-T bonds and preferred stock in exchange for their Northwestern holdings. With that, the Wichita Falls & Northwestern Railway Company disappeared as a corporate entity. The former satellites of the WF&NW then passed to the Missouri-Kansas-Texas Railroad of Texas (M-K-TofT), charted on January 23, 1923, under Texas law. Yet the satellite roads, unlike their parent company the WF&NW, did not lose their corporate identities. To be sure, the Wichita Falls Railway, the Wichita Falls & Northwestern of Texas and the Wichita Falls & Wellington companies were only leased to the M-K-Tof T. Of course, the entire operation of these lines was fully assumed by the Katy. Wichita Falls remained the major terminal and traffic hub, but the general offices disappeared, as also did the several official positions associated with the Wichita Falls Lines. To secure office and warehouse space formerly provided by the Wichita Falls Route, the Katy in 1923 built a new freight house and office building, costing $107,676.53, at Ninth and Ohio Streets, hard by Union Station.[11]

In reality, the WF&NW enjoyed only a brief tenure as the main line of an independent company. As soon as the Katy assumed stock control of the WF&NW, the road became little more than a branch line appendage of a major carrier. During the years of receivership, Katy maintained that the Northwestern operation resulted in heavy losses. Yet there was no attempt to dispose of the property, as was the case with the Wichita Falls & Southern and numerous other feeders which were acquired during Katy's period of expansion and then released during and after its receivership. On the contrary, the management of the Katy concluded that there was real promise in the WF&NW lines. Thus the trackage north of Wichita Falls was retained and properly identified by the M-K-T as its Northwestern District—unromantic and unheralded branch lines, except during the Burkburnett Boom.

By January, 1919, Burkburnett's population had risen, according to one estimate, to 8,000. *Author's collection*

Perhaps the largest group of people to arrive in Burkburnett were ex-servicemen, released by the Armistice and then lured to Boomtown by the prospect of sudden riches. *Author's collection*

54

Bottles of Bourbon, Barrels of Oil:
The Burkburnett Boom

"In short order there were derricks scattered thickly over the little town, pointing upward like so many pins in a cushion."*

The little train drifted down to the Red River and onto the long pile trestle. Safely across, the engineer reopened the throttle; the sharp exhaust of the 4-4-0 belied her diminutive size. Soon the train was within sight of Burkburnett, only four miles from the river. L. C. Rodgers detected that something about the town was different—something had happened since he went through it the day before as fireman on a northbound run. The station platform now thronged with people. As the engineer brought the train to a stop in front of the depot, Rodgers leaned out of his cab window and inquired about the excitement. The mail messenger, then positioning a four-wheel cart next to the door of the RPO car, paused and said, "Haven't you heard? 'Fowler's Folly' came in!"[1]

Drilling for oil had been a part of life in North Texas since the dawn of the twentieth century. Often, however, the discovery of oil was a collateral or even a serendipity development. The original Red River Uplift Well was sunk in 1902 by a farmer who was seeking an adequate water supply. Instead, he brought in the Henrietta oil field. Five years later the Petrolia field came in; that was followed in 1911 by the discovery of the Electra pool. There was seemingly no end to the petroleum resources of north Texas. The Iowa Park field was developed in 1913, and on July 29, 1918, "Fowler's Folly" ushered in the fabulous Burkburnett boom.[2]

Until the Fowler well roared in, Burkburnett was much like dozens of other small towns in the Southwest. Insofar as the Wichita Falls & Northwestern Railroad Company was concerned, it amounted to little more than an average way station. To be sure, oil production had been a part of the local scene for some time. The first well in the immediate vicinity of Burkburnett came in on July 1, 1912. The Corsicana Oil Company immediately made locations for offsets, and there was the usual rush for leases. By December, 1917, the Burkburnett oil field covered approximately 60 square miles. Some wells were reportedly put down in 36 hours and produced up to 15 barrels a day. More than 1,000 oil-field workers lived in Burkburnett, and since ordinary people could still get into the oil business, some of these laborers hoarded their wages in the hope that they, too, would become "oil tycoons." Other laborers were soon hired by the Burkburnett Oil Refinery which was ready for production before 1918. It had a daily capacity of 3,000 barrels of crude which was refined into gasoline, naphtha, and other petroleum products. Nevertheless, the real boom was in the future.[3]

The Fowler well was so spectacularly productive that it yielded 100 barrels every 40 minutes. Similar ventures were summarily initiated as the word spread. This naturally resulted in a rush to secure town lots and to organize oil companies. Derricks shortly were scattered over the town and across the surrounding areas. On land which S. Burke Burnett had earlier sold to Joseph A. Kemp and Frank Kell—and which they had resold to hundreds of settlers without retaining mineral rights—it seemed that the earth's crust was only a superficial cover over a vast pool of black gold.[4]

The Burkburnett townsite pool proved to be

*Burkburnett [Texas] Star, January 3, 1919.

55

About 90 per cent of the oil pumped from the Burkburnett field came from the 17,000 acres sold by S. Burke Burnett to Kemp and Kell back in 1906. *Author's collection*

4,000 feet wide and three miles long, with the village squarely in the middle. By January, 1919, Burkburnett's population had risen, according to one estimate, to 8,000. People thronged the streets, and its stores were open 24 hours a day. Oil companies were formed on sidewalks and in streets. Hotels, rooming houses, and private homes were filled. Sleepy visitors were obliged to pay $10 per night for the privilege of staying the night on porches or in cellars. The constant and heavy traffic over the community's roadways reduced them to a deplorable state; rain turned them into veritable arteries of mud. Conditions were so bad that in 1919 a mule bogged down in front of the First National Bank and expired before it could be extricated. There simply was no time to make repairs. During the spring of 1919, the townsite pool was producing 55,000 barrels per day. Dry holes began to show up, however, and it appeared likely that the boom would soon be over.[5]

Then another field—the northwest extension—was located nearby in what had been Burke Burnett's west pasture. It was five miles long and two miles wide; every inch of it was within the original 6666 Ranch. In time, other patches were located, but about 90 percent of the oil pumped from the Burkburnett field came from the 17,000 acres sold by Burnett to Kemp and Kell back in 1906. At its apex, the Burkburnett field produced almost $10 million in oil per month. During 1924, there were seven crude-oil refineries and fourteen casinghead gasoline plants in operation within the confines of the field. In that same year, the townsite pool and the northwestern extension collectively produced 20,000 barrels per day. Yet, in reality, the boom ended two years earlier in 1922. Extensive drilling continued, but it had resolved into an orderly and methodical operation by big companies such as Magnolia, Texas, and Gulf.[6]

The impact of the Burkburnett Boom on the daily operation of the WF&NW was both immediate and dramatic. As the news of the boom spread, the railroad was besieged by patrons wanting to secure passage, especially between Wichita Falls and Burkburnett. The road initially tried to handle the heavy volume by adding coaches to its regularly scheduled trains each day. By February of 1919, however, the WF&NW was forced to schedule three additional daily round-trip trains between Wichita Falls and Burkburnett. One observer noted that more than 300 persons arrived in Wichita Falls from Fort Worth each morning aboard the cars of the Missouri, Kansas & Texas and the Fort Worth & Denver City roads. These passengers plus "three or four times that number then swarmed onto the morning train for 'Burk.'" Many were speculators, but others were merely observers. Perhaps the largest number were ex-service men, released from military burdens by the Armistice and then lured to Burkburnett by the prospect of sudden riches. A stranger who happened by Wichita Falls Union Station one morning was surprised at the number of people then buying tickets for Burkburnett and asked if the train was an excursion. He was told that it was the regular train and that it would be followed by another in just a few minutes. These two trains, one a through run for Forgan, Oklahoma, and the other a usual Burkburnett train, both returned in the evening with weary laborers from the oil fields. At one time, the railroad used as many as six ticket-takers per train. They picked up tickets or sold cash fares for 45¢ to patrons as they boarded the cars. Passengers frequently presented 50¢ pieces or dollar bills as payment and in the flush spirit of the times or perhaps because of their great desire to "dust the cushions," they often told the ticket-takers to keep the change. Other passengers, however, proved to be "tough customers." A few timid trainmen avoided confrontation with them, but most of the regular conductors and brakemen carried blackjacks which produced some civility among the unruly.[7]

By mid-July of 1919, the railroad reduced to two the number of round-trip trains between Wichita Falls and Burkburnett. At the same time, however, it added a new through operation between Wichita Falls and Oklahoma City in conjunction with the St. Louis-San Francisco Railroad. This new train, christened the BURKBURNETT SPECIAL, carried sleeping cars, coaches, and chair cars and operated on a convenient overnight schedule via Frederick. It connected at Oklahoma City with trains arriving from Tulsa and thereby provided comfortable transportation to Burkburnett for the oil nabobs of Oklahoma. Not surprisingly, the Wichita Falls-Oklahoma City train was the pride of the line, its only "flyer," and employees were warned not to delay its speedy passage. The lifespan of the BURKBURNETT SPECIAL corresponded with that of the boom itself; the train expired on February 10, 1923. The two Burkburnett locals, known infor-

Wrapper from the type of bottle which was frequently delivered to Boomtown by the WF&NW cars. *Author's collection*

mally as the "Polly," were similarly discontinued as the boom passed. Nevertheless, the through Wichita Falls-Oklahoma City standard sleeper—previously handled by the BURKBURNETT SPECIAL—was transferred to another set of night trains. Such service persisted until shortly before the Great Crash of 1929.[8]

Clerks on the Forgan and Wichita Falls R.P.O. were literally swamped with mail for Burkburnett. Often the volume was so heavy that the mails were carried by that station and worked back by another train. Express messengers were similarly overburdened. Seemingly every nature of parcel was shipped into Boomtown by express. Two examples are representative. Before national prohibition, and even thereafter, trains from Wichita Falls brought countless quarts of liquor to Burkburnett. Trains were often delayed while carton after carton of the precious spirits were transloaded from the express car to the four-wheel carts, lined up and waiting at the Boomtown depot. One item which the express messengers fortunately did not have to handle except in record books was a "bull-wheel," ordered from a manufacturing plant in Pennsylvania by a Burkburnett oil man. This heavy piece of equipment was loaded on a flat car and handled all the way to Texas by passenger train. Such expeditious handling resulted in express charges which exceeded the cost of the machinery. Nevertheless, the oil man willingly paid the price.[9]

Oil derricks were everywhere in Burkburnett, even next to the railroad station platform and all along the right-of-way. In 1919, twelve pipe line companies served the Burkburnett region, and three refineries were located at or near the townsite. The railroad, of course, was called upon to deliver the pipe for the pipe lines and the machinery for the refineries. Frequently, there were from 60 to 100 cars on the sidings waiting to be unloaded. Most contained derrick timbers, oil well casings, drilling machinery, and other equipment incidental to the boom. In 1919, the railroad reported its freight business at Burkburnett to be $25,000 per day.[10]

Before 1918, the WF&NW owned a 97′x 20′ combination depot at Burkburnett. It served well until the boom, but then the railroad was forced to utilize box cars as offices and quarters for the 13 new employees sent there to handle the mushrooming business. In February 1919, the railroad completed a new 30′x30′ passenger depot south of the original structure. At the same time,

it converted the former combination station into a freight depot, extended the building by 100,′ and built a new freight platform. After the boom the new passenger station was leased in 1924 to American Railway Express Company, and the freight depot once again became a combination station.[11]

Throughout the boom period, extra gangs labored to install new tracks. Records indicate that at one time there were no less than 63 tracks in and around Burkburnett. Of these, 45 were built to serve a variety of oil companies, among them Magnolia, Skelly, Humble, Texaco, Sinclair, Gulf, and a host of lesser known concerns. This new trackage sprouted from the main line beginning at a point some two miles south of town and extending to a location approximately three miles north of that community. The main line through Burkburnett was double-tracked, and wye tracks and engine house tracks were also installed. Most of this track construction began in 1919, and virtually all of it was utilized until 1923.[12]

In addition to the twelve regularly scheduled passenger trains which served Burkburnett during its salad days, there were numerous through freights plus the usual locals. Additionally, there were day and night switch engine assignments. Some of these switch crews were based in Burk-

Express business at Burkburnett, Texas during the boom was so heavy that entire cars were often lined up for unloading. *Author's collection*

burnett, others came up from Wichita Falls, and yet others serviced Boomtown from Frederick. The exact volume of tonnage which originated at Burkburnett during the boom is impossible to determine. However, at one time, four trains per day were necessary to move casinghead gasoline from just the Charles F. Noble Oil & Gas Company's plant. Much of this tonnage moved over the Northwestern to Woodward, Oklahoma, from where it was conveyed to California outlets by the Atchison, Topeka & Santa Fe. Other trains handled crude oil and gasoline from various Burkburnett loading racks to Frederick, Elk City, Hammon, and Wichita Falls where the cars were delivered to other carriers. When traffic became particularly heavy, as it frequently did, railroaders warned each other that "the bullets are really flying."[13]

Earlier, in 1919, a well owned by J. A. Kemp and Frank Kell near Mangum, Oklahoma —farther north along the WF&NW—came in at 700 barrels per day. As a result, Mangum fully anticipated a boom similar to that of Burkburnett. One scribe noted that the WF&NW happily brought the capital of Greer County, Oklahoma, "in touch with all points north and south and renders special service in that a three-hour journey can bring Ranger and Burkburnett investors into the Greer County fields." However, it was not Mangum but Wichita Falls which fully benefitted from the location of the oil fields in relation to the WF&NW. That city had risen to prominence essentially because of the numerous railroad lines which either ran through it or radiated from it. In this development, Kemp and Kell had played the major roles for they had fostered the creation of most roads, including the Wichita Falls & Northwestern. Wichita Falls thus was already a strong commercial and transportation center when the surrounding oil fields began to come in and, therefore, it quite naturally became the hub of the North Texas oil region. Evidence of its growth came in the form of new refineries, equipment houses, hotels, major business concerns, and spreading residential areas. In 1919, there were nine refineries in Wichita Falls processing 27,000 barrels of crude oil from the nearby fields. As could be expected, many of these were located next to or close to the railroad right-of-way. During the boom, most investors and promoters commuted to Burkburnett but made

Wichita Falls their headquarters. Similarly, most of those local residents who "made it big" during the boom later left town; to this day, there is no "Silk Stocking Row" in Burkburnett. Many took their money with them and "settled" in Wichita Falls.[14]

Burkburnett's boom was short-lived but sufficiently bawdy to attract Hollywood writers of a later day. In 1940 Metro-Goldwyn-Mayer released a film entitled *Boom Town*, starring Clark Gable, Spencer Tracy, Claudette Colbert, and Hedy Lamar. It told a tale of wildcat drilling in what it postured as the mud-and-shanty frontier town of Burkburnett, circa 1919. Explosions, high-powered deals, heartbreak, and quick millions all combined to make the film a box office favorite. Nevertheless, critics gave it mixed reviews. Interestingly, the man who eventually became known as Clark Gable and who starred in *Boom Town*, had been one of the multitude who actually toiled in the Burkburnett field during the boom years.[15]

Burkburnett's boom was short-lived but bawdy enough to attract Hollywood writers of a later day. *Author's collection*

Clark Gable, one of the stars in *Boom Town*, had once toiled as a "roughneck" in the Burkburnett fields. *Author's collection*

The Burkburnett boom provided the only brush with romance that the Northwestern ever experienced. The volume of freight and passenger business generated at or destined for that station during those brief, hectic years was impressive: aboard its cars moved rich and poor, high and humble, capitalist and crook, roughneck and ràscal, bottles of bourbon and barrels of oil. Yet for the railroad, as for the town which gave its name, the Burkburnett boom was a flash in the pan. The only lasting legacy for the railroad was the regularized movement of petroleum products in significant volume along southern portions of its line. This was done in the typical fashion of a branch line; it originated the traffic and passed it on to the main line or yielded it to other carriers for ultimate delivery. There was nothing romantic about that. It was just a part of the workaday world of branch line railroading.

The Beaver, Meade & Englewood Railroad:
The Home Road: 1912-1923

"Beaver citizens had enviously watched the rise of neighboring railroad towns. They knew that they must have a railroad if they maintained their urban leadership in the Panhandle. But how?"*

No area of the Southwest has a more checkered or interesting history than Oklahoma's Panhandle. For several years of the national experience, it was unclaimed by neighboring political entities and attached to none. Small wonder, then, that it was called No Man's Land. While other parts of the Southwest were opened to homesteading, No Man's Land was believed to be owned by the Cherokees and the area remained generally devoid of white population. Cattlemen, mostly from Kansas, eventually paid the Cherokees for the privilige of grazing their cattle on the luxuriant grasses of the area. Then an enterprising lawyer from Denver discovered that title to the land did not rest with the Cherokees but rather with the government. With this news squatters began to occupy the country; "soddies" seemingly erupted everywhere as the squatters took up residence. As always, the "sodbusters" spelled doom for the open range cattle industry.[1]

The invasion of No Man's Land by the squatters began in 1886 and was in full swing by the following year. Three seasons later, on May 2, 1890, President Harrison signed into law the Organic Act which completely reorganized Indian Territory and set up territorial government for Oklahoma Territory. No Man's Land was included as a part of Oklahoma Territory despite the fact that the two areas were separated by the Cherokee Strip. When "old" Oklahoma was thrown open to settlement under the Homestead

Law on April 22, 1889, more than 6,000 squatters left No Man's Land for the rush. When the Cherokee Strip was similarly opened four years later, additional squatters from No Man's Land departed. They did not return. In 1897, the population of Beaver County, comprising all of No Man's Land, was only 4,778; two years later it had dropped to 2,548. However, the prospect of statehood for Oklahoma and the construction in 1902 of the Chicago, Rock Island & Pacific Railway across the midsection of Beaver County created a spirit of rising expectations. Indeed, by 1907, the population of Beaver County had grown to 35,000, and all of its best farmland was occupied.[2]

Beaver City was long recognized as the capital of No Man's Land. When boosters proposed to convert the region into the romantic sounding but ill-fated State of Cimarron, Beaver City was naturally selected as the state capital. Although these aspirations never reached fruition, Beaver City did eventually become the seat of Beaver County. Enterprising citizens from Wichita, Kansas, first developed the area in 1886 by forming the Beaver Townsite Company. Within two months after the town had been platted, no less than 20 soddies were counted. The government established a land office there during 1890, and this added to the strategic importance of the village. Cowboys and teamsters made regular calls at Beaver City, and the town grew in population and in importance until 1902, when

*Carl Coke Rister, *No Man's Land* (Norman: University of Oklahoma Press, 1948), p. 172.

the Rock Island crossed the county to the west. Then Guymon became the largest town in the county. Beaver City's influence was further diminished when Oklahoma gained statehood. Before that time Beaver County and the Oklahoma Panhandle were one and the same. With statehood, however, the Panhandle was divided into three counties. Beaver City remained the seat of Beaver County, the easternmost of the three and the smallest in size.[3]

The absence of adequate transportation plagued No Man's Land from the time of its settlement. Many of Beaver County's early inhabitants had arrived at railheads in Kansas, such as Englewood, Meade, and Liberal, and then had to undertake lengthy overland journeys to reach their destinations. All supplies had to come from these and other distant railroad towns. This meant frequent and difficult trips for all who lived in the area. The construction of the Rock Island through Guymon alleviated the difficulties only for those who lived in the midsection of the Panhandle. Thus a number of schemes to bring the amenities and conveniences of railroad transportation to the region were considered.[4]

In 1888, the management of the Atchison, Topeka & Santa Fe Railway told its stockholders that "the history of Western railroad construction for the past quarter of a century has demonstrated that successful results can only be attained by occupying territory promptly. . . ." During that year, or perhaps late in 1887, one of its satellites reached Englewood, Kansas, hard by the border of No Man's Land and some 40 miles from Beaver City. Santa Fe records indicate that several surveys were made to extend the line, but strangely this was never done. Englewood remained an end-of-track town; in this case, the Santa Fe failed to make good on its philosophy of "occupying territory promptly."[5]

In 1904, the Oklahoma & Northwestern Rail Road Company was chartered to build a road from an unspecified point in Roger Mills County northwestward to another undisclosed point in Beaver County. This firm also hoped to build a branch to the South Fork of the Red River. Apparently the incorporators of the road hoped to forge a line from the Rock Island's east-west road to Beaver City, but all plans came to naught. Soon Beaver City was excited by a considerably bolder scheme. On October 14, 1907, the Beaver

Valley & North Western Railroad received a charter to build a line of road from Oklahoma City through Beaver City to La Junta, Colorado, where a connection could be made with the AT&SF for all points west. The road was capitalized at $4 million. All the incorporators were from Beaver City, although Bailey Wagoner, a representative of the Missouri Pacific Railway, apparently masterminded the operation. However, the general economic slump of the period conspired against success, and the BV&NW never laid a rail. Still another road was projected for the Panhandle between 1905 and 1910. This one, strange to say, intended to build from west to east—from the coal fields in northeastern New Mexico on a route designed to pass via Hooker, Gate, Woodward, Watonga, Guthrie, and Oklahoma City. Also planned was a branch from Gate to connect with the Santa Fe at Englewood, Kansas. Promoters of this scheme were also the operators of the Yankee Fuel Company located near Raton, New Mexico. Their plan, like those before it, also failed, and the Panhandle remained devoid of adequate transportation service.[6]

When it appeared that the Wichita Falls & Northwestern was entertaining notions of building into the Panhandle, Beaver City sent representatives to Frank Kell hoping to persuade him to locate the WF&NW extension along the south bank of the Beaver River to their community. But they were sorely rebuffed. Kell built into Beaver County on the north side of the river, contending that construction on the south side would be more difficult and expensive. Indeed, there were significant bridging problems on the southern route, but these were minuscule compared to those already conquered by the WF&NW. In truth, Kell felt that more money could be made from townsite development along the northern route. He cared little for the heritage of Beaver City, and instead of favoring that community he promoted Forgan, a rival townsite a few miles north of Beaver City. Kell obviously considered that the WF&NW could have Beaver City's traffic without building the line directly to it. At the same time, Kell considered, Forgan would prove to be a lucrative townsite project. Thus Beaver City saw the arrival of the Northwestern's steam cars into the area on September 12, 1912, as no more than a mixed blessing.[7]

Earlier, on December 28, 1911, leading citi-

Promoters of the BM&E asked for donations to start building a grade. Area farmers agreed to do the work, using their teams and the county's road machinery. *Veldo H. Brewer collection*

zens of Beaver City had held a meeting to discuss their transportation problems. Out of this meeting came a decision to form the Beaver, Meade & Englewood Railroad Company (BM&E, the Beaver Road, or the Beaver). Accordingly, a charter was obtained which allowed the company to construct, maintain, and operate a line of railroad from Beaver City to "such a point or points as may be necessary or convenient in the towns of Meade, Kansas, and Englewood, Kansas." The company was also authorized to construct extensions and branches. The two proposed lines of the BM&E, both emanating from Beaver City, were each expected to be 40 miles in length. The road was capitalized at a mere $25,000.[8]

The successful completion of the BM&E to Englewood would, its boosters contended, provide a direct link with that village—long an important entrepot for the Panhandle—and concomitantly forge a connection with far-off Kansas City via the AT&SF. Completion of the other proposed route, to Meade, similarly would afford a bond with Kansas City, although by way of the CRI&P. Completion of both legs of the road would grant two important ties with Kansas City, by way of two competitive trunk lines. Even if the BM&E failed to reach either Kansas community, it was absolutely necessary to link up with the WF&NW at Forgan. To do less was to forfeit the existence of Beaver City.

Meanwhile, delegations met with representatives of the Rock Island and the Santa Fe roads. Both companies were interested but not to the point of granting financial assistance. Rebuffed in their long range plans, Beaver Citians had to fall back to the short-range goal. They naively

reasoned that the mere completion of the home road to Forgan would force the Northwestern to purchase and operate the line. Yet by 1913, very little meaningful labor had been expended to bring these plans to fruition. This can be explained by the absence of necessary funding abilities, a condition which was greatly aggravated by Oklahoma laws which did not permit the voting of bonds for the promotion and construction of railroads. To circumvent this situation, the people of Beaver City voted bonds for the installation of a light and water plant and then diverted part of the proceeds for the acquisition of materials necessary for the construction of the BM&E.[9]

The promoters then asked for donations in order to commence building a grade. Area farmers agreed to do the work, using their teams and the county's road machinery. In return, they received two dollars per day for feed and board plus an additional two dollars per day in the railroad's stock. Numerous others donated feed, labor, food, and money. During the winter of 1913, as many as fifty farmers toiled on the grade and soon the route to Forgan was one-half finished. However, residents of the Forgan vicinity had little interest in the road and failed to donate lands necessary for the right-of-way. Had adequate money been available, these lands could have been purchased by condemnation proceedings. Unfortunately for the home road, the money had simply run out.[10]

At this juncture, the promoters contacted President C. E. Schaff, whose Missouri, Kansas & Texas Railway had recently acquired the capital stock of the WF&NW. Schaff was told

Jacob A. Achenbach, circa 1930. *Leonard J. Achenbach collection*

that the partially completed right-of-way would be given to the Katy if only that road would finish the project. The Katy president demurred but advised that if the road was finally completed the MK&T would consider taking it over for operation as a part of its WF&NW. Thus encouraged, the promoters redoubled their efforts. Holidays were often declared in town, and everyone put in time working on the railroad. Then the till was empty once more. Schaff was contacted again and a contract was drawn whereby the MK&T was to assume the total assets of the BM&E. Frank Kell, however, intervened. Kell was still an official of the WF&NW, and he advised the MK&T Board of Directors that completion of the BM&E to Forgan would be detrimental to the Northwestern. Kell argued that the WF&NW was getting the traffic anyway; additional mileage would be redundant. Moreover, fulfillment of Beaver City's dream would prejudice Kell's aspirations for Forgan, one of his pet projects. In the end, Kell won out and the contract was not consummated.[11]

It was a glum Beaver City which learned of Katy's decision. Without a railroad, the fate of the community was clearly sealed. It had to have a railroad in order to survive. Residents of Beaver City cared little if it was a trunk line, a branch, or an independent short line. In 1912, they even considered an interurban electric line between their community and Forgan. Now, however, it appeared that all of their labors had gone for naught; and they were broke. Then when everything seemed lost, a former resident visited Beaver City and, learning of the railroad problem, referred the promoters to a friend of his in Kansas, Jacob A. Achenbach.[12]

Achenbach was born in Germany on March 22, 1846. When he was six years of age, his parents moved the family to the United States and settled in Green County, Illinois. By 1883, Achenbach had become a successful farmer in that state. Yet he wished to expand his operations and, as opportunities for the acquisition of agricultural land in Illinois were limited at that time, Achenbach moved to Kansas. In 1884, he owned 6,300 acres of land in Barber County. Two years later he purchased another nearby 640 acres, formed a townsite company, and organized the town of Hardtner. This area, in south-central Kansas, proved to be excellent for growing wheat, and

the region prospered. Achenbach's new town prospered likewise, but it had no railroad, and much potential business flowed to Kiowa and other neighboring railroad towns. Achenbach and others eventually urged the Santa Fe to build to Hardtner from its main line at Kiowa. That company proved to be uninterested in the proposal, undoubtedly feeling that the Hardtner traffic would naturally flow to Kiowa and its line anyway. The Missouri Pacific, then building a branch from Wichita to Kiowa, was also contacted but, like the Santa Fe, had no inclination to promote a short stub to Hardtner.[13]

Achenbach, however, was not to be denied. As early as 1906, he was talking about the creation of an independent road to link Hardtner with Kiowa. Two years later, by-laws were drawn governing the Kiowa, Hardtner & Pacific Railroad Company—the title of which implied both short-term and long-range goals. In 1909, lands were condemned; on June 8-9, 1910, Hardtner held a gala celebration honoring the inception of rail service to that point. One month later, Achenbach leased the KH&P to the Missouri Pacific, a concern which operates that line even today. Jacob Achenbach planted the first wheat grown in Barber County, Kansas, developed his own town, and brought needed rail service to the country. He was exactly the type of man needed by Beaver City in its quest for a railroad.[14]

Achenbach listened to what the Beaver City emissaries had to say, yet after consideration, he told them that he was not interested. Nevertheless, he undertook a survey of the Panhandle's potential—and soon thereafter consented to finish the road between Beaver City and Forgan. Achenbach and his good friend Ira B. Blackstock of Springfield, Illinois, then purchased all of the company's capital stock, amounting to $25,000. It was then agreed among the several parties that all of the BM&E's previous obligations were to be waived. Thus the new owners received the property on a debt-free basis. The original promoters had finished the grade between Beaver City and Forgan and had laid 3.06 miles of used 56-pound (to the yard) and 65-pound rail south of Forgan between 1912 and 1914. Achenbach and Blackstock completed the remaining 3.77 miles to Beaver City with used 52-pound steel. The road was completed in 1915 and opened for business the next season. Achenbach then offered the com-

Ira B. Blackstock, circa 1925. *Illinois State Histroical Library collection*

pleted railroad to the MK&T for a nominal price. The Katy at that time was in the hands of a receiver and declined the offer. But in doing so, the MK&T took a condescending attitude, saying that it would be foolish to pay for a railroad which had been so recently offered to it on a gratis basis. Furthermore, Katy management doubted that the road would ever "earn sufficient revenue to buy grease for the engine." Neither Achenbach nor Blackstock had any experience as railroad operators; they had been only builders and promoters. With Katy's recalcitrance, that was about to change.[15]

Ira B. Blackstock was born in Illinois on April 3, 1886, and remained a resident of that state to the time of his death. He met Achenbach by way of mutual friends in Illinois, and together they became partners in numerous business ventures. Blackstock served as President of the Kiowa, Hardtner & Pacific and Vice President of the BM&E. Nevertheless, both railroads were nominally Achenbach enterprises; Blackstock provided some capital, minor advice, and moral support but little else. Indeed, Achenbach tried to keep the financial aspects of both roads a family matter insofar as he was able to do so. When the BM&E's capitalization was raised to $75,000, he and Blackstock purchased the entire issue. Yet August E. Achenbach, one of Jacob's sons, was a member of the road's board of directors, and when the company needed additional financial support "the whole Achenbach family chipped in."[16]

No accounting records were kept by the BM&E prior to January 1, 1919. Consequently, there are few resources from which to draw an adequate picture of the road's initial years. The company later advised the Interstate Commerce Commission that it had acquired 31 parcels of land necessary for the construction of the line. Of these, 19 were considered as aids to construction. The others were acquired at a total cost of $3,032.75. Before mid-1918, the BM&E acquired two used locomotives, one used freight car, and one open-vestibuled passenger car. The WF&NW co-operated by supplying freight cars when ordered, and station and yard facilities at Forgan were shared with the Northwestern under a contract which called for an annual payment of $1,200. As early as July, 1916, the *Hardtner Press* reported that the road was "doing almost a

The BM&E was completed from Beaver to Forgan in 1915 and opende for business the next season. This was the first revenue run from Beaver. *Veldo H. Brewer collection*

capacity business hauling merchandise and carload commodities into, and grain and other products out of Beaver." With expanding revenues and without bonded indebtedness, the Beaver Road proved to be at least a marginally profitable enterprise almost from the beginning.[17]

The development of railroads in the Panhandle was a persistent theme during the first three-and-one-half decades of the twentieth century. In the summer of 1913 many observers expected the WF&NW to be extended, while residents of western Kansas communities proposed lengthening to Forgan a railroad already serving Scott City and Garden City. At the same time, the Dodge City & Cimarron Valley Railway, a predecessor of the AT&SF, opened a line from Dodge City to Elkhart, Kansas, and seemed poised to invade the western portion of the Oklahoma Panhandle. Two years later, a group of businessmen from Alva, Oklahoma, proposed to build a short road from Rosston, on the WF&NW, eastward twenty miles to Buffalo. On April 10, 1916, the Buffalo Northwestern Railway received a charter to construct a line of road between Des Moines, New Mexico, and Tulsa, Oklahoma. The Alva Road and the Buffalo Northwestern both were locally sponsored. The former remained a "paper company," but the latter did some grading near Buffalo. In time, the Buffalo enterprise was reorganized and completed a road between Buffalo and Waynoka. When finished, it was conveyed to the Santa Fe. In another area, wheat farmers from La Kemp, in southern Beaver County, incorporated the La Kemp & Northwestern Railroad Company on August 7, 1915. They hoped to build a road connecting on the west with the Rock Island at Guymon and on the east with the AT&SF at Gage. A branch to tap the WF&NW at May was also a part of the project. Most of these were locally sponsored dreams— born of a desire and need to give the Panhandle adequate transportation resources. Most, too, were the result of local frustration with the established carriers, which were strangely hesitant about building into the Panhandle.[18]

Jacob Achenbach also pored over maps of the region and dreamed of expanding the BM&E. He still considered the Englewood option, but the idea of building to Meade was dismissed. Another alternative was that of building south from Beaver City to the lines of the AT&SF. Achenbach first considered lengthening the BM&E in a southerly direction in 1916; later he personally directed a study of proposed routes. Three years later, however, he was primarily interested in reaching the markets and commercial houses of Wichita, Kansas. This could best be accomplished via the Santa Fe at Englewood, but Uncle Jake, as Achenbach was commonly called, also considered a connection with the Rock Island at Liberal.[19]

The contemporary operations of the BM&E and the long range strategy of its owners were not

The Achenbach family crest. *Leonard J. Achenbach collection*

By 1920, the Beaver Road was doing a good business. In this view one sees a considerable volume of broomcorn ready for loading in the BM&E yards at Beaver. *Veldo H. Brewer collection*

68

BM&E locomotive #2 near Beaver during the "high water" in 1919. *Frank O. Kelley collection*

admired by all. The *Wichita Beacon* even made fun of Achenbach and his Beaver Road; it suggested that the officers of the road also doubled as the train crew. Moreover, stated the *Beacon,* "when they are not busy operating the train the officials 'work section.'" These accusations infuriated the editor of Achenbach's home town weekly, the *Hardtner Press,* who hotly replied that the story showed "how unreliable that paper can be when it wants to be." The Hardtner editor boasted that all Uncle Jake needed was "a 'brass collar' and a special car to transport himself and

stenographer, to identify him as a railroad magnate."[20]

The advent of World War I precluded immediate expansion, and the subsequent economic distress further postponed construction. Meanwhile, the BM&E operated two regularly scheduled daily-except-Sunday trains in 1918 and 1919. This service was reduced in 1920 to a single daily-except Sunday train, and reduced further in 1922 to a tri-weekly operation. Additional trains were operated, of course, but on an as-needed basis. BM&E schedules were designed

BM&E locomotive #1 at Beaver in 1919. *Frank O. Kelley collection*

BM&E #2 bucking snow between Beaver and Forgan on December 24, 1918. *H. E. Cross collection*

to coincide with passenger train schedules of the WF&NW at Forgan. Tickets were sold at the Beaver City depot and by the Northwestern agent at Forgan. Cash fare tickets could be obtained from the conductor by those who arrived too late to purchase the regular tickets or by those boarding at McKee, a point midway between the terminal stations. Reductions in regular service implied a greater reliance on public roadways by those wishing to use the Northwestern trains at Forgan. Freight volume, on the other hand, remained stable.[21]

Between 1919 and 1925, the BM&E owned only two locomotives and two cars. Additional motive power and freight equipment frequently were provided by the Northwestern and later by the Katy. A one story 22'x80' combination station, which also served as the road's general office, was constructed at Beaver City. An impressive 7'x15' vault was installed for the safe keeping of company records and currency. Achenbach, Blackstock, and General Manager Carl J. Turpin were frequent visitors, but the daily operation of the road was left in the hands of local officers: Robert H. Loofbourrow, General Attorney; Fred C. Tracy, Secretary; E. E. Booth, Superintendent;

and W. E. Martz, General Agent. Late in 1921, however, the general offices were moved from Beaver City to Oklahoma City. In a sense, this represented the BM&E's growing maturity and implied its future growth. On the other hand, the importance of Beaver City to the BM&E decreased accordingly.[22]

70

BM&E West: 1924-1927

"I saw the possibilities of developing the Oklahoma Panhandle through railroad facilities and decided to extend the road which split the Panhandle wide open." Jacob A. Achenbach*

Operation of the Beaver, Meade & Englewood resulted in a modest profit each year through 1921; in 1922 and 1923, there were minor losses. Jacob Achenbach determined that the seven-mile BM&E was "too short to operate without a loss in overhead expenses." As he saw it, there were two choices: sell the line or expand it. The Wichita Falls & Northwestern, the only likely suitor, and the Missouri, Kansas & Texas, its parent and in 1923 its successor, were either unable or unwilling to acquire the Beaver Road. Thus in the summer of 1922, Achenbach authorized surveyors to make preliminary studies on routes leading west from Forgan. At the same time, all earlier proposals to extend the line elsewhere were shelved.[1]

One of the most encouraging signs, one which certainly caught Achenbach's eye, was the increasing success which Panhandle wheat farmers were having. In 1902-1903, Sam Kerns of near Gate enjoyed two successive years of bountiful wheat production. Farther west, G. W. Riffe sowed the first wheat in northern Texas County during 1903. Farmers harvested a fair crop in 1906 and a good crop in 1910. Four years later a combination of good growing weather and a rising market, accentuated by the coming of World War I, caused Panhandle wheat to score a phenomenal success. A mad gamble in land and wheat followed. In 1921 and again in 1924 and 1926, Texas County, Beaver's neighbor to the west, claimed to be the banner wheat-producing county in the United States. Without doubt, wheat

was big business in the Panhandle by this time. Another factor which drew Achenbach's attention was the manifest need for coal in western and central Oklahoma. Numerous plans had been advanced to facilitate the transportation of coal from the fields in northeastern New Mexico to Oklahoma. To date, however, none had been successful.[2]

After lengthy consideration, the BM&E asked the Interstate Commerce Commission on August 4, 1923, for permission to build a 39.2 mile line from Forgan to Hooker. Such a line, the company contended, would fill a transportation void in the Panhandle, connect the Panhandle with the rest of the state, and furnish a direct route for grain to the ports of Galveston and New Orleans. Construction of the proposed line, it also was argued, would benefit farmers in an area of nearly one million acres by reducing the rates paid for the transportation of their produce. Commercial advantages would also be offered, and new towns would be created.[3]

There was general support in the Panhandle for the BM&E's application. Liberal, Kansas, and the Kansas & Oklahoma Railway opposed the request, however. The K&O earlier had received permission to build a road from Forgan, Oklahoma, through Liberal, Kansas, to the Colorado border. Accordingly, it paid the WF&NW for the construction of a 268' connecting track northwest of the Forgan depot, and it completed some grading north of that town. Eventually, the company did place in service some 19 miles of rail-

*Kiowa [Kansas] News-Review, April 8, 1935.

71

road from the Oklahoma-Kansas line to Liberal but then it fell on hard times. The *Liberal News* took the position that construction of the BM&E from Forgan to Hooker would "mean nothing but a big detriment to Liberal." Some observers urged that the K&O be turned over to the BM&E. Many others argued in favor of the Hooker line and an extension of it through Boise City to the New Mexico coal fields. In any event, the regulatory agency ruled in favor of the BM&E's construction proposals on January 29, 1924.[4]

Hooker wanted another railroad. The town had been founded by the Chicago Townsite Company in 1904, two years after the Chicago, Rock Island & Pacific had pushed through its line from Liberal, Kansas, to Dalhart, Texas. It had prospered from the outset, but it was always second in importance to Guymon, 23 miles to the southwest on the same CRI&P route. Should the BM&E be completed, Hooker not only would be served by a transcontinental line but also by a road connecting the Oklahoma Panhandle with the rest of the state. It had been rumored that Achenbach would ask Hooker for $50,000, but on April 18, 1924, Uncle Jake Achenbach announced that "as soon as Hooker delivers into our hands deeds of contract for the rights-of-way, we will be ready to start construction within five days." Shortly thereafter, Achenbach and his associates entered into a contract with several citizens of Hooker, later referred to as the Hooker Guarantors, which called for Hooker to provide either free land for rights-of-way or the money necessary to gain the land by legal process. For its part, the BM&E deposited a $25,000 bond in assurance that it would complete the road to Hooker. R. F. Baker, Dr. W. J. Risen, and other leading citizens of Hooker immediately began to solicit the necessary properties between their village and Forgan. They hoped that most of the land owners would donate rights-of-way, and this generally proved to be the case. Only four condemnation suits were necessary in the first 14 miles west of Forgan. It was Hooker's responsibility to raise the money for the prosecution of whatever number of condemnation suits were necessary and for payments under such settlements. To show the progress in securing this money, R. F. Baker announced that a large dial would be painted on a blackboard to be located on Gladys Avenue in downtown Hooker. The

editor of the *Hooker Advance* was euphoric: "At last there looms upon the horizon an east and west road—Hooker's hope of hopes."[5]

The Beaver Road amended its articles of incorporation on April 29, 1924. It was recapitalized at $325,000, reflecting the decision to move west. Achenbach and Blackstock held all of the stock save the single director's shares issued to August E. Achenbach, C. J. Turpin, F. C. Tracy, H. N. Lawson, and J. N. Ticher. On the same day, Achenbach and Blackstock filed incorporation papers forming the Panhandle Construction Company. This firm was authorized "to do a general construction business, including construction of railroads . . . telegraph and telephone lines. . . ." In addition to Achenbach and Blackstock, the directors of the construction company included C. J. Turpin, August E. Achenbach, J. M. Gayle, A. Carey Hough, and F. A. Achenbach. On May 6, yet another company, having the same directors, was formed. This one, the Panhandle Townsite Company, was created "for the purpose of locating, laying out, and improving townsites, and buying and selling real estate therefore, including the sale and conveyance of the same in lots, sub-divisions, additions, or otherwise." Achenbach was clearly contemplating the same tactics that had been utilized successfully by countless other railroad developers in the trans-Mississippi West. He was pushing a railroad into an already settled but not entirely developed area; he was using his own construction company to build his own railroad; and he was using his own townsite company to create new villages and shipping points along the railroad. Achenbach was not prone to take risks; he saw profit in each of these enterprises.[6]

The I.C.C. approved the issuance of securities to facilitate the Hooker extension on June 26, 1924. All construction was eventually performed by the Panhandle Construction Company or subcontractors responsible to it. The entire issue of the BM&E's $320,000 First Mortgage Seven Per Cent Bonds plus $240,000 of the railroad's capital stock was turned over to it in payment. Earlier, on May 12, work on the grade had begun near Forgan. On the first day of work, 60 teams of mules and equipment made one-half mile of grade. Uncle Jake's son, August, who was the Hardtner, Kansas, representative for the Hart-

Parr Tractor Company of Charles City, Iowa, also was on hand to unload one of his 70-horsepower tractors at Forgan for work on the grade. Although the harvest soon interrupted work on the railroad as men left for the wheat fields, the grading to Floris was nearly completed by the Fourth of July.[7]

Floris, ten miles west of Forgan, became the first new townsite on the Hooker extension. Another town bearing the same title had been located about three miles north of the railroad in 1903. The old town evaporated with the arrival of the BM&E, and many of its residents moved to new Floris. Achenbach's town boasted four streets and four avenues, most of which were named for local landowners. The steel gang reached Floris late in the summer of 1924. Farmer's Union Equity of Forgan established a branch elevator at the new station, and by the end of September several cars of the 1924 wheat crop had been shipped. A bunk house for section men, an 8'x10' station, and a tool house were soon built there for railroad purposes.[8]

Achenbach calculated that his most important townsite should be located equidistant between Forgan and Hooker. Consequently, another new town, christened "Turpin" after the BM&E's General Manager, came into existence. The first lot was sold to George Probst for an elevator site on August 15; Tom Snyder purchased the first business lot two weeks later. The village streets and alleys were graded in the fall. Local farmers, anticipating the imminent arrival of the BM&E, had held their grain and broomcorn that season. Indeed, it was piled high along the railroad grade awaiting shipment. Before the end of November, the rails were within one mile of Turpin. J. R. Butcher, General Manager of the Panhandle Townsite Company tacked up posters around Hooker advertising a celebration in Turpin on Saturday, December 6, to coincide with the arrival of the railroad. A dance was held; land was purchased; and the BM&E accepted its first freight shipments. Two days later George Probst sent the first cars of wheat eastward on the newly laid rails of the Beaver Road.[9]

The BM&E earned a very modest profit in 1924, but operations for 1925 resulted in a deficit of over $10,000. This partially explains why the BM&E languished at Turpin for more than 15 months; the company and its promoters were temporarily low on funds. Furthermore, Hooker had not yet completed rights-of-way acquisitions or funding for necessary condemnation proceedings. Finally, the Interstate Commerce Commission authorized the construction of a new Rock Island line from Amarillo, Texas, to Liberal, Kansas. This competition was slated to cross the BM&E's projected survey at right angles 7.7 miles west of Turpin at the future townsite of Baker. The Amarillo-Liberal line was conceived to help the Rock Island maintain its grip on the heavy grain traffic of Texas County. It also was designed to connect at Amarillo with the CRI&P's east-west line which bisected Oklahoma via Oklahoma City, El Reno, and Elk City. Collectively, this would diminish the importance of the M-K-T's Northwestern District and negate the claim that only the BM&E and the M-K-T together connected the Panhandle with the rest of Oklahoma.[10]

Meanwhile, H. G. McClure built a 16'x60' frame combination station for the BM&E at Turpin. A well, pumping station, and an 18,000 gallon water tank also were installed. At the same time, Achenbach re-examined the prospects of westward expansion and concluded that it was still justified. It would be necessary to ask the I.C.C. for an extension of the deadline for completion of the project. It also would be necessary to find short-term financing for purchasing the necessary rail. The regulatory agency twice extended the deadline, to December 31, 1926, and later to December 31, 1927. The Katy then found an unusual way to bolster the BM&E's temporarily sagging finances.[11]

Under two contracts, dated April 13 and August 4, 1926, the Misouri-Kansas-Texas Railroad leased 17 miles of 60-pound and 63-pound rail and fastenings to be laid by the BM&E westward from a point near Baker. The total value of the leased material was only $44,217.84, upon which the Beaver Road paid the usual six percent interest. These agreements included an option proviso whereby the BM&E was later able to purchase all of the leased items. Katy's seeming benevolence was easily understandable. The BM&E was tapping new and burgeoning trade areas which would be tributary in large measure to the M-K-T via the Forgan gateway. Moreover, the newly authorized Rock Island line from Amarillo to Liberal threatened the continued

73

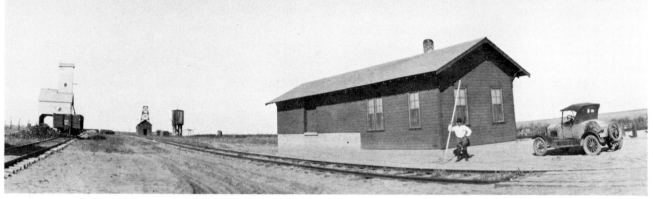

At Turpin, Achenbach authorized the construction of a 16' x 60' frame depot, a well, a pumping station, and an 18,000 gallon water tank. *M-K-T collection*

prosperity of Katy's own Northwestern District. By aiding the BM&E, the larger road was risking little but expecting much. After all, what was good for the Achenbach road was good for the Katy.[12]

Steel gangs renewed their labors during the summer of 1926, and by the end of August, 65 cars of wheat had been shipped from the new station at Baker. The Panhandle Townsite Company platted the village during the summer, and by fall it was able to announce that a lot sale would be held on October 20. The town was named after Reuben F. Baker of Hooker, who owned the quarter-section where the townsite was located. Baker was also the leader among Hooker residents who helped bring the BM&E to Texas County.[13]

Another resident of the Oklahoma Panhandle, Stacy R. Miller, a farmer and contractor, received many of the subcontracts let for grading by the Panhandle Construction Company. Miller was a good-sized man who was easily able to handle men, draft animals, and machinery. He

was generally paid in cash, but once he accepted $5,100 in BM&E securities as a partial payment. Another subcontractor was Guy Winn, who worked no less than 80 head of mules on his fresnoes and road plow. Winn's crew included eight men, who drove 4-mule teams, pulling fresnoes with only one-quarter yard capacities. Another man drove the 8-mule team which drew the heavy road plow, itself operated by another employee. Two others hauled the necessary water, grain, and hay. Winn's crew also included a foreman and a man-and-wife cook team. All, including the mules, slept in tents. Winn purchased oats and hay from local farmers and grain dealers, who thus found yet another reason to rejoice at the coming of the steam cars.[14]

Mr. A. Carey Hough, the BM&E's General Counsel, was in Hooker to address the Citizens' Railroad Committee on October 23. Hough exuded optimism and pledged the assistance and co-operation of the company which he represented. Hough predicted that great volumes of coal, petroleum, and agricultural produce would

74

eventually move via the Hooker gateway. There was good reason to be confident, at least in terms of the region's agricultural production. Farmers in Texas County harvested a huge 7.5 million bushel wheat crop in 1926. This resulted in the shipment of 4,851 carloads of wheat from Texas County elevators; 1,550 carloads were shipped from Hooker alone.[15]

While Hooker dearly wanted the BM&E, the Rock Island, which already served the community, did not. In November, 1926, the BM&E sought permission to cross the CRI&P at grade north of town and the Oklahoma Corporation Commission gave its blessing on December 17. The Beaver Road delivered materials to the cross-

ing site, but the Rock Island delayed installation by appealing the decision. Its Superintendent, H. P. Greenough, even posted guards lest the BM&E accomplish the task under cover of night. The Commission reaffirmed its decision on March 5, 1927, and the crossing was effected by crews of the BM&E and the CRI&P shortly thereafter. All costs were divided equally for the two carriers.[16]

H. C. Baird of Oklahoma City was appointed General Agent for the BM&E at Hooker in April; one month later, the road delivered the first freight shipment to the Pierce Oil Company. Still the road was not officially opened for business between Baker and Hooker. One problem

Except for a few curves near Forgan, and a short reverse curve between the Rock Island crossing and the Hooker depot, the BM&E route between Forgan and Hooked, Oklahoma provided a straight track built on the center-section line. *M-K-T collection.*

BM&E locomotive #229 shows a clear stack prior to its departure from Hooker in 1928 with a short train for Forgan and Beaver. *M-K-T collection*

remained—legal difficulties regarding abstracts. These prevented opening the line in time for the 1927 grain season and caused Achenbach to feel that the Hooker Railroad Committee had not carried out its promises. The newly appointed agent eventually was recalled, and the weeds grew high in the Hooker yards. Then the abstract problems appeared to be solved, for the BM&E finally established train service to Hooker in the late days of October 1927. The editor of the *Hooker Advance* then gloated: "There is more incoming and outgoing freight from this point, than any other point in the west." This was a totally inaccurate calculation but one which might be forgiven, considering the exuberance of the moment. Nevertheless, the arrival of the BM&E promised to make Hooker more than just "a good Saturday night town." The BM&E's agent at Beaver (City had by now been dropped from the corporate title), R. H. Dorsey, was transferred to Hooker in November. Right-of-way fence between Forgan and Hooker was built, and a transfer track between the CRI&P and the BM&E was installed at Hooker. Meanwhile, the line between Baker and Hooker was operated unofficially until December 31, when it was fully opened to revenue service.[17]

Uncle Jake Achenbach had built a road nearly devoid of curves, bridges, and heavy grades. Except for a few curves near Forgan, and a short reverse curve between the Rock Island crossing and the Hooker depot, the route provided a perfectly straight track built on the center-section line. There were only two bridges between Forgan and Hooker and but one major grade, Nash Hill eastbound. Westbound there was a gradual rise in elevation of about 11 feet per mile.[18]

Throughout this period, the BM&E operated tri-weekly round-trip service between Beaver and the end-of-track. Another train, powered by engine number 229—leased and then purchased from the Katy—handled construction duties. During the harvest rush, additional power was leased from the Katy, and Superintendent Booth hired any boomer railroader who would work. Normally, however, the BM&E's lone engine and regular crew were sufficient to handle the daily traffic. Payday rituals were handled as informally as hiring practices in the years before the road reached Hooker; employees were simply paid in cash each Saturday night at the Beaver depot.[19]

The Panhandle Construction Company performed all obligations on borrowed capital provided by Achenbach, his two sons, Blackstock, Turpin, the Panhandle Townsite Company, the BM&E, and friendly bankers. Achenbach and his sons provided the bulk of these funds. In every case, the lenders were fully repaid at eight percent interest. The Panhandle Construction Company was paid at the rate of $14,273.25 per mile, plus ten percent, in stocks and bonds of the railroad company. Later changes and additions required of the construction company were paid on the basis of actual costs plus ten per cent. The ulti-

76

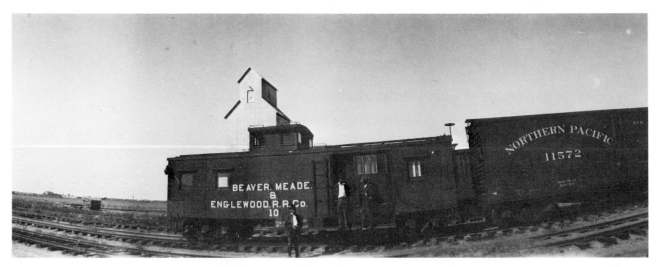

The BM&E's side door cabooses were functional if not elegant. *M-K-T collection*

mate expense of constructing the extension from Forgan to Hooker plus the salaries of general officers totaled $556,130.09, but under the terms of the construction contract, the BM&E paid out $632,046.06. Thus there remained a profit from construction of $75,915.97, easily sufficient to acquire the 17 miles of rail and fastenings originally leased to the BM&E by the Katy. In sum, the entire extension had been financed by Achenbach and his associates; they owned the entire railroad, the construction company, and the townsite company; and they profited through salaries, interest payments, and the growing equity of their securities. Moreover, the railroad had turned a tidy profit on its operations for 1926. The results for the following year were less impressive, but the future looked rosy.[20]

The future looked good, too, for the BM&E trade area. With the completion of the extension, no point in Beaver County was more than 30 miles from a railroad. In the twelve-month period following September 1, 1928, a total of 450 carloads were shipped from Turpin. Coincidental with the arrival of the railroad in that community, area schools were consolidated in 1927. Two years later, there were several businesses in Turpin, including three elevators, a bank, a general store, a lumber yard, and several other establishments. Beaver, progenitor of the BM&E, shipped to market nearly one million bushels of wheat in 622 cars and another 66 cars of other assorted grains between September 1, 1928, and August 30, 1929. Within the same period, the Beaver agent also billed 92 cars of broomcorn, 20 cars

of hogs, plus numerous shipments of cattle and other commodities. Before Uncle Jake had finished the home road in 1915, it appeared that Beaver City might pass in favor of Forgan. However, the BM&E gave the Beaver County capital new life; Forgan's importance had peaked by 1919 and then it declined. On the other hand, a partial listing of commercial establishments at Beaver in 1929 included five elevators, four groceries, three hardware firms, three dry goods establishments, three drug stores, and a theatre. As Beaver and the surrounding area matured and prospered, so did the railroad that was the Panhandle's own.[21]

77

On the High Plains, the windmill means life. Near the BM&E right-of-way between Hough and Hovey. *Author's photograph*

Panhandle Odyssey:
The BM&E: 1928-1931

"Today's railroad, like other great utilities are intended to serve—serve the public—and the BM&E must serve—will serve—the Panhandle of Oklahoma." A. Carey Hough*

In 1924, while construction crews toiled on the route west of Forgan, officers of the BM&E in the Grain Exchange Building at Oklahoma City mapped long-range strategy. President Achenbach was optimistic about extending the road west of Hooker, but was concomitantly cautious. The great wheat crop of 1924 suggested that adequate revenue would derive from the movement of agricultural produce originating in the country west of Hooker. Yet Achenbach realized that the average annual rainfall on the High Plains in western Texas County and in all of Cimarron County, Oklahoma, was less than 17 inches. He had been a farmer in Illinois and in Kansas and was fully aware of the inherent risks in agriculture. He also understood that the gamble in husbandry was even greater in lands closer to the mountains. Thus any railroad built into those areas and dependent on the revenue gained from the carriage of agricultural produce grown there would be subject to financial rewards as dictated by capricious weather conditions. This liability could be offset somewhat, however, if the projected railroad was able to capture other regular sources of traffic or if it could be connected with trunk lines willing to give it heavy bridge traffic. Apparently the BM&E officers never contemplated the latter option, but the former possibility was elementary to the carrier's ultimate goals as early as the fall of 1924.[1]

Several previous railroad projects had been sponsored by those interested in connecting the coal fields of northeastern New Mexico with the

markets of central and western Oklahoma and the Panhandle. Yet no such railroad project had been carried to fruition despite the fact that coal traffic from New Mexico would constitute a steady and remunerative source of revenue. Achenbach considered this potential traffic as the cushion necessary to justify any significant extension of the Beaver Road beyond Hooker. Thus on October 24, 1924, General Counsel A. Carey Hough filed papers with the Interstate Commerce Commission which asked permission to construct a line of road from Hooker, Oklahoma, to Des Moines, New Mexico. Reflecting Achenbach's cautious judgment, however, Hough requested that the proceedings be held in suspension until the end of 1927. The Governors and Corporation Commissions of both Colorado and New Mexico, as well as regional members of Congress, fully supported the BM&E's desire to become an interstate carrier. The regulatory agency accommodated Hough's request and did not hand down its decision until March 13, 1928. In sum, the I.C.C. permitted construction of a new line from Hooker to Keyes, in Cimarron County, Oklahoma, but denied without prejudice the request to build west from Keyes into New Mexico. The decision thus authorized extension of the BM&E into an agricultural region which Achenbach regarded as capable of supporting the railroad on its own merits. Furthermore, the long-range goals of the road were not denied—merely postponed.[2]

When the I.C.C. made its decision, the happy news was relayed to the *Hooker Advance*

*Hooker [Oklahoma] Advance, October 23, 1926.

79

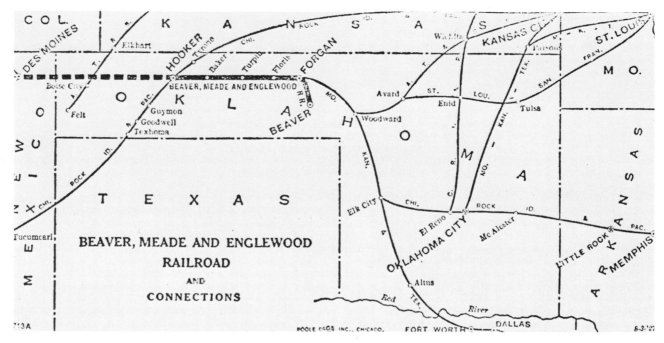

Map of the BM&E, August 3, 1927. *Author's collection*

by Congressman M. C. Garber. A few days later, General Manager Carl J. Turpin wrote an open letter to the citizens of Hooker thanking them for the support which they had given the railroad in its recent application before the regulatory agency. Turpin promised that the line, when completed to Keyes, would "make the Panhandle a part of the great state of Oklahoma in fact as well as name." The BM&E official asserted that the construction of the Beaver Road from Forgan had stimulated other railroad promotions in the Panhandle by two trunk carriers, the Santa Fe and the Rock Island. Finally, Turpin pleaded for the continued co-operation of Panhandle residents, especially in the matter of soliciting right-of-way lands.[3]

The editor of the *Hooker Advance* counseled his readers to assist the enterprise in any way possible. Such support was justified because thousands of dollars had been saved by farmers in the areas around Turpin and Baker since the arrival of the BM&E to those points "and thousands of dollars will be saved by the farmers along the proposed western extension by nearer markets and shorter hauls." Additionally, property throughout the area would rise in valuation on completion of the lines to Keyes. This spelled progress as far as the Hooker journalist was concerned. "Hooker is in the midst of her brightest future," bubbled the editor.[4]

Earlier, in the fall of 1927, President Achenbach had spent considerable time making preliminary surveys between Hooker and the New Mexico border. On this trip, he was accompanied by his son August and Morris Burke, then the company's civil engineer and principal contractor. They considered three routes: via Keyes, via Boise City, and via Kenton. Surviving records do not indicate why the Boise City and Kenton options were discarded. A route through Boise City would have provided the most direct link with Des Moines, but by 1927, Boise City was "a Santa Fe town," which may explain why it was rejected. The Kenton route would have taken the line over more broken country than the other two. The route chosen, to Keyes, passed through some of the finest wheat land in the Panhandle. Except for some rough country near Goff Creek, between Hough and Tracy, the survey was made along the half-section line.[5]

Before April 1, 1928, Achenbach awarded several contracts. One, for the construction of a 20'x80' wood-frame combination depot at Hooker, went to H. G. McClure. Another was awarded to Morris C. Burke for grading the first 20.2 miles from Hooker to Hough. Stacy R. Miller and August E. Achenbach received the two subcontracts. Miller began grading west from Hooker, while Achenbach started near Hough and worked toward the east; the official ground-

The wood-frame combination depot at Hooker was erected under a contract let to H. G. McClure. *M-K-T collection*

breaking ceremony occurred on April 26. The rail was down as far as Mouser, 11.2 miles, before the Fourth of July. As a result, two Hooker residents, Ed Hopkins and J. H. Mason, built a 25,000-bushel elevator at Mouser in the summer of 1928. During mid-July, they shipped the first dozen cars of wheat from that point. Two months earlier, Hooker had received no fewer than 50 carloads of freight on the BM&E in a one-week period. Moreover, 30 cars of wheat were loaded on the BM&E at Hooker each day during the first week of July by the Wheat Pool Elevator.[6]

As soon as the BM&E had passed from local control in 1915, Jacob Achenbach clearly emerged as the strongest of the buyers. Achenbach was a frequent visitor on the property, but the day-to-day operations were in the hands of his trusted lieutenants—Carl J. Turpin, General Manager, and A. Carey Hough, General Counsel. Turpin and Hough were also officers of the Panhandle Construction Company and the Panhandle Townsite Company. On May 18, 1928, Turpin and Hough negotiated the acquisition of nearly 40 acres of land from Alfred C. Mouser which subsequently was platted as the Mouser townsite. At Hough, named for the railroad's general counsel, the same process was followed. Nearly 40 acres were acquired by the townsite company from Edward Eden on June 16 and platted a month later. Lots there were sold for businesses and residences; one parcel brought $500.[7]

In May, 1928, the *Hooker Advance* proudly proclaimed that "only a few condemnation" proceedings were necessary to procure right-of-way lands on the new line. Indeed, between Hooker and Hough nearly all lands were secured under warranty deeds. Surviving corporate records indicate that the extension from Hooker to Hough was turned over to revenue operation as of July 1, 1929, but the line was clearly in service before that time. The railroad built a number of permanent structures at Hough, including a pump house, water tank, section house, and other buildings for maintenance of way equipment. Then the contractors disbanded their crews while Uncle Jake contemplated the future of the road.[8]

A number of factors conspired to make the Oklahoma Panhandle increasingly a wheat-producing area. Just as The Great War began, weather conditions on the Southern Great Plains fostered bountiful crops of wheat. While national leaders said that wheat would win the war, many farmers felt that the tractor could remake the plains. As Vance Johnson put it, "the weather was ideal for the great wheat expansion. The nation demanded it. The tractor made it possible." On May 1, 1915, wheat sold for $1.15 per bushel; but two years later, wheat grown by farmers on the southern Great Plains was bringing $2.15 per bushel. For better or for worse, such growth caused 64 percent of the growers to become dependent on cash crops—wheat in particular—for a living. More land was placed in production, and much more machinery, including trucks and combines, was purchased. One observer noted that "tractors, combines, trucks, and all the other appurtenances of modern wheat production, made possible—and in a sense compelled—a vast expansion in" the farmer's operation. Overproduction followed; it resulted in lowered wheat prices for the farmer, but it also resulted in an increased volume of traffic that served to profit the BM&E by its carriage. As a result, the Beaver Road boasted a net profit of $38,516 in 1928.[9]

In 1929 and 1930, the BM&E and its owners became involved in two major law suits. On November 27, 1929, the Beaver Road brought suit against R. F. Baker and 45 other residents of Hooker who were collectively labeled the Hooker Guarantors. In April 1924, the BM&E and the Hooker Guarantors had entered into a written agreement whereby the defendants promised to procure, without cost to the plaintiff, the entire right-of-way from Forgan to a point ten miles west of Hooker. In return, the BM&E promised to build its line to Hooker. To expedite construction, the BM&E advanced $25,460.94 to the defendants for use in purchasing the required lands. By 1929, only $7,972.11 had been repaid, leaving a balance due of $17,488.83. Additionally, the BM&E alleged that it would need another $2,500 to satisfy all additional right-of-way claims. The trial lasted for five days before the jury found for the defendants on November 25, 1929. The case was appealed to the Oklahoma Supreme Court, but a decision from that body did not appear until 1934. The records of the case suggest that the Hooker Guarantors acted in bad faith, but the Supreme Court upheld the lower court's ruling nevertheless, saying that the contract was not binding since insufficient numbers of Guarantors had signed the instrument. The earlier love affair between residents of Hooker and the BM&E had evaporated.[10]

The second suit was filed in January of 1930 by Joseph A. Tack; Jacob A. Achenbach and Ira B. Blackstock were the defendants. Tack had been the intermediary between the Beaver Railroad Committee and Achenbach in 1915. Achenbach had been told by Tack that the citizens of Beaver would willingly turn the BM&E over to him if he would agree to purchase the entire $25,000 stock issue of the broke and incompleted railroad. Achenbach and Blackstock had then put up the $25,000 and authorized Tack to complete

the road on their behalf—with, Tack claimed, the proviso that all three men eventually would share equally in the ownership of the property. Tack subsequently had received $10,000 in payment for his work, and this, Achenbach and Blackstock contended, was payment in full. They denied that Tack had any further interest in the road. Records of the company filed with the Interstate Commerce Commission and the Oklahoma Secretary of State fail to mention Tack's name either as a holder of BM&E capital stock or of its first mortgage bonds. Tack maintained, nevertheless, that an oral contract had been made. The jury, in February of 1931, saw otherwise and found for the defendants.[11]

There was considerable other railroad construction in the Oklahoma Panhandle during the last half of the 1920s and first half of the 1930s. Some of it was undoubtedly prompted by the construction of the BM&E, but much of it reflected the rounding out of secondary trunk line systems by the Rock Island and Santa Fe companies. The Amarillo to Liberal line of the CRI&P, begun in 1926, was completed at 7:30 p.m. on Saturday, July 26, 1929, when the last spike was driven at the center of the bridge spanning the Beaver River between Hardesty and Adams. The Beaver Road had protested the construction of this line but had been overruled by the I.C.C. The two lines crossed at a grade in Baker, where in 1928 the BM&E had originated some 800 cars of wheat. Without doubt, the competition of the second Rock Island route in Texas County would hurt the BM&E.[12]

Farther west, Cimarron County became a bastion of Santa Fe power. In 1925, the diagonal line of the AT&SF from Dodge City, which had languished at Elkhart, Kansas, since 1913, was extended 59 miles through Boise City to an obscure village named Felt. The first train arrived in Boise City, the county seat, on October 3, 1925. Six years later the road was extended to Clayton, New Mexico. Trackage rights over the Colorado & Southern Railway then were obtained from Clayton to Mount Dora, and from there additional construction by the AT&SF provided service to Farley. The Santa Fe hoped eventually to finish another 35 miles to Colmor, a station on its original transcontinental route. The Dodge City-Boise City-Colmor line would have saved 69 miles on the Santa Fe's main line and would have allowed overland traffic to avoid the tortuous grade over Raton Pass. Unfortunately, the depression intervened and the dream was never consummated. Indeed, the long stretch from Boise City to Farley would be abandoned in 1942. In 1931, the AT&SF also completed a road from Amarillo to Boise City. After a lapse of six years this line was lengthened northward from Boise City to Las Animas, Colorado. A junction there with the AT&SF's LaJunta-Pueblo-Denver line allowed the Santa Fe to compete effectively with the C&S/FW&DC Gulf-to-Rockies route. The Santa Fe built no east-west routes in the Oklahoma Panhandle. Yet it constructed north-south lines on the eastern and western edges of the region and east-west routes to the north and to the south. The BM&E "split" the Panhandle, but the AT&SF effectively boxed it in.[13]

Early in the fall of 1927, the Beaver Road announced a tri-weekly schedule for its mixed trains between Beaver and Hooker. Train number one was slated to leave Beaver on Tuesdays, Thursdays, and Saturdays at 8:00 a.m. It spent the noon hour switching at Hooker and returned to Beaver as train number two at 5:20 p.m. Extra trains were called as needed. One year later, the BM&E advertised the same time table but increased its service to a daily round-trip basis. However, in the summer of 1929, the road instituted a significant alteration in its operations. Beginning on June 16, train number one departed from Forgan daily-except-Sunday at 6:00 p.m.,

made a Hooker turn, and returned to Forgan via Beaver as train number two at 4:00 a.m. Irregular service was offered between Hooker and Hough. This service meshed nicely with the schedules of the M-K-T at Forgan and afforded Panhandle shippers convenient and reliable service.[14]

The management of the Beaver Road did not favor business other than carload freight nor did it solicit any. Carl Turpin announced in mid-1928 that the company would not provide full passenger service on the Hooker extension. For that matter, the earlier policy of operating BM&E trains on schedules designed to connect with the Katy passenger trains at Forgan long since had been discontinued. Indeed, paying passengers were a rare item on the road by 1928. Those who did show up were carried on the cushions of its side-door cabooses. During the grain season, BM&E crews were especially hospitable; trains were stopped anywhere along the line to pick up or drop off "harvest hands." It was important to do whatever was necessary to assist in the harvest and, whether it was official policy or not, these itinerant workers often were transported gratis.[15]

Unsolicited though it may have been, less-than-carload (LCL) freight and express was also handled on BM&E trains. Both express and LCL shipments from Forgan to Beaver were especially heavy. The Rock Island likewise supplied heavy transfer shipments at Hooker. Much of the LCL and express traffic flowing through this gateway originated at Amarillo, Texas, and Hutchinson,

It is nearly "train time" at Beaver in this 1920 view. *Veldo H. Brewer collection*

Kansas, and also was destined for Beaver merchants. LCL shipments included general freight and merchandise such as hardware, canned goods, flour, and even candy. Candy was shipped in pails, and merchants often complained that the containers were not completely full when delivered. The management of the BM&E grudgingly paid the resulting claims and pledged more diligent surveillance of train crews. Later, when the road was extended westward from Hough, donuts and bread were shipped on the BM&E from Les Rickman's bakery at Hooker to the grocery store at Eva.[16]

Carload business, without question, provided the company with its principle revenue. Inbound shipments included combines, petroleum products, and livestock. Outbound loadings were essentially livestock and grains. Wheat consigned to grain dealers in Kansas City, Missouri, Hutchinson, Kansas, and Enid, Oklahoma, moved to junction points with the CRI&P at Baker and Hooker. Most of the wheat, however, went to Gulf ports via Forgan and the M-K-T.[17]

All traffic on the road was handled by locomotives owned by the BM&E or borrowed from trunk carriers. Before the summer of 1929, the Beaver Road owned a total of five second-hand locomotives acquired during various stages of its growth from the M-K-T. The first of these, appropriately given the number "1" by the BM&E, was a very light 2-6-0 built by Baldwin Locomotive Works in 1891. This machine was purchased in 1915 and was followed by number "2," a similar locomotive that was acquired a year later. Number 454, a light 2-6-0 outshopped by Baldwin in 1901, arrived on the property late in 1924. Four years later, the BM&E leased and then purchased number 229, a modest 4-6-0 constructed by American Locomotive Company in 1904. It was followed by number 237, another Baldwin product originally purchased by the Katy in 1905. It is doubtful that all five of these locomotives were ever in running order at the same time. The BM&E once used a Rock Island 1400-class engine as a "loaner" but the M-K-T provided the majority of the extra power during the annual wheat rushes. Originally the Beaver Road borrowed Katy's 400-class 2-6-0 engines because Superintendent E. E. Booth feared that the Katy's larger 500-series moguls were too heavy for the Beaver's track. Louis Baker, Achenbach's secretary, leased some 500s anyway, and they proved to be perfectly acceptable.[18]

Goff Creek, looking north toward the BM&E's trestles. *Author's photograph*

Early in 1929, General Counsel A. Carey Hough appeared before the Interstate Commerce Commission with a request that the BM&E be permitted to issue securities sufficient to finance construction of the road to Keyes. The I.C.C. promptly authorized the issuance of $591,000 in first mortgage six percent gold bonds in denominations of $1,000. It also allowed the company to increase its capitalization by $605,700. However, not until February of the following year did Achenbach announce that the extension program actually would be pursued. By June 1, 1930, the bonds were issued, and Uncle Jake was ready to sign construction contracts. A few days later, the BM&E again amended its charter to permit the new construction beyond Hooker to Keyes. However, no mention was made of any long range plans to build into New Mexico. The company also was formally recapitalized at $930,000. Achenbach took 1413 shares, Blackstock 1168, Turpin 204, and August E. Achenbach 184, while one director's share each was awarded to Jule G. Smith of Fort Worth, and H. A. Dockum of Wichita, Kansas.[19]

The route between Hough and Eva, 20.4 miles, covered a terrain that was more broken than any other on the line. Construction Engineer E. C. Quickel therefore was forced to locate the right-of-way on a path that departed from the usual center-section line. This also meant that the road ran at angles which unfortunately interfered with farming and ranching operations. As a result, most of the lands necessary for right-of-way were secured only by condemnation proceedings that forever alienated the affections of many property owners. The most difficult construction problems on the entire road were encountered about six miles west of Hough; these were occasioned by the presence of Big Goff Creek, a normally dry stream bed, and its tributaries. In order to reach the valley of the main stream, the Panhandle Construction Company found it necessary to carve a deep and lengthy excavation—known as Hovey's Cut—through the surrounding hills. Two bridges of 7 panels each and a third of 17 panels were necessary to span Big Goff and its attendant creeks. The ruling grades on the entire BM&E proved to be at Hovey, in both directions from this valley.[20]

The road was completed to Eva before the end of 1930 but was not turned over to full revenue operation until March 1, 1931. A frame combination station, a pumphouse, water tank, section house, and bunk house were subsequently erected at Eva. Eight miles east of that station, at mile post 77, Construction Engineer Quickel returned the survey to a route that followed the center-section line, and farmers west of that point generally co-operated by granting title for right-of-way lands without a quarrel. From mile post 77, the survey extended west on a perfectly straight line to mile post 103.5, where a slight jog to the northwest was necessary to take the railroad into Keyes. From Eva to Keyes, the terrain was flat to slightly rolling, with a constant but gentle rise in elevation toward the west. The area was devoid of streams and dry creek beds, and engineers found it unnecessary to construct any bridges whatsoever between Goff Creek, mile post 73.2, and the end-of-track at Keyes, mile post 105.[21]

Nearly 30 percent of the grading between Eva and Keyes was completed in 1930. In March of the following year, Stacy R. Miller accepted a contract to complete the remaining grade. This work was easy for Miller's motorized machinery; little excavation was necessary. Steel gangs followed closely behind Miller's graders, and on June 25 the road was completed to Keyes. It was placed in service five days later. A depot similar to that at Eva, a section house, and a tool house soon were constructed there. Even before the rails had arrived, H. E. Knight was dispatched to Keyes as agent, and on the first day of business, he billed three cars of wheat.[22]

Achenbach found opportunity for townsite development at Tracy and Eva, and to a lesser

Fred C. Tracy served as the BM&E's Secretary for several years. *Eleanor Tracy collection*

extent at the community which the railroad temporarily labeled South Keyes. At the latter point, the BM&E's station and yards were located four blocks south of the Santa Fe's Keyes depot. The intervening distance was partially filled by William A. Miller, the landowner, who on November 18, 1930, platted the area and labeled it "Keyes' Cimarron Heights Addition." The connection between him and Achenbach, if any, is unknown. Farther east, the townsite of Tracy, named for Fred C. Tracy of Beaver, the road's secretary, was platted on May 1, 1931. The railroad built a depot and stock pens there, but the village failed to prosper; by 1933, it had even been renamed "Muncy." Eva proved to be more suitably located, and the Panhandle Townsite Company did a good business in lot sales at that point.[23]

By the time it reached Keyes, the BM&E owned and operated 105 miles of railroad and was truly the Panhandle's private transportation servant. The dreams of reaching the New Mexico

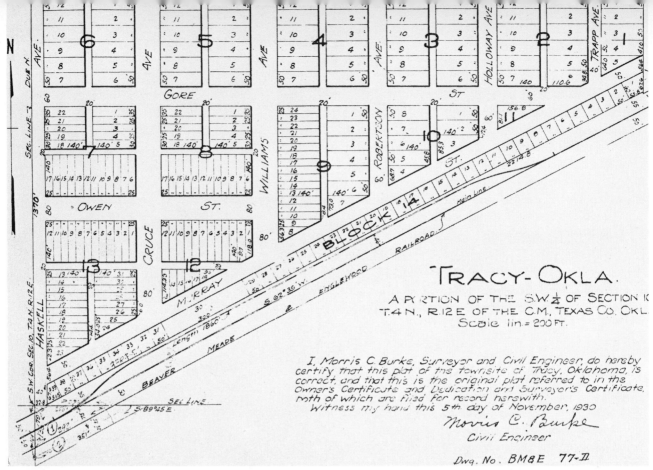

Tracy—a project of the Panhandle Townsite Company—was named for Fred C. Tracy of Beaver, the BM&E Secretary. *Author's collection*

coal fields were only infrequently recalled by BM&E officials after 1929. They did, however, authorize a survey from Hough to Elkhart, Kansas, sometime after April 1930, but this project also was discounted. The road had been built with private, if outside, capital for the twin purposes of satisfying the transportation needs of an area poor in transportation devices and of gaining profits for the owners. Both goals were met. In 1930, the BM&E moved its operational headquarters to Hooker—nearly at the center of the Panhandle—and was operating convenient daily-except-Sunday round-trip service between Hooker and Beaver on an afternoon and early evening schedule. The road also operated trains to Keyes after the line was opened to that village in 1931, but only on an irregular basis. It had been constructed economically and efficiently and was not overcapitalized. The entire railroad was laid with light relay rail on mostly untreated ties bedded generally in earthen ballast. Yet the line's traffic pattern meant only heavy track wear during the harvest season and, if properly maintained, would be fully serviceable for a protracted period of time. Although its productivity

was irregular, the Panhandle already had proved its value as a "breadbasket." If the Panhandle prospered, so did the Beaver Road; if the Panhandle languished, so did its railroad. In 1929, the BM&E's nearly $100,000 profit mirrored this relationship. The lesson was not lost on two of the area's trunk carriers, the Rock Island and the M-K-T. Both were profit-seekers and both came to covet the BM&E. A lengthy and bitter struggle for its control followed.[24]

BEAVER, MEADE AND ENGLEWOOD
RAILROAD COMPANY
1929   No. B 46
PASS Lawrence A. Downs, President

ACCOUNT Illinois Central Railroad
Company

UNTIL DECEMBER 31, 1929 { UNLESS OTHERWISE ORDERED AND SUBJECT TO CONDITIONS ON BACK

FIRST VICE PRESIDENT

The "Orphan" No More:
Sale of the BM&E

"It is a fair inference from the evidence that but for the offer of the Rock Island to purchase the BM&E interests, the M-K-T would have made no move to that end. As long as it could get all the BM&E traffic anyway, it was willing to forego any obligation or burden. . . ."*

Jacob A. Achenbach was a farmer, not a railroad man. In large measure he was forced into the railroad business when trunk carriers refused to build into the area of his residence near Hardtner, Kansas. At the age of 64, however, Achenbach set about the task of linking Hardtner with Kiowa, the nearest railroad town. The result was the Kiowa, Hardtner & Pacific Railroad Company, completed in June of 1910, consisting of ten and one-half miles of track. At no time did Uncle Jake ever exhibit any enthusiasm for the personal operation of the KH&P. With the aid of a few financial associates, he had taken the risks of construction, but when the line was completed, he was perfectly willing to lease the property to the Missouri Pacific. In this manner, Achenbach succeeded in gaining a railroad for his town and in making both short-term and long-range profits without shouldering the responsibility of operating the KH&P.[1]

Achenbach expected to handle the Beaver, Meade & Englewood in like fashion. When he and his associates purchased that road's capital stock in 1915, they expected little difficulty in peddling the completed road to the Missouri, Kansas & Texas, then the lessee of the Wichita Falls & Northwestern Railway. Earlier, when the KH&P had been leased to the MP, that road had simply moved its terminal from Kiowa to the KH&P's end-of-track at Hardtner. Achenbach assumed that the Katy would gladly take the BM&E and then move its WF&NW terminal seven miles from Forgan to Beaver. But the MK&T was bankrupt at that time and was in no condition to assume even an insignificant lease such as that which Uncle Jake offered. Furthermore, the Katy management took a haughty attitude, saying that the BM&E would never earn a profit.

His Teutonic temperament thoroughly antagonized, the 69-year-old Kansas railroad builder immediately purchased a locomotive, a coach, a couple of box cars, and a caboose. In this fashion, he became a railroad entrepreneur. Indeed, there was little choice. Unless the BM&E could be extended beyond Forgan, there were no prospective suitors other than the Katy; yet at that time, Uncle Jake had no cash in the till for additional construction. Some observers scoffed at the BM&E, calling it "Jake's fool project," but the enterprise struggled along and by 1924 was ready to begin further construction. Three years later, it reached Hooker, thereby forging a connection with the Chicago, Rock Island & Pacific Railway.[2]

About the time the BM&E was approaching Hooker, Achenbach renewed exploratory negotiations with the Katy. This reportedly resulted in a spontaneous decision which led him to make an unannounced trip to St. Louis to meet with the M-K-T president. On this trip, he unfortunately

*Before the Interstate Commerce Commission, Finance Docket Nos. 7624 and 7680. *Brief of the Applicant, the Chicago, Rock Island & Pacific Railway Company,* September 12, 1929, p. 22.

was dressed in his usual offhand way, and his countenance and general demeanor offended the railroad's receptionist—who refused to allow the Kansan beyond the outer office. Achenbach responded with an outburst of colorful if obscene Germanic oaths and was subsequently ushered from the premises. He doubtless never forgot the incident. Apparently the Katy was not serious about purchasing the BM&E anyway, for its president stated that "acquisition of the line would be of no advantage to the M-K-T."[3]

In 1927, however, the Katy presidency passed to Columbus Haile, who soon renewed contact with the BM&E by way of Carl J. Turpin, its General Manager. At the same time, the M-K-T was involved in an important consolidation plan which would have combined the Katy with the St. Louis Southwestern and Kansas City Southern companies. Until these negotiations were finally terminated, there was no real bargaining between the BM&E and the Katy. Then on November 3, 1928, Turpin asked Haile if the M-K-T was interested in procuring the Beaver Road. Haile responded two days later by saying that the Katy "would not be interested just now in the acquisition of the BM&E." After a lapse of four months, Haile inquired as to the current status of the road; Turpin replied that his company had "made no effort whatever to dispose of the property and are not particularly anxious to do so as our folks thought they would like to complete the extension as far as the Santa Fe [at Keyes]." Turpin did admit that he had received numerous other inquiries. According to the BM&E's General Manager, he had told all parties that, while they were not anxious to sell, the owners might accept an offer of $20,000 per mile. On April 27, 1929, President Haile asked Turpin to meet with him to "discuss the possible purchase of the BM&E." Haile advised Turpin that he understood that both the Rock Island and the Santa Fe were considering the purchase of Achenbach's "orphan road." The Katy president asked Turpin to delay any action until such time as they could "get together and talk the matter over." On the other hand, Turpin was evasive and declined to meet with Haile even in Oklahoma City.[4]

Turpin had reason to be evasive. On April 3, President J. E. Gorman of the Rock Island had secured permission from his board of directors to purchase the capital stock and bonds of the BM&E at the rate of $20,000 per mile, or approximately $1,310,000. A sales agreement then was drawn and signed on April 28 with $25,000 in earnest money deposited in favor of the BM&E owners. Subsequently, on May 25, the CRI&P management filed the necessary application with the Interstate Commerce Commission. A few days earlier, President Haile of the Katy had learned of these developments and had told a Rock Island representative in New York that the M-K-T would "oppose the granting of such an application and would, in our own interests, feel compelled to use every effort against it."[5]

The headlines of the *Hooker Advance* for May 23, 1929, seethed with the message: "CRI&P Buys BM&E Road." There was fear in Hooker that the Rock Island would tear up the newly built BM&E, although a representative of that company told a meeting of the Hooker Lions Club that the CRI&P planned to complete the road to Keyes, "and if conditions justify, to complete the road to its western end [Des Moines, New Mexico]." Nevertheless, 75 residents gathered in mid-June at the Masonic Hall to hear Katy's Z. G. Hopkins weakly explain why his company had been slow to act. Hopkins maintained that "as long as the BM&E Railroad was operated under its present management," it had not been advantageous for "the M-K-T to acquire its property." Hopkins implied that the Katy management felt somehow betrayed by Achenbach's recent actions. The city sided with the Katy; it did not wish to lose the railroad competition which it had so recently gained.[6]

A few days later, H. G. Clark, a Rock Island Vice President, was in Hooker to explain the case for his company. He advised that under the Rock Island plan the BM&E would remain a separate company, although numerous improvements in facilities and service would be made. However, Clark did not promise that the road would be extended to Keyes as had been asserted earlier, and his presentation was unnecessarily abrasive. He had been sent to Hooker to quiet resistance in that community, but he left by saying that "if we cannot gain your consent, we intend to purchase the road anyway." The BM&E had given Hooker shippers, especially wheat growers, better rates; purchase of the road by the Rock Island clearly meant the end of such favorable conditions. The editor of the *Hooker Advance* labeled the gathering opposition as a "bitter protest" against Achenbach's unconscionable attempt to sell the Beaver Road to the CRI&P—the very company whose clutches Hooker had tried to escape by assisting the construction of the BM&E. The Hooker editor contended that area citizens had placed in the hands of BM&E officials right-of-way lands, moneys, and labor in the amount of $150,000—but admitted that competitive rates in 1928 alone had saved Texas County wheat growers $144,000 as against the rates of 1926 (before the Beaver Road had reached Hooker). Both figures appear to be inflated; indeed, those who had entered into a contract to assist the BM&E eventually voided their earlier commitment (see Chapter XIII). Nevertheless, the town of Hooker and the county of Texas energetically fought the acquisition of the Beaver Road by the Rock Island.[7]

Meanwhile, the M-K-T filed an intervening petition in opposition to the CRI&P's application. On June 19, the Katy Board of Directors authorized President Haile to make an application for authority to acquire control of the BM&E for the same consideration and upon the same terms and conditions as the Rock Island had agreed to. The board also authorized Haile to advise the I.C.C. that the M-K-T would proceed with the extension of the line to Keyes. Such an application was filed with the regulatory agency on June 26.[8]

During the summer of 1929, the Rock Island took a strong hand in the management and operation of the BM&E. At its La Salle Street Station headquarters in Chicago, Rock Island management made plans to rehabilitate and generally upgrade the road. A CRI&P locomotive was loaned to the Beaver Road, and Rock Island gangs were used to make certain improvements on the property. At Hooker, W. H. Wells, the cashier for the BM&E, was transferred to the Rock Island depot. At the same time, the Interstate Commerce Commission held hearings in Oklahoma City to decide whether the Rock Island or the Katy was to receive permission to purchase the Beaver.[9]

All parties agreed that there was no issue as to whether the BM&E should be made a part of a larger system. The Rock Island pointed out that it held a sales agreement with the owners of the Beaver Road; the M-K-T did not. Moreover, the CRI&P boasted that it was "one of the premier grain carrying roads in the West," and control by that road would, it was argued, give the grain farmers and elevator operators of the BM&E trade area a wide range of competitive markets in Kansas, Texas, and Oklahoma. Cecil Munn, President of the Enid Terminal Elevator Company, pointed out that in the event of Rock Island control, his firm would be "permitted to move wheat from BM&E stations to Enid and transit it without penalty." S. J. Cole of the Amarillo Chamber of Commerce, representing the grain dealers and wholesale houses of that city, also favored the Rock Island's application. However, most of the wheat shipped on the BM&E moved to Fort Worth, a destination which was 92 miles farther via the CRI&P than it was on the Katy. Yet, as the Rock Island representatives demonstrated, Fort Worth was merely an initial destination for transit purposes; the real destination was Gulf ports, and the Rock Island's haul to those destinations was only 25 miles farther than the Katy route. Finally, the CRI&P agreed to operate the BM&E in connection with its main line at Hooker, whereas the Northwestern District of the Katy offered only tri-weekly freight service over its dirt track railroad.[10]

Katy's President Haile responded by asserting that his road's long-standing position had been that when Katy "matured its plans for further extension it would acquire the property of the Beaver Road, which would constitute an extension of the WF&NW as originally planned." He admitted that "so long as the Beaver Road was operated as an independent short line, the Katy officials felt that the traffic from that line would naturally move via Forgan and the Katy." The connections established with the Rock Island at Baker and Hooker and the anticipated connection with the AT&SF at Keyes changed all that. The Katy now considered the BM&E vital to its welfare, particularly because of the support it gave to its Northwestern District. Earnings on traffic which the M-K-T interchanged with the BM&E in 1928 alone amounted to $647,080.11. "If the BM&E tonnage is diverted from that part of our line," Katy's counsel warned, "it would have the effect of reducing the earnings on our Northwestern District very substantially and will seriously impair the ability of our company to furnish adequate transportation service to the shipping public served by that line."[11]

The Katy attorneys argued that the "natural" movement of grain from BM&E origins was to elevators and mills in Oklahoma and Texas, and directly to Texas Gulf ports for export. Their figures showed that the vast majority of the BM&E's outbound traffic in 1928, 92.3 percent, was consigned to Texas and Oklahoma points. Some grain dealers maintained that, due to certain transit privileges, BM&E billing occasionally gained from 1 to 10 cents more per bushel for them as compared to grain loaded on the Rock Island. Kimball Elevator Company of Fort Worth favored the Katy application because it could use transit privileges on back-haul and/or substitute tonnage on grain moving eventually to Chicago, Minneapolis, and California. Union Equity Exchange, Farmer's Co-operative Elevators, Equity Elevators, Oklahoma Wheat Pool Elevator Corporation, and the Oklahoma Wheat Growers Association likewise favored the Katy request. A number of elevator operators in the Panhandle testified that the BM&E, with co-operation from the Katy, seemed better able to supply box cars for loading at peak harvest periods. The Rock Island owned more box cars than the Katy, but owned fewer in terms of cars per mile of operated railroad. Should the application of the Rock Island be granted, Katy counsel summarized, there would be no competition for the vast bulk of the Panhandle's rail traffic.[12]

No less than ten communities on the Northwestern District of the M-K-T protested against the Rock Island's application. Residents there perceived that the loss of traffic from the BM&E would negatively affect service to them by the Katy. Katy then was spending $500,000 on the Henrietta Subdivision, between Whitesboro and Wichita Falls, Texas, to upgrade that line which connected its Northwestern District and its main line. This was partially justified by the reasonably constant traffic of oil from Burkburnett and Wichita Falls, but that business was not permanent. Agricultural traffic originating on the BM&E would, it was argued, justify additional betterments on the Henrietta Subdivision and on the Northwestern District as well. Representatives from the Panhandle stressed the element of competition which was offered to them by the presence of the BM&E and vigorously favored Katy's application. The Rock Island boasted that it offered "superior service," but a Hooker attorney pointed

out that the CRI&P had not been able to hold the traffic of the territory against the competition of the BM&E. Indeed, the Rock Island's own George E. Snitzer testified that the majority of the grain business in the Panhandle then was handled by the BM&E.[13]

In mid-November the Commerce Commission decided in favor of the Katy's application. It noted that the bulk of the BM&E's outbound traffic was to the south and concluded that the M-K-T's Northwestern District heretofore had provided a satisfactory avenue for this commerce. The I.C.C. considered that the BM&E was a natural extension of the M-K-T and that diversion of tonnage from the Katy would prejudice adequate service to the stations of its Northwestern District. Moreover, the Katy seemed better able to supply grain cars at harvest time. Too, passage of the Beaver Road to the Katy would guarantee the future of rail competition in the Panhandle. In granting it permission to purchase the BM&E, the I.C.C. ordered the M-K-T to preserve existing routes and channels of trade; to maintain existing gateways for interchange; and to continue the neutrality of handling traffic by the Beaver Road.[14]

The news of the Commerce Commission's decision did not reach the Panhandle until after Thanksgiving. Almost simultaneously, Hooker learned that the legal suit brought by the BM&E against the Hooker Guarantors had been decided in favor of the defendants. As a result, the November 28, 1929, issue of the *Hooker Advance* was ceremoniously printed on pink paper and boasted dual headlines reading "Hooker Victorious" and "BM&E to Katy." The editor considered both decisions a singular "victory over the BM&E" and took great pride in announcing a forthcoming banquet in honor of R. F. Baker, the primary defendant in the law suit and chief spokesman for Hooker at the recent I.C.C. hearings. Clifford W. Ferguson of Hooker wrote to Charles S. Berg of Katy's legal department saying that Hooker was "just about to go wild." The optimistic editor of Hooker's newspaper expected the M-K-T to assume control of "the orphan" by the first of the year. Reportedly, Jacob Achenbach was ready to sell the Beaver Road to the Katy for the same amount which the Rock Island had promised—plus the amount that he and his associates had lost in the recent court battle with

Achenbach and his associates made a profit of $2,000 per mile from the sale of the BM&E. Here Uncle Jake is receiving the payment check from Katy's Z. G. Hopkins. *Author's collection*

the Hooker Guarantors. Later, however, the independent-minded president of the BM&E demanded an additional $40,000 which he represented as the accrued profits earned by the BM&E in 1929. On the other hand, Katy was not authorized to pay more than the recent Commerce Commission decision had allowed. As a result, the entire issue again was in doubt.[15]

After some delay, Achenbach announced that the BM&E would begin an extension program in the spring. Meanwhile, the CRI&P reiterated its desire to obtain the BM&E. Rock Island Vice President MacKenzie maintained that if the M-K-T did not secure the road, his company would; and in that event, he gave assurances that the line would be extended. In Dallas, C. C. Huff, M-K-T's General Solicitor, reported

that the Katy would meet all I.C.C. directives and the CRI&P's offers as well. Yet Achenbach refused to sell to the M-K-T. Indeed, he concluded a lease contract with the Rock Island to provide 41 miles of used rail and other equipment sufficient to take the BM&E to Keyes. At the same time, Achenbach attempted to woo another suitor. In 1910, he had succeeded in leasing the Kiowa, Hardtner & Pacific to the Missouri Pacific. Twenty seasons later he wrote to MP President L. W. Baldwin suggesting that the KH&P, still under lease, be extended 110 miles from Hardtner, Kansas, to the BM&E at Beaver. Baldwin, as could be expected, declined the invitation.[16]

The BM&E experienced an extremely good year in 1929. The proved earning capacity of "Jake's fool project" and the extension of the road toward Keyes combined to make the property considerably more valuable than before. Achenbach intended to bide his time, and he did so for awhile. Then in mid-October in 1930, Uncle Jake announced that he would be glad to sell the BM&E to the Katy. Perhaps he was beginning to feel old, as was reported, or possibly he was prompted to negotiate due to the increasingly serious illness of Ira B. Blackstock, his long-time friend and partner. More likely, however, Achenbach felt that the optimum time for sale was at hand. The Great Crash had occurred a year before, and the effects of the depression were beginning to appear. The wily 85-year-old president of the BM&E possessed an uncanny capacity for timing, a talent that served him well when on January 24, 1931, he agreed to sell the 65 percent of the company which he and his son August held.[17]

The other owners quickly agreed to sell their holdings, and an agreement among all parties was signed on February 26. The BM&E owners agreed to pay one half of the ad valorem taxes for 1931 and to pay the Rock Island for all materials acquired under lease agreements made to lengthen the road from Hough to Keyes. For its part, the M-K-T agreed to purchase all capital stock and bonds of the BM&E and to pay up to an equivalency of $22,000 per mile of owned main line, or a total of $2,310,00. For Achenbach and his associates, this represented a profit of $2,000 per mile—on the sale of a property which earlier Katy managements had labeled as incapable of earning enough to pay for the grease on one locomotive. The editor of the *Hooker Advance* considered that Katy's victory was also Hooker's victory; competition for grain traffic had been vouchsafed. Yet, ironically, the headlines of the next week's issue read: "The Paramount Issue in the Panhandle is Highways."[18]

Control of the BM&E passed to the M-K-T at 12:01 a.m., July 1, 1931, only a few days after the road had been opened all the way to Keyes. No longer was the BM&E "the orphan" railroad of the Panhandle. It survived as a corporate entity, but its offices were moved to the Railway Exchange Building in St. Louis and to 25 Broad Street in New York City. The sale of the BM&E, an obscure country railroad in the remote country of the Southern Great Plains, was sufficiently newsworthy to attract the attention of the national news media; even *Time Magazine* carried the story. Meanwhile, in the Oklahoma Panhandle, the biggest news item was the price of wheat; it had dropped to 29¢ per bushel.[19]

The Belle Epoque:
KATY Northwest: 1923-1949

"The passenger station at Hammon was clearly visible from my schoolroom window. And every time I heard a train whistle I went to the pencil sharpener to watch the little old steamer come into town. The teacher never questioned the diligent student who wrote so much that his pencil needed sharpening so often."*

When the Missouri-Kansas-Texas Railroad fully absorbed the Wichita Falls & Northwestern in 1923, residents and shippers along the Northwestern route heartily applauded. They expected that the Katy would upgrade the lines and expand the services on them. Unfortunately, the Katy had just emerged from a lengthy and painful receivership. It was still overcapitalized and unable to make most of the anticipated betterments. The Katy's inability to provide adequate ballast and heavier rail left the Northwestern District a dirt track railroad even in its halcyon days. Yet it performed well, if not spectacularly, as an ordinary day-in-and-day-out branch line railroad.[1]

Increased traffic, particularly that originating at Burkburnett, did force the expansion of yard facilities at Wichita Falls. In 1921, North Yard, where trains from the Northwestern District were handled, boasted 13 tracks, a 3-track coach yard, a 6-track machine shop, and an 8-stall roundhouse. Additionally, there were rip tracks, a boiler house, a storehouse, dormitories, and a 55,000-barrel fuel storage tank. Tracks extended to the nearby refineries of American Petrofina Company of Texas, Eagle Refining Company, Texhoma Oil & Refining Company, Red River Refining Company, and Lone Star Refining Company. Three tracks also were built to serve the Panhandle Steel Products Company, whose property adjoined North Yard. Railroad employees of all classes ate their meals at the eating house—variously labeled the "beanery" or "greasy spoon"—located near the east dormitory. Several regular switch engines shuffled cars around the yard on a 24-hour basis. Even with expanded facilities, North Yard frequently became plugged with traffic, and switching operations often spilled over into the older and smaller downtown yard.[2]

Passenger trains used the Fort Worth & Denver City between North Yard and Wichita Falls Union Station. By 1922, the Wichita Falls-Burkburnett locals, "The Polly," had been dropped as Burkburnett's boom faded. One year later, daily through service was offered between Wichita Falls and Forgan on a daytime schedule which required 13 hours and 50 minutes for the 305.1-mile route. An overnight turn was also advertised between Wichita Falls and Elk City. These trains handled the usual coaches plus an Oklahoma City sleeper, which was given to the Frisco at Altus. On the Wellington Branch, service was offered on a convenient schedule which featured close connections with the day trains on the Wichita Falls-Forgan route. This pattern obtained until the fall of 1928, when the evening trains were discontinued. At that time, regular sleeping car service on the Northwestern ended forever.[3]

Earlier, during World War I, passenger extras had started at Forgan and stopped at every station to pick up men who were answering

*Dr. Forrest D. Monahan, Jr., former resident of Hammon, Oklahoma, May 1, 1972, to the author.

93

Photographer Harold K. Vollrath found Katy #314 on the point of southbound train #53 at Elk City. July, 1939. *Harold K. Vollrath photograph*

Woodrow Wilson's call to make the world safe for democracy. One of these lads, A. P. Cummins of Buffalo, had boarded the train at Rosston on September 5, 1917, and was taken to San Antonio for induction. There were other extra movements, too, like the "Millionaire's Special" which brought a trainload of investors to the oil towns of Grandfield, Devol, and Burkburnett. After this group of nabobs had been delivered safely to Wichita Falls, each trainman and engineman was given a $20 tip by the passengers, whom they had greatly pleased by their competent handling of the train. There were also extras for circuses, fairs, and football games. The railroad always provided its best equipment for Chamber of Commerce specials, such as those sponsored by the merchants of Wichita Falls. Big crowds met these trains at every station between Wichita Falls and Elk City. The Rock Island then took the cars to Oklahoma City where they were transferred to the Santa Fe. The Katy then returned the entourage to Wichita Falls from Gainesville, Texas.[4]

In the 1920s, the railroads still provided the primary means of passenger transportation. This was as true on branch lines as it was on main lines. One public school teacher from Hollis, who was required to attend summer school in order to retain her certification, used the Katy as far as Altus, transferred to the Kansas City,

Mexico & Orient for Clinton, and finally arrived at Weatherford on the Rock Island some 24 hours later. A child long captivated by the romance of the passing trains was thrilled with her first train ride, 31 miles from Hammon to Carter. A man from Missouri took his family's household goods and farm tools to Knowles and was soon joined by his family, who reached Beaver County via the rails of Katy's Northwestern District. In 1922, six members of the Laverne Merry Matrons Embroidery Club used the Katy trains in order to visit Mrs. P. W. Doherty of Forgan. Residents of Camargo gleefully boarded the northbound local whenever a circus was playing at Woodward. In those days, high school baseball teams from Camargo used the morning train to reach Trail, four miles distant, where their game was played; the athletes returned on the afternoon train. Cattlemen who accompanied their stock to market usually spent a few days "in the city" before returning to their ranches via the Katy cars.[5]

Romance, too, rode the rails. P. O. Parks, a brakeman on a passenger run, was attracted by Helen Pursell, a teacher from May who used the train to commute on weekends to Rosston. They subsequently were married. Laverne residents took the train to Woodward, spent the day shopping, and returned home late in the afternoon

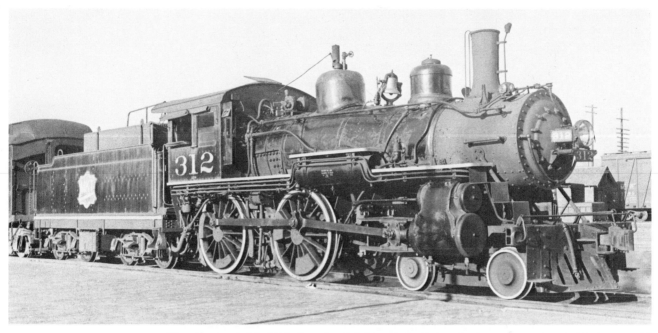

Katy's trim 4-4-0 #312 dozed at Wichita Falls Union Station on January 1, 1941. *Harold K. Vollrath photograph*

on the westbound passenger. Throughout the period, the state hospital at Supply brought a brisk passenger trade to that station. During the mid-1920s, one eager youth from Dunlap commuted to Supply on regular trains so that he could attend school. Passenger traffic on the Wellington Branch was particularly heavy each year when transient laborers headed for the cotton fields along that line. Extra coaches were added to the regular trains in order to accommodate the seasonal traffic. The M-K-T frequently gained $2,700 per month in ticket revenues from the Wellington station alone during the harvest seasons of the 1920s.[6]

Dairying became extremely important in Beaver County and elsewhere along the Northwestern District during the late 1920s. Farmers routinely sent their cream to market by express, and local Katy agents were pleased to receive the commissions from such shipments. In 1929, no less than 14,480 gallons of cream were shipped from Knowles alone. Many of these consignments were destined for the Armour plant at Elk City, but cream also was shipped to Oklahoma City and to creameries as distant as those in Wichita, Kansas, and Fort Madison, Iowa. Bread from the largest bakeries of the region was shipped to on-line grocery stores by express. An outdoorsman at Tipton once received a crated wildcat, much to the chagrin of the express messenger

who had the task of unloading the animal from the train to the depot's freight room—and to the great surprise of the station agent who later found him there. Numerous pedigreed greyhound racing dogs were billed from the same station at one time. Prior to the passage of Oklahoma's "Bone Dry Law" and the later national experiment with prohibition, a large volume of individual liquor shipments were handled on the express cars. The Oklahoma law and the Noble Experiment did not completely dry up this traffic, however, as shipments still were made between distilleries and licensed drug houses. Under this arrangement the druggists distributed the whisky; individuals no longer picked up their booze at the Katy depots. Of course, not all shipments were delivered as intended. On weekends or when draymen were too busy to make prompt deliveries, the liquor was locked up in the depot's freight room. By the time delivery could be made, however, the express company frequently was faced with a claim for an unaccountable loss of the spiritous merchandise.[7]

The express service also was used for less honorable purposes. Using fictitious names, some farmers ordered calves to be delivered by express, C.O.D. Upon arrival of the livestock, the agent was of course unable to locate the party who had placed the order. He then sold the animals for the express charges, ordinarily to the man who actually had made the order. This satisfied the express company and the agent, pleased the farmer, and disappointed only the hapless shipper. Fish companies on the Gulf Coast used the express service in a somewhat similar but less clandestine fashion. When their inventories were too high they made C.O.D. shipments to some fictitious person at a random station on the Northwestern. The agent sold the fish for whatever amount he could get and remitted this, less the express charges, to the fish company. Everyone was satisfied with this irregular arrangement: the fish company moved its excess inventory, the agent received a commission (and usually some fish, too), and the express company gained a revenue shipment. As was then the custom, agents along the line remitted railroad and express company money in charge of the train's express messenger. The envelopes containing this currency were closed, labeled by wax seals, and signed for by the expressman prior to the consignment in the heavy steel safe aboard the train. During the Burkburnett oil boom, one express messenger attempted to rob one of these safes. Knowing that it contained over $100,000, he moved it to the car door and pushed it out into a gully as the train sped along. He then knocked himself out, later to report that he had been robbed by three desperate men. Unfortunately for the dishonest expressman, section men and law officers discovered the safe and the inept thief received a jail sentence.[8]

Baggage in all forms was handled on the passenger trains. Baggagemen had the unpleasant task of handling coffins bearing remains shipped to on-line stations for interment. The Katy charged the usual rate—"one full fare regardless of the age of the deceased." Through this period the Post Office Department authorized Railway Post Office service between Wichita Falls and Forgan and between Altus and Wellington. The mails were particularly heavy at Grandfield, Mangum, and Frederick, and transfer mails (to and from other RPO lines) were heavy at Elk City and Altus. At Gate, and no doubt at many other stations on the Northwestern District, most of the population met the westbound evening train and then adjourned to the Post Office to await the distribution of mails into the authorized boxes. Many patrons were particularly interested in receiving a favorite newspaper, often the *Kansas*

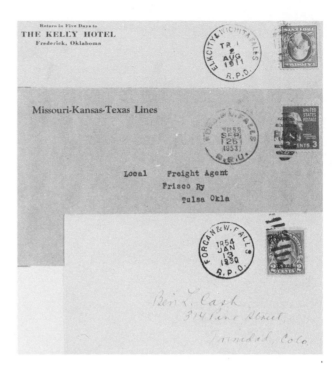

Postmarks from the RPOs which operated over the Northwestern District. *Author's collection*

City Star. The train did not stop at the tiniest villages along the line, but non-stop mail exchanges were made at many locations such as Hester, Moravia, Carpenter, Dunlap, and Mocane. At Mocane, Everett Evans became so disenchanted with this arrangement that on one occasion he flagged the speeding westbound train. As it ground to an unscheduled halt, Evans handed up a letter to the startled RPO clerk. Then he innocently explained to the fuming conductor that he needed to get that letter to a party in Forgan and had stopped the train only for that purpose. The RPO clerk willingly serviced the letter but the railroaders understandably took a dim view of this highly personalized mail service.[9]

During the hard times of the 1930s, tramps frequently slept in station waiting rooms. Railroad employees generally did not molest them, for they were viewed as people merely down on their luck. Yet if these men could not pay for a night's lodging, neither could they afford to buy railroad tickets for transportation. They "rode the rods" instead. During the early 1930s, passenger revenues plummeted on the Northwestern District. The depression was the main factor, although people increasingly availed themselves of the automobile for their shorter trips. On

Train #54 after its arrival in Woodward on September 5, 1949. *H. S. Tyler photograph*

September 4, 1935, the usual daily passenger train on the Wellington Branch was replaced by a daily-except-Sunday mixed, or "hog and human," train. Passengers then were handled on that line in side-door cabooses; the RPO authorization was terminated, but express still was handled. The Wellington mixed connected with the passenger run from Wichita Falls, but schedule changes on the south-bound train from Forgan unfortunately did not permit connection between these two operations. By April of 1940, full daily passenger train service north of Woodward similarly was terminated, with tri-weekly mixed train service on that part of the Northwestern substituted thereafter.[10]

Katy officials frequently rode the passenger trains to inspect the tracks, stations, and other facilities. When the general officers toured the lines, business cars were attached to the passenger or mixed trains. Special inspection trains, operated especially for Katy's board of directors, were less frequently scheduled. However infrequent they were, there was never any delaying of these trains. During the Dust Bowl days, the swift movement of these specials appeared to employees and local residents as a tornado moving down the track. Locomotive engineers understandably took particular pride in receiving these assignments.[11]

Road building and highway construction in the area served by the Northwestern District was slower to develop than in other areas of the country. The roads that were available frequently were of poor quality and often impassable. Even those who ordinarily relied on automobiles for transportation were thankful for the reliable service offered by the Katy. In sum, the passenger train service offered on the Northwestern was still considered crucial to the area's welfare. The importance of these trains increased during the war years as road construction diminished and as both gasoline and tires were rationed. Such rubber tires as were available for private use ordinarily reached their destinations via express. Baby chickens also were conveyed to farmers by express and by parcel post as well. In 1943, Mrs. Earl Kerns of Gate ordered a single dairy calf which was delivered by Railway Express. It was the first of several calves which Mrs. Kerns shipped in to build a Grade A dairy herd. The railroad between Camargo and Trail even facilitated service to local residents when the trains were not operating. If water on the South Canadian was so high that automobiles could not ford it, and if no trains were scheduled, residents of Camargo simply walked over the long railroad bridge to reach the other side. On one such occasion, a ball game was scheduled between Leedey and Camargo. In order that this crucial contest be held, coaches, players and spectators all fearlessly scrambled to the yonder side courtesy of the Katy's spindly timber trestle.[12]

World War II also prompted frequent special movements to the military bases and the one prisoner of war camp located on the line. The most important of these facilities was Shep-

97

During World War II and for a while thereafter, local passenger service was still considered crucial of the Northwestern's service area. Fragile-looking but ordinarily reliable 4-4-0s drew these trains except on rare occasions when a 500 substituted for them. These remarkable sequential views by R. W. Richardson were made in and near Wichita Falls on a December day in 1946 when the usual power was laid up. *Everett L. DeGolyer, Jr., collection*

pard Field, near Burkburnett, which was opened on October 17, 1941. Entire trainloads of airmen were transported to and from this base throughout the war years and even thereafter. Generally a switch engine crew from North Yard handled the train between that point and the base. Special movements also served the bases at Frederick and Altus, while German prisoners of war were delivered to and from a confinement area near Tipton. The most unpleasant of all tasks fell to railroaders during these years. Agents at most Katy stations also were Western Union operators, and when a casualty message was received it was the agent's duty to hand-carry the wire to its recipient, often a personal friend or acquaintance of the agent. Trainmen and station employees also were called upon to handle the remains of those who perished in the conflict and were returned to their home towns for burial.[13]

The handling of freight of course was always the major task of the Northwestern District. In the early days of rail service to Burkburnett, corn in the shuck was piled high in the streets near the depot while shellers labored night and day to ready the grain for shipment. Later, during its boom period and after, Burkburnett's traffic consisted mainly of oil and petroleum-related prod-

ucts. A plethora of tracks were built north and south of the town to serve the burgeoning petroleum industry. Beginning in 1923, however, many of these tracks were abandoned as the oil production of the area was rationalized by the surviving companies. By 1934, only a few major petroleum shippers remained at Burkburnett; four years later, only two natural gasoline plants and two refineries were producing traffic there for the Katy. Nevertheless, it was not unusual to bill 100 cars of oil from that station in the late 1920s and after. Seven miles north, across the Red River at Devol, Oklahoma, no less than 15 individual tracks were necessary to serve the eight petroleum industries at that point. One refinery near the Red River had sufficient tracks to load 50 cars in 6 hours, 24 hours a day. Many of the laborers at this plant were of Greek descent and proved to be friendly toward the train crews which served the facility. Railroaders frequently were asked to dine with the refinery workers at their nearby dormitories. Six miles farther, at Grandfield, five other petroleum firms had tracks to serve their needs. Throughout the 1920s and 1930s, the Katy handled single carloads as well as entire trainloads of crude oil and refined gasoline from these three stations to other carriers at Wichita Falls,

Frederick, Altus, Elk City, and Hammon Junction. The petroleum traffic on the Northwestern District was high in volume and high in revenue generated. Until the reserves began to fail, petroleum and petroleum-related products accounted for nearly as many carloadings on the Northwestern as did the products of agriculture.[14]

However, over the entire history of these lines, agriculture always was king. Harvests varied, of course, according to weather conditions. Wheat was first planted in the Panhandle during the first decade of the twentieth century. In 1908, J. D. Key, a farmer in Beaver County, received 60 cents per bushel on a harvest that yielded 15 bushels per acre. Using a McCormick-Deering header, Key cut his wheat, elevated it into header barges, and stacked it. In this fashion, the wheat was stored to await the arrival of a threshing crew. After the railroad reached Forgan, the growing of wheat grew in popularity. As long as the harvest season was prolonged by the use of threshing machines, the grain moved to market each fall in an orderly way. The tractor, combine, and farm truck changed that into an annual wheat rush which troubled the railroad thereafter early every summer. A predictable pattern followed. In anticipation of the rush, extra cars, locomotives, and crewmen were recruited from other Katy divisions. At Vici, Brinkman, Knowles, and elsewhere, farm trucks and wagons were backed up for blocks awaiting a turn to dump at the trackside elevators. Meanwhile, Katy crews labored day and night to keep the grain moving. Not all of it moved during the rush, but before elevators expanded their storage capacities, the vast bulk of it did. In the early days, much wheat went to eastern points, but gradually the majority of it moved to Oklahoma and Texas mills and to Gulf ports for export. During the 12-month period immediately prior to September 1, 1929, 2,331 cars of wheat were shipped from Beaver County alone. More than one-half of these were shipped on the BM&E; but of the rest, 631 carloads originated at Forgan, Knowles accounted for 273, and 170 were billed at Gate. These same Northwestern stations also shipped 255 cars containing other grains plus 31 carloads of broomcorn during this period. On May 10, 1945, the railroad reported that its stations on the Northwestern District and the BM&E together had generated a total of 7,508 carloads of grain from the 1944 crop.[15]

The trade area serviced by the Northwestern District, particularly the Texas and Oklahoma Panhandles, was also cattle country. In 1903, the cattle industry in the area was revolutionized by the introduction of cottonseed cake, or "oil cake." Ranchers used the railroad to ship in their supplies of this and other feed but, more important, the rails were employed to move the cattle themsevles. There were numerous stations which acquired reputations as heavy cattle loading points, but more cattle were reportedly shipped from tiny Mocane, just east of Forgan, than from any other station on the District. Certainly some of the largest ranches of the Panhandle were nearby. One of these was the well-known Barby Ranch. Otto N. Barby, its founder, was born in St. Louis in 1865 but moved to the Panhandle 31 years later. There, near Beaver, he acquired 160 acres, the humble beginnings of an empire that was later expanded to more than 50,000 acres. Barby and his sons annually grazed 3,000 head of cattle, somewhat less than the rule of thumb which called for 15 acres per animal. The operation gave employment to 15 cowboys. Barby shipped in heifer calves from Texas and Colorado, but most of his shipping was outbound. In October, stocker cattle which had been sold to farmers in Iowa, Illinois, Indiana, Ohio, and Pennsylvania were driven overland to the pens at Mocane or Knowles for loading. Frequently, the volume was great enough to warrant a special train. Slaughter cattle were consigned to the Kansas City Union Stockyards; these shipments usually were made at the end of a week on a carlot basis. In all cases, the Barby cattle moved eastward via Woodward and the AT&SF.[16]

There were numerous smaller cattle shippers along the route. At Supply, there was a heavy shipment of cattle each fall. In the spring, ranchers from near that station received shipments of Mexican steers, frequently brought in by the railroad. Most of the slaughter cattle went to market in carload lots from the various stations. In early years, an extra was called at Woodward late in the week to peddle stock cars at every station to Forgan. The next day these cars, now loaded, were picked up by the same crew and handled to Woodward where most were given to the Santa Fe. On the same day, the northbound local on the "Long Barrel" began picking up stock at each

Otto N. Barby, Sr. *Ralph Barby collection*

station above Elk City. Upon its arrival at Woodward, interchange cars were given to the Santa Fe, and the remaining loaded stock cars were combined with whatever southbound stock remained from the recently arrived extra from Forgan. Another extra then wheeled these cars, mostly consigned to Fort Worth packers, southward toward Texas. Back in the bouncing caboose, the usually fearless cowboys who were accompanying the cattle to market braced themselves, cursed the engine driver who was rapidly propelling them toward what appeared to be an uncertain destiny, and yearned for the sanity of the open ranges now far behind. After they had delivered the cattle, and after "shootin' 'em up" in the big city for a few days, these same cattlemen boarded the cars of the Katy's passenger trains for a more civilized if less colorful return voyage.[17]

Other livestock also went to market over the rails of the Northwestern. Jacob C. Holmes, proprietor of the Holmes Livestock Company, was an independent hog buyer and shipper who purchased these animals at various stations along the Katy and the BM&E, particularly at Beaver, La-

verne, and Vici. Most of these animals were taken by the M-K-T to Woodward where they were billed to Los Angeles slaughterhouses. Holmes also shipped entire carloads to Fort Worth, a lengthy and remunerative line haul for the Katy. Prior to the depression, nearly every farmer in the area had a few hogs, and Holmes was never at a loss to fill out his weekly carloadings. At Vici, the sales barn shipped large numbers of horses and mules during the 1930s. This reflected more the financial disaster which had befallen most area farmers than it did a switch to mechanized farming. Also at Vici and at Forgan too, poultry cars were loaded several times per year until the late 1930s when this traffic disappeared for all time.[18]

A wide variety of other carload shipments also were handled. Coal was carried to fuel merchants at nearly every station. The Railway Ice Company at Forgan (not a part of the M-K-T or the BM&E) received ice by the carload. Virtual trainloads of pipe were unloaded at Knowles and elsewhere as the area became perforated by pipe lines. In 1926, 12 cars of eggs and cream were billed from Forgan. Pure white volcanic ash was found near Gate, and in the late 1920s a firm was established to gather and ship this material. In 1929 alone, 80 carloads of this volcanic ash—ordinarily mislabeled as silica sand—was conveyed to distant points by rail. During the same year, the agent at Gate counted over 300 inbound carloads for various customers in addition to the usual LCL commodities. The three cotton gins at Burkburnett in 1927 provided a heavy flow of cotton traffic from that station. Later, in 1932-1933, the area experienced a veritable "cotton boom" due to an unusual temporary rate structure. The construction of various highways and flood-control projects during the depression and after precipitated a large flow of building materials to Supply. Hay was received at May, and alfalfa seed was billed from Tipton. At Vici, Earl Wiedman, a local merchant, received citrus in carload lots. But the most unusual freight movement on the line may have been to Camargo. In the early 1920s, that village did not have a water supply other than "gyp water"—a very foul-smelling liquid unsuitable for human consumption—and such rain water as could be entrapped and stored in cisterns. When these reservoirs went dry, Katy transported drinking water from Woodward to Camargo by the tank-car load. Whether carrying water, stock, or wheat, the lines were crucial to the well-being of both the M-K-T and the area which they served. In 1938, the Northwestern District and the BM&E together originated 15,621 carloads of freight. This amounted to 10.7 percent of all cars loaded on the M-K-T that year.[19]

Less-than-carload (LCL) bilings on the Northwestern District and on the BM&E for 1938 amounted to 2,834 cars. For the railroad, this business was labor intensive and only marginally remunerative. Before the advent of hardtop roads and over-the-road trucking, however, the railroad's LCL service was absolutely indispensable to the people living in the area. Through the 1920s and 1930s and even into the following decade, five and six cars of LCL were delivered to Burkburnett each day. Receipts from LCL shipments also were high at Frederick, Altus, and Woodward. Shipments to the smaller stations were handled in line (or way) cars. These were placed either immediately behind the locomotive or just ahead of the caboose. At every station, except the largest ones, the agent and the train crew loaded and unloaded consignments before the train did its other work. Packing house products (PHP) were similarly handled. Salesmen for the major packers sold orders to the grocery stores and meat markets along the line and then mailed or wired these to their respective plants. Line cars then were loaded and dispatched, particularly from Fort Worth and Oklahoma City, and were handled in local freight service. Agents and trainmen were responsible for the unloading of these shipments, but as many older heads later explained, "the count frequently was short," especially during hard times.[20]

Despite the depression, Katy located eight major new shippers on the Northwestern District in 1938. These were expected to originate an additional 385 carloads of traffic per year. Also in 1938, the Northwestern and the BM&E had eight stations which boasted annual freight earnings of over $100,000. They included:

Wichita Falls	$1,765,658
Burkburnett	201,146
Grandfield	459,028
Frederick	139,334
Altus	172,231
Hollis	149,300
Woodward	127,511
Beaver	130,110[21]

Cotton, wheat, and livestock were the three commodities that traditionally moved to and from stations on the Wellington Branch. During the 1920s, the scheduled eastbound freight train picked up from 20 to 50 cars of stock each Tuesday and Saturday at the various stations between Wellington and Altus. Most of these cars contained hogs billed to Oklahoma City packers and were moved via Altus and the SL-SF. Slaughter cattle from shippers on the Wellington Branch ordinarily were sent to Oklahoma City, Fort Worth, or Kansas City. Cotton shipments were especially heavy at Hollis and Wellington. During the 1920s, most of the cotton loaded at Hollis was sent either to Altus for compression or to plants in southeastern states. The primary wheat-loading stations on that line were Victory, Duke, and Gould.[22]

Five or six cars of LCL arrived in Hollis each morning, the contents to be distributed by Jim Thompson, a local drayman. Express shipments were delivered by another firm. Wellington received a similar volume of LCL consignments. In the late 1920s, Hollis and Wellington were growing and prospering. Numerous businesses were developing, and residential housing was scarce. It was not unusual for the railroad agent at Hollis to receive between 50 and 75 Western Union wires daily. In addition to these and other duties, the agent frequently sold $300 in passenger tickets each day during this pre-depression era. At Wellington, trackside shippers included oil companies, coal companies, elevators, cotton gins, and a general warehouse firm. Yet in 1931, the effects of the depression were evident, and shortly thereafter, as one resident later recalled, "the bottom dropped out" of the local economy. This naturally affected revenues on the railroad. Then as if to add insult to injury, the Fort Worth & Denver City built a 111-mile line from Childress, on the FW&DC's main line, to Pampa, in the Texas Panhandle. This new road, opened for business in 1932, passed through Wellington and served to drain much needed traffic away from the Katy line.[23]

Traffic patterns on the Wellington Branch for the period between 1938 and 1942 reflect a number of interesting developments. Statistics for these years show not only the upswing in the

Until the advent of hardtop roads, the Hollis Oklahoma depot was an extremely busy place. Even in later days a number of four-wheel express carts stood waiting although increasingly they merely slumbered in the sun. *M-K-T collection*

national economy and its local counterpart, but the end of Dust Bowl conditions and the changing general designs of transportation service in the rural areas as well. Fewer cars of cotton, cotton-related products, and wheat moved during 1938 than in any of the other four years, but weather and marketing conditions both improved subsequently, and carloadings of these commodities increased significantly thereafter. Livestock loadings bottomed out in 1939 and then increased. On the other hand, traffic in refined oil and gasoline dropped each year after 1938, while traffic in new automobiles and trucks was totally absent by 1942. In general, the traffic mix thinned while the "big three" commodities—cotton, wheat, and livestock—maintained their importance. Interestingly, too, inbound traffic for the period peaked in 1939 and then dropped dramatically. Meanwhile, outbound shipments remained steady. Thus there were more cars handled on the line in 1938 than were handled in 1942. These patterns persisted throughout the war years and later.[24]

Two decades earlier, on August 8, 1920, fire had destroyed part of the coal chute at North Yard in Wichita Falls. It mattered little since

the railroad had nearly finished converting the locomotives which were assigned to Wichita Falls from coal burners to oil burners. The fire in the coal chute had merely hastened the conversion process. Between the time that Katy acquired the capital stock of the WF&NW and the time that it fully incorporated the Northwestern into the M-K-T in 1923, locomotives belonging to the WF&NW were headquartered at Wichita Falls and were assignend to the Forgan line and to the Wellington Branch. However, Northwestern power was insufficient to handle even the regular traffic of the lines, and Katy was forced to add some of its locomotives to the Wichita Falls pool. A WF&NW dispatcher's sheet dated August 18, 1917, shows that 60 percent of the power on the lines for that date was of Northwestern ancestry. When the WF&NW lost its corporate identity in the early 1920s, Katy automatically inherited its three 2-6-0s, seven 2-8-0s, and four 4-4-0s. Former Northwestern employees recalled that these machines had leaky boilers and were poor steamers; and in 1924, the M-K-T chose to sell or scrap most of them. However, the four American Standard machines outshopped by Baldwin in

After the Wichita Falls Route passed to history, the Katy decided to sell or scrap most of the former Kemp and Kell locomotives. Before that time, however, entire trainloads of wheat, oil, and cattle had moved to market behind the drawbars of mills such as #20. *Eugene R. Dowdy collection*

1910-1911 remained on Katy's roster until 1932. Two other WF&NW locomotives, both 4-6-0s, had been sold to the Clinton & Oklahoma Western as early as 1912.[25]

A number of adjustments had to be made when the locomotives were converted from coal fuel to oil. Dismounted tank cars were placed as refueling stations at strategic intervals along the line, and coal tipples were dismantled. Enginemen who initially were unfamiliar with oil-fired locomotives sometimes misgauged the distance that they could cover between refuelings. As a result, there were a few embarrassing moments when it was discovered that tenders were empty several miles from the nearest oil supply. On his first trip with an oil burner, one fireman let his fire go out when he neglected to turn the valve which heated the oil prior to its passage from the tender to the firebox. After they adjusted to the new fuel, however, enginemen had few problems. Conversion from coal to oil brought no alteration in the types of locomotives assigned to the Northwestern District. Pert little American Standard locomotives still drew the few passenger runs, while 400 and 500 class Moguls handled the freights. Occasionally a 600-class 2-8-0 also ventured out, usually to do battle with snowbanks which period-

ically plugged the lines. None of the locomotives which toiled on the Northwestern trailed large tenders. In order to avoid stopping at every water tank or simply to get from one to another with heavy trains, Katy frequently added one and even two auxiliary tanks to locomotives assigned to the Long Barrel between Elk City and Woodward and to the Top End between Woodward and Forgan. The track then was well groomed, and passenger trains were allowed to travel at a maximum of 40 miles per hour over most of the Northwestern, but freight trains were restricted to 25 miles per hour on most of the District. However, engineers who knew the track exceeded these speeds safely. Due to several difficult hills, locomotives usually assigned in freight service had a limited rating of 1,600 tons over most of the trackage. However, between Mangum and Altus, Leedey and Hammon, and Thompson and Supply, the ratings were two and three times greater due to downhill pulls. During the harvest season, this resulted in leap-frogging tonnage to Mangum, Leedey, and Thompson, where it was gathered and taken later in huge trains to Altus, Hammon, and Supply. Then the whole process was repeated.[26]

The Katy's financial record for the first half

Locomotive #306 with southbound train #53 at May, Oklahoma in December, 1937. This view characterizes the small town/small train syndrome, typical of branch line operations everywhere in the country. Note the tumble weed temporarily captured on the locomotive's pilot. *Frank O. Kelley collection*

MK-T locomotive #594. Woodward; November, 1934. *Frank O. Kelley collection*

Wichita Falls, June 4, 1949. P. Dailey photograph; *Everett L. DeGolyer, Jr. collection*

of the twentieth century was checkered indeed. President C. E. Schaff headed the Katy from 1912 to 1926. The road suffered bankruptcy during his tenure, but Schaff implemented a plan for the reorganization of its finances and simultaneously promoted a $50 million improvement program to rebuild the property. Prosperity returned, and in 1924 the road resumed dividend payments on its preferred stock. These were continued through 1931. In 1930, *Railway Age* reported that the Katy proper was in good physical condition and that the road was operating efficiently. The company paid $3.00 on its common stock in 1930, but one year later it omitted similar dividends and also declined to pay quarterly dividends on its preferred issues. An outside analyst observed that significant losses in revenue had "pushed the Missouri-Kansas-Texas to the extreme limit of retrenchment in the apparent purpose to earn fixed charges and to preserve so far as possible the company's cash reserves." Expenditures for maintenance of way and for maintenance of equipment dropped precipitously; on November 15, 1931, 23.4 percent of Katy's locomotives were "bad ordered." The M-K-T had begun a long day's journey into night which ended only when prosperity returned with the accompaniment of World War II. Between 1933 and 1940, Katy completed a seven-year stretch during which earnings failed to cover fixed interest charges by almost $12.5 million. In 1940, 43 percent of its locomotives and 12 percent of its

freight cars were laid up awaiting major repairs. Although interest was never defaulted, Katy's first mortgage bonds sold on the New York Stock Exchange for as little as 19¢ on the dollar; its common stock was available for 25¢ per share.[27]

Then in 1938, the Reconstruction Finance Corporation grudgingly granted the road a loan, and the gathering clouds of world conflict promised future growth in traffic. In 1942, its total revenues were 113 percent above 1940 levels. President Matthew Scott Sloan then began a rehabilitation program which involved plowing every available dollar back into the property. By 1945, $100 million had been so spent. By refurbishing its plant, Katy was able to handle the growing war traffic while concomitantly preparing for the postwar years. At the end of the war, M-K-T was physically in good condition and was an active participant in the Southwest's continuing economic boom. In 1941, Katy's traffic volume was 291,192 cars; seven years later, after the war, it handled 550,781 carloads. The same pattern in microcosm was reflected on the Northwestern District throughout these years. But nowhere on the Katy System were the mercurial transitions from prosperity to poverty to prosperity more evident than on the Beaver, Meade & Englewood.[28]

For Better or for Worse:
The BM&E: 1931-1949

"No one who remembers the wheat crops of 1926, 1929, 1931, can possibly regard this as submarginal land."*

The Missouri-Kansas-Texas Railroad assumed control of the Beaver, Meade & Englewood at 12:01 a.m., on July 1, 1931. Three hours later, Superintendent C. W. Watts ordered veteran BM&E conductor T. J. Robb to take a Katy engine and train of cars piled high with company material from Forgan to Keyes. Aboard the cars was everything required, in Katy's view, to operate a standard branch line railroad "in an up-to-date and efficient manner." Telephone and telegraph apparatus was installed quickly at the various BM&E stations; and within two weeks, butterfly train order boards were similarly installed at all telegraph stations. This special train also distributed fuel oil, grease, gasoline, nails, and a variety of cooperage materials.[1]

A bridge gang from the Katy's Northwestern District soon was sent to rebuild the Beaver River bridge near Beaver, and a ditcher was dispatched to clean the cuts between Tracy and Hovey. At the same time, Katy suggested that the existing light-weight rail would be replaced with heavier stock and that the roadbed would be ballasted with material other than dirt. Before the M-K-T assumed control, the BM&E offered daily-except-Sunday mixed train service between Beaver and Hooker but only irregular service west of Hooker. It also was implied that Katy would make improvements in the periodicity and quality of this train service. Keyes and other communities on the BM&E asked the M-K-T to extend full passenger service to them and urged the Post Office Department to authorize Railway Mail

Service over the Beaver Road. "If the patrons of our roads desire this service, they certainly will get it, as we are here to serve," replied Superintendent Watts. Meanwhile, Watts issued a mimeographed timecard which, it was claimed, would serve "until an employees' time table in regular form" could be provided. Thus the immediate change of ownership was characterized by the implementation of certain betterments and the promise of more to come.[2]

The sale of the Beaver Road to the Katy naturally resulted in numerous changes in personnel. The entire membership of the road's board of directors changed so that the new composition was almost entirely Katy officials and prominent shippers from its main line; the Panhandle was represented only by J. B. Doolin, one of the lawyers who helped facilitate the sale of the BM&E to the Katy. E. E. Booth, former superintendent, was retained as Mr. Watts' assistant, and R. H. Dorsey, former general agent at Hooker, was continued as assistant auditor and timekeeper. The two BM&E train crews, the nine section foremen, and all track laborers likewise were retained. However, former Katy men were placed in every depot along the Beaver Road. Those so assigned were:

> J. C. Parks, former cashier at Frederick, agent at Beaver
> C. J. Morahan, former cashier at Altus, joint agent at Forgan
> C. M. Templin, from Katy's Southern Division, agent at Turpin

*Caroline A. Henderson, "Letters From the Dust Bowl," *The Atlantic Monthly,* Vol. 157 (May 1936), p. 543.

E. B. Parks, former cashier at Elk City, agent at Hooker

J. E. Fulmer, relief agent on Northwestern District, agent at Tracy

L. W. Self, former agent Duke, agent at Eva

H. L. Knight, from Katy's Southern Division, agent at Keyes

J. C. English, from Katy's Southern Division, cashier at Hooker

J. Gilardi, former agent at Forgan, BM&E traveling agent

The former Katy engine watchman at Forgan, G. L. Davis, was transferred to Hooker on the BM&E, and F. A. Hanson, a Katy lineman, accepted a similar position on the BM&E at Hooker. Katy engine and train crews appeared on the line in 1931 to help move the massive grain shipments of that season, but after the rush they returned to their regular positions.[3]

The former Katy employees did not take a condescending attitude toward the Beaver Road, but they did poke fun at it. Virtually every railroad has been labeled with a humorous epigram designed to fit its own corporate initials; the Denver & Rio Grande Western (D&RGW) has been called the "Dangerous & Rapidly Growing Worse," the Texas Central (TC) was known as the "Tin Can," and the Minneapolis & St. Louis (M&StL) was referred to as the "Midnight & Still Later." Katymen christened the BM&E the "Butter, Milk & Eggs." Not to be outdone, Beaver employees identified the MK&T as the "Meat, Kraut & Taters" and jokingly referred to themselves as "Bilious Monkeys & Eggheads."[4]

Most residents of the Panhandle were pleased when the M-K-T secured control of the BM&E. "It is just what this section needs—a progressive, enterprising railroad management, alive to our needs and ready to provide the best service permitted by conditions," stated R. F. Baker of Hooker. In 1931, Katy likewise seemed happy to share in the future of the Panhandle. "We are well aware of the fact," said President Cahill, "that this portion of Oklahoma is only now coming into its own and that the future presents a very strong prospect. . . . It is our earnest hope to serve this section in a way that will attest the interest we so long have had in it."[5]

Yet the BM&E did retain its corporate identity. After July 1, 1931, it was operated as a separate if wholly owned subsidiary of the M-K-T.

Earlier, in 1929, when the Katy was hoping to acquire the Beaver Road, it had maintained that the entire overhead or supervisory expense incurred by the BM&E would be eliminated inasmuch as the M-K-T expected to operate the line as an extension of its Northwestern District. One Katy official argued then that the traditional terminal at Forgan would merely be moved west on the BM&E and thereby complete a through freight division from Woodward. Nevertheless, Katy management later altered its position, perhaps due to rate divisions that made a separate corporation more profitable.[6]

The oft-stated long range goal of the BM&E was the coal fields of northeastern New Mexico. This had been an on-again, off-again project, but on March 12, 1931, the editor of the *Hooker Advance* confidently asserted that the Katy, as new owners of the BM&E, would build the road to Des Moines, New Mexico. To the fuel-starved residents of the Panhandle, who still called cow chips "Hereford Coal," this was good news indeed. Apparently, however, the Katy never seriously considered extending the line as far as Des Moines, although it may have contemplated construction as far as the New Mexico border. The January 2, 1932, issue of *Railway Age* intimated that Katy anticipated no "prospective extension" of the line. It was a wise decision. Coal mining in the Raton area gradually diminished, and the connecting railroad between Raton and Des Moines, on which the BM&E would have depended for coal traffic, was abandoned in 1935. In fact, Katy management was even unwilling to allow the BM&E to build a transfer track with the Santa Fe at Keyes, apparently feeling that such a connection would have short hauled the Beaver Road on most interchange traffic moving via that gateway. As early as October of 1932, a meeting was held at Hooker to protest the absence of an interchange track at Keyes. Delegates at this meeting were particularly interested in securing for themselves lower rates on coal and oil. Nevertheless, not until the autumn of 1936 was a 389-foot connecting track placed in service west of the BM&E depot at Keyes.[7]

In all three counties of the Oklahoma Panhandle, the number of farms decreased each decade after 1910. By 1930, there were only 887 farms in Cimarron County, 2,020 in Texas County, and 2,047 in Beaver County. Yet the production of wheat increased, depending, of course, on the capricious whims of the weather. Farmers in the area learned to carry surpluses of fat years over to lean ones. One long-time resident recalled that the accepted yardstick of agricultural success in the Panhandle was:

> One crop in three years—people can get along
> One crop in two years—prosperity
> One crop per year—Boom!

By the late 1920s, 64 percent of the farmers in the heart of the southern Great Plains were dependent on cash crops—usually wheat—for a living. In Cimarron County, farmers produced only 590,000 bushels of wheat in 1924, but four seasons later the production had risen to nearly 2.5 million bushels. Then came what one writer called the "super-duper, ultra-terrific wheat year" —1931. Unhappily, this was a mixed blessing. On June 10, 1931, number one wheat at Amarillo brought 50¢ per bushel; but as the bounteous harvest of new wheat reached the elevators, the bottom seemingly dropped out of the market. At Keyes, wheat sold for only 24¢ per bushel later that summer; it resulted in bankruptcy for numerous farmers. The total wheat production for Cimarron County alone was nearly 6 million bushels in 1931.[8]

Katy expected that no fewer than 6,000 cars of wheat would be originated on the BM&E as a result of the 1931 bumper crop. By early July, 4,936, cars already had moved on the Katy System; of these, 3,000 had been loaded on the BM&E and on the M-K-T's Northwestern District. Despite this volume, those farmers who could do so were holding their wheat; Katy officials estimated that 60 percent of the harvest would be stored for future shipment. On July 1, 1931, the day that Katy assumed operation of the Beaver, 96 unbilled and unsold cars of wheat— loaded at Mouser and Hough—plugged the Hooker yards. With the price of wheat depressed and their bins filled to capacity, elevator operators had loaded these box cars subject to billing on consignment. They were then moved to Hutchinson, Kansas, or to Houston, Texas, or to other points while the consignees hoped for a rise in prices on the grain market. The contents of these cars eventually were sold enroute, although the process was time consuming and wasteful of ton miles. In August, farmers received a paltry 20¢ per bushel at Amarillo. After 15 months, and another growing season later, Hooker elevators were paying only 26¢ per bushel. The full force of the depression had come to the Panhandle.[9]

Nature then attempted a total eclipse of the region. As early as 1895, the *Alva Review* had taken note of a severe dust storm which had whirled into the area from the north. Another preview of the "Dirty Thirties" occurred in the Panhandle in March of 1923 when a devastating wind swept in from the north and west. "We do

Keyes, Oklahoma at 7:00 p.m., May 21, 1937. *Author's collection*

The famous "duster" of March, 1923, at Hooker.
George L. Risen photograph

not think the scene will be witnessed again for generations to come," opined the always optimistic editor of the *Hooker Advance*. "Blissful peace and happiness," he continued, "is always found on the prairies, where man finds contentment and prosperity." His prophecy was sadly in error. In 1932, the winds were strong—strong enough on April 17 to blow down the BM&E's engine house at Beaver. The following year was hot, dry, and windy. The wheat harvest for the three-county Oklahoma Panhandle averaged but 18/100 of a bushel per acre. Near Hooker, some 60 cattle per day died of a disease brought on by the dust storms, 40 of which had been recorded in the vicinity during the first six months of 1933. An April storm in 1934 dumped dirt from the Panhandle on the Capitol in Washington, D.C. Yet there was ample rain that season to produce a 3.5-million-bushel wheat crop. Unhappily, the small harvest gave only false hope, for the rains then failed again. By the Fourth of July, cattle in the area were shot daily, while entire dairy herds were sold and shipped east from stock pens at BM&E stations. Beef cattle, too—at least those which were still healthy—were shipped to the Kansas City Union Stockyards by the carload,

and even by the trainload, from points on the Beaver Road. One farmer who stayed in the Panhandle during the Dirty Thirties simply because he had no other place to go sent one shipment of cattle to Kansas City and received a mere 3¢ per pound for them.[10]

In prior years, the average annual rainfall in Cimarron County had been 16.8 inches. In 1930, the county received 21.09 inches of moisture, and in 1931 it produced a bulging 5,920,500-bushel wheat crop. However, only 8.62 inches fell on Cimarron County farms in 1934, and not one grain was harvested there in the next year. Land values in the county dropped so low that property could not be sold. On April 14, 1935, a black blizzard hit Beaver County, a harbinger of things to come. The term "Dust Bowl," by this time had become common. Farmers "harvested" Russian thistles (tumbleweeds); then even these died, as did the jackrabbits. On the BM&E and on the other roads too, railroaders complained that the dust was stopping their precision watches. A total of 61 storms hit the Panhandle in 1935.[11]

At Baker, the Rock Island agent learned to keep an eye on the weather from her depot-home near the BM&E crossing. When she saw "smoke-like clouds billowing up almost to the dome of heaven and appearing to suck up the whole earth," she deserted the depot, gathered the family and dog, and waited out the storm in a neighbor's dug-out. If a storm developed during the night, sheets were dampened and hung like a pup-tent over the beds. A farm wife near Eva used oil cloths on the window sills and between the upper and lower sashes in a vain attempt to forestall the movement of dust into her home. The combination of economic depression and Dust Bowl conditions drove people from the land without mercy. In one Texas County township along the BM&E, only eight places out of a possible 136 were still occupied by those who made the original homestead entry. Early in March of 1936, a newspaper in that county carried two notices of foreclosure proceedings and nine notices of sheriff's sales. Although leaving the homelands was a tragic experience, remaining, too, was a grim business. One veteran BM&E section foreman who stayed through those dark days later said, "We lived through it, but I don't know how."[12]

With no grass and only a few weeds on his 640 acres, one farmer near Eva decided in May, 1935, to ship his few remaining cattle to more fertile pastures in the central part of Oklahoma. His 27 head, comprising a partial load, were billed on the BM&E for $46. These same animals were returned to him in the fall on a special 85 percent drought rate. A weary but helpful train crew unloaded them in the dead of night, and an even wearier owner drove them home at dawn. Meanwhile, the wheels of government finally ground out some assistance. One thoughtful contemporary observer commented that "the benefit payments under the AAA and the wage payments from Federal work projects are all that have saved a large territory" in the Panhandle from abandonment. Another government project fostered the development of shelter belts. The first of these was begun near Brinkman on the Katy's Northwestern District in southwestern Oklahoma.[13]

During 1936, a total of 45 storms roared across the Panhandle. Prospects for recovery looked bleak, and one group of experts recommended that the government purchase and permanently retire 2.25 million acres of land in the affected area. Later in the year, President Franklin D. Roosevelt received a report which chronicled the origins of the Dust Bowl conditions. In summary, government researchers determined that:

A) Too much marginal land had been plowed up.
B) The grasslands had been overstocked.
C) Cash crop farming had disastrously led to a lack of crop rotation and to an overdependence on wheat.
D) Farmers had engaged in improper methods and techniques of farming, land management, and water conservation.

Even as the New Deal attempted to ameliorate these problems, weather conditions worsened in 1937. Storms began as early as January, continued in February, and intensified in March. On March 21, schools in the Panhandle and those

Dust storms, like this one at milepost 102 near Keyes, frequently buried the BM&E track. *M-K-T collection*

as far east as Woodward were forced to close due to a severe dust storm. Before the year had ended, no less than 110 "destructive dust storms" had raked the Panhandle. Cimarron County experienced crop failures in 1937 and 1938, although Beaver and Texas counties each had partial crops both years. More than 70 storms hit Cimarron, Texas, and Beaver counties in 1939; yet while the frequency dropped in 1939, the dirt blizzard of March 11, 1939, was proclaimed the worst of all.[14]

These rampaging storms naturally interfered with the normal operations of the BM&E. A former engineer on the Beaver Road later recalled that it was necessary to "switch by sound"; signals, ordinarily passed visually, were shouted during dust storms. Frequently, it was necessary for section men to patrol the track ahead of the trains. On one occasion, a section man from Keyes, John Walters, used his motor car to inspect the track between Keyes and Hopkins. When he arrived at Hopkins, he boarded the locomotive of a westbound train to tell the engineer that the road to Keyes was clear. A storm was in progress, however, and visibility had dropped to zero. The train headed toward Keyes, but one mile west of Burton it slammed into a cut and derailed in a five-foot drift of dirt. Less than an hour before, Walters had passed through that same cut on his tiny motor car without difficulty.[15]

A few years earlier, before the vicious nature of the wind was fully evident to railroad employees, an even more bizarre incident took place on the western portion of the BM&E. During the dark hours before dawn, the crew of a west-bound train spotted a number of grain cars for loading at the Hopkins elevator, mile post 95.2. Sleepy brakemen did not set hand brakes on the cars and neither did they set the derail behind the cars. During the next afternoon, a fierce wind developed which literally blew the cars out of the siding, through the switch, and onto the main line. Aided by a slight descending grade, the cars gathered momentum as they headed east. Twenty minutes later a dumbfounded elevator man at Eva stared at the fast-approaching but locomotiveless train of cars. He ran to tell Hugh Parks, the local section foreman, and together they gave chase in a Model A Ford. Parks had earlier placed a 12-mile-per-hour slow order on a stretch of track near Muncy, but as the cars hit the downhill grade

toward Goff Creek they safely passed over the "slow" track at more than 50 miles per hour. Meanwhile, a thoroughly alarmed W. C. Anderson, the agent at Eva, warned the Hooker office that he had just seen boxcars flying by his bay window. The agent at Hooker, E. B. Parks, passed the message to section foreman J. R. Bone, who promptly removed a rail at the west end of the Hooker yard. Thankfully, a forced derailment was unnecessary. The itinerant cars negotiated the bridges over Goff Creek but slowed on the uphill grade near Hovey. By this time, Parks and the elevator man had caught up with them. The cars were boarded and the hand brakes set lest they continue on their unauthorized voyage. The dispatcher then issued an order that brakes be set thereafter on all cars spotted at sidings along the BM&E.[16]

Throughout the history of the line, crews were admonished to operate their trains "under full control between mileposts 73 and 77 expecting to find sand over the rails." This four-mile stretch was always troublesome, but farther west at milepost 103, the cuts became so thoroughly filled with dirt in 1937 that two steam shovels were dispatched to clear them. Operated by what BM&E crews called "Dinky Skinners," these Katy men and their steam shovels spent several days opening the road. Meanwhile, service to Keyes was indefinitely suspended. Elsewhere, many shallow cuts simply disappeared when the track was jacked up to rest on the dirt ballast recently deposited there by a passing storm. Section foremen at Keyes and Eva frequently hired local men as well as drifters when it became necessary to shovel sand from the right-of-way. From 1936 through 1939, it was not unusual to see between 25 and 30 men, assisted by two or three teams with fresnoes, digging out the line. The capricious wind also played tricks on the maintenance-of-way people. Cuts reportedly filled with sand at the end of one day often were clear when laborers arrived the next. A subsequent evening storm or shift in wind would mysteriously relocate the shifting sands.[17]

The BM&E did whatever it could to assist the Panhandle during these difficult years. Rates were lowered to help livestock owners who wanted to farm out their cattle during the dry summer months but who wanted them returned in the fall. In 1931, merchants and farm-

At milepost 103, the cuts became so thoroughly filled with dirt in 1937 that two steam shovels were dispatched to clear them. *Byron Bates collection*

The capricious wind frequently played tricks on the maintenance of way people. Cuts cleared on one day would be filled the next. *Byron Bates collection*

ers at Hooker donated a carload of wheat to the Red Cross. The grain was milled free by the Altus Milling Company and distributed to needy drought sufferers. The BM&E and the Katy happily assisted in this project. Trainmen found another way to help; they obligingly allowed hoboes to ride with them. Indeed, one engineer frequently stopped the train between stations to pick up hoboes. Hooker was the favored destination for these men, for they could "catch" trains on the Rock Island's Golden State Route at that point.[18]

With the coming of hard times, all of Katy's plans for improving the physical facilities of the Beaver Road disappeared. Anticipated improvements in train service also evaporated. In fact, the periodicity of movements suffered after the M-K-T purchased the BM&E. Regularly advertised trains disappeared by 1932. In lieu of scheduled trains, the BM&E offered "irregular mixed train service" throughout the period. However, the usual pattern was to operate a night run over the BM&E to complement the daylight freight schedules of the M-K-T at Forgan. The Rock Island agent at Baker simply learned to expect BM&E trains only when she saw them.[19]

Residents of the Panhandle received a particularly welcome Christmas present late in 1939 when 14 inches of snow blanketed the area. Soaking rains followed in the spring of 1940, and the area's wheat production reached 46.8 million bushels. The 1942 harvest exceeded even that of 1931, but the next harvest was slightly below normal in the Panhandle. Then followed three successive bumper crops. The Dirty Thirties—

the infamous Dust Bowl Days—had passed. Yet its effects were evident. Cimarron County attained its maximum population in 1930. Ten years later, the census revealed a loss of 1,754 people for that county. In the same decade, Beaver County's population dropped by 2,804, while Texas County had 4,304 fewer inhabitants after the Dirty Thirties. Moreover, there were 1,282 fewer farms in the Panhandle in 1940 as compared to 1930.[20]

Uncle Jake Achenbach had considered the acquisition of brand new equipment to be a consummate extravagance when similar inexpensive second-hand items were available. Thus at the time of its acquisition by the M-K-T in 1931, the Beaver Road owned five used locomotives:

Number 1—2-6-0, acquired in August, 1915

Number 2—2-6-0, acquired in October, 1916

Number 229—4-6-0, acquired in May, 1928

Number 237—4-6-0, acquired in May, 1929

Number 454 — 2-6-0, acquired in December, 1924

These elderly mills were then in various stages of disrepair, and, except for number 237 which survived until 1934, all were scrapped in 1932. Numbers 1 and 2 had been stored unserviceable on weed-grown tracks east of the Forgan depot and were quickly cut up and shipped from that location. The three spindly box cars owned by the BM&E likewise were scrapped, but the road's two venerable side-door cabooses were retained and decorated in Katy livery. As replacement locomotives, the M-K-T sent its own 400- and 500-class engines, used extensively on its Northwestern District, to fulfill the power needs of the BM&E. Occasionally, however, a few 600-class 2-8-0s reached the Beaver's rails. These machines, heavier and more powerful than the 2-6-0s, usually were employed as snow plows but also were used to power ditchers. The BM&E's rolling stock needs were supplied from the Katy's general car supply.[21]

Before the depression deepened, many carloads of hogs were shipped to market from Beaver. This traffic, like livestock traffic generally, deteriorated during the Dirty Thirties. However, as rainfall amounts returned to normal, so did the BM&E's livestock business. Stock pens were located at Beaver, Hough, Muncy (changed from Tracy in 1933), Eva, and Keyes. At Baker and at Hooker, an arrangement was made with the Rock Island to use its stock pens and tracks. Cattle from Mexico and Texas moved into the Panhandle on the Beaver Road each spring. If consigned to ranchers whose land adjoined the right-of-way, portable chutes were employed to unload the cattle. If not, the cars were taken to stock pens at the various stations. In the fall, many of these animals were reloaded for shipment, generally to Kansas City or to St. Joseph, Missouri. Cattle consigned to these points were delivered to the Santa Fe at Keyes, the Rock Island at Hooker, or the Katy at Forgan. Sheep also were shipped in; ordinarily they were "jumped" from the cars to the adjoining grazing areas.[22]

With the return of prosperity, fewer and fewer hoboes availed themselves of the Beaver Road's personalized passenger service. Harvest hands were carried as always, and occasionally a paying passenger showed up. Even less frequently, a Katy official arrived with his private car for an excursion over the Butter, Milk & Eggs road. On one occasion, however, a board-of-directors special passed over the entire line; and on another occasion, a genuine passenger train was handled by the Beaver Road. A photograph owned by T. J. Robb, Jr., a former BM&E engineer, shows a ten-car train pulled by a diminutive Katy passenger locomotive arriving in the Forgan yards. This unique movement, a "Wichita Boosters Train," had been brought over the BM&E from

the Rock Island at Hooker and was forwarded to Woodward on the M-K-T. Individual passenger service of quite another type was utilized by the agent at Keyes. Before the construction of reliable highways, Albert Dowdy used a motor car to get from Keyes to the elevators at Burton and Hopkins. Dowdy picked up the bills of lading from these shippers, cranked up his "putt-putt car," and returned to Keyes. At Keyes and elsewhere, station agents had to provide their own transportation in order to deliver Western Union wires. As better public roads became available, LCL shipments declined in volume. Yet through the war years and even later, LCL and Railway Express traffic was handled in line cars or in the caboose. The use of line cars to move packing-house products ended by the mid-1940s, however.[23]

In the 1940s, a large traffic of non-recurring shipments moved over the light rails of the BM&E. In 1943, tracks were built for a new Cities Service Transportation and Chemical Company plant at Straight, 13.3 miles west of Hooker. This facility promoted the subsequent movement of materials necessary for the construction of the pipe lines which soon laced the area. The Cities Service Oil Company built a loading track at the same location in 1945, and this gave new but sporadic business to the BM&E. In the same period, the Beaver handled trainloads of gravel and asphalt for road construction projects.[24]

Dust storms were not the only problems of nature with which the BM&E had to deal. Snow and water presented almost perennial difficulties. The blizzard of 1937 was monumental, but any snow that was accompanied by wind usually filled the right-of-way cuts. Strangely, the BM&E never owned or operated a snow plow. When it was necessary to clear the line, a locomotive was dispatched to do the job. Some of these were equipped with pilot-plows, but in most cases the pilot was merely "chained up" and, as one veteran engineer described it, "we let 'er rip." He also recalled that in these snow-removal operations, crew members often "rode the engine all day and never saw the track." Frequently, however, the locomotive became stuck in the drifts and had to be dug out by section men before it could "make another run" at the snowy barrier. Adding to the difficulty, snow coming up through the damper often killed the fire. Bucking snow

This unidentified locomotive had just arrived at Hooker after opening the line from Forgan in January, 1932. *T. J. Robb, Jr. collection*

Katy locomotive #495, stuck in the snow at milepost 42. *A. E. Bauman collection*

A supreme effort was necessary to plow deep cuts. Milepost 69; January 19, 1932. *Hugh Parks collection*

Sometimes a supreme effort was inadequate. Milepost 69; January 19, 1932. *Hugh Parks collection*

Two 600-class engines were required to open the Katy line from Woodward to Forgan in March of 1932. Succeeding in that, they went west to do battle with drifts on the BM&E. *T. J. Robb, Jr. collection*

Locomotive #492 stuck in a cut west of Hough on January 19, 1932. *Hugh Parks collection*

Plowing the line. Turpin; January 21, 1944. *Charles E. Gardiner collection*

was always a difficult and dangerous job. Two events illustrated this. The January 13, 1944, issue of the *Hooker Advance* reported that 35.5 inches of snow had fallen there since early December. Six days later, after the BM&E line had been blocked by what had become hard, packed snow, engine number 553 turned over near the Hooker depot as it was attempting to plow the line; fortunately crew members sustained only minor injuries. Nevertheless, it was necessary to call "the big hook" from Wichita Falls to rerail the locomotive. A few years later, two locomotives were dispatched to open the road following another storm. All went well until they reached mile post 67 west of Hough. Then, instead of easing into this cut as they had done all day with others, the men decided to "really hit this one," although with a lone engine. Unfortunately, a crust of ice underlaid the snow, and when the charging locomotive made contact, the ice and not the iron horse was the victor. Luckily there were no major injuries to the enginemen—except a loss of dignity. Again the wrecker was summoned.[25]

Although raging water sometimes reached as high as the caps on bridges over Goff Creek, damage there was rare. At Beaver, however, damage to the long, pile trestle over the Beaver River

was frequent and extensive. On at least one occasion several bents were swept away during a flash flood. Farther west at "Elmore Lake," between Baker and Hooker, water often covered the track. For much of one winter, and at other times too, BM&E trains detoured over the Rock Island, using its trackage from Baker to Liberal and back to Hooker. As might be expected, BM&E engineers took particular delight in racing their trains over the heavy steel of the Golden State Route.[26]

Above all else, the Beaver Road was the Panhandle's premier grain carrier. Even Rock Island representatives admitted that the BM&E always made it "tough competition" for the wheat traffic. Together with its Katy parent, the Beaver reached the right places with the right rates. During harvest season, the total energies of the road were devoted to the movement of grain. Engines, cars, and men were borrowed from the Northwestern and other Katy operating divisions for the annual ritual, at least after the Dust Bowl years. Engineer C. W. Dowdy was one of many Northwestern employees who temporarily were assigned to the BM&E. He labeled the Panhandle country as "high, dry, and windy" and, like many others who worked there during World War II, not altogether good-naturedly referred to the

Accidents will happen. *Leon H. Sapp photographs*

On January 19, 1944, locomotive #553 turned over near the Hooker depot as it was attempting to plow the line; fortunately, crew members sustained only minor injuries. *A. E. Bauman and George Crosby collections*

As long as BM&E section men were allowed to keep up the track, wrecks like these were few. *Lester W. Barnett and T. J. Robb, Jr. collections*

The bridge over the Beaver River near Beaver required frequent attention. October, 1941.
Lester W. Barnett collection

During May of 1951, high water knocked the Beaver River bridge out of line. *Lester W. Barnett collection*

124

The BM&E's distinctive side door cabooses were repainted in Katy's Matt Sloan yellow during the mid-1940s. *Lester W. Barnett collection*

Extra 550 east, with 33 cars and 1460 tons, is nearly home. Near Forgan, 1946. *Lester W. Barnett collection*

Engine facilities at Forgan, circa 1945. *T. J. Robb, Jr. collection*

BM&E as the Burma Road. These "foreigners" indeed often found the Panhandle hot and windy. Yet they enjoyed the generally cool nights and discovered that on many days it was perfectly calm; one seemingly could hear a pin drop, and exhaust reports from hard-working locomotives were heard long before the train came into sight.[27]

The Katy men always found the BM&E track neatly groomed and in fit condition to carry the burden of frequent and heavy trains during the harvest periods. The maximum speed allowed between Forgan and Keyes was 18 miles per hour. Regular enginemen who knew the road rarely paid attention to this rule, however. One veteran took a five-car train from Floris to Forgan, 10.3 miles, in 12 minutes without difficulty. On a later trip with 90 loads of wheat, this engineer's luck ran out when 17 of these cars derailed as he vainly made a run for troublesome Nash Hill west of Forgan. Except for Nash Hill and the Goff Creek hills, 500-class engines could, the men boasted, "pull anything you could pump the air off." Indeed, with well-manicured track, easy grades, and a talented engineer, these machines could pull amazingly long trains except over the hills mentioned. However, even under the best conditions, a 500 could handle only 15 loads eastbound out of the Goff Creek bottoms. As a result, a siding at Hovey, mile post 72, was constructed for doubling purposes.[28]

From June until October, the BM&E ordi-narily operated two daily trains in each direction, supplemented during the harvest period with one or two other daily trains. A BM&E crew handled one train each way daily, while a second Beaver crew was used on an evening turn-around operation. Katy crews manned all other movements. The following itinerary is representative of the tight schedules to which BM&E's number two crew was subject during the wheat rush:

Extra 552—July 29, 1944—departed Forgan   5:20 p.m.
Extra 552—July 30, 1944—arrived Keyes   5:15 a.m.
Extra 552—July 30, 1944—departed Keyes   2:15 p.m.
Extra 552—July 30, 1944—arrived Forgan   7:35 p.m.
Extra 552—July 31, 1944—departed Forgan   1:05 p.m.
Extra 552—August 1, 1944—arrived Keyes   1:05 a.m.
Extra 552—August 1, 1944—departed Keyes   11:30 a.m.
Extra 552—August 2, 1944—arrived Forgan   1:00 a.m.
Extra 552—August 2, 1944—departed Forgan   3:15 p.m.
Extra 552—August 2, 1944—arrived Forgan   11:00 p.m.
Extra 596—August 3, 1944—departed Forgan   6:40 p.m.
Extra 596—August 4, 1944—arrived Keyes   9:15 a.m.
Extra 596—August 4, 1944—departed Keyes   5:15 p.m.
Extra 596—August 5, 1944—arrived Forgan   7:00 a.m.

Later, on October 7, 1944, a train left Forgan at 9:05 a.m., turned back from Keyes at 5:15 p.m., and was in Forgan at 12:05 a.m. Thus in 15 hours, this crew covered 210 miles and did all the necessary local work. The traffic mix for this run, and others like it during the period, included

126

Forgan as seen from the M-K-T fueling tower. Doubleheader (541/535) is preparing to leave for a wheat-gathering expedition on the BM&E. Circa 1945. *T. J. Robb, Jr. collection*

wheat, barley, maize, merchandise, sand, chat, gravel, coal, engines, soybean cake, cottonseed cake, pipe, cement, and cattle. Nevertheless, the Beaver Road's bread-and-butter traffic was grain. As the 1945 harvest began, Katy reported that 7,508 cars of grain from the previous year's crop had been loaded on its Northwestern District and on the BM&E.[29]

The impact of the Dirty Thirties and the change to prosperity in the 1940s was reflected in the BM&E's balance sheets. In 1931, when Katy acquired the Beaver Road, it earned a profit of $35,801. Operations for the next year resulted in a deficit of nearly $100,000, and for the following five years the BM&E failed to earn even its operating expenses. Deficits were trimmed between 1938 and 1942 as prosperity gradually returned to the Panhandle, and in 1943, the Beaver turned a modest profit of $27,452. In 1944 and in 1949, profits exceeded $100,000 and surpassed $200,000 in 1947 and 1948. Smaller profits resulted from operations in 1945 and 1946. As the decade of the 1940s drew to a close, the BM&E was still a dirt track railroad but nevertheless was in remarkably good physical condition. The road was willing and able to handle the volume and nature of traffic which then was attracted to it. The Dust Bowl era was only an ugly memory; the 1940s brought prosperity; the future looked even better.[30]

Paul O. Parks. *Author's collection*

Of Men and Events:
The Northwestern District

"Katy has found the parable 'as you sow, so shall ye reap' has a place in the business world as in personal life."*

Construction of the Wichita Falls & Northwestern fostered the development of Wichita Falls as an important commercial and transportation center. It also served to open a large new territory, and it provided useful and efficient transportation for that area. Its construction and operation resulted in diverse employment opportunities for people in agriculture, industry, commerce, and many other fields. Additionally, the railroad provided direct employment for several hundred workers. A list of employees for the company's transportation department indicates that 657 people found permanent jobs on the Northwestern District in that branch of service alone. Most of these were trainmen, enginemen, and station employees. Not included on this list were those who worked only briefly in that department. Nor were maintenance-of-way employees, bridgemen, shop workers, carmen, general office personnel, or supervisors included. While additional statistical data do not exist, it seems clear that the Northwestern District offered, over the years, employment of one type or another for a minimum of 2,000 people. It also provided temporary work for at least that many and probably more.[1]

Some of these employees formerly held permanent jobs on other railroads: Samuel A. King left the Abilene & Southern to become agent at Hollis. Some had been boomers: C. P. Parks alternately was a telegrapher and a fireman on numerous roads before coming to the WF&NW as a brakeman. Others simply lived along the line and took advantage of the employment opportunities which it offered: as a 16-year-old young-

ster, L. C. Rodgers hired out in the Wichita Falls roundhouse as a helper. These three men, with diverse backgrounds, are representative of those who found permanent employment on the Northwestern. All eventually retired from the line after lengthy service.[2]

In the earliest days of the line's existence, the road was, as one veteran later recalled, "desperate for workers and hired all comers." Almost always well received were the boomers, many of them "running under a flag" (using assumed names or forged service letters). C. W. Dowdy, who spent over 40 years in engine service on the Northwestern, recalled that "nine out of ten were good men." C. P. Parks considered them "the best railroaders that ever lived." These itinerant railroaders were especially helpful during the WF&NW's construction years and later during the annual harvest rushes. Ordinarily, however, they worked only long enough to earn a "pie card" before searching again for the "Big Rock Candy Mountain."[3]

The boomers added a romantic flavor to the Northwestern District, but they left little visible record. Rather, it was the local labor supply which contributed a regular flow of both temporary and long-term manpower. For example, Walter R. Smith was hired as a helper by the regular depot employees at Vici. His duties were to help find and load freight. Smith later left railroading and eventually served as superintendent of schools at various towns along the Northwestern District. A decade later, Clifton Kay hung around the same depot and learned the station

*Willard V. Anderson, "Katy Serves the Southwest," *Trains*, Vol. 9 (April 1949), p. 25.

business from Walter W. Roan, the agent. Initially, Kay was hired to "bed" stock cars, a task which paid him 25¢ per car and took two hours each. Later he spent five years as an extra agent-telegrapher on the Northwestern before leaving to become a dispatcher on numerous other railroads. P. A. Johnston was hired by the M-K-T in 1923 "after hanging around the depot at Burkburnett." Johnston stayed with the company until he retired on November 30, 1971. For Wesley P. Altland, the case was similar. A native of Woodward County, Altland was the oldest man on the seniority roster when he retired on January 31, 1972.[4]

Promotions came quickly during the early days and later during the Burkburnett boom days. After only three months as helper in the Wichita Falls roundhouse, L. C. Rodgers was promoted to fireman. Thrilled at the prospect of a road job, he quickly purchased "new overalls, a jumper, a blazing red bandana, and a nice stiff cap" and reported for duty. C. P. Parks was promoted from brakeman to conductor after being with the WF&NW for only 27 days. Dan B. Cullen and P. O. Parks both entered train service before World War I and were senior men before the boom at Burkburnett. Existing records do not admit an accurate evaluation of the number of train crews that were assigned to the Northwestern during these years. However, sketchy payroll records suggest that there were 22 train crews assigned between Wichita Falls and Altus in May, 1922. Most veterans feel that there were twice that many two years earlier when the boom was at its peak. As the boom passed and traffic was adjusted, however, the number of employees on the line dropped sharply. Men promoted earlier were demoted, and junior men were forced to resign.[5]

Each steam locomotive is said to have had its peculiar personality. So it was with their drivers. Each had his own way of handling the machine. Some, like Sam Creecy, were truly "whistle artists." Creecy had a way of making the whistle sound eerie, particularly at night; everybody knew that he was at the throttle by his "lost boy whistle." Creecy was also known as a fast runner. It was said that in chain-gang service (first crew in, first crew out) he could make two miles while other crews made one. Small wonder, then, that he is the best remembered of all Northwestern engineers. Another engineer, Fred Cook,

frequently was assigned to passenger-train service. Cook always tried to arrive in Burkburnett a few minutes early. Succeeding in that, he would remove his gloves, place them on the brake valve, light up a cigarette, and lean back in the seat for a few minutes relaxation. Most engineers had a favorite piece of track where they liked to make up lost time. John C. Coldwell's favorite race track was between Moorewood and Hammon. Others found the flat plain near Tipton more to their liking.[6]

The men of the Northwestern always enjoyed spinning yarns about themselves and others who had labored on those lines. One story concerned a hefty brakeman who bragged that in unloading LCL from a box car he had carried out a barrel of oil under each arm. A diminutive brakeman standing nearby is said to have verified the story, adding that he had followed his mighty colleague from the car while he himself had carried a piano on his back. On another occasion an engineer during steam days is reported to have committed a cardinal sin by running out of water near milepost 190. Leaving the train there, he took the locomotive to Vici and filled the tank. Later, when he returned with the train—now considerably delayed by his earlier absent-mindedness—the agent handed up a message from the dispatcher which pointedly asked, "Why did you cut off and run for water?" The huffy engineer scribbled out a return wire which read, "No water available at milepost 190." Sectionmen delighted in telling of correspondence between two fictional railroaders, Superintendent Finnegan and Section Foreman Flannigan. According to the story, Flannigan always sent lengthy, detailed reports to the Superintendent whenever he derailed his motor car. Finnegan requested that future reports be abbreviated. Thus the next report read: "Supt. Finnegan. Motor car off again. On again. Gone again. Flannigan."

P. O. Parks considered the WF&NW "exceptionally good to work for." Parks' evaluation extended to the M-K-T as well and represents the prevailing thought of those who worked on the Northwestern District. As a result, a rather unusual loyalty developed between the company and its employees. Perhaps it was because most officials took a personal interest in the welfare of "the men." In 1921 when the agent at Sharon wanted to complete a course in telegraphy at

Chillicothe (Missouri) Business College, Superintendent F. W. Grace granted him a leave of absence and provided him with free passes. Moreover, a succession of superintendents did everything possible to retain in service even the most flagrant violators of company rules. One engineer who had a long record of poor performance was fired in 1920 for delaying a train. A year later, several senior engineers and the union's local chairman convinced company officials to reinstate him. Eventually he retired after more than a half-century of service. Another engineer was fired in 1931 for violation of the "infamous" Rule G—drinking while on duty. This man, too, was reinstated because company officials knew that he was "hard up" and because of his "previously good record." In 1939, he again was removed from service for drinking, but one month later he was back at work. At least two station agents were dismissed for violating Rule G and then rehired after petitions were received by the company from prominent citizens of their respective communities. Morale among employees in all branches thus remained high over the years. Few employees looked forward to retirement. Many were like James I. Burt, who reluctantly "pulled the pin" in 1960 after spending 48 of his 77 years with the railroad.[7]

While few employees were permanently dismissed, fewer still had perfect records. Company officials did keep a battery of stenographers busy typing and mailing demerit reports to offending personnel. This was the railroad's way of disciplining its help; as Superintendent F. P. Blount told a concerned shipper at Laverne in 1935, "the matter of discipline is paramount in handling employes and unless such discipline is maintained the morale of the entire organization suffers." Often demerits were given for minor offenses. One agent received 10 demerits when he failed to "comply with Rule J at Laverne, August 8, 1924, by not wearing agent's cap while working train #53." At another station, an agent received a like number of minus marks when an official discovered him smoking while working the same passenger train. Superintendent D. C. Dobbins assured the offender that "there is absolutely no excuse for this and we are not going to tolerate employes smoking on duty." E. B. Parks, who was considered by many of his peers to be the best telegrapher on the line, received 10 demerits at

Hollis in 1925 when the Western Union operator was unable to transmit a wire to him. In 1931 the agent at Sharon was chagrined to learn that he had earned five demerits for failing properly to date his waiting room's bulletin board. The same man earlier had failed to have a fire built in the waiting room stove prior to the arrival of a passenger train; for this his personal record was assessed 10 minus marks. However, when the safe at Laverne was robbed because the agent had left it unlocked, only 20 demerits were given. Finally, one hapless employee earned no fewer than 190 demerits in 18 years, but was retained in service and finally retired in 1957 after 47 years with the company.[8]

Station agents often were considered pillars of the community in which they worked. This is easy to understand, for prior to advanced telephone service and modern highways they were the local representatives of the only available commercial communication and transportation companies. The fact that they could send and receive messages via telegraph implied a certain superiority. As "lightning slingers," these men were the first in town to know the latest news as well as the latest gossip. Express and LCL shipments were handled by them, and in order to ride the passenger trains, one even had to buy a ticket from them. Thus everyone in the community knew the "depot agent." During the depression, agents were frequently considered to "have money" since they were among the few residents of smaller communities who received regular incomes. As late as 1963, 56 people at Grandfield signed a petition asking that Eugene R. Dowdy be continued there as agent; Dowdy had been displaced by a senior employee when the Hammon station was closed.[9]

The depression brought economic dislocation to railroaders and nonrailroaders alike. At Vici, ordinary law-abiding folks boarded coal cars when freight trains stopped there for water. Before the train began to move they threw off what fuel they could and then detrained to pick it up. At Camargo, a young girl used a gunny sack to gather coal that had fallen from passing trains onto the company's right-of-way. Residents there and elsewhere also sought used ties as fuel during those hard times. Friendly section men frequently placed them where they could easily be found by those whom they knew to be the most needy.

Many railroaders, especially those in train service, were laid off during the hard times of the 1930s. Even men who had 20 years and more of service were furloughed. Engineers were reduced to firemen and then completely released. Between 1932 and 1941, many of these men were used, if at all, during harvest season or at other times on an emergency basis. One engineer found temporary employment as a policeman at Altus; but when business increased in the early 1940s, he returned to the railroad. In 1941 and through 1943, many Northwestern enginemen were loaned to mainline divisions due to heavy wartime traffic. As the area served by the Northwestern slowly recovered from the combined effects of the Dust Bowl and the depression, these men returned to handle trains at Wichita Falls, Altus, and Woodward.[10]

Between 1930 and 1935, annual picnics were held at Woodward for all Katy employees and their families. These were gala affairs. Long tables were set up to hold a bounteous supply of culinary delights; athletic contests occupied the younger set; and, prohibition notwithstanding, those with thirst settled the dust in their throats with an occasional slug of whisky. Perhaps this was "Canyon Run," distilled illegally in the scrub oak area near Camargo. As one former resident of that area explained it, "prohibition never came to Dewey County." This fact was universally applauded by the railroad's bridge gangs, who frequently were sent to Camargo to maintain or repair the lengthy timber trestle over the South Canadian River nearby. Many trainmen likewise rejoiced in this happy situation. Carrying a covered wicker basket, one local bootlegger regularly met the freight trains. To camouflage his nefarious dealings, he always announced to the eager railroaders: "Here are your cackleberries." Inside the basket, of course, was a bottle of "Canyon Run," the local moonshine or white lightning.[11]

Undoubtedly one of the most widely known and clearly one of the most colorful of all Northwestern employees was Paul O. Parks. As a youngster, Parks was known at Vici as a sign painter, an adept amateur athlete, and a consummate practical joker. He gained employment on the railroad in 1915, served in the Army during World War I and, after returning to railroad service, was promoted from brakeman to conductor during the Burkburnett boom period. Parks was a well-dressed, even flashy, passenger brakeman and conductor, although he spent most of his years in freight service between Woodward and Forgan. Every shipper knew him as did most of the others who lived along the line. At Laverne, Mrs. Jacob C. Holmes recalled that Parks spoiled her children by bringing treats for them every time a shipment was made by the Holmes Livestock Company. "P. O." always was a Woodward booster. Whenever he had a chance to do so, he distributed promotional material at on-line stations. But railroading eventually interfered with his work, and he retired in 1952. Then he busied himself as a Sergeant-at-Arms of the Oklahoma State Senate, as promoter of annual Fourth of July shows at Woodward, and as the town's Santa Claus during the Christmas season. With his long, flowing white hair, bushy eyebrows, mustache, and goatee, he was a natural for the role of Santa. One of his continuing interests has been the popular Woodward rodeo; on its behalf he has traveled more than 50,000 miles. Parks was never much of a horseman himself; rather, the hustle and bustle of rodeo time was what appealed to him. The indefatigable Parks was 87 years young in 1974.[12]

Only a few women were employed on the Northwestern District, most of them in station service. Between 1926 and 1932, Elizabeth C. Thomason acted as relief agent at Carter while her husband John G. Thomason, relieved other agents on the line for their annual vacations. During the depression, she was unemployed, but as the war drew increasing numbers of men into the service and as her husband had become disabled, Mrs. Thomason again entered station service. She retired in 1960. Another woman agent was Bertie L. Denton. She worked at a number of stations during the 1920s, resigned, and like Mrs. Thomason, returned to the Katy during the war to stay there until retiring in 1967. Probably the first woman to be employed on the Northwestern was Julia V. Roan. Although the railroad apparently had a prohibition against hiring women at that time, the agent at Laverne employed her to do clerical work at that station anyway. Payroll records listed her simply as J. V. Roan, and officials were unaware for some time that they had a woman working on the line. Later she learned telegraphy and was fully employed as an agent-telegrapher. When she arrived at Knowles as agent, the local elevator manager promptly and bitterly protested to the railroad that the work there was too heavy for a woman. Some time later, when she was promoted to another station, the same shipper protested her departure. Railroading was practically a tradition in Ms. Roan's family. Two of her brothers, Walter W. and Norman C. Roan, also were agents on the Northwestern, and her husband, Grover C. Pyle, was Chief Train Dispatcher at Wichita Falls. She retired after many years with the railroad.[13]

In August, 1910, L. C. Rodgers made his first trip as a locomotive fireman. He was on duty that trip for 25 hours before he was released for a few hours rest. When Rodgers retired in 1960, federal regulations which limited to 16 hours the maximum time that train crews could be on duty without rest had long been on the books. Later the maximum was lowered to 14 hours; and as of 1973, employees in train service could work no more than 12 consecutive hours before rest is required. As a fireman in 1918, Rodgers was paid according to this daily rate of pay:

Passenger service,	$5.12
Way freight service,	$6.08
Switching service,	$5.72

As a locomotive engineer in the same year, Rodgers was subject to this daily pay schedule:

Passenger service,	$6.56
Way freight service,	$8.04
Switching service,	$7.20

Overtime payments were unknown in 1918. In 1973, the rate of pay that Rodgers would have received had he still been working, was computed on a mileage basis, 100 miles equaling an eight hour day. Thus, he would have received $42.55 per day as an engineer or $37.39 per day as a fireman. Both figures were subject to overtime rates after the first eight hours.[14]

Other crafts enjoyed similar pay increases over the years. In 1922, boilermakers earned between 49¢ and 80¢ per hour, depending on their ratings. When steam disappeared thirty years later, boilermakers were earning from $1.90 to $1.97 per hour. Carmen made from 47¢ to 80¢ per hour in 1922; but by 1973, they were paid between $5.42 and $5.54 per hour. Section laborers were paid $39.25 per month in 1920; 43 years later, they earned $693.43 per month. Monthly salaries for agents always have differed according to stations, but all have risen sharply, as this schedule shows:

Station	1922	1973
Grandfield	$220.00	$1,070.58
Frederick	$215.00	$1,093.16
Altus	$240.00	$1,124.20
Elk City	$175.00	$1,069.63
Woodward	$190.00	$1,077.21[15]

Of the many men who began their railroad careers on the Northwestern, few were more competent than Charles C. Huff. Appointed as General Attorney for the WF&NW in 1908, Huff accomplished the many difficult legal tasks necessary in launching and operating a new railroad. In 1914 he became General Attorney for the MK&TofT and was appointed General Solicitor for the entire Katy System in 1931. He died unexpectedly in 1943 while still serving in that capacity. Possibly the most popular operating official on the Northwestern was Frank W. Grace. Many employees considered Grace to be a competent official and a friend as well. One former engineer recalled that Grace was "stern but realistic." He was Katy's Vice President and General Manager when he passed away in 1945. A Superintendent who greatly admired habits of punctuality and attention to detail was D. C. Dobbins. His initials, DCD, were transcribed into "Don't Come Dragging" by employees who accorded him only grudging respect. In later years, a popular and effective official was C. W. Robbins, an Assistant Superintendent who retired in 1970 after 42 years with the Katy. The last operating official assigned directly to the Northwestern District was Albert Dowdy. Appropriately he was a man who cut his eyeteeth on the line. Dowdy was hired on April 4, 1939, as a telegrapher at Welon Yard (Altus), but spent 1940 and 1941 on the BM&E as agent at Keyes. After the war, he served numerous stations on the Northwestern District before becoming Trainmaster at Wichita Falls in the early 1960s. Dowdy remained in that capacity until February 1, 1973, when he was reassigned to Fort Worth.[16]

Disasters on the Northwestern were few in number and thankfully mild in nature. On August 22, 1922, the depot at Mangum was destroyed by fire. It was replaced by a 24'x130' brick veneer structure costing $18,957. A tornado hit the passenger station at Woodward on April 9, 1947,

Albert Dowdy, trainmaster on the Northwestern District. *Author's photograph*

and did considerable damage, but later the building was fully repaired. Major derailments likewise were few. A major catastrophe was avoided on Christmas Eve, 1917, when a farmer looking for some stray stock near the North Fork of the Red River found that a rail had been turned over by a freight train which had just passed; the alert farmer then rushed up the track to flag a heavily loaded southbound passenger train which he knew to be approaching. During the mid-1920s a

northbound passenger train, assisted by a 600-class helper assigned to guarantee passage through snow-filled cuts, derailed near Knowles. The helper engine turned over while the passenger engine and the trailing RPO-storage car were derailed. Happily there were no major injuries. In the late 1930s, a section crew pulled its motor car onto a siding at Willow, but then forgot to close the switch. Meanwhile, the engine crew of train number 53, the southbound passenger, did

134

Wesley P. Altland, station agent on the Northwestern District. *Author's photograph*

Wreck of WF&NW freight train at milepost 166 south of Leedey. March 3, 1911. *Mrs. Dorothy Peters collection*

During the mid-1920s, a northbound passenger train, assisted by a 600-class helper assigned to guarantee passage through the cuts, derailed near Knowles. Luckily there were no major injuries to crew or passengers. *Hugh Parks and Mrs. Leota Hodges collections*

not see the open switch until remedial action was quite out of the question. The result was a demolished motor car, a derailed locomotive, and an absolutely speechless section crew. Later, shortly before the passenger train was removed north of Woodward, patrons on the cars were startled one day near Gate when outside their windows a veritable blizzard of feathers appeared. Unfortunately, 300 turkey poults belonging to Mrs. Earl Kerns had ventured onto the Katy tracks coincidental with the passage of the morning train. In this case, the simultaneous arrival resulted in a victory for the iron horse, for the hapless birds suffered a premature slaughter.[17]

Freight train accidents were more frequent and more dramatic. The first railroad wreck in Beaver County occurred on August 1, 1913, when a local freight derailed two miles east of Forgan. In this accident, caused by spreading rails, four wooden box cars were demolished, and four others plus the locomotive tender were de-

railed. Brakeman Lawrence Baker was injured but fortunately recovered. Three decades later, the second section of a grain train plunged into the swirling waters of the Elm Fork of the Red River after a violent rain storm in Texas had sent waters cascading into unsuspecting Oklahoma. This flash flood tore out the Katy bridge north of Mangum under cover of night and went undetected until it was discovered by the searching headlight of the onrushing train. The engineer and fireman jumped clear before the locomotive and trailing cars shot into the boiling waters. However, the head brakeman, riding in the "dog house" atop the tender, had little warning and was forced to ride his mobile perch into the churning waters. He miraculously escaped and was rescued downstream; a broken leg was his only injury. In the 1960s, as the track deteriorated, derailments became much more frequent, if less dramatic, due to slower train speeds.[18]

Through the Dust Bowl days, agent W. P.

Negligent section men left a switch open at Willow with dire consequences. *Cliff Kay collection*

Altland often found it necessary to light lamps in the depot during daylight hours. Blizzards of dirt outside would cut visibility to near zero. Yet dust storms on the Northwestern District were not nearly as bad nor as frequent as those experienced on the BM&E. However, blizzards of snow periodically paralyzed the Northwestern in the same fashion and in the same magnitude as those which hit the Beaver Road. Each morning after the usual 11:00 a.m. time check, Western Union followed with a CND report—the weather summary. When weather conditions were threatening, Western Union kept telegraphers along the line apprised of the situation. These operators, in turn, passed the word to other railroaders and local residents as well. As blizzards developed, officials attempted to get trains off the line and into terminals until the storms had passed. Thus few trains were stranded in drifts along the line. When a freight train infrequently was stuck in a drift, enginemen ordinarily kept the locomotive hot while waiting for help. Meanwhile, trainmen had more comfortable quarters in the caboose. Indeed, until quite recently, trainmen slept and ate their meals in the caboose; it served as a rolling motel and cafe. Newt Branyon and George W. Ford are recalled as excellent caboose cooks. Branyon's specialty was spaghetti and meatballs. Thus waiting for help to arrive usually was no great inconvenience for the trainmen. On one occasion, however, a freight train was stuck in a drift near Vici for several days. The crew eventually ran out of food and survived only by breaking into the LCL line car ahead of the caboose and locating shipments of sardines and crackers.[19]

North and west of Gate, the railroad passed through a long cut on a curve which traditionally filled with snow. In 1918 or 1919, a freight train became stuck in that cut and, having no way to extricate it, the crew left the train and took the engines to Forgan. Meanwhile, a tripleheader, dispatched from Woodward to keep the line open, plowed into the caboose of the stranded train. At another time, a plow engine became buried in the same cut, and before it could be removed, another storm hit the area; 16 days were to elapse before the locomotive finally was removed and the line reopened. The 1937 blizzards in Beaver County were legendary, but April storms that same year also filled the several extensive cuts between Leedy and Trail. Three years later, veteran conductor Dan B. Cullen spent five 16-hour days on a work train which was charged with opening the line after a particularly violent blizzard. At Gate and near Mocane, drifts were over ten feet high; on one day, Cullen's train cleared only five miles of track. This operation was typical of the ones undertaken during those days. Two 500-class engines were assigned; one was the plow engine, and the other was the drag-out engine, used to extricate the plow engine whenever it became stalled in the heavily packed snow of troublesome cuts. Several cabooses were used to carry the section men who were picked up at every station as the plow train worked westward. These unheralded laborers had the unpleasant task of digging out locomotives whenever they could not remove themselves from unusually difficult drifts. Strangely, neither the WF&NW nor the Katy ever assigned snow plows to the Northwestern District. A few locomotives were equipped with pilot plows, and for that reason, they were eminently better for snow removal operations than the diesels which replaced them later.[20]

Of all the problems faced by railroaders on the Northwestern District, none were more troublesome than high water and flash floods.

Traffic was frequently disrupted when the approaches and the bridges themselves were threatened or even washed away by swiftly flowing streams. In August of 1917, a passenger train was stopped by high water on the North Canadian River at milepost 259, four miles north of Laverne. Four years later, 40 loaded cars were placed on the trestle over the Red River north of Burkburnett in an effort which saved most of that structure. Nevertheless, 17 bents on the south end of the bridge were installed five months later—after the rampaging Red had carved away approaches on that side of the stream. The devastating flood of April 4, 1934, on the Washita River did not take Katy's bridge over that stream north of Hammon Junction; however, several people were drowned in that disaster, and one body was found in the debris that accumulated against the piling of the railroad's trestle. A number of Bureau of Reclamation projects in the Texas Panhandle later eased flood threats on the South

High water north of Laverne in 1917 caused considerable aggravation. Opposing passenger trains met on either side of the swollen stream and passengers were obliged to cross the bridge on foot to get to the other train. Note the hat check properly displayed in the band of the hat worn by the man on the right. *C. W. Criswell collection*
The South Canadian River, barely a trickle in these views, could and did at times become a raging force. *Author's photographs*

The South Canadian River, barely a trickle in these views, could and did at times become a raging force. *Author's photographs.*

In 1921, the bridge over the South Canadian was out for ten days while crews replaced 46 bents. *M-K-T collection*

After the washout disasters of 1923, the Katy installed considerable steel jetty protection upstream from its South Canadian bridge. *M-K-T collection*

Fire destroyed seven bents in 1913. *Mrs. Pearl Rogers collection*

Canadian and on the Elm Fork of the Red River. The Fort Supply Lake project, an undertaking of the Army Corps of Engineers, also reduced flood threats on Wolf Creek near Fort Supply and on the North Canadian at Woodward. The Optima Dam flood control project, authorized in 1936 but not expected to be operative until 1976, was designed to lessen water damages on the Beaver and North Canadian Rivers.[21]

Nowhere on the Northwestern District was there more difficulty with water than on the South Canadian River at milepost 183 south of Camargo. In 1973, the bridge structure over that river was 271 panels, or 3,767' in length. It stood only 23' above the river, and its piles rested in the pure sand which characterizes the streambed at that location. An abbreviated transcript reveals the interesting history of this bridge:

A) March 13, 1913, fire destroyed seven bents. Bridge out for two days.

B) June 7, 1921, 46 bents and 25 panels washed away. Bridge out for ten days.

C) May 18, 1922, completed the driving of 114 bents and the renewal of 98 deck panels.

D) May 1923, washout of north side approaches. Added 83 panels "to provide adequate waterway for handling drainage."

E) September, 1923, another flood washed away 48 panels then under construction after May flood. Re-

newal not fully completed until February 13, 1924, although rail service resumed much earlier.

F) October 30, 1930, north side embankment washed out. Bridge extended by 121 feet.

G) June 1936, washout of north embankment. Bridge extended another 70 feet.

H) June 1937, washout resulted in extending bridge to the north by an additional 210 feet.

I) September and October, 1941, washouts necessitated extending the bridge by 570 feet. Structure reached its maximum length, 4,660 feet, or approximately .88 mile.

J) May 21, 1953, completed filling 70 panels, leaving 272 panels.[22]

In 1913, when the bridge over the South Canadian burned, the WF&NW borrowed a bridge crew from the MK&T and had the structure in shape for traffic within 43 hours. Meanwhile, the company transferred mail, express, and passengers by ferrying them over the river. Eight years later, disaster simultaneously struck the Camargo trestle and the bridge over the Red north of Burkburnett. Within hours, a pile driver was at work on the north side of the South Canadian while a special train was speeding another such machine to the Red. In all cases, bridgemen were pushed to the limit of human endurance and pile drivers were operated 24 hours per day until the road was opened once more. Since its

High water took out several bents in 1913. It was, indeed, a bad year for the bridge.
Mrs. Dorothy Peters collection

pilings rested on sand instead of on a firm foundation, the Camargo structure tended to shift, settle, and rise according to the volume of water in the stream or the weight of trains passing over it. Trainmen naturally were apprehensive about the bridge, and others like it on the line, and unhesitatingly circulated campaign stories regarding its spooky idiosyncrasies. In later years, electric color lights were installed to protect trains approaching bridges over the Elm and North Forks of the Red River. Such protection was never afforded at the other major stream crossings.[23]

Katy herald, circa 1950. *Author's collection*

The last steam passenger train on the Northwestern District. Elk City; June 17, 1950.
P. A. Johnston photograph; Old Town Museum ʌElk City, OklahomaQ collection

144

Deramus and Damnation

"Cut all personnel to the lowest possible number that will permit daily conduct of business." President William N. Deramus, 1957.

"You can't starve a railroad into prosperity." President John W. Barriger, 1966.*

Agent P. A. Johnston took his camera to work with him at Elk City on June 17, 1950. The last steam-powered passenger train was scheduled for that warm day, and Johnston wanted to secure a pictorial record of that historic event. The following day a gas-electric motor car was the prime mover on the Northwestern District's single remaining passenger train. Schedules also were changed so that the new motor train could make a daily round trip between Wichita Falls and Woodward. It left Wichita Falls at 6:00 a.m. and arrived in Woodward, 220 miles distant, eight hours later. Returning, the train left Woodward at 3:00 p.m. and arrived in Wichita Falls at 11:05 p.m. The replacement of steam by internal combustion power on the passenger trains was symbolic of even greater changes that were to characterize the Northwestern District between 1950 and 1969.[1]

When engine 314 pulled the last steam passenger train through Elk City in 1950, it was a venerable but yet well maintained piece of machinery; even its tires were daintily trimmed in white. The dirt track over which it rolled was immaculately manicured; nary a weed grew between the ties. Nevertheless, 19 years later, Katy's Northwestern District offered no passenger service whatsoever; its box cars were often ill-coopered; its tracks had nearly disappeared in a sea of weeds and dirt; and most of it had experienced or was facing abandonment.

Although steam disappeared from passenger service on the Northwestern in 1950, it continued to provide motive power for all freight assignments in that year. Locomotives of the 500-class ordinarily drew these trains, although a sprinkling of 400-class machines also were stabled in the on-line roundhouses. Number 479 was typical of this class. It was built by American Locomotive Company in 1902 and had a tractive effort rating of 30,200 pounds. Locomotives 541 and 596 frequently were visitors on the lines north of Wichita Falls and were representatives of the 500 class. Number 541 was outshopped by Baldwin Locomotive Company in 1904 and had the same tractive effort rating as the 479. However, the 596—a Baldwin product of 1906—was rated at 31,750 pounds tractive effort. All had 63-inch drivers, and each trailed tenders holding only 6,000 to 8,000 gallons of water.[2]

Early in 1949, Katy officials expected that steam would long rule on the Northwestern District because of its extremely light rail and its superficially ballasted roadbed. The engineering department then felt that locomotives having an axle loading of more than 52,000 pounds would severely damage the track. Six-axle diesel locomotives would have eased this problem and were available at that time. Katy management ruled against the acquisition of them, however, as they were "not interchangeable with the balance of Katy's diesel motive power." Moreover, they were

*Railway Age, Vol. 142 (April 29, 1957), p. 9; Parsons [Kansas] Sun, November 15, 1966.

145

Locomotive #479 was typical of the 400-class machines which worked the Northwestern District. *John J. Siller photograph*

A typical sight on the Northwestern District during the wheat season was doubleheaded freight trains. Here is one, with locomotives 596 and 530, near Altus, Oklahoma on June 15, 1946. *Preston George photograph*

Locomotive #555 was well manicured on April 27, 1946 when photographer Preston George found her in Welon Yard at Altus.

146

Top. Steam was near its "last hurrah" when locomotive #559 roared into Fort Supply on December 27, 1950. Bottom. The same locomotive had an auxiliary tank on July 7, 1951 at Laverne. *H. S. Tyler photographs*

The dubious task of drawing the last steam powered train out of Forgan fell to locomotive #521 on February 9, 1952. *W. O. Gibson photograph; Everett L. DeGolyer, Jr. collection*

Moguls 541 and 596 were typical of that type locomotive used extensively on the North-western District. Top, Everett L. DeGolyer, Jr. collection. Bottom, R. W. Richardson photograph; *Everett L. DeGolyer, Jr. collection*

After June 17, 1950, the Katy used its M-12 and a trailer coach to provide passenger service between Wichita Falls and Woodward. Here the setting is Elk City in the summer of 1950. *P. A. Johnston photograph*

deemed cost prohibitive. Nevertheless, on February 21, 1951, a 1,500 horsepower GP-7 locomotive, having a 60,000-pound axle loading, was used for a test on a local freight between Wichita Falls and Altus. After analyzing the results of this run, Katy engineers agreed that the operation of four-axle GP-7 locomotives was permissible even on this light rail. Following this decision "diesel locomotives were placed in regular service on the Northwestern. . . ." There were a number of advantages to a diesel operation as opposed to steampower. As the statistics below indicate, not the least of these was the increased tonnage ratings for the diesel locomotives:

Northbound	500-Class Steam (ratings in tons)	1,500 hp. GP-7 (ratings in tons)
Wichita Falls-Altus	1,275	2,200
Altus-Woodward	1,275	2,000
Woodward-Forgan	1,275	2,000
Southbound		
Forgan-Woodward	1,275	2,200
Woodward-Altus	1,275	2,000
Altus-Wichita Falls	1,820	2,200

The conversion from steam to diesel was surprisingly swift. Sturdy 500s assisted with the harvest rushes of 1951, but on February 9, 1952, locomotive number 521 pulled the last steam-powered train out of Forgan. For that matter, the entire Katy System was completely dieselized shortly thereafter. On the Northwestern District, the final curtain for its steam era came in 1953 when the boiler plant, water facilities, and fuel stations at Wichita Falls were retired. The eight-stall roundhouse there already had been retired in August, 1952.[3]

Steam and then diesel locomotives powered the daily-except-Sunday mixed trains on the Wellington Branch. Subsequent to June 17, 1950, Katy's M-12, a heavy gas-electric motor car built by the St. Louis Car Company in the early 1930s, handled the Wichita Falls-Woodward passenger train. Behind the M-12's motor room was a section for baggage, express, and storage mail, plus a 15-foot R.P.O. apartment. The volume of mail always was heavy because of the large amount of local mail distributed to on-line and nearby offices. The Woodward & Wichita Falls R.P.O. connected with another branch line route, the Oklahoma City & Quanah, at Altus. It also dispatched to and received mail from trunk line RPOs, including the McAlester & Amarillo RPO

Wichita Falls Union Station about the time full passenger service ended on the Northwestern District. *Author's collection*

at Elk City, the Amarillo & Fort Worth RPO at Wichita Falls, and the Newton & Amarillo RPO at Woodward. While the mail volume remained high, express shipments declined in the face of highway competition. Nevertheless, station agents still forwarded their railroad and express remittances in the time-honored way. Envelopes bearing cash and negotiable instruments were closed with banker's wax bearing impressions from the station's wax seal. These were then given to the train's express messenger for safe delivery.[4]

The end of gasoline rationing and the creation of new and better highways spelled doom for passenger service on the Northwestern District, however. Conductor C. P. Parks, with an omnipresent carnation in his buttonhole, greeted fewer and fewer patrons as passenger volume decreased. By 1950, numbers 53 and 54 were little more than mail trains. Mrs. Allen D. Wherritt of Trail and others like her continued to use the train "whenever local roads were in bad shape." Yet roads proliferated in number and quality, and the automobile's popularity increased accordingly. South of Camargo, completion of the

Johnston-Murray Bridge promised uninterrupted highway traffic parallel to the entire length of the Northwestern. Thus the inevitable occurred on March 31, 1954. On that day, the single old steel coach on train number 53 bounced and swayed as it rolled along the curving road south of Vici. Back in one of the rear seats, Conductor Dan B. Cullen stared out of the windows at the hills and landmarks which had been a constant part of his life since he had been hired by the railroad in 1913. Up ahead, Engineer Tom W. Goen, another veteran employee, whistled for the station at Camargo, and several people on the platform there bestirred themselves as the train approached. Conductor Cullen got up, stretched, opened the heavy door, and stepped out to the vestibule. A cloud of dust rolled up behind the decelerating train. When it stopped, Cullen dropped off and positioned the step box for those who were getting on and off. His face brightened when he helped aboard Mrs. Phil Hocker, who had ridden the first Wichita Falls & Northwestern passenger train into Camargo 42 years earlier. As soon as mail, express, and passengers had all been

150

loaded, Cullen intoned ". . . Boooard!" and lifted his left arm in the traditional "highball." The gasoline engine cackled and snorted, and the train began to move. As it rounded the curve south of the depot, Cullen waved one last time to those who stood transfixed on the depot platform watching as the train passed from view. Several hours later, when it drew to a stop in front of the Wichita Falls Union Station, regular passenger train service on the Northwestern District ended forever. However, the Katy did agree to haul such passengers as offered themselves on side-door cabooses assigned to local freights—now classified as mixed trains. Even that service eventually ended in Texas, as it did on June 20, 1958, in Oklahoma.[5]

In 1952, Katy's official biographer, V. V. Masterson, proudly maintained that the Katy management at that time was "busy with recapitalization plans that would free its securities from a mountain of back debt, which could so easily have been sloughed off by voluntary bankruptcy during the depression years." The solution to Katy's financial problems, in Masterson's view, was to "design the property for efficient, economical operation [so] that it will be able to support comfortably 'out of current earnings,' its present capital structure, and at the same time reduce steadily its past obligation to investors." Indeed in 1952, it appeared that the road might succeed in that venture. Masterson went so far as to assert that "the Katy's future never looked brighter."[6]

Unfortunately, however, the road's financial problems evaded solution. Some observers suggested that the road might have solved its difficulties by negotiating a merger with another carrier. Almost three decades earlier an ambitious plan had been postured to merge the Kansas City Southern Railway, the St. Louis Southwestern Railway, and the M-K-T into a sprawling but powerful system. The federal government frowned on the venture, however, and it was abandoned in October of 1928. Merger speculation again was renewed late in 1956 and heightened early in 1957 when President William N. Deramus, III, left the Chicago Great Western Railway to become Katy's chief executive. A merger of the two roads, the CGW and the Katy, may have been logical, but Deramus lost no time in repudiating such reports. The M-K-T, he said, would go it alone. But the road alone was bumpy. *Railway Age* reported that "Katy hit a few rough spots in 1956, with net estimated around $2 million, off around a third from 1955." A long and severe drought in the road's territory plus unpaid dividends then approaching $160 per share on its seven percent preferred stock were blamed for the company's economic tailspin.[7]

William Neal Deramus, III, was born in Pittsburg, Kansas, on December 10, 1915. Before World War II, he earned an A.B. degree at the University of Michigan and an LL.B. at Harvard. By 1946, he had become Assistant to the General Manager of the Kansas City Southern, perhaps because his father was the Chairman of the Board and President of that firm. In 1948 he went to the CGW, and one year later he was its president. When he became Katy's president in 1957, Deramus told *Railway Age* that his only objective was to "get the railroad back on its feet." He then suspended publication of the road's monthly employees' magazine and abolished the public relations department. The idea, he said, was to cut all "frill" expenses. Then he sent an order to department heads which read: "Cut all personnel to the lowest possible number that will still permit daily conduct of business." In 1953, the M-K-T had 10,123 employees. In 1956, the number stood at 8,000. By mid-1960, three and one-half years into the Deramus tenure, the number of jobs was down to 2,817. As early as 1958, however, Deramus's three-part Spartan railroad philosophy—minimum facilities, longer freight trains, and no frills—was fully evident. As the youthful president slashed at what he considered unnecessary expenses, morale sagged, track deteriorated, engines failed, the ire of the State of Kansas was raised, the on-line press exploded, passengers and shippers revolted, and the Katy was expelled from the St. Louis Chamber of Commerce. A writer for *Railway Age* observed early in 1958 with gross understatement that Deramus had become "a controversial executive."[8]

Katy's problems were complex. When the road emerged from bankruptcy in 1923, its directors and management alike resolved never to enter the courts again. Though it earned well in the 1920s, dividends were few. Ultraconservative purchasing kept equipment trust obligations at a low level, and Katy husbanded its money for the early retirement of its bonded debt. Thus it was able to avoid receivership during the depression

Weeds grew high in front of the Forgan depot after maintenance forces were reduced in the mid-1950s. *Author's photograph*

when most of its competitors succumbed. Yet its recapitalization in 1923 saddled the company with a burden which could be handled only in the best of times. Wartime traffic postponed an inevitable crisis, which was further deferred by the postwar boom in the Southwest. Katy dieselized, bought block signals for the main line, streamlined the TEXAS SPECIAL, and purchased a few box cars. On the surface, all appeared well with the M-K-T. However, the Korean War traffic benefited the road little and then all but vanished with the truce in 1953. Furthermore, a drought descended on much of Katy territory beginning in 1950, and lasted for eight years. Meanwhile, three million inadequately treated ties, installed during the war, aged prematurely, posing an overnight system-wide rehabilitation problem. Even the motive power situation was clouded by the fact that the diesel roster was composed of a plethora of models built by a number of manufacturers. This lack of standardization resulted in a parts inventory problem and continual nightmares for maintenance men. By 1959, fully one-third of Katy's diesel fleet was awaiting repairs. Two years earlier, the dividend arrearage on the preferred stock had reached a staggering $10,722,830. Finally, in that same year, 1957, the first season of the Deramus era, the profit and loss results were posted in red ink.[9]

On the Northwestern District, a number of telegraph operators, cashiers, clerks, switchmen, enginemen, trainmen, agents, and section men suddenly found themselves unemployed. Normal operations were not immediately affected. Nevertheless, weeds grew where none had grown before, telephones rang longer before they were answered, box cars were less adequately coopered, ordinary bridge care was deferred, and morale— traditionally high from the inception of the road —plummeted. The real crunch came in the maintenance of way department. Entire sections were eliminated, and remaining crews were given impossibly lengthy territories. President Deramus promised to ameliorate the situation by assigning mechanized track gangs to supplement the section crews. Few of these gangs ever saw the Northwestern District, and those that did provided little assistance—dirt track railroads and mechanized equipment simply do not mix. The track always took a beating during the harvest rushes. Afterward, section laborers previously had used the rest of the year to get their trackage renewed, to maintain proper drainage, and to keep down the weeds. Supervisors had been easily able to fix responsibilities, for section districts were short and the boundaries well known. With longer districts, fewer men, and scant materials, supervisors no longer could demand precise maintenance. Amazingly, the track held up well despite an absence of proper grooming. In the summer of 1958, locals frequently ran from Wichita Falls to Altus in six hours, from Altus to Elk City and return in twelve hours, from Elk City to Woodward in five hours, and from Woodward to Forgan in four hours—and did the work at all way stations. Such performance reflects the care which section men had given the line over the years; no greater compliment could be theirs.

On July 1, 1960, the Missouri-Kansas-Texas Railroad Company and the Missouri-Kansas-Texas Railroad Company of Texas were consolidated. This merciful act helped to unclutter its corporate structure, but surprisingly, the WF&NWof T and the Wichita Falls Railroad were not included in the consolidation. Then one year later William N. Deramus suddenly returned to the Kansas City Southern as its President. The financial interests which had brought Deramus to the M-K-T in 1957 thought that his brand of railroad medication would help. They had been proved wrong. Nevertheless, Claude T. Williams, a longtime Katy official but one who wholeheartedly embraced the Deramus philosophy, was elected the new President. Few operational changes were forthcoming. The Northwestern District's physical condition continued its eclipse, and service naturally faltered. This occurred despite the fact that in 1960 Deramus had admitted to stockholders that Katy's health was directly tied to the quality and volume of the annual wheat crop. It was a tacit acknowledgement of the Northwestern District's crucial position relative to the financial health of the entire Katy System.[10]

Between 1950 and 1952, the M-K-T purchased a total of 71 diesel road switchers from four manufacturers: General Motors (33), American Locomotive Company (15), Baldwin Locomotive Works (18), and Fairbanks-Morse (5). At various times, models from each of these companies labored on the Northwestern. The Baldwin and the Alco locomotives had heavier axle loadings and usually were restricted to service between Wichita Falls and Altus, where the bridges had high Cooper ratings. Road units, such as GM F-3 and F-7 models, also paid periodic visits to the Northwestern, and when the bad-order line at Denison lengthened in the late 1950s, a few borrowed Chicago Great Western engines wandered into Woodward. In an effort to standardize the road's motive power, the Baldwins

were rebuilt by GM in 1958-1959. Some Alcos were similarly treated, while others later were scrapped or traded for high horsepower main line power. By the early 1960s, the Northwestern District universally employed General Motors GP-7 model power, numbered 91 through 123.[11]

On the Northwestern, the first casualty of changing traffic patterns and Katy's inability (or unwillingness) to provide adequate maintenance and ordinary renewals came in 1958 when the Wellington Branch was abandoned. In actuality, the beginning of the end had been prompted by the invasion of the trade area by the Fort Worth & Denver City in 1932. The depression further distressed the health of the branch, as did the construction of better roads and highways throughout the area. As early as 1943, Katy management contemplated abandonment of the line, but shelved the plan until a decade later when President D. V. Fraser ordered another evaluation. However, a committee of Katy officials unanimously opposed abandonment at that time. Then two years later, the committee agreed that abandonment was warranted but suggested that such proceedings move slowly. To circumvent the provisions of the Burlington Agreement (an early employee protection case), which the Katy officials expected as a condition imposed by the Interstate Commerce Commission should the abandonment request be granted, the committee suggested that on-line stations be closed prior to the filing of a formal application. As a result, the agencies at Gould and Duke soon were closed. In August 1955, however, a new variable had to be considered; it was reported that the Kaiser Gypsum Company was considering the construction of a plant near Duke. Fraser then ordered a study to determine the feasibility of abandoning the road west of that station. But before any decision could be made on that proposal, a flood on the Salt Fork of the Red River carried away the approaches to and part of bridge 80.7 between Altus and Victory.[12]

As a result of this washout on May 28, 1956, traffic on the Wellington Branch was reversed. On June 11, President Fraser announced that a detour arrangement had been devised whereby a daily-except-Sunday mixed train was scheduled to service the line from Wellington to Victory and return. A connecting train was operated from Wichita Falls to Wellington over the FW&D.

153

Bridge #80.9 on the left, bridge #81.0 on the right—after the disastrous flood of May 289, 1956 on the Wellington Branch. *M-K-T collection*

When the frame depot burned at Gould, it was replaced by Katy's T-100, a dismounted passenger car. May, 1957. *M-K-T collection*

154

Although extant Katy records on the subject are silent, many employees feel that T-100 (see lower left) was formerly M-10, a gas-electric car outshopped by St. Louis Car Company in 1925. There is no evedence that M-10 ever operated in revenue service on the Northwestern District. It is shown here at Parsons, Kansas in October, 1939. *Everett L. DeGolyer photograph*

Fraser cautioned that this was merely a provisionary measure; he promised another decision after the wheat rush. During the summer, Katy officials attempted to determine exactly what plans Kaiser Gypsum had regarding the rumored plant at Duke. They could not secure a clear indication from Kaiser, however, so Katy management urged abandonment. Thus early in December, the boards of the M-K-T, M-K-TofT, and the Wichita Falls & Wellington Railway all authorized management to seek abandonment of the entire branch. On December 20, the process was begun.[13]

Agents along the line could have predicted this move by their decreasing workload. Wesley P. Altland had worked at Hollis during the depression; in 1954, he returned as agent. During the intervening quarter-century, a number of dramatic changes had occurred in railroad operations at that point. The LCL business had nearly evaporated, and Western Union telegrams no longer were handled. Full passenger service had ended long ago, and in 1955 only 2,151 paying travelers boarded the side-door cabooses for transportation over the line. In 1956, the number dropped to 61, partly the result of the reversed traffic flow occasioned by the washout. Even carload freight traffic was down, and the movement of livestock to and from stations on the branch had nearly disappeared. On the other hand, the volume of cotton-related business probably was higher in the mid-1950s than it had been 25 years earlier. Outbound traffic remained stable but inbound traffic in 1956 dropped to just over 100 cars. Traffic statistics for the Wellington Branch, circa 1953-1956 are shown below.

Katy service to Wellington, Texas would last slightly more than a year after this view was made on May 25, 1957. *M-K-T collection*

Top. By 1957, LCL business on the Wellington Branch had nearly evaporated. Yet on this day, the train crew was called upon to deliver a few shipments at Duke. *M-K-T collection*

Bottom. Transloading LCL freight from a motor transport at Victory, Oklahoma on May 25, 1957. *M-K-T collection*

Rancher T. A. Judy shipped countless head of cattle on the Katy from Mocane, Oklahoma. *Author's photograph*

COMMODITY	1953	1954	1955	1956
Wheat	260	391	140	394
Hay	131	6	8	3
Sorghum grains	82	56	166	13
Cotton	12	50	46	23
Cotton linters	9	17	45	32
Cottonseed cake, meal	191	58	74	5
Cottonseed oil	16	58	34	45
Cantaloupes	0	0	6	4
Lumber	16	18	29	32
Stone and rock	143	22	18	0
Implements and tractors	15	7	20	18
Cement	20	28	14	18
Others	*	*	*	*
Total Cars Terminated	457	125	177	110
Total Cars Originated	515	642	480	522
Total Cars	952	767	654	632

*Numerous other commodities under ten cars per year.[14]

The Interstate Commerce Commission found that the Wellington Branch earned net deficits of $34,964 in 1955 and $29,612 in 1956. Katy estimated that it would need $81,750 to repair the damages to bridge 80.7 and to install necessary jetty protection. The regulatory agency judged that "to rehabilitate the line to enable operations at minimum maintenance costs are not justified by the prospects of the line in the forseeable future." Nevertheless, the statement acknowledged that agricultural production for the previous several years had been inhibited by a drought that was then just lifting. Indeed, the I.C.C. noted that "the prospects for the area, in terms of agricultural output . . . are brighter than at any other time during the past 20 or 30 years." Claude Brown, a Duke banker and one of those who had protested against Katy's application, fully agreed. He contended that, whether or not the branch was making money for the Katy, the residents and businesses along the line were highly dependent upon the railroad. He argued, too harshly perhaps, that shippers on the branch had been well served "until Deramus." In any event, the I.C.C. gave permission to abandon the line on February 17, 1958, but Katy willingly agreed to keep the road open through the coming harvest season. On July 31, Claude Brown, his wife, and a few others strolled down to the depot to watch the last Katy train. As it disappeared into the distance, Brown realized that the line somehow had to be resurrected. In time his efforts, and

those of his associates, resulted in the creation of the Hollis & Eastern Railroad (see Chapter XIX).[15]

Changing traffic patterns were evident elsewhere, too. As late as the fall of 1947, the Barby Ranch near Knowles had shipped an entire trainload of cattle over the Northwestern District. Nevertheless, the construction of hardtop roads and the development of over-the-road trucking meant the end of the era when cattle were driven overland to the railroad's stock pens for loading. Barby and another rancher, T. A. Judy of near Forgan, continued to ship a few cars from Knowles and Mocane until the mid-1950s, but the end of all livestock shipping was clearly at hand. Even the Holmes Livestock Company of Laverne, which had shipped hogs to market on the Katy since 1925, stopped using the railroad for its transportation needs about 1960. According to Jacob C. Holmes, the proprietor, there were several reasons for the switch. These included the development of sale barns, changing patterns of agriculture, good roads, and big trucks. In 1959 and again in 1965, Ralph Barby contemplated the construction of a spur track near Rosston which could have been used to unload carload lots of cattle feed directly into his warehouses. High construction costs prevented this, with the result that Barby and other ranchers began receiving their feed by truck. In 1959, the stock pens at Mocane were retired, and those at Knowles, Rosston, and Supply were similarly disposed of in 1962 and 1963. For that matter, Katy's entire livestock tariff was cancelled on June 7, 1972.[16]

Between July 21 and November 7, 1948, a total of 23,380 carloads of crude oil were dispatched from oil-loading racks at Morfa, a few miles east of Wichita Falls on the Henrietta District. The oil racks were fed by pipe lines from Jal, New Mexico, Midland, Texas, and from nearby wells; they were capable of loading 440 cars daily. These cars then were sent to refineries in trainload lots. Other refineries at Wichita Falls were giving Katy additional petroleum traffic; and although Gulf, Magnolia, and Skelly were all pumping their crude in pipe lines from Burkburnett, the La Salle Company continued to operate its refinery south of that station. A quarter-century later, however, Morfa, its loading racks, and even the railroad had disappeared. Gone too

Liquid petroleum gas (LPG) loading racks were installed at Mocane, Oklahoma in 1966. *Author's photograph*

The Bell Refinery at Grandfield, Oklahoma was closed during 1962. *M-K-T collection*

was most of the petroleum business at Wichita Falls and Burkburnett. The inevitable had occurred; most of the available crude had been used, and what remained was piped out. Some of this went to the Bell Refinery at Grandfield. That plant shipped 2,407 carloads of petroleum products in 1958 and 2,127 cars in 1959. Much of this traffic moved south, but after the advent of jet engines, large quantities of jet fuels were shipped to Altus Air Force Base, 48 miles north. Unfortunately, the Northwestern District was deprived of this important revenue after the Grandfield plant closed in 1962.[17]

As if to supplant the rapidly disappearing oil traffic, three important liquid petroleum gas (LPG) plants were located on the Northwestern District. The first of these, a Shell Oil facility at Hocker, 6.5 miles south of Elk City, was opened in 1947. The other two, a Sun Oil plant at Laverne and a Warren Petroleum facility at Mocane, began production in 1959. During the late 1940s, the Hocker plant shipped 25 cars per day. The combined traffic statistics for 1967-1968 indicate that LPG loadings accounted for 59.6 percent of all outbound shipments on the Northwestern

District for those years. The following data shows the volume of LPG shipments from each plant for the years indicated:

HOCKER LAVERNE MOCANE

Year	(Shell)	(Sun)	(Warren)
1958	1,874	—	—
1959	787	N.A.	N.A.
1962	1,276	1,997	N.A.
1966	235	815	75
1967	198	678	183
1968	304	70	120
1969	145	77	154
1970	176	14	8
1971	130	135	0
1972	94	77	0[18]

As marketing conditions changed, as pipe line service became available to them, and as Katy increasingly was unable to satisfy their demands, all three of these plants vastly curtailed their rail shipments. Strangely, the LPG business proved to be a mixed blessing to the Northwestern District. Admittedly, these shipments were remunerative and helped to cushion the loss of petroleum business from Grandfield,

The first of the LPG plants to be located on the Northwestern District, the Shell plant south of Elk City, began production in 1947. *Author's collection*

Locomotives #91 and 101 doing station work at Laverne in August, 1968—the era of the LPG boom on the Northwestern District. *H. S. Tyler photograph*

Burkburnett, and Wichita Falls; however, LPG ordinarily was shipped in "Jumbo Tanks," and these heavy cars with their even heavier cargoes unmercifully pounded the Northwestern's already weakened track structure. Previous to the slashing of their numbers by President Deramus, trackmen had been able to renew the road after every harvest rush. However, LPG moved constantly rather than on a seasonal basis, and, as a result, there was no time to rebuild the track even if men had been available. In sum, Katy had become so hard up that it had neither the men nor the material to repair the road. The situation deteriorated so badly that in 1964 the road had to be removed from service temporarily. As a result, the Interstate Commerce Commission issued Service Order Number 957 on December 10, 1964. This order allowed the M-K-T to re-route any shipment on the Northwestern District to connecting carriers. This, too, was a mixed blessing. By short-hauling itself, the Katy deprived its Northwestern District of revenues which it so desperately needed. However, handling these heavy shipments over the length of the District risked the total destruction of the road. For Katy it was a "no win" situation; deferred maintenance had ruined its ability to handle and profit adequately from the carriage of LPG and, for that matter, other heavy cars and their cargoes. Meanwhile, Katy's deteriorating condition heightened the LPG shippers' desire to seek other means of transportation.[19]

For a variety of reasons, the Northwestern District was becoming a marginal branch line operation. During the period 1961-1964, revenues from its operation dropped dramatically. In

The Shell plant south of Elk City was a busy loading point when P. A. Johnston made this photograph during the summer of 1952.

161

During drought periods Katy's Welon Yard at Altus was a sleepy place. *Author's photograph*

1964, only one station earned more than it had in 1961; three earned essentially the same; and the remaining ten suffered serious reversals in revenue. The following statistics tell the tale:

STATION	1961	1962	1963	1964
Altus	$635,992	$515,615	$356,786	$474,694
Burkburnett	$185,704	$ 79,516	$111,451	$ 42,457
Camargo	$ 96,967	$114,432	$ 44,889	$110,429
Elk City	$816,481	$751,820	$486,751	$441,409
Forgan	$116,471	$ 51,538	$103,519	$ 62,524
Frederick	$318,550	$333,629	$230,357	$293,427
Gate	$339,734	$ 94,869	$ 69,785	$ 70,249
Grandfield	$275,748	$114,581	$116,335	$150,064
Hammon	$ 57,137	$ 94,276	$ 5,387	— *
Laverne	$637,461	$917,881	$653,721	$603,980
Leedey	$ 49,834	$ 73,242	$ 33,125	$ 49,450
Mangum	$163,315	$125,531	$148,399	$ 81,199
Vici	$112,576	$205,895	$ 60,345	$ 30,268
Woodward	$387,972	$429,622	$295,723	$245,845
Total	$4,193,942	$3,902,447	$2,724,593	$2,655,995

*Hammon was closed in 1963.

A drought during this period did seriously curtail the usually more voluminous and lucrative agricultural traffic. Yet it is unmistakably clear that the earlier and more broadly based traffic mix had ended; by the mid-1960s the Northwestern District had become almost exclusively a carrier of grain and LPG. Grain traffic fluctuated widely according to the whims of nature, and the LPG traffic was declining in volume and in remuneration due to track conditions and the resultant I.C.C. Service Order Number 957.[20]

In 1950, Katy offered daily-except-Sunday way freight service between Wichita Falls and Altus, and tri-weekly way freight service on the "Long Barrel" between Altus and Woodward as well as on the "Top End" from Woodward to Forgan. These trains were authorized to travel at a rate of 25 miles per hour except between Altus and Burkburnett where they were restricted to 20 miles per hour. In 1950, track conditions warranted faster running conditions than the company allowed, and few engineers kept their trains to these speeds. The pattern of daily-except-Sunday service from Wichita Falls to Altus and the tri-weekly service operation north of Altus obtained until August 17, 1964, when the Wichita Falls-Altus service was reduced by half. For a while in 1965, only one round trip each week was operated from one end of the line to

Revenues at Gate dropped from $339,734 in 1961 to $94,869 in 1962. *M-K-T collection*

Track scene in 1965 at milepost 180 near Trail, Oklahoma. *M-K-T collection*

the other. However, on August 16, 1965, tri-weekly operation was instituted from Wichita Falls to Elk City, and a bi-weekly schedule was implemented between Elk City and Forgan. Finally on October 25, 1968, bi-weekly service was instituted on the whole line. This scheduling utilized only two train crews; they exchanged through traffic at Elk City. In 1968, trains were restricted to a maximum of 15 miles per hour over the entire route from Wichita Falls to Forgan—and few engineers ignored the restriction. Meanwhile, most of the line's stations had been closed as this partial listing indicates:

STATION	DATE OF CLOSING
Brinkman	April 1, 1955
Supply	March 25, 1958
Sharon	March 25, 1958
Knowles	March 25, 1958
May	March 25, 1958
Willow	March 25, 1958
Carter	Cctober 22, 1959
Tipton	October 27, 1960
Hammon	— , 1963[21]

Each year that a line of railroad is used, a certain amount of its physical life is used up. Regular and adequate maintenance is necessary; otherwise the line eventually will become worn out, and its essential components, if not replaced, will collapse under moving trains. When all service life is exhausted, the track simply becomes inoperable. In the fall of 1964, operations on the Northwestern nearly came to a complete standstill after repeated rains thoroughly softened the roadbed. Inadequate ballast, deteriorated conditions, and ineffective drainage due to lack of maintenance combined to allow the rails to spread under the passage of heavy loads. Derailments were frequent and rerailing operations difficult. As noted previously, this resulted in the issuance of an I.C.C. Service Order which allowed the M-K-T to divert traffic. The same document authorized temporary suspension of all service between Wichita Falls and Hocker, site of the Shell plant south of Elk City. The ink barely was dry on this order when Katy applied to abandon the entire Northwestern District. Two weeks later, it also sought permission to abandon the entire BM&E as well.[22]

Nearly a decade of deferred maintenance

by 1965 had left the Katy System a railroad in name only. Train service on all lines was deplorable, and shippers largely had blackballed the road. Understandably, employee morale was zero. In short, Katy was dying; it faced not bankruptcy but liquidation. The company needed a doctor of sick railroads—and it found one in John W. Barriger who signed on as its chairman and chief executive officer effective March 11, 1965. President C. T. Williams resigned in April, and Barriger then assumed that position too. What Barriger found when he arrived on the property in March was a situation of appalling neglect. In his words, "housekeeping was so neglected that the property looked like a transportation slum." In his view, the previous managements had been goaded or were panicked by the road's top-heavy financial structure into undoing the very plant and service which alone could rescue the line. He insisted that you "can't starve a railroad into prosperity." Barriger maintained that the Deramus and Williams administrations had hacked instead of pruned. He charged, moreover, that "fictitious earnings derived through deferred maintenance are in reality not income but unreported liquidation of capital." Thus Barriger's first duty was to reverse the trends of previous years. He faced the Herculean task of re-establishing the Missouri-Kansas-Texas as a successful railroad in the eyes of patrons, employees, investors, communities, and management alike.[23]

John Walker Barriger was born on December 3, 1899, and took a B.S. degree at Massachusetts Institute of Technology 22 years later. During his summer vacations away from MIT he worked in the Pennsylvania Railroad's Altoona shops. Always a controversial figure, Barriger has been associated with ten different railroads since 1917. He ultimately served as President of the Monon, Pittsburgh & Lake Erie, and the M-K-T. Upon leaving the Katy in 1970, he would become chief executive officer of the Boston & Maine, and in 1974 the Special Assistant to the Federal Railroad Administrator. Earlier he had been associated with Kuhn, Loeb & Company, Bullock & Company, Fairbanks-Morse, and the Reconstruction Finance Corporation. In 1933, he collaborated in the preparation of the "Prince Plan of Railroad Consolidation" which urged that the national rail net be reduced to fewer but larger rail systems. In 1956, he authored an important study entitled *Super Railroads*. In John Barriger, Katy thus found a man of unquestioned talent whose contacts and breadth of experience were absolutely necessary in rebuilding the road. In large measure, "Doctor" Barriger was successful. Nearly a decade of deteriorating property conditions, service standards, traffic volume, and earning power was brought to an end during 1965. In April of that season, Barriger made his first system-wide inspection. In the Panhandle and all along the Northwestern District, he found that rains had brightened crop prospects after several lean years. Barriger did not wish to prosecute the abandonment petition filed earlier "until he had his feet on the ground," particularly in view of a potentially profitable grain-movement year. Moreover, withdrawal of the abandonment application would be a public relations coup; it would demonstrate that the new management embraced a philosophy of service quite different from that which had been offered by previous administrations. On April 27, the M-K-T thus requested dismissal of the applications. It was granted without prejudice on June 9. Meanwhile, President Barriger traveled to Mangum in May to discuss the fate of the railroad and to announce that the applications had been withdrawn. A year later he was optimistic about "retaining indefinitely some 400 miles of railroad in the Wichita Falls, Northern Texas and Oklahoma districts." However, Barriger cautioned, the situation would be reviewed on a year by year basis. On the line, emergency crews filled the worst holes, but contrary to rumor there was no over-all plan to rebuild the road. At the same time, the authorized speed was dropped from 25 to 15 miles per hour in an attempt to reduce the burden which passing trains placed on the nearly shattered trackage.[24]

From 1965 to 1968, wheat was the Katy System's number one commodity in terms of total cars handled and also in terms of revenue earned. In 1968, however, wheat slipped into second place as Katy's traffic mix became more diverse. Still, the movement of wheat was crucial to Katy's financial health. In 1967, a short and disappointing wheat crop reduced Katy's revenues below forecasts. With a normal crop, Barriger announced, the Katy would have had a small profit instead of a loss for that year's operations. Grain loadings on the Northwestern District plus those of the Hollis & Eastern and the BM&E usually contributed from 20 to 25 percent of all grain handled on the Katy System during the 1960s. Carloadings of grain from the Northwestern District, H&E, and BM&E were as follows:

1958 - 8,290	1966 - 4,114
1959 - 5,681	1967 - 3,606
1960 - 7,631	1968 - 4,007
1961 - 6,483	1969 - 3,810
1962 - 4,218	1970 - 4,232
1963 - 4,400	1971 - 1,981
1964 - 3,516	1972 - 2,703*
1965 - 7,100	

*Loadings for calendar year

Through the 1950s and 1960s, Katy was forced to lower its grain rates in order to meet competition by truckers. Thus, as the following statistics indicate, many rates dropped by more than 50 percent between 1954 and 1968:

Rates In Cents per 100 pounds on Wheat and Sorghum Grains to Houston for Export

From	Commodity	10/54	8/57	11/59	6/62	1/65	5/68
Brinkman	Wheat	59	67½	50	40½	35½	28
	Sorghum	44	44	44	44½	35½	28
Elk City	Wheat	59	67½	50	44½	40	29
	Sorghum	44	44	44	44½	40	29
Woodward	Wheat	61½	70½	54	47½	44	36
	Sorghum	52	52	52	47½	44	36
Forgan	Wheat	65½	75	54	47½	46	38½
	Sorghum	53	53	53	47½	46	38½

The origin of grain loadings which were handled on the Northwestern varied according to crop conditions. The following is a breakdown for the three-year period 1966-1968:

Origin	1966	1967	1968
Hollis & Eastern	713	535	752
Northwestern District	2,075	1,372	1,913
BM&E	1,326	1,699	715

Wheat accounted for 30.3 percent of outbound loadings on the Northwestern District for 1967-1968. Of this total, nearly one-third was loaded at Brinkman alone. In an effort to provide an

165

adequate number of cars for grain traffic at Brinkman and elsewhere, the M-K-T lined 274 of its stock cars with plywood and pressed them into grain service during 1965-1966. Unfortunately, heavier cars with gross weight exceeding 117 tons were restricted from the entire District, and this kept Katy from utilizing the new jumbo covered hoppers on the Northwestern. The use of these high-capacity cars would have been economically advantageous to the M-K-T and to the elevators which it served. Moreover, their greater efficiency would have resulted in an expansion of volume and simultaneously would have reduced the box car shortage. In the late 1960s, as had been the case for years, loaded grain cars were bunched during the harvest rush at Fort Supply, Woodward, and Hammon due to heavy southbound grades. Extra trains then were authorized to shuttle these cars over the road to Wichita Falls.[25]

Other than shippers of grain and petroleum, there were few major patrons on the Northwestern during the 1950s and 1960s. Still, there were numerous small shippers who relied on the railroad for their transportation needs. Sheppard Air Force Base received or dispatched 194 cars in 1962. Elsewhere, droughts and crop failures during the 1950s caused the farmers and ranchers of Beaver County to ship in large quantities of baled hay, oats, and straw. At Gate, Mr. and Mrs. Earl Kerns were able to hold together their Grade A dairy herd during those times only by shipping in hay from Minnesota. At Mangum, carload after carload of cotton was shipped from the Trader's Compress in the 1950s, but this business was reduced to a trickle by 1969. A similar compress at Elk City was not opened after 1966. In 1968, 437 carloads of pipe were handled, but this was nonrecurring revenue. A steady and remunerative shipment of bulk clay nobin (bentonite) was made annually from Camargo by the Fisher Grain Company of Woodward; perhaps aggregating 100 cars per year, this commodity was destined for Jackson, Mississippi, where it was processed into a desicant used in the manufacture of baby powder and other products. Farther north, the Axtell Mining Company at Gate used the railroad for 98 percent of its shipping needs. Many carloads of Axtell's volcanic ash were consigned to manufacturers and jobbers in St. Louis and Kansas City, and these shipments gave the M-K-T a long

line-haul. Cement by the hundreds of carloads was unloaded at Woodward for distribution in western Oklahoma and the Panhandle. Although these cars were loaded by a plant on the Katy's main line and were unloaded by the Katy at Woodward, the long intervening haul was on a competing carrier due to the dilapidated condition of the Northwestern's track.[26]

Nancy Ford, writing in the October, 1965, issue of *Modern Railroads* asserted that "in no area is the Katy's new president more gifted than in customer and public relations." Two events associated with communities along the Northwestern District contributed to the verification of Ms. Ford's contention. The 60th anniversary of Burkburnett's founding came in 1967, and Barriger arranged for the Katy to play a major role in the celebration. Indeed, the entire proceedings centered around a special train which Barriger authorized to take railroad officials, local civic leaders, business dignitaries, and Lt. Governor Preston Smith from Wichita Falls to Burkburnett. The depot at Burkburnett was painted, the weeds in the yard were cut, and the track was inspected. At 9:45 a.m., on June 15, 1967, the shiny special, pulled by engine number 98 and trailing a string of newly painted cars, including Barriger's private business car, departed from the historic Wichita Falls Union Station. According to one of the invited guests, Barriger served a "sumptuous brunch" consisting of watermelon balls, roast beef, ham, potato salad, chocolate cake, ice cream, and candy as the special rocked along toward Burkburnett. Up ahead, engineer T. H. Edmiaston whistled gaily at a group of mounted bandits who attacked the train by firing blank ammunition at it. A throng of people, including

"Banditti" greeted the Burkburnett anniversary train, June 15, 1967. *Author's collection*

Katy officials (left to right, Richey Cring, John W. Barriger, and R. B. George posed in front of Wichita Falls Union Station prior to departure of the Burkburnett anniversary train. *Author's collection*

Children, many of whom had never seen a passenger train at Burkburnett, inundated the anniversary train when it arrived as part of the Boom Town celebration. June 15, 1967. *Author's collection*

Arrival of the anniversary train at Burkburnett. *Author's collection*

Preston Smith (Lt. Governor of Texas), Katy President John W. Barriger, and other dignitaries posed for this photograph before the departure from Wichita Falls of the Burkburnett anniversary train. June 15, 1967. *Author's collection*

169

In 1967 the M-K-T depot at Laverne underwent general refurbishing at President Barriger's direction. All of this was in honor of Jayne Anne Jayroe, the Laverne girl who became Miss America that year. *Author's photograph*

the 761st Air Force Band from Sheppard Field, met the train at the Burkburnett depot. Before the band had finished playing the national anthem, people swarmed aboard the train, even invading Barriger's private car. For many, it was the first time that they had seen a passenger train at Burkburnett. A reception, parade, rodeo, and several speeches—including one made by President Barriger—followed a noon barbecue. A few months earlier, Jayne Anne Jayroe of Laverne had been crowned Miss America for 1967. The *Laverne Leader-Tribune* used unheard of 144 point type to blaze this good news in two-inch headlines across the front page of its September 15, 1966, issue. Said its editor: "Laverne residents could no longer contain themselves after the television show was completed and everybody knew the results." Automobiles with horns blaring invaded the business district, the town siren was set off, firecrackers were ignited, and people "generally made a noisy time of it." The town's board of trustees immediately renamed Main Street "Jayne Jayroe Boulevard," and several groups were mobilized to make "the Home Town of Miss America . . . spic and span." When President Barriger learned of Miss Jayroe's corona-

tion, he ordered that the ramshackle old station at Laverne be repainted and flower boxes placed in the windows. Additionally, the tracks in front of the depot were ballasted, lined, and surfaced and, in Barriger's words, "other things done to make the M-K-T presentable and reasonably worthy of the distinction of serving the home town of Miss America." The editor of the *Leader-Tribune* acknowledged that Laverne's townspeople were delighted with the results. Indeed, "you wouldn't know the place," said he. "Beautiful ladies are characteristic of Katyland," asserted Barriger in the road's *Annual Report* for 1967. Furthermore, he proudly noted, Katy's depot at Laverne was located at the head of Jayne Jayroe Boulevard.[27]

A few months after the public relations triumphs at Burkburnett and Laverne, an unrelated incident near Sharon told a more factual story of conditions on the Northwestern District. In October, 1967, a 1,200-pound bull was startled by the approach of a southbound train near mile post 211. In a blatant error of judgment, the bull charted a collision course with Extra 112, the whistled warning from Engineer Byron Bates notwithstanding. Presently the bull and engines 112

The stillness of an early rural morning was shattered by the passage of Katy's weekly train south of Woodward. November, 1971. *Author's photograph*

Extra 117 rumbled southward through Sharon, Oklahoma with a respectable train in the autumn of 1971. *Author's photograph*

Extra 101 eases a train of wheat and LPG out of the hills and onto the flats west of Woodward on a beautifully bright afternoon in October, 1971. *Author's photograph*

Engineer Byron Bates had legitimate concern for both the location and condition of Katy tracks as his train passed beneath stately Chinese elms near historic Fort Supply, Oklahoma in the fall of 1971. *Author's photograph*

and 94 were in the ditch, considerably worse for the wear. For the bull the encounter with the iron horse was terminal, for crewmen it was embarrassing, and for the railroad it was expensive. Collisions between trains and domestic livestock rarely resulted in damaging derailments, even on the Northwestern in its later days. Nevertheless, derailments had become more frequent as the road's track structure deteriorated. Barriger's earlier optimism vanished with poorer than usual crops in the region and with greater than expected headaches on the main line. When a stray dollar floated into the Katy till, Barriger considered that it could be put to only one use—to build up the main gut of the road. Unfortunately, there simply were too few dollars to rebuild the Northwestern as well. Thus in 1968, Barriger sadly admitted defeat and ordered the Katy legal department to

begin preparations for abandonment proceedings. Formal applications to terminate all service north of Altus and to fully abandon the BM&E subsequently were filed on April 1, 1969. Some observers recalled that Lucien C. Sprague, another "Doctor of Sick Railroads" had followed a similar course in tending to the needs of the Minneapolis & St. Louis Railroad some three decades earlier. Sprague was forced to trim a number of M&StL branches, but in the end, the company's main trunk operations emerged in a completely rejuvenated condition. Barriger obviously had the same idea for the Katy System.[28]

From Branch Line to Short Line:
The Hollis & Eastern Railroad

"The Hollis & Eastern is a living example of what can be accomplished when communities work together for a common cause."*

For Claude Brown, the decision of the Interstate Commerce Commission to allow the abandonment of the Missouri-Kansas-Texas Railroad's Wellington Branch came as a rude shock. Brown, a banker in Duke, Oklahoma, had joined with others from Jackson and Harmon Counties and residents of Collingsworth County, Texas, in protesting Katy's application to drop service over its 55.4-mile branch which extended westward from Altus, Oklahoma, to Wellington, Texas. Brown and the others considered their cause just: they needed rail service. After all, reasoned the protestants, the area had suffered greatly in the hard times of the Dirty Thirties, and, while great strides toward economic recovery had been subsequently made, the loss of transportation service offered by the Katy line probably would be the knockout blow which the combined forces of the Dust Bowl and Great Depression had failed to deliver. Thus they trusted that the regulatory agency would rule against the railroad company —justly, they considered—and for the territory which it served. So confident in the sanctity of their cause were they that the protestants failed to wage the strongest opposition to the railroad's petition. As a result, they were surprised, even shocked, when, on February 17, 1958, the I.C.C. gave its permission to abandon the entire line. When service finally ended on July 31, 1958, Brown, his wife, and a few others went down to the depot at Duke and watched the passage of Katy's final trains.[1]

As the cars disappeared into the distance, Claude Brown resolved to mount a personal campaign for the resurrection of rail service on the Altus-Wellington line. Soon he was joined by other civic leaders, businessmen, farmers, and shippers who heretofore had been lethargic. Like Brown, they were galvanized into action only after the Katy trains had run their last miles. The collective efforts of Brown and his neighbors eventually resulted in fruition when, with the assistance of "foreign" capital, they were able to acquire the property. Soon thereafter most of the route was again in revenue service—but now as the Hollis & Eastern.

Brown had been in the banking business at Duke since 1923. He had seen the building up of the area in the 1920s and he had witnessed its nearly total eclipse during the 1930s. Early in the following decade, Brown's confidence in the region was renewed when a local farmer, Ivan Owen, drilled the first irrigation well near Duke and thereby initiated new hopes for agricultural prosperity in the area. By 1950, shallow-well irrigation had largely made these dreams a reality. Irrigation ended the domination of the country by cotton; increased acreage was given over to the planting of wheat and the production of livestock. As a result, the economy became more balanced and less prone to disturbance by the whims of nature.[2]

Claude Brown maintained that the area always had been—and it continued to be—"dependent on the railroad." He also acknowledged that this dependence had been altered in recent years to the carriage of freight in carload lots. Yet, he asserted, irrigation would result in greater

*Wichita Falls Times, Features Magazine, June 28, 1959, p. 13.

173

E. S. Stephens, President of the Hollis & Eastern Railroad. *Courtesy E. S. Stephens*

agricultural production and thus in an even greater need for rail service. Brown claimed that the patrons along the Wellington Branch had been well served until William N. Deramus became president of the Katy in 1957. In actuality, however, President Deramus had little to do with the abandonment of the line. Its possible demise had been contemplated by other presidents early in the 1940s and again a decade later. By the time Deramus arrived on the property, the die already had been cast; so far as the railroad was concerned, its fate was sealed on May 28, 1956, by a flood which swept away approaches end even portions of bridge 81.0 located a few miles west

174

Claude Brown, Vice-President and General Manager of the Hollis & Eastern Railroad. *Courtesy Claude Brown*

of Welon Yard in Altus. This was particularly serious, as trains for the Wellington Branch traditionally originated at Welon, where the branch was connected to the main line of Katy's Northwestern District. After the washout, until abandonment, Katy was forced to operate "reverse" daily-except-Sunday round trip mixed train service from Wellington, nominally the end of the line, to Victory, the first station west of Altus. Traffic to and from points on the line had to be carried by a special train between Wichita Falls and Wellington over the Fort Worth & Denver Railway or simply interchanged with that company. This was an expensive and unprofitable process which served only to assign more red ink to the branch's ledger. Authorization for abandonment followed. The I.C.C. could hardly have ruled in any other way, especially in view of Katy's then rapidly deteriorating financial fortunes.[3]

In granting the railroad's request for abandonment of the line, however, the regulatory agency stipulated that its permission was subject "to the condition that any part of the line" could be sold by the Katy to "any responsible person, firm, or corporation . . . at a price not less than the net salvage value of the property. . . ." Katy set that amount at $269,856, a figure which dampened enthusiasm for acquisition except by a few hard-core proponents who advocated independent operation of the route. While these local civic leaders were attempting to locate the necessary funds, an outsider, E. S. Stephens of Fort Smith, Arkansas, expressed an interest in the project. Stephens knew President Deramus personally and in a conversation between the two, the status of the far-off Wellington Branch was discussed. Earlier in his life, Stephens had been a telegraph operator and then a dispatcher for the Union Pacific Railroad, and, although he had no experience as an entrepreneur in that industry, he became intrigued with the idea. He telephoned Brown, and it was agreed that he, Brown, and a few others would form a corporation to acquire the Wellington line. To this end, the Hollis & Eastern Railroad Company was incorporated under the laws of Oklahoma on October 15, 1958. Initially capitalized at $50,000, its first directors included Mr. and Mrs. E. S. Stephens, Mr. and Mrs. Claude Brown, and Oklahoma City attorney Dan M. Welch.[4]

At the first board meeting in Oklahoma City on November 28, 1958, Stephens suggested that the H&E purchase only the 34 miles of road between Altus and Hollis. This could be done for $55,000. He pointed out that there were only two stations west of Hollis—Dodson and Wellington, both in Texas. Furthermore, Wellington shippers were guaranteed continued rail service by the FtW&D under provisions of the I.C.C.'s order permitting abandonment of the branch. After comparing the advantages of intrastate versus in-terstate operation, it was decided to acquire only the Altus-Hollis portion, all in Oklahoma. Subsequently, on December 9, 1958, the H&E applied to the I.C.C. for authority to acquire and operate the trackage in Jackson and Harmon Counties. It also asked to acquire trackage rights and joint use over 3.66 miles of main line, 1.3 miles of wye track, and terminal facilities owned and operated by the M-K-T at Altus. The Commerce Commission gave its blessing on February 3, 1959. It noted that the earlier salvage price was much higher, but concluded that $55,000 represented the line's "estimated salvage value, less cost of removal and shipment to market." Moreover, the H&E asked to purchase only 34 miles of the original 55.4-mile line. On the basis of its performance circa 1955-1958, the H&E expected to originate or receive an average of 714 carloads annually. If contemporary freight rates were maintained the H&E anticipated annual revenues of $268,812. The M-K-T and the H&E had earlier agreed that the new road was to enjoy a 25 percent division on all freight revenues, exclusive of switching charges, accruing to Katy on interchanged cars. Accordingly, $67,203 was projected as H&E's average annual division based on the branch's traffic for the years 1955-1958. That amount had been clearly insufficient to bring a profit to Katy during its ownership, but the I.C.C. acknowledged that "due to lower costs of operation as a short line railroad, the applicant's revenues derived from the line will be sufficient to pay its expenses." Finally, the regulatory agency decided that "if the shareholders of

> "if the shareholders of the applicant have such confidence that they are willing to risk their personal funds in an effort to furnish service to the communities and shippers formerly served by the Katy, we are of the opinion that they should be afforded an opportunity to do so."[5]

For its part, the M-K-T was pleased with the arrangement. By selling the 34-mile portion abondoning the rest, Katy divested itself of what had become an unremunerative branch line.

However, with independent operation of the largest portion of the line, Katy logically expected to retain the average annual traffic (amounting to 714 cars) that moved to and from it. This continued business was welcome indeed on Katy's Northwestern District, to which the former Wellington Branch was connected, for the traffic posed no burden; instead it brought much needed revenue. Additionally, the H&E agreed to pay the M-K-T the sum of $5 for each loaded freight car that it moved or switched on the trackage owned by the Katy at Altus. The larger road then agreed to lease one of its GP-7 locomotives, number 103, to the H&E for the paltry sum of $10 per day. Finally, the M-K-T affirmed that it would supply necessary cars on liberal per diem agreement.[6]

Before March 1, 1959, the H&E's authorized stock had been raised to $75,000, and all of it had been subscribed. A total of 96 individuals, companies, and organizations purchased the entire offering at $10 per share. Many bought only one share; several purchased a few; the Altus Chamber of Commerce bought 175 shares; and E. S. Stephens purchased 6,000. Within a few months, minor shifts in ownership occurred. Stephens increased his holdings by 500 shares, Claude Brown acquired 100, and ten on-line residents held the remainder. With 86.6 percent of the stock, Stephens unquestionably controlled the new company, but he was an absentee owner; Brown, as Vice President and General Manager, was left in charge of operations. At its meeting at the Duke Masonic Hall on May 20, 1959, the board of directors re-elected Brown and Stephens and added as members three on-line representatives: Emory S. Crow, Jr., of Gould, Paul Horton of Hollis, and Howard Cotner of Altus. Prior to this, it had hired Kenneth R. Langford of Denison, Texas, an employee of the M-K-T, as bookkeeper and accountant.[7]

With its entire offering of stock subscribed and with $25,000 in the till as the result of a loan made to it by City National Bank & Trust Company of Kansas City, the H&E was ready to draw a contract with the M-K-T for the purchase of the road. Such an instrument was signed on February 10, 1959. As a result, the H&E received a quitclaim deed on the 33.97 miles of railroad extending from the west wye track switch at Altus (Welon Yard) to Hollis. The total consideration

was $57,807. Katy estimated that the "original cost of property includible in primary road and equipment account" was $587,583.54. A few days later the M-K-T and the H&E entered into another agreement whereby the new company purchased "all rail, fastenings, and all other components" on the remaining 20.17 miles between Hollis and Wellington. The total sales price was $32,193. The H&E subsequently dismantled the road beyond Hollis, except for 2.21 miles of main track and sidings at Wellington which the FW&D had purchased earlier from Katy. The H&E did not acquire the right-of-way and other lands beyond Hollis, however. Even in 1974, the Katy still owned parcels of land between Hollis and Wellington where it held warranty deeds.[8]

Except for the considerably damaged bridge at the crossing of the Salt Fork of the Red River west of Altus, the line was in fair condition when the H&E purchased it. There was little to do in making it ready again for business. Instead of driving a new bridge at the washout, the directors decided to substitute an embankment. As a result of this decision, a contract was drawn on March 13 between the railroad and the S. E. Evans Corporation of Fort Smith, Arkansas. Meanwhile, J. G. "Jess" Evans of Altus, a man who had been employed by the M-K-T for 39 years, was hired as Assistant General Manager. In actuality, Evans would also be a conductor, engineer, and section foreman. The new embankment was ready late in May, and the first train was scheduled to begin spotting empty grain cars at the elevators in anticipation of the coming wheat harvest. Then another flash flood washed out bridge approaches on the Salt Fork, and the H&E was back where it had started. Nevertheless, emergency crews were rushed to repair the damage, and on June 16, officials of the line rode their own train from Altus to Duke and officially opened the Hollis & Eastern for business. One observer noted that crops from Jackson and Harmon Counties again had "easy access to markets." It was an accurate assessment. During the next year alone, more than 1,000 cars of wheat grown in these two counties moved over the tracks of the H&E.[9]

By 1961, the road's Board of Directors authorized annual salaries of $6,000 for President E. S. Stephens, $5,400 (plus $1,800 as expense money) for Vice President and General Manager

Conditions at the crossing of the Salt Fork of Red River looked like this when the H&E acquired the property in 1959. *Author's collection*

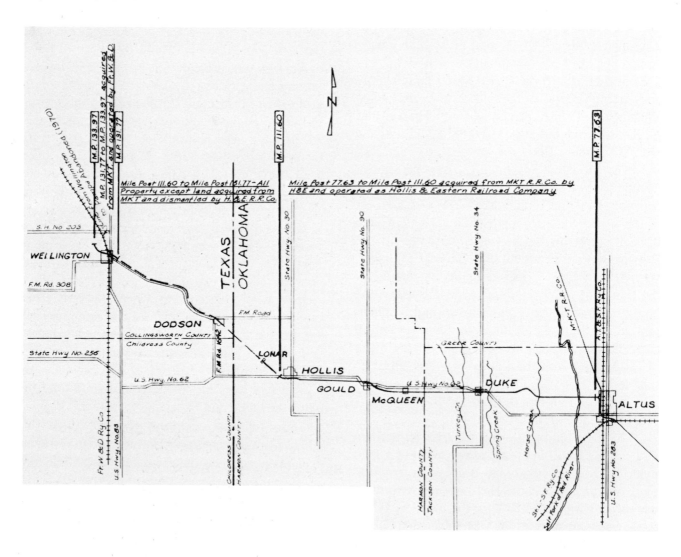

Map of the Hollis & Eastern. *Author's collection*

Notices of H&E stockholder meetings are baldly direct. *Author's collection*

Claude Brown, and $100 for Secretary Prebble Brown. The directors also voted to pay themselves $5 per meeting (up to $60 a year) but, in a burst of unrestrained extravagance, later doubled their stipends. Assistant General Manager Evans received $5,700 per year, but in 1963, he was granted a $600 raise. These salaries remained constant for the remainder of the decade. The board always was frugal, even to the point of being tight-fisted. Meetings were held variously at small cafes, restaurants, and elsewhere in the little villages served by the H&E, but usually they were held at Kirby's Restaurant in Hollis "because the steaks there were the best." At these gatherings, all bills, no matter how small, were considered and approved. Late in 1964, the board agreed to pay a local farmer for the labor and material necessary to fix the right-of-way fence along his property. According to the minutes of that meeting, "the Board of Directors thought it would be cheaper to buy the posts and pay for the labor and get the fence repaired than to run over and kill the cattle." At the same meet- ing, the board approved a $1.84 bill for a lock and chain. Earlier, on July 1, 1963, an H&E train had run over a man who eventually filed a claim against the company. The board considered the man to have been a trespasser, and only after lengthy debate, considerable correspondence, and expensive litigation did they grudgingly agree on an out-of-court settlement which partially satisfied the injured man's hospital bill.[10]

During the first five years of the H&E's existence, its traffic mix greatly resembled that of previous years when the line was a part of the Katy System. The road generally depended on the movement of wheat and cotton-related products for its subsistence. Happily, its yearly carload average ordinarily exceeded that which Katy had enjoyed from 1955 to 1958; this was despite the fact that abandonment had removed two stations from the former branch line. In the second half of the 1960s, grain loadings alone exceeded, with but one exception, the total traffic averages for the 1955-1958 period. According to M-K-T records for the years 1965-1969, it received the

179

The opening of Republic Gypsum's plant west of Duke, Oklahoma in September, 1964 was exceedingly good news for the H&E. *Author's photograph*

following numbers of grain loads from the H&E:

1965 - 781	1968 - 752
1966 - 731	1969 - 764
1967 - 535	

However, one formerly important element of traffic completely disappeared from the line after 1965. In the spring of that year, 16 carloads of cattle were shipped out, but thereafter livestock was absent from the H&E's traffic mix.[11]

During the summer of 1963, important news, which was to have both an immediate and long-term effect on the road's history, reached the owners of the H&E. The oft-rumored construction of a wallboard plant at Duke was verified in August. Belying the excitement which that news brought, the road's secretary glibly recorded that "the expected increase in business is gratifying." This news was sufficient to prompt the H&E's board to authorize the purchase of 3,747 ties as well as the payment for surfacing certain portions of its track. The total cost of these betterments was $22,253.72, of which the road was forced to borrow $15,000 in order to pay the bill. However, it was expected that the company would be able to redeem this debt "in July or August after the harvest."[12]

The board's optimism was well founded. Business prospects in the following summer of 1964 were very promising. By June 18, 545 cars of wheat had been loaded. Additionally, the mill at Hollis was shipping large quantities of cottonseed oil, and a number of cars bearing material for the construction of Republic Gypsum's wallboard plant were arriving at Duke. H&E officials anticipated that the new plant would open in September and gleefully concluded that "we should have a good business from then on." As expected, wallboard traffic added an important new element to the line's thin traffic mix, and it likewise contributed materially to the company's financial health. Indeed, the contemporary and future potential of the wallboard traffic encouraged H&E owners to strengthen the approaches to the bridges over the Salt Fork. In the late 1960s, the road engaged in a contract by which the M-K-T constructed an expensive but permanent partial steel-span bridge over that troublesome stream. Moreover, the new wallboard traffic increased revenues so spectacularly in 1965 that the usually conservative directors voted a 20 percent or $2.00 per share cash dividend on the road's stock. Thus the road which had been sponsored "for service and not for profit" was, in 1965 at least, able to provide both.[13]

In 1966, the second full year of production at the Duke plant, wallboard was second only to wheat in terms of carloadings on the H&E. That same year, cottonseed hulls for the Hollis Cotton Oil Mill led inbound traffic. The full shipping record for 1966 was as follows:[14]

Carloads Forwarded, 1966

Commodity	Jan	Feb	Mar	Apr	May	June	July	Aug	Sept	Oct	Nov	Dec	Total
Wallboard	62	43	67	74	66	64	33	51	28	47	41	25	601
Cottonseed oil	4	8	9	7	9	3	1				2	7	50
Cottonseed linters	1	7	4	2	3	3	3	5	4			7	36
Wheat	12	11	15	6	60	642	10		3		2	8	769
Cotton pickers							2						2
Miscellaneous											2		2
TOTAL	79	69	95	89	138	712	51	54	31	47	47	47	1460

| Carloads Received, 1966 | | | | | | | | | | | | | |
Commodity	Jan	Feb	Mar	Apr	May	June	July	Aug	Sept	Oct	Nov	Dec	Total
Combines & impl.	1	4		2					2		4		13
Fertilizer	2	6	10	8	2	1	4	2	8		6	4	53
Gypsum products	4	1	1	4	4	2	2	2	1	1	3	2	27
Cottonseed hulls			5			16	10	17	14	7	9	8	90
Miscellaneous		3	4	4	2	3	1	11	6	5	2	1	43
TOTAL	7	14	21	15	12	22	17	32	31	13	24	15	226

By 1971, a combination of age and illness persuaded Claude Brown to contemplate his withdrawal as an active member of the H&E's management team. Since 1958, he and E. S. Stephens had worked closely in the successful and sometimes modestly profitable operation of the road. Brown was located in Duke, on the line, but Stephens was far removed. Nearly all correspondence between the two, including discussions of operating and entrepreneurial philosophy, was carried on by way of the telephone. Each trusted the other, and Stephens, the President and major stockholder, was an exceedingly rare visitor on the property. Thus when Brown wished to resign, Stephens decided that it was an opportune time to divest himself of his interest in the road. This prospect thoroughly distressed the Republic Gypsum Company, which feared that the road might fall into the hands of less reputable owners. Despite the fact that E. S. Stephens, a "foreigner," had controlled the road, the H&E had always been a local enterprise dedicated to performing necessary rail service for the shippers and citizens of the area which it served. However, new owners might bring more mercenary entrepreneurial attitudes to the operation of the road. Indeed, due to the idiosyncrasies of the tax laws, new owners might find it more profitable to abandon the property than to operate it for transportation purposes. The owners of the Republic Gypsum Company thus considered it wise to consult with Brown and Stephens regarding this problem.[15]

After preliminary discussions with the principal owners of the railroad and after considerable study, the Republic Housing Corporation (Republic Gypsum's parent company) determined that its own interests could best be served by the outright purchase of the H&E's controlling interest. Republic Gypsum accordingly executed a stock purchase agreement and gave Stephens $5,000 in earnest money on September 13, 1971.

In sum, Republic agreed to purchase Stephen's entire holdings in the H&E, 6,500 shares, or 86.6 percent of the capital stock. On October 23, Stephens waived all claims. Thus he got back his $65,000—dollar for dollar. His only profit was an annual salary, modest interest on a promissory note from Republic, a few dividend checks, and a considerable pride in saving what he considered to be necessary railroad service for an area which would have been greatly distressed by its loss. In announcing the transfer of control the President of Republic Gypsum said that "acquisition [of the H&E] would help improve freight distribution from the company's Duke plant." He might have put it more strongly; ownership of the H&E by Republic guaranteed continued dependable rail service to its plant. Republic's President also affirmed that the railroad would continue to serve all other shippers on the route.[16]

The new officers of the H&E served simultaneously as officers of Republic Gypsum; none had previous railroad experience. Four of these officers also served on the new H&E board of directors and, representing 86.6 percent of the capital stock, easily controlled the organization. Except for Stephens, all former directors, representing on-line communities, were retained. Until early 1971, the H&E had shared office space at the Katy's depot in Altus, but it subsequently rented facilities elsewhere in that city. When conrol passed to Republic Gypsum, the railroad ofices immediately were moved to the plant site near Duke. Other changes followed. The earlier agreement between the H&E and the M-K-T by which the larger road leased one of its GP-7 locomotives to the Hollis Road on a per diem basis was terminated in February 1972. At that time, the H&E acquired its own locomotive, number 100, an 80-ton center-cab diesel-electric machine outshopped by General Electric in 1942. Unfortunately, number 100 developed mechanical difficulties in the summer of 1972 which necessitated extensive shopping. While its own locomotive was being repaired, the H&E leased a 45-ton GE product which had been built in 1941. This strange-looking machine, constructed for and originally operated by the U.S. Army Corps of Engineers, was returned to its owner, the Texas Tank Car Company, in February, 1973, after number 100 was returned to service.[17]

Very few operational changes were instituted

Locomotive #7427 was leased by the H&E in 1972 after its own locomotive developed mechanical problems. It is shown above dozing at Katy's Welon Yard engine facility in Altus on November 15, 1972. Below, it is shown hurring along on the following day west of Duke with a two car train. *Author's photographs*

By the summer of 1973, H&E's locomotive #100 had been returned to service. On a hot July day it was performing revenue service east of Gould, Oklahoma. *Author's photograph*

under the new management. Charles Onan had earlier replaced J. G. Evans as Assistant General Manager; he assumed the same multitudinous responsibilities that had been handled by his predecessor. In 1974, Onan and Dan R. Knight comprised the total train and engine crew roster; both were paid on a salary basis. The road also employed a section foreman and two laborers; they were guaranteed a 40-hour week. None of the railroad's employees were represented by unions. As a result, salaries earned by H&E employees were lower and side benefits were fewer than those for railroaders working elsewhere under union contracts. Furthermore, craft lines were obscured on the H&E; Onan and Knight frequently assisted in track maintenance when not involved in train service. Such efficient utilization of manpower had been considered mandatory by the previous owners, and Republic adopted a similar view. During May and June, when the wheat harvest moves to market, the H&E operates around-the-clock using two two-man crews. The second crew is ordinarily recruited from current or former Katy employees at Altus. When work is necessary on the line's bridges, it is performed by Katy crews on a job-contract basis. Overhead is further lowered by doubling plant management as railroad management. For example, Jerry Neilson is Republic's Vice President and General Manager, Plant Manager at Duke, and he also serves as the railroad's chief executive. Similarly, John L. Rodda is the Administrative Manager for the plant and is the railroad's accountant as well. Clerical and stenographic help likewise is drawn from plant staff. Thus while "featherbedding" may exist elsewhere, it is totally absent on the Hollis & Eastern.[18]

The H&E's future is very difficult to predict, but the road does face certain difficulties. The M-K-T, the only carrier with which the H&E has a direct connection and the road which supplies the vast bulk of its necessary car supply, abandoned its line above Altus in January 1973. Earlier, in 1970, Katy's former Whitesboro-Wichita Falls line, connecting the Northwestern District with its main artery, was similarly removed from service. Thus the remaining Wichita Falls-Altus line is isolated. However, the M-K-T does have trackage rights over the FW&D between Fort Worth and Wichita Falls. Nevertheless, it seems questionable that Katy will operate an uncon-

nected line such as this for very long. Except for harvest season, only two trains per week are necessary to handle what business there is on the Wichita Falls-Altus line. Fortunately for the H&E, Altus is also served by the Atchison, Topeka and Santa Fe and the St. Louis-San Francisco companies, and although Katy offers better rates and routings for traffic originating on or destined for points on the H&E, alternative arrangements could undoubtedly be worked out with the remaining carriers if Katy abandons its operations. A second problem is the thin traffic mix which has characterized the line since the advent of hardtop roads and long-haul trucking. Currently the road's major shipments include items incidental to the operation of Republic's plant as well as wheat and cotton-related products. There is little likelihood that this pattern will change in the foreseeable future. Nevertheless, agricultural shipments always vary according to the whims of nature. Shallow-well irrigation lends some stability to agricultural production, but the long-range effects of this on the water table are not clear.

Changes within the building trades industry and within Republic itself could alter the H&E's future. On the plus side, it is likely that the Duke plant will eventually increase its capacity; this would undoubtedly result in additional rail traffic. Moreover, there is a 50-year known reserve of raw gypsum—on the basis of current usage—near Duke. However, rail shipments of wallboard decreased sharply in 1972 after Republic purchased a similar plant already in operation near Rosario, New Mexico. This deprived the Duke facility of its West Coast market, which was ideally suited for rail movements. Currently Republic's own truck fleet moves the majority of the wallboard production from the Duke plant. Surprisingly, however, inbound shipments have become more important than outbound transportation to the competitive position of the Duke operation. These inbound shipments, about 10 carloads per month, originate at distant points, are bulky, and are hard to handle. They are generally transported more inexpensively and easily by rail than by truck. This seemingly insignificant factor is, nevertheless, crucial to efficient production at the Duke plant.[19]

On balance, then, the Hollis & Eastern appears to have at least moderate prospects for continued life. The directors representing Republic and those representing on-line communities still embrace the same philosophy. They view the road's continued existence as necessary to the efficient and profitable advancement of both regional agriculture and the wallboard plant at Duke. They are pleased when small profits are earned; they are relieved when the road breaks even; and they tolerate small losses. For them the railroad remains an important tool—a means to an end and not merely the end in itself.

The road originally was purchased and operated simply to sustain the agricultural economy of a two-county area in an obscure part of the Great Plains. In that development alone, the creation of the Hollis & Eastern was a landmark case. It was one of the first instances where an abandoned branch from a major trunk railroad —serving primarily agricultural interests—was successfully transformed into a viable independent short line railroad. All major trunk carriers currently are engaged in what they label as the rationalization of their plants. As a result, numer-

ous lines like Katy's former Wellington Branch will be lopped off and thereby become fair game for short line operation. Because of its early development, the Hollis & Eastern was truly a harbinger of the future. In 1973, 15 years after the incorporation of the H&E, farmers and agribusinessmen in Iowa similarly were forced into the railroad business when the Chicago, Rock Island & Pacific abandoned its 64-mile Montezuma Branch. The similarities between the Oklahoma and Iowa cases are striking.[20]

A writer for the *Wichita Falls Daily Times* once observed that "the Hollis & Eastern is a living example of what can be accomplished when communities work together for a common cause." It is that—and more. The original idea was locally conceived, but funding came mostly from an outsider, E. S. Stephens, whose infrequent visits to the property cast him as an absentee owner. Pessimists might have expected Stephens to milk the line and let it die, using it as a tax write-off. On the contrary, Stephens' conduct as

An unkown optimist attached a horseshoe to the H&E train order board at Hollis. It did little good; the depot was dismantled in 1973. *Author's photograph*

an absentee entrepreneur refutes, admittedly in microcosm, the oft-heard charges that railroad owners are robber barons. The purchase of the controlling stock of the H&E by the Republic Housing Corporation in 1971 adds yet another significant dimension to the interesting legacy of the road. The Republic firm builds mobile homes, manufactures gypsum products, and processes lumber. It has a sales network in 15 midwestern and southwestern states. Its major interest is hardly running a railroad. Nevertheless, when Republic felt threatened by the prospect of a new and possibly damaging entrepreneurial philosophy, it hesitated not at all in adding a short line railroad to its web. The H&E has successfully provided necessary economical and reliable rail transportation for shippers of agricultural products and for the Republic Gypsum Company as well. In the process, it has become the prototype of similar ventures in all areas of the country.[21]

An Early Autumn:

The BM&E: 1950-1969

The little station flipped by in the darkness; tall elevators suddenly stood out like ghosts in the night as the Jeep's headlight caught them momentarily. Finally. just a little past midnight, we stopped before a frame depot whose signboard proclaimed 'Keyes, Oklahoma,' the last outpost to the far frontier of Katy's domain."*

On September 21, 1968, Conductor Lester W. Barnett sent a wire to Superintendent C. W. Robbins which read: "Front end of engine 117 went on ground at M.P. 10.5. Engine was not damaged. Nobody injured." There was nothing dramatic about this accident, yet it represented what had become an altogether too frequent event on the Beaver, Meade & Englewood Railroad in the late years of the 1960s. Indeed, in the three-year period 1967-1969 there were 24 derailments on the road, and as a result it once was closed to operation for 41 days. In 1969, John H. Hughes, Chief Engineer for the Missouri-Kansas-Texas Railroad, the BM&E's parent company, admitted that track conditions on the Beaver Road were "deplorable." This condition had developed, said Hughes, because "over the past twelve years there was no effective roadbed maintenance program." In sum, deferred maintenance by 1969 had resulted in "a railroad that was not dependable and was badly in need of rehabilitation." Unfortunately, Katy then was struggling for its corporate survival, and in 1969 the Beaver Road did not earn enough revenue to cover even its operating expenses. Thus when the M-K-T sought permission to abandon its Northwestern District above Altus on April 1, 1969, it likewise asked to abandon the entire operation of the BM&E.[1]

Nineteen years earlier, in 1950, the BM&E had been a well-maintained dirt track railroad. Its locomotive engineers unhesitatingly ignored company speed restrictions and safely operated heavy freight trains at 40 miles per hour and faster. In that same year, the Beaver Road earned a modest profit of $38,866. Steam power pulled all trains, LCL and express was handled, passengers still were welcome aboard the aging side-door caboose, and Western Union telegrams were yet dispatched from BM&E stations. However, steam power vanished quickly after the Katy discovered in 1951 that it could employ diesel-electric locomotives having a 60,000-pound axle loading on the Northwestern District and on the BM&E as well. Water and fuel stations for steam locomotives were not fully retired until 1953, but the locomotives themselves had disappeared forever a year earlier. By 1960, little express was handled, and the Western Union service had been terminated. For that matter, the BM&E's fragile telegraph wires crumbled beyond repair in the late 1950s, although they were not officially retired until 1967. LCL shipments declined and finally were restricted by a 6,000-pound minimum tariff regulation. With the passage of the express and LCL business, the side-door cabooses lost their special utility and were scrapped. Passenger service similarly was terminated, although an unusually brave hobo occasionally volunteered as a rider.[2]

In 1950, the volume of traffic was sufficiently high to demand the use of train orders to govern movements over the line. Six years later train crews merely were expected to "report for clear-

D. Keith Guthrie, August 25, 1958, to Richard S. Prosser (a personal letter loaned to the author).

187

The Beaver Road's venerable side door cabooses disappeared with the demise of express and LCL traffic. *Howard E. Cross photograph*

Wichita Falls   February 20, 1969

GENERAL ORDER

All trains operating over Beaver, Meade & Englewood tracks will not exceed 15 Miles Per Hour.

C.W.R

ance before leaving Forgan and Keyes." By the mid-1960s, however, all trains were operated without clearance or train orders. As track conditions deteriorated, the authorized speed was correspondingly lowered to 15 miles per hour in 1969 and to 10 miles per hour in 1970. Only the barest number of slow orders were issued; engineers simply were expected to know where the worst spots were located. The loss of LCL, express, Western Union, and even carload traffic eventually resulted in the reduction of open stations. Floris, Baker, Mouser, and Muncy had been closed for several years; but on March 28, 1958, Eva was the first major station to be closed. Less than 10 years later, the road's first station, Beaver, was locked up. In 1967, the historic depot building at that point was retired, sold, and moved to Hooker where it became a garage. At the depot site in Beaver, only the 7x15 concrete vault safe remained as a grotesque reminder of an important era now passed. Finally, the agency at Turpin was abolished in the first days of 1971.

Thereafter, only Hooker and Keyes had open stations.[3]

Beginning in 1952 and continuing through 1957, the operation of the BM&E resulted in net losses. The road even failed to earn operating expenses in 1953, 1955, and 1956. In the last mentioned year, the Beaver Road had revenues of only $55,273 while posting a net deficit of $163,328. These conditions generally were prompted by a thinning traffic mix and a disastrous drought which cut deeply into revenues from the transportation of agricultural commodities. These also were lean years for the M-K-T System, and, in an effort to return it to prosperity, various financial interests fostered the nomination of William N. Deramus, III, as president. The youthful Deramus arrived on the property in January, 1957, and promptly ordered department heads to "cut all personnel to the lowest possible number that will still permit daily conduct of business." As a result, nearly all of the BM&E section men were dismissed, the number of sections

188

BM&E Board of Dirctors' meetings were held "off-line." Late in the 1930s, this one was held at the Katy station in Muskogee, Oklahoma. *John T. Griffin collection*

was reduced, and those which remained were stretched to levels that negated any possibility of adequate maintenance. The usual comprehensive maintenance program was junked, the section men performing only day-to-day service. At the same time, requests for materials were categorically denied. In 1958, the second year of the Deramus regime, only 238 ties were inserted along the Beaver's 105 miles of track. Nevertheless, previous managements had demanded a well-maintained track; this guaranteed a lengthy incubation period before the telling effects of deferred maintenance became troublesome. In the late 1950s, BM&E crews were still making a Forgan-Beaver-Keyes turn, 210 miles, within 16 hours as prescribed by federal law. A guest passenger who rode over the line in 1958 observed that the engineer frequently had the train moving "at a brisk forty miles per hour, in blatant and nonchalant disregard of the authorized speed."[4]

After the M-K-T purchased the BM&E from Jacob Achenbach and his associates in 1931, the

Beaver Road's Board of Directors was made up of Katy officials and shipping friends. In the early 1950s, the board consisted of Katy's board chairman, its president, its vice president and general manager plus shipping and banking representatives from Tulsa, Muskogee, and McAlester, Oklahoma; Joplin, Missouri; and Dallas, Texas. One of the directors was Bryan Cole, an executive of the Griffin Grocery Company of Muskogee, Oklahoma, who served from 1944 until his death in 1972. He succeeded John Taylor Griffin, President of the Griffin Grocery Company—the largest wholesale grocery company in the Southwest and an important shipper on Katy's main line—who had been appointed to the directorate in the early 1930s. Remuneration for the directors was meager: a pass good on Katy passenger trains, an elegant dinner served in conjunction with the annual meeting, and, perhaps most important, considerable pride in being a director of a railroad company. The BM&E trade area was not represented on the board, and there is no

189

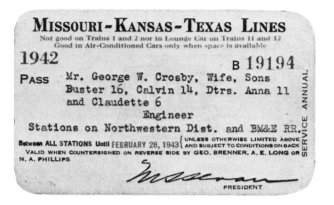

record which suggests that the annual meetings, usually aboard a Katy business car, ever were held on the railroad itself. Muskogee, Oklahoma, was a favored location for several years.[5]

There was generally a very positive, even warm, relationship between the officials and employees of the BM&E. Jacob Achenbach was respected by his employees, although they recognized that he was more a farmer than a railroad operator. They were more skeptical of Carl J. Turpin, General Manager under Achenbach, whom they considered an able railroader but one who was prone to "go by the book." Always neatly dressed, the bespectacled Turpin was stern and had a hard time retaining good men, particularly in the maintenance of way department. E. E. Booth, who worked for Turpin and later for the M-K-T as a BM&E official, was well liked. A consummate cigar smoker, Booth had been a mechanical officer for the Wichita Falls & Northwestern and later for the Katy at Wichita Falls before joining the BM&E's official family in the mid-1920s. Locomotive engineers especially liked Booth, for he "let the crews roll," although the speed limit was only 18 miles per hour. Overhead expenses on the BM&E were reduced after Katy purchased the road. This was done by doubling the M-K-T's Northwestern District officials in duplicate roles on the Beaver Road. F. W. Grace, who later became Katy's Vice President and General Manager, was an instant favorite on the BM&E. He enjoyed making inspection tours on his private car, and BM&E employees looked forward to his visits. Engineers also appreciated C. W. Campbell, who liked to board the locomotive and take his hand at the throttle. Ironically, the last of the BM&E's operating officials, Albert Dowdy, spent two years as agent at Keyes in the

early 1940s. A man who was much admired on the BM&E, Dowdy had the very distasteful task of closing down its operation in 1973.[6]

The BM&E offered both temporary and permanent employment for station agents, enginemen, trainmen, and section laborers. Owing to its low pay and heavy seasonal traffic, however, it experienced an extremely large turnover in help. Senior employees often joked about management's recruiting tactics. One favorite story involved an unemployed drifter who happened into Forgan during World War II and was immediately drafted into the BM&E's service as a brakeman. He was forthwith dispatched to Keyes on an overnight wheat run, but upon returning to Forgan after a bone-jarring 16-hour tour of the BM&E, he went AWOL without drawing his salary. Boomers flocked to the road during its annual harvest rush; although most of them moved on to become permanent hands. One of these was George W. Crosby, who came to the Beaver Road in 1927 as an engineer and retired there 36 years later. As a youth in the eighth grade, he had been an engine watchman for the WF&NW at Elk City in 1912 and 1913. Soon thereafter he quit school to enter engine service on the Northwestern; later he spent two years on the AT&SF and nine years on the Katy before signing on with the Beaver Road. Crosby was clearly the most colorful of the BM&E employees. The stories of his fast running are legendary. Perhaps a bit careless at times, he had something of a devil-may-care attitude. But when it was necessary, Crosby was the man for the job. He took particular delight in frightening the daylights out of a new man or a Katy man who was temporarily assigned to the BM&E. Another boomer who found a permanent home on the Beaver Road was Charles H. Gardiner who retired as agent at Forgan in 1972. Gardiner was born in the Rock Island depot at Isabelle, Oklahoma, where his mother was agent; his father also was a Rock Island agent. After working for several roads, Gardiner hired out on the BM&E in 1943. He moved to Forgan after the Beaver station was closed in 1967.[7]

Several others, like Thomas J. "Zip" Robb, Sr., were not boomers but did have previous railroad experience. Robb had been an official on the Clinton & Oklahoma Western before joining the BM&E as a conductor in 1929. Hugh H. Parks had been in charge of a Katy extra gang prior to his employment as a section foreman on

During the summer of 1945 several BM&E employees posed together with locomotives 541 and 535. Left to right, engineer Charles Suttle, trainman Ira Darus, and trainman Cecil Tedder. Fireman T. J. Robb, Jr. is in the cab of #541. *T. J. Robb, Jr. collection*

BM&E train and engine crew—the entire roster—in 1972. Left to right, engineer T. J. Robb, Jr. conductor Lester W. Barnett, and brakeman L. E. Smith. *Author's photograph*

Engineer T. J. Robb, Jr. patiently takes locomotive #112 and a train of empty grain cars through a sea of weeds between Mouser and Hough on June 28, 1972. *Author's photograph*

L. E. Smith and T. J. Robb, Jr. compared watches in time-honored fashion prior to leaving Keyes on July 26, 1972. *Author's photograph*

L. E: Smith at the controls of a GP-7 type locomotive west of Hooker on June 2, 1972. *Author's photograph*

BM&E station at Turpin, Oklahoma. June, 1959. *B. K. Hendricks collection*

C. H. Gardiner was the joint M-K-T/BM&E agent at Forgan in 1971. *Author's photograph*

The paint on the depot at windblown Keyes, Oklahoma was nearly gone by 1971. The television aerial speaks volumes regarding the informal nature of railroading on the BM&E. *Author's photograph*

At Keyes, a man-and-wife team shared the agent's job. Elsie W. Walters was half of that team. *Author's photograph*

the Beaver Road in 1930. A few local residents also found work on the railroad. W. H. Wells spent a few years as cashier for the company at Hooker shortly after the road arrived there. Byron Bates was a jack-of-all trades for the BM&E at Forgan before entering engine service on the M-K-T. Lester W. Barnett of Forgan hired out as a brakeman in 1938 and was promoted to conductor five years later. T. J. Robb, Jr., followed his father's footsteps in 1944 when he secured employment on the BM&E as a fireman. In 1946, another Panhandle resident, L. E. Smith, was hired as a fireman. Barnett, Robb, and Smith comprised the entire train crew and engine crew roster when the Beaver Road was abandoned in 1973. The railroad also brought economic opportunities to C. W. Suttle of Forgan, who was the company's official watch inspector, and to Dr. W. J. Risen, who was the company surgeon at Hooker.[8]

Informality was the word which best char-

acterized labor relations on the Beaver Road. Whenever the BM&E was "covered up with wheat," many Katy crewmen, such as engineer C. W. Dowdy of Mangum, helped out until the rush was over. Katy crews derisively referred to the line as the "Burma Road" but grudgingly marveled at the ability of the Beaver's train crews when it came to moving wheat. During hard times, unfortunately, many regular BM&E employees were frequently without work. John B. Arrington, a former boomer, worked for the BM&E as a fireman between 1928 and 1941, but only on an as-needed basis. G. H. McMahon similarly was called to work when the movement of grain peaked but was otherwise unemployed. Men with the most seniority held the few regular jobs, but others with less seniority sometimes were hired to perform other tasks on the railroad. For instance, extra brakemen and firemen were used interchangeably as section laborers until 1957. Even George H. Capehart, normally an engineer,

195

At Hooker, F. W. Topinka was the BM&E agent, assistant auditor, and time keeper.
Author's photograph

periodically toiled on a section crew. During World War II, the BM&E happily welcomed women to its employment rolls. In 1943, the *M-K-T Employes' Magazine* announced that an attractive clerk, Miss Lois Kirkhart, had been assigned to the Hooker office. In the same year, Clinton U. Walters, agent at Eva, was drafted. In his absence, his wife Elsie, then pregnant, filled the job. When the baby was born, Mrs. Walters' mother acted as a substitute agent at Eva and later accepted the agency at Keyes. In 1952, Mrs. Walters' husband became agent at Keyes, and his wife retained the Eva position. After Eva was closed in 1958 and until the BM&E was abandoned in 1973, Mr. and Mrs. Walters shared the Keyes agency. Walters bought some land near Keyes and engaged in farming during part of the year while his wife held the railroad job. During the remainder of the year, Mrs. Walters was a housewife while her husband returned to railroad work. This unusual arrangement was

satisfactory to the Walters and to the railroad as well. The BM&E also approved a similar arrangement at Hooker when Mrs. F. W. Topinka, a fifth-grade teacher from Forgan, filled in for her husband during his annual vacation. Topinka himself had earlier been a section laborer and brakeman before transferring to station service in 1955. At Hooker he was the BM&E's agent, assistant auditor, and time keeper.[9]

Katy officials seem to have been more lenient with BM&E employees than with their own help on the Northwestern District. One time, after a severe derailment which was aggravated by excessive speed, it appeared that George Crosby would be dismissed. On the contrary, not even a demerit mark was assessed against his record. As with its own employees, however, Katy officials were loath to interfere with the personal lives of BM&E workers. Shortly after the Katy assumed control of the Beaver Road, a laundress at Beaver complained to Superintendent C. W.

196

Watts that a BM&E section foreman had failed to pay a small bill owed her. Watts advised the foreman, "I dislike to receive letters like this, and wish you would do whatever necessary to keep your personal affairs out of this office." Nevertheless, Watts did not have unlimited patience. In 1931, a merchant at Baker complained that the BM&E agent there owed him money and had given him bad checks in payment. Watts told the agent that he was "disappointed in his conduct" and urged that he "square accounts." Several later complaints exhausted Watts' good humor, and the employee was eventually dismissed because, in the words of the superintendent, he was "unable to satisfactorily perform the duties of the position." This case, it should be noted, was extremely unusual. Perhaps Katy officials felt compelled to exercise a loose rein on BM&E employees because of the difficulty of retaining men on the line or perhaps because the entire operation was so far removed from the Wichita Falls offices. In any event, Katy supervisors embraced a philosophy which permitted almost anything as long as the traffic moved smoothly and they received no complaints. For their part, the BM&E workers appreciated this philosophy and ordinarily performed well.[10]

While working relations generally were good, wages and benefits were not. Until recent times, no BM&E employees were protected by union agreements; and in 1973, such protection was accorded only to agents and section men. Traditionally, the BM&E paid salaries on a monthly basis, except for maintenance of way laborers who were paid on an hourly rate. In 1941, these workers were paid a paltry 30¢ per hour, and their wages were frozen during the war. Earlier, in 1929, trainmen and agents both had been paid $100 per month. In 1942, the agent at Keyes earned only $122 per month. Section foremen were offered $105 per month in 1938, and in the same year conductors received $150 every 30 days. Shortly before Pearl Harbor, firemen were given a raise from $128 to $150 per month. All salaried employees were subject to call twenty-four hours per day, seven days a week. In 1948, the Order of Railroad Telegraphers was certified to represent the telegraphers on the BM&E after an investigation by the National Mediation Board. The company, nevertheless, refused to formulate rules regarding specific working conditions. On the other hand, when national agreements were signed, the BM&E generally granted wage increases, vacation improvements, and health and welfare amendments to its station employees. Finally, in 1967, a contract was written to cover the BM&E's three agents at Turpin, Hooker, and Keyes—a traditional agreement except that agents were assigned a six-day work-week. Maintenance of way personnel gained a union shop contract in 1950 which fixed monthly salaries for foremen at $224.97 and hourly rates for laborers at $1.16.[11]

The two BM&E bond issues, one maturing in 1954 and the other due in 1960, were paid on time; Katy thereby became the outright owner of the road. The parent company happily reported that beginning in 1958 and continuing through 1963, the Beaver Road earned profits totaling $1,030,242. In every year, fixed operating expenses were low. In 1958, for instance, the BM&E had a profit of $217,465 on total earnings of $370,026.[12]

The Oklahoma Panhandle had recovered from the devastating Dust Bowl days. In 1950, there were fewer residents in Beaver and Cimarron counties than had lived there 20 years earlier, but Texas County had a greater population in 1950 than it had in 1930. In the tri-county area of the Panhandle, there were fewer farms in 1950 than there had been earlier, but their total production was greater than before, and modern agricultural practices coupled with irrigation promised a bright future for the area. Additionally, petroleum production, particularly that of liquid petroleum gas (LPG), had increased very substantially in the Panhandle. Part of this prosperity was registered in the BM&E's profit and loss statements for the period 1958-1963. Yet maintenance of the property had nearly disappeared, and the roadbed reflected this neglect. William Deramus left the Katy in 1961, but he was replaced as president by C. T. Williams who continued the same management policies. Nearly a decade of deferred maintenance by 1964 had left the Katy System a railroad in name only. The situation was as critical on the BM&E and on the Northwestern as it was on the main line. The nearly prostrate Katy was faced with a cruel dilemma: it had no money to patch even its main artery, let alone its western branches and the BM&E. Then, reversing the trend of the previous six years, 1964 proved to be disastrous for the BM&E as it lost nearly $100,000. As a result, in

Track conditions during the spring of 1965 near Hooker. Material changes had taken place since 1928 (see illustrations on page 75 for comparison). *Author's collection*

December, 1964, Katy chose to petition the Interstate Commerce Commission for permission to abandon the entire Northwestern District and the BM&E as well. Before the case could be heard, however, Katy's board of directors brought in a "Doctor of Sick Railroads," John W. Barriger, who stoutly maintained that, in their zeal to economize, Deramus and Williams had hacked instead of pruning. Barriger insisted that "you can't

starve a railroad into prosperity." After making a system-wide inspection and after reviewing the crop prospects for 1965, Barriger asked the I.C.C. on April 27, 1965, to dismiss the abandonment application; the regulatory agency quickly obliged. The new Katy president cautioned, however, that the case would be reviewed on a year by year basis. Out on the line, emergency crews hurried to fill the worst holes in anticipation of the harvest rush.[13]

Fortunately, the assessors in the counties through which the BM&E passed took note of the increasingly deteriorated condition of the road. The value of the road in Cimarron County for 1932 was set at $93,195. In 1950, it was assessed at $50,980; but in 1972, it was only $7,388. In 1950, the BM&E paid Cimarron County $1,332.47 in taxes; but 22 years later, it paid only $426.58. In Texas County, the pattern was similar. For 1959, the BM&E paid that county taxes amounting to $8,719.38 on property assessed at $229,716. In 1972, the assessed valuation had dropped to $32,353 on which the railroad paid only $1,728.92 in taxes. Although statistics for its entire history are unavailable, it is clear that the Beaver Road was an important taxpayer in the Panhandle. For the years 1943-1972, inclusive, the BM&E paid a total of $190,385.22 in taxes to Texas County alone.[14]

Before 1967, one very traditional commodity totally disappeared from the BM&E's traffic mix. The haulage of livestock, particularly hogs and sheep, had gradually eroded in favor of trucks. Changing marketing conditions likewise served to diminish the use of the railroad in the transportation of cattle. Thus in 1967, the last stock pens, at Beaver and Muncy, were retired. That same season, the M-K-T removed the last 298 stock cars from its equipment roster and converted most of them to box cars by sheathing their sides. Many of these rebuilt cars were used on the Beaver Road to move grain from Panhandle elevators. For a short period of time, it appeared that over-the-road truckers might capture even the grain trade from the BM&E. However, grain always was the road's life blood, and it responded to this threat by instituting a series of rate reductions which all but drove truckers from the field. Between 1954 and 1968, certain grain rates were lowered by nearly 50 percent, as the following statistics indicate:

Tumbling tumble weeds. Milepost 69 near Hovey. Spring, 1965. *Author's collection*

WICHITA FALLS, TEXAS JUNE 4, 1969

BULLETIN BOOK B-M-E

ALL VACATIONS ARE POSTPONED FOR TRAIN AND ENGINE MEN
UNTIL AFTER HARVEST.

C W ROBBINS

235PM 4th

Rates in Cents per 100 Pounds on Wheat and Sorghum Grain to Houston for Export[15]

From	Commodity	10/54	9/57	10/60	6/62	7/64	5/68
Turpin	Wheat	65½	59	54½	47½	46	38½
	Sorghum	53	53	54½	47½	47½	38½
Hough	Wheat	72	61	54½	47½	46	38½
	Sorghum	53	53	54½	47½	46	38½
Keyes	Wheat	72	61	56½	47½	46	38½
	Sorghum	55	55	55½	47½	47½	38½

With highly competitive rates, the BM&E held the grain trade until 1968. Between 1965 and 1967, the road delivered no less than 4,848 loads of grain to the M-K-T at Forgan. This was an annual average of 1,616 cars. However in 1968, only 715 loads of grain were given to the Katy; and in 1969, the BM&E originated only 1,000 carloads of that traffic. Part of this drop is explained by the usual variance in crop conditions, but another factor was more crucial. In the late 1960s, numerous Panhandle livestock owners became feedlot operators, using locally grown grains for their feeding purposes. This change was reflected in the BM&E's traffic statistics for 1967-1969; in 1967, a total of 996 cars of milo were billed; but the following year, the Beaver Road moved only 280 loads of that grain. Even bargain rates could not reclaim that traditional and remunerative traffic. And there were other factors which worked against the BM&E's continuance as the Panhandle's premier grain carrier. On-line elevators, including those which were locally owned, as well as those which were a part of Oklahoma or Texas chain operations, previously had a loyalty to the BM&E and to grain terminals which could be reached by its parent, the M-K-T. However, in the late 1960s and thereafter, many of these elevators passed to the Perryton Equity Company of Perryton, Texas—a concern which had neither loyalty. Moreover, due to its light rail and rapidly deteriorating roadbed, the BM&E could not employ the new jumbo hopper cars. This conspired against shippers on the BM&E, for it made them less competitive than

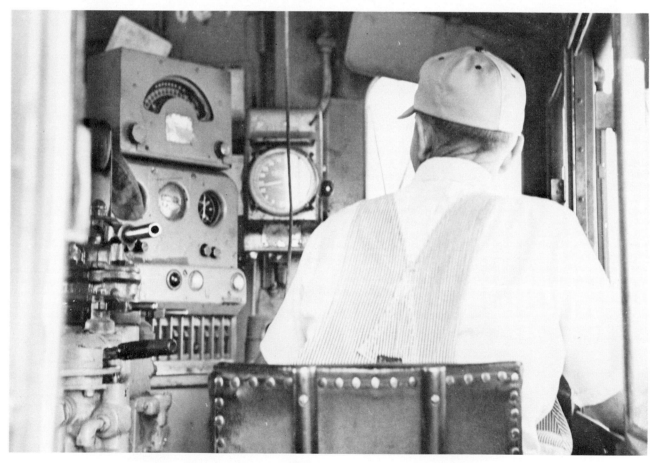

L. E. Smith, usually the BM&E brakeman, also substituted as conductor or engineer—whichever was necessary. On this day in June, 1972, he was the engineer—making 13 miles per hour with locomotive #107 near Mouser. *Author's photograph*

their rivals on the Santa Fe and Rock Island lines. For instance, the Stafford Elevator Company at Keyes, a long-time shipper on the Beaver Road, began ordering covered hoppers from the AT&SF for its loadings. As a result of the consolidation of country elevator companies and the inability of the BM&E to utilize the more efficient covered hoppers, the area from which it drew grain was narrowed to a strip a few miles on either side of its line.[16]

In 1968, a fertilizer mixing plant was located west of Straight by the Gulf Oil Company. This new facility did develop a modest traffic for the BM&E. In the same year, a total of 211 carloads of pipe moved to destinations on the road. Unfortunately, this was nonrecurring traffic and, in fact, when installed as part of the pipe-line operation, soon drained away the very important LPG business which had been a major contributor to the Beaver Road's traffic mix since the mid-1960s. In 1964, the Mobil Oil Corporation entered into a private track agreement with the BM&E for two 185' tracks to serve loading racks located at milepost 68 west of Hough. A smaller plant was installed at approximately the same time near milepost 4, between Beaver and Forgan, by the Cabot Corporation. Between 1967 and 1969, these two plants contributed 33.3 percent of all loadings on the railroad. Strangely the LPG traffic proved to be a mixed blessing. Due to economic considerations, shippers favored the use of heavy jumbo tank cars for these movements. Although such cars generally were employed in this service, the BM&E's light rail and earthen roadbed, long deprived of adequate maintenance, increasingly were unequal to the task. In reality, the movement of these heavy loads served to hasten the complete physical deterioration of the railroad.[17]

Most of the LPG business from plants located on the BM&E was consigned to destinations which would have given the Northwestern District, and indeed the entire Katy System, profitable long hauls. Late in 1964, however, the Katy's Northwestern District simply collapsed due to the combined effects of deferred maintenance, unusually wet weather, and heavy traffic. The M-K-T then sought and received a car service order from the I.C.C. which allowed it to divert traffic to connecting but competing carriers. This move deprived the BM&E's parent of much needed revenue, which it would have received as a

Milepost 105—Keyes—end of the BM&E line. *Author's photograph*

Unhappily, the BM&E had become—by the late 1960s—a broken down, decrepit railroad. Derailments such as this one were the natural result. *Author's collection*

matter of course had it been willing or able to maintain its lines responsibly in years gone by. Under the I.C.C. order, the majority of the LPG originated on the BM&E was given to the Rock Island at Baker. Cars destined for Fort Worth and billed in transit, however, were carried all the way on the Katy. These cars were sandwiched between grain loads to reduce wear on the track and bridges whenever possible. Then, nearly as quickly as it had started, the LPG traffic on the BM&E evaporated. In the three years prior to 1969, the Cabot plant had shipped an annual average of 253 cars over the Beaver Road; but late in 1968, pipe-line facilities became available and Cabot never again used the railroad. Mobil billed 437 cars from Hough in 1967, but three years later it shipped only 124 cars. After receiving pipe line service in 1969, Mobil soon terminated the use of rail transportation for the delivery of production from the Hough plant. The precarious condition of the BM&E may have hastened the decisions of the gas companies to make the switch to pipe-line transportation, but, as a Mobil representative explained it, the ultimate "reason was purely one of economics." In the transport of LPG, the pipe-line was inherently

more efficient than the flanged wheel and the steel rail.[18]

In 1967 and 1968, loadings of sorghum grains amounted to 38.7 percent of all billings on the Beaver Road; and in the same two years, LPG shipments accounted for an additional 33.3 percent. Most of the sorghum-grain business was lost thereafter when Panhandle feedlot operators began using the milo for their feeding purposes. At the same time, the LPG plants shifted their transport to pipe lines. The loss of the two commodities which had, as late as 1967-1968, furnished 72 percent of its traffic was a crushing blow. Unhappily, the BM&E had become a broken-down, decrepit railroad with its major sources of traffic gone. Moreover, the road lost money on its operations every year since 1963, except for 1966 and 1968 when it earned very modest profits. While the M-K-T may have had certain reservations about the abandonment of its Northwestern District, it had no compunction about seeking the abandonment of its wholly owned Beaver, Meade & Englewood Railroad. On April 1, 1969, the Katy sought such permission.[19]

Decision for Euthanasia:

The Death Warrant

"We therefore conclude, and find, that the continued operation of these lines would impose an undue burden on the subject carriers and upon interstate commerce. The basic rationale for our decision can be described as finding that the present and future public convenience and necessity does not justify the continued operation of marginally profitable lines where the rehabilitation burden outweighs the public need shown for the retention of this service. . . ."*

Angry opposition had developed when the Missouri-Kansas-Texas Railroad asked the Interstate Commerce Commission for permission to abondon its entire Northwestern District and its wholly owned Beaver, Meade & Englewood Railroad in 1964. On May 14, 1965, John W. Barriger, Katy's new president, was in Mangum to discuss the fate of the lines north of Wichita Falls, and was able to announce that he earlier had ordered the applications withdrawn. Emergency crews were directed to patch the worst holes in order that trains could safely traverse the weary trackage at a mere 15 miles per hour. One year later, Barriger was in Wichita Falls, and the "Grand Old Man of Railroading," as the *Wichita Falls Times* called him, was optimistic about "retaining indefinitely Katy's railroad in the Wichita Falls, northern Texas, and Oklahoma district." Barriger was cautious, however, saying that the entire situation would be reviewed on a year-to-year basis. Unfortunately, the entire M-K-T System had become so completely run down that Barriger's problems defied immediate and, for a while it appeared, even long-term solution. The main line offered shippers the shortest rail route between Kansas City and Dallas, but had become uncompetitive due to the deferred maintenance of the previous several years. Thus when Barriger located a stray dollar, it naturally was used to bolster Katy's sagging main stem.[1]

By 1968, it was clear that the M-K-T simply had too many route miles to renew. In an effort to prune marginally productive trackage, the Barriger administration announced at mid-year that it would seek to divest itself of the Henrietta Subdivision from Whitesboro to Wichita Falls. This 105.9-mile stretch of track included the historic Wichita Falls Railway built by Joseph A. Kemp in 1894 and was the connecting link between the Northwestern District and Katy's main line. Unlike the Northwestern District and the BM&E, the Henrietta Subdivision boasted heavy steel, gravel ballast, and was in at least average physical condition. However, there was little on-line industry, and the route was primarily useful as a bridge between the main line and the Northwestern. Moreover, the road paralleled the Fort Worth and Denver for several miles, making it at least partially redundant. In making the announcement, Barriger contended that it had become impossible for the Katy to maintain all of its trackage because of the company's weak financial condition. If cuts had to be made, this was the place to do it, Barriger implied. Furthermore, said the Katy president, the M-K-T was taking this action so that funds would be available to rehabilitate the Northwestern District. Nine years earlier, all passenger service on the Henrietta Subdivision had ended; and in 1967, the proud Union Station at Wichita Falls faced

*U.S. Interstate Commerce Commission, *Finance Reports,* Volume 338 (Washington: U.S. Government Printing Office, 1972), p. 748.

203

The sands of time were accurately accounted for by this Seth Thomas clock in the Katy depot at Elk City. *Author's photograph*

demolition after the FW&D's TEXAS ZEPHYR was discontinued. Finally, on January 2, 1970, the entire road between Whitesboro and Wichita Falls was abandoned, the tracks to be dismantled shortly thereafter. Trackage rights over the FW&D were then obtained between Fort Worth and Wichita Falls in order to maintain a connection between the Katy main and the Northwestern. Somewhat earlier most of the former Texas Central, which had become an important Katy feeder, tapping the area northwest of Waco, similarly was abandoned. A portion of that line, between Stamford and Rotan, was temporarily retained and serviced by trackage rights over the Denver Road from Wichita Falls. Late in 1969, the Katy asked for and received permission to abandon these trackage rights and then sold its interest in the old Texas Central line. With that, Katy's single remaining owned operation in the Wichita Falls area was the Northwestern District —still an important feeder but physically a wreck, unconnected with the M-K-T main stem except by trackage rights and tied on the other

end of its line to the increasingly unprofitable BM&E.[2]

Before the projected benefits from the abandonment of the Henrietta Subdivision could accrue to it, most of the Northwestern District itself faced Valhalla. On November 8, 1968, Katy's Board of Directors voted to seek abandonment of the trackage north from Altus to Forgan and the entire BM&E from Beaver to Keyes as well. Included were a total of 330.99 miles of railroad. Katy's legal department filed the appropriate forms with the Interstate Commerce Commission on April 1, 1969. Due to the magnitude of the application, the case drew considerable local, regional, and even national attention. The I.C.C. originally scheduled hearings in September, but subsequently these were postponed to the first week of December when an examiner took testimony at three locations, Altus, Woodward, and Guymon.[3]

Katy's first witness at the hearings was President John W. Barriger, who pointed out that the Northwestern District and the BM&E had

By 1972 the bridge over the South Canadian River at Camargo had deteriorated badly. Vegetation even grew from one of the timbers. *Author's photograph*

"received only minimum essential maintenance immediately necessary to permit operation." He recalled the situation which he found when he arrived on the property in 1965 as "one of appalling neglect of maintenance of track, structures, and equipment." This was the case on all Katy lines, Barriger testified, not just on its western branches. Indeed, the M-K-T at that moment in 1965 "was on the brink of bankruptcy, if not actual physical disintegration." Consequently, a major rebuilding program had been instituted on the main line, but there was little money to repair the Northwestern District and the BM&E; now they were approaching the point where their service life was exhausted. Barriger stoutly contended that ". . . it would be a gross misuse of M-K-T's meager financial resources to permit any diversion of funds otherwise available for main line work to subsidize the operation of these branch lines which have no hope of successful operation. In turn, this misapplication of rehabilitation funds would have an adverse reaction upon the recovery of main line traffic that M-K-T badly needs in order to survive." In sum, the Katy president asked that the M-K-T and the BM&E be relieved of the obligation of continued operation of these lines before they reached the absolute end of their physical existence.[4]

Chief Engineer John H. Hughes later testified that the aggregate length of the 117 bridges between Altus and Forgan was 18,887 feet. The average age of these bridges in 1969 was 32 years, and Hughes judged that their general condition was poor. In further testimony, Katy's engineer revealed that 8 percent of all rails and 25 percent of all angle bars on the Northwestern District then were broken. Moreover, 64.7 percent of the line's ties were in need of replacement. Due to deferred maintenance, the track unhappily had become center bound, and the cut ditches had filled so that there was no effective drainage system to carry water away from the track. On the BM&E, where only used relay rail had been employed in its construction, the situation was equally bad—if not worse. In general, track conditions on both lines according to Hughes, were "deplorable." In order to rehabilitate these 330.99 miles and restore them to branch line standards permitting speeds of 30 miles per hour, Hughes estimated that it would take $8,506,260 for the Katy line and $3,599,170 for the BM&E. However, the estimated current salvage value of the M-K-T line was $401,600, and $250,400 for the BM&E.[5]

A number of studies were submitted which demonstrated that on both lines the traffic in general commodities had declined greatly in the previous decades and had totally disappeared with respect to many items. Livestock traffic, for example, had disappeared some years previously; milo, originated on the BM&E and moved overhead on the Katy line, was down to 141 cars in 1969. The LPG business similarly had dried up when the several plants on both lines took advantage of pipe-line transportation as it became available to them. Furthermore, under I.C.C. Car Service Order No. 957, issued in December 1964, these heavy loads were diverted at the nearest junction due to the poor track conditions on the Northwestern District. A heavy cement traffic to Woodward similarly was diverted, and the use of covered hopper cars for the movement of grain was banned on both lines because of the heavy weight of these cars when loaded. In other words, the Northwestern District above Altus by 1969 was used almost exclusively for the movement of wheat outbound and a small amount of supplies and fertilizer inbound. The movement of wheat, of course, was no unimportant matter; Oklahoma ranked third among all states in the production of this grain, much of it grown in the area affected by the twin abandonment applications. In the seven year period 1963-1969, encompassing good, bad, and ordinary crop years, an average of 2379 carloads of wheat moved to market each year over these lines. Of these, an average of 1141 were originated at Katy stations, and an average of 1238 moved overhead from the BM&E. However, in order to retain this important traffic, both railroads had greatly reduced their rates. Testimony from numerous elevator operators demonstrated that they would always use the least expensive transportation service, either truck or rail, depending on current rates. Indeed, as little as one-half cent per bushel, delivered price, often determined the sale of grain and the means of its transportation. Katy's counsel therefore concluded that the elevator operators saw the railroad as necessary only to provide competition for trucks—cheap rates—and not to furnish transportation *per se.*[6]

The deterioration of traffic mix was even more dramatic on the BM&E. By 1969, Katy considered it to be "a grain carrying line, transporting only negligible amounts of other commodities." Carload traffic statistics for 1967 and 1969 bolster this contention:

Commodity	1967	1969
Grain	1688	1192
LPG	695	173
Pipe	4	31
All Other	201	96
TOTAL	2588	1492

In Katy's view, the BM&E not only had experienced a marked decline in traffic and rapidly increasingly deficits, but was able to survive only because funds, equipment, and services were supplied to it by the parent company. The last good year which the BM&E had experienced was 1962, when the road earned profits amounting to $151,925. Thereafter earnings exceeded expenses only in 1963, 1966, and 1968. Between 1964 and 1970, inclusive, the company sustained a net loss of $255,593. The Beaver Road clearly had become a drag on the economic health of its parent. Because it was considered an independent carrier, the determination of its case was a simple matter. All that was necessary was to prove that the road had become unprofitable. On proof of such loss, the Commission no longer had the right to exercise its discretion or to consider other factors because, as Katy's counsel pointed out, under such circumstances the railroad whose entire line is operated at a loss has a constitutional right to terminate its business.[7]

A number of protestors contended that western Oklahoma was on the verge of important economic expansion, but Katy's attorneys contended that "rosy predictions based on fond hopes are poor substitutes for quantitative analysis based on actual movements and the trends demonstrated in such movements." In sum, the Katy argued that the most significant aspect of the two applications involved the deteriorated and worn-out condition of the tracks. Its representatives testified that both lines had reached the end of their useful lives; they had either to be rebuilt or abandoned. The second most important aspect of these applications, in Katy's view, was the financial crises then facing both applicants. These problems had resulted from years of deficit operation and the financial inability of either applicant to provide funds necessary to restore the lines to proper condition. In other words, the M-K-T was financially unable to retain in operation this part of the Northwestern District and the BM&E. Moreover, in the unlikely event that funds were made available to rehabilitate these lines, the costs of such rebuilding would, in Katy's estimation, result in even greater deficits from their future operation. Finally, in the case of the BM&E, the application was warranted "primarily because of constitutional requirements."[8]

For their part, the protestors took the position that the final or sole test was whether the abandonment of these two operations was consistent with the public conveniences and necessities, "present and future prospective needs of the public, and loss and inconvenience resulting from this abandonment, weighed against any losses which may accrue to the applicants from their continued operation." They considered the continued operation of the two lines not to be an undue burden on interstate commerce, and they maintained further that the lines served "a substantial and essential public need in connection with the movement of agricultural products and other commodities to and from" points on those lines. Moreover, the combined operation of the two lines in question provided the most direct route from western Oklahoma and the Panhandle to the export terminals on the Gulf. They also pointed out that there were only five connecting railroads on the entire 330.99-mile route which the M-K-T and the BM&E proposed to abandon. This meant that there were railroad junctions only at an average of every 66 miles, effectively negating the applicant's claim that the area was oversupplied with railroad services. Shortly before filing the twin applications for abandonment, President Barriger contacted six regional competitors and offered to sell to them any portion or the entire railroad from Whitesboro, Texas, through Wichita Falls to Keyes, Oklahoma, at not less than scrap value. Only the Rock Island responded affirmatively. It agreed to purchase some trackage at Mangum on the Katy and a short spur on the BM&E at Baker, but refused to buy a 9.8-mile portion of main line from Mangum to the high volume elevators at Brinkman. Nor did it offer to purchase another 10-mile stretch of main line from Elk City to the Shell Oil plant near Hocker.[9]

Statistics clearly proved that the area served by these lines had experienced a reduction in population over the years, but the protestors demonstrated that the property values had risen during the same time. Brinkman, for example, had a population of only 14 people but ordinarily produced more revenue from wheat loadings than any other country elevator point on the Northwestern District. The M-K-T admitted that western Oklahoma might have economic potential but felt that it was only a remote possibility. Protestors, however, showed that numerous plants had recently been located in the area. One of these was located at Woodward on the AT&SF and would have been placed on the M-K-T "had this abandonment not been pending." Furthermore, financial deposits in the affected counties were up by 200 percent since 1948. In the Panhandle, the growth of feedlots had made it a feed importing area—a fact which Katy's BM&E had not taken advantage of. An M-K-T witness testified that there was no reason to expect larger volumes of grain from the region. Yet in the Panhandle, there had been a 35 percent increase in the number of irrigation-well installations in the single year 1968. According to those people opposing abandonment of the BM&E, irrigation promised to stabilize the economy of the area and to increase crop production. Finally, due to the combined effects of fertilizer, irrigation, and intensified research, the average wheat yield had risen in the area from 12.7 bushels per acre in 1953 to an average of 28.5 bushels per acre in 1969. Several protestors considered that there was no reason to believe this trend would not persist.[10]

It was on behalf of the wheat farmers and elevator operators that the protestors waged their strongest campaigns to save the lines. Claude G. Rhoades, a representative of the Oklahoma Wheat Commission, testified that Oklahoma ranked third among all states in producing wheat and that wheat was Oklahoma's number one farm crop. The counties served by the lines in question produced one-quarter of the state's entire crop, and, in Rhoades' opinion, the granting of the two abandonment applications "would discriminate against 9,500 wheat farm families by depriving them of railroad service and penalizing them financially." These two connected rail lines were the primary wheat movers in their respective areas and provided the most direct route to the Gulf. Rhoades pointed out that the vast bulk of all the Oklahoma wheat crop, some 80 percent, was exported. Inexpensive rail transportation to

Gulf ports, of the type supplied by these two lines, encouraged such exportation and thus assisted the United States in its balance of payments problem. Railroad officials responded by asserting that regional trucking services were adequate for the movement of grain from the area. But the protestors proved that, in 1969 at least, trucking was inadequate. Moreover, they demonstrated that several independent companies and even chain organizations such as Bunge Elevator Company used rail service almost exclusively.[11]

Without doubt, the farmers and elevator operators in the Panhandle would be those most affected by the proposed abandonment. Many farmers who ordinarily marketed their grain at Knowles would have to truck their wheat to Booker, Texas, a round trip of more than 50 miles. Custom combine operators would necessarily have to raise their rates, as they would have longer truck hauls from the grain fields to the elevators and then longer waits at those elevators. The Riffe-Gilmore Company, with elevators on the BM&E at Baker, Mouser, and Hough, shipped its wheat to Fort Worth and to the Gulf via BM&E and the M-K-T. Without rail service, its Hough and Mouser facilities, with a total capacity of 1.12 million bushels, would be hard hit. Wheat from those areas would have to be trucked to a competitor at Hooker, whose facilities would be overburdened by the additional volume. The elevator operator at Eva stated that, if the abandonment request was granted, he would have to truck grain from his facility to Elkhart, Kansas, for rail loading; this would mean an additional expense of from three to six cents per bushel, a charge which eventually would be borne by the farmers. In Beaver County, George Kamas had a $1 million investment in 9,000 acres of land, and said that if he was compelled to truck his annual grain production to Englewood, Kansas, he might be forced out of business. The protestors calculated that grain producers in all of the affected counties in 1969 were subject to an average 7.5-mile haul from their farms to rail-loading facilities. Should the I.C.C. grant the applications, they would be burdened with an average 25-mile haul to railroad points. Of course, wheat farmers were not alone in their fears. At Gate, the Axtell Mining Company which shipped volcanic ash in carload lots contemplated its extinction if the rails disappeared from that location.[12]

The protestors hotly charged that the Katy

had "milked" these lines as long as possible without properly maintaining them. Now they were in deplorable condition. This was caused, many said, by habitual neglect ordered or at least condoned by Katy management over a long period of time. Thus the protestors asked: "Can the condition of the trackage, admittedly brought about by Applicant's own neglect, their own lack of sufficient and adequate maintenance over many years, be used as a basis and justification to abandon the lines and deprive the shippers and users of that which they have a right to expect, when such absolute duty has been voluntarily assumed?" That the lines needed repairing and rehabilitating was never in question either by the railroads or the protestors. However, they did differ as to the cost of such upgrading. An independent and well-respected Oklahoma engineer, H. E. Bailey, estimated that "to completely rehabilitate the lines and all bridges and roadway" so that heavily loaded LPG tanks and covered hopper grain cars could be handled at 30 miles per hour, it would be necessary to spend at least $5,869,767—about one-half of what Katy officials had suggested. The protestors acknowledged that all railroads, and particularly the Katy, were experiencing difficult times. On the other hand, they contended that "these are likewise and in the same breath critical times for all businesses, individuals, towns, and communities." Therefore, they argued, "comparison should be made between investments which the railroads would be required to make, as compared with the valuations of farm lands" and other investment of those who would be negatively affected by the abandonment of these lines.[13]

On October 16, 1970, the I.C.C. examiner who heard the case announced his recommendations. He favored approval of the applications, but with severe restrictions. One of his recommended conditions was that the line be retained in operation for two years, after which period the applicant again would be required to submit filings. Both the railroads and the protestors filed exceptions to the examiner's report, and the case was referred to the entire Commission "because of the importance of the matters involved." The M-K-T and the protestors alike criticized the examiner's use of the I.C.C.'s "50 percent formula." This formula was applied—with the assumption that the abandonment application would be granted—in an attempt to determine the expense in transporting shipments over Katy's remaining lines. By way of example, if a 300-mile "line haul" shipment (moving exclusively over Katy's rails) passed over 100 miles of railroad proposed for abandonment and over 200 miles of unaffected line, two-thirds of the revenue was assigned to the unaffected line (or balance of the system), and—under the 50 percent formula—one-half of this revenue was viewed as the expense of transportation over the unaffected line. The formula clearly constituted no more than a "rule of thumb"; thus the controversy. Nevertheless, on this issue the full Commission upheld its examiner. Correspondingly it found "that Katy's net income from operation of the line from Altus to Forgan for 1967, 1968, and 1969 was, respectively, $125,492, $213,191, and $171,307." However, the M-K-T had spent only $1,400 per mile to maintain this portion of the Northwestern District during those same years, while $2,400 was considered by the I.C.C. the average annual expenditure for branches of this type. Had the Katy spent the normal amount for maintenance during the period 1967-1969, the Commission calculated the line would have been operated at a net loss. On the BM&E, the case was clear; it had become an economic burden to its parent. Thus after lengthy consideration, the I.C.C. decided on November 18, 1971, that the two applications for abandonment would be granted.[14]

In making its decision, the I.C.C. asserted that it was impossible to "over-emphasize the critical financial condition of the Katy on a system-wide basis." In view of this, the cost of rehabilitating the line was a major issue with which the regulatory agency had to deal. Eventually, the commission had become "convinced that an expenditure of $12 million, as claimed by the applicants, or even the lesser figure of $6 million which the protestants feel would be sufficient, is not justified under the circumstances. . . ." The I.C.C. agreed that the hard-pressed Katy had to establish priorities in allocating its limited rehabilitation funds and further agreed that these monies rightly should be spent on its main line; "to do otherwise would jeopardize Katy's entire system," concluded the Commission.[15]

At the hearings, numerous protestors charged that the railroads had an affirmative duty to maintain tracks and facilities in reasonably good operating condition but had not done so. They alleged that the two roads had engaged in negli-

Extra 117 rolls through the hills near Vici late in 1971. *Author's photograph*

gent "nonmaintenance" or had deliberately downgraded service so as to rid themselves of traffic which ordinarily would have flowed to them. The Commission dismissed these allegations, but, as the position advanced by the protestors was frequently heard by the I.C.C., and as the Katy situation provided "a dramatic example of the general problem," the Commission finally decided to create distinctions "between economizing and the deliberate downgrading of service." In this landmark decision, the Commission stated that the essence of the problem was the carrier's intent: whether it deliberately downgraded a viable line or merely neglected it out of financial necessity. "We are of the view that the effect of a carrier's act can best be judged in terms of the over-all needs of the carrier," said the I.C.C. Therefore in answering future allegations of deliberate downgrading, the I.C.C. announced that it expected the railroads to be prepared to demonstrate their needs to economize according to these criteria:

A) Whether, on a system-wide basis, the carrier is either only marginally profitable or is operated at a deficit.

B) Whether the particular line under consideration is marginally profitable, operated at a deficit, or would have been operated at a deficit were it not for deferral of maintenance and rehabilitation costs.

C) Whether the carrier can clearly show that its available funds for maintenance and rehabilitation are required for those portions of the lines within its system for which a greater public need has been demonstrated and which offers a larger profit potential for the carrier, and that carrier has definite proposals as to how such expenditures are being or will be made.

In summary, the Commission said that in the future it would look to the following factors in making its decisions regarding the downgrading of service issue:

A) The nature of the services and the public need shown in the past for the services.

B) The effect of the carrier's act.

C) The need demonstrated by a carrier to economize under the implied intent test.

D) Any evidence as to a specific intent to deliberately downgrade service for the purpose of turning what ordinarily would be a profitable operation into a deficit operation in perfecting a case for abandonment.[16]

The I.C.C. admitted that the abandonment

210

After picking up several loads of wheat at Vici, extra 117 was ready to depart. *Author's photograph*

"would work a hardship on some shippers, especially elevator operators," and that many shippers would "have to make major adjustments in their transportation patterns." To cushion the blow and to accord shippers a reasonable time to make such adjustments, the regulatory agency demanded continued operation of the lines until June 30, 1972. It also provided that the M-K-T could "sell the line to any responsible person, firm, group, organization, association, or corporation, including the State of Oklahoma or any agency thereof, prior to June 30, 1972, for continued operation (upon approval of this Commission) for not less than the net salvage value of the property to be abandoned." On behalf of the affected Katy and BM&E employees, the I.C.C. imposed "the Burlington conditions," modest job protection provisions. Later, as it became apparent that the newly created Oklahoma Railroad Maintenance Authority was acting in good faith to acquire these lines from the Katy, the I.C.C. modified its order to assure continued operation through August 30, 1972. Then, in an act of good faith on its own, Katy voluntarily guaranteed operation until January 15, but the lines were finally and officially abandoned on January 31, 1973. Thereafter, only the trackage between Wichita Falls and Altus remained in service under the Katy banner.[17]

In large measure, the proceedings involving the abandonment of these 330.99 miles of rail-road, reportedly the largest branch line abandonment to that date, served to focus national attention on the general problem of the closing of rail service to rural areas. Prompted by the I.C.C.'s decision to allow the abandonment of these lines, Senator Henry Bellmon (R-Oklahoma) introduced a bill in Congress entitled the Rural Railroad Assistance Act of 1972. Under this proposed legislation, the Department of Transportation would have been authorized to make loans and loan guarantees to state and local public bodies for the establishment or re-establishment of rail service in rural areas. Such loans could have covered up to 80 percent of the cost of such projects, but, while the legislation was passed in the Senate, it died for lack of action in the House. Earlier, Senator Walter F. Mondale (D-Minnesota) introduced similar legislation entitled the Rural Transportation Act of 1972; this legislation was not enacted, either. Nevertheless, the efforts of Bellmon and Mondale suggest that the problem of branch line abandonment in rural areas eventually will receive a full airing. This undoubtedly will result in the passage of comprehensive legislation to deal with the problem.[18]

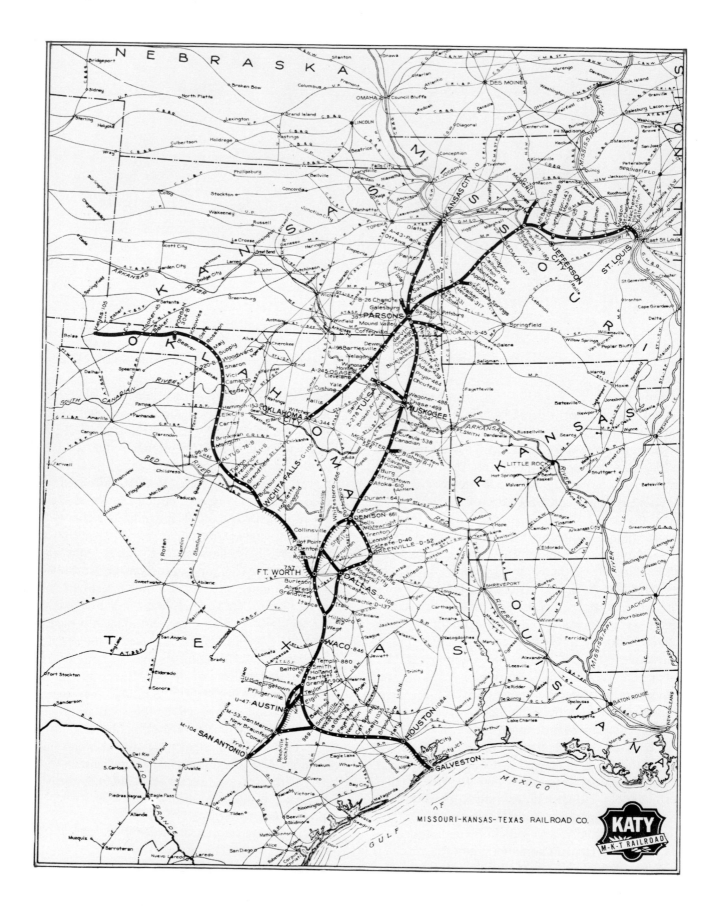

Map of the Katy System, circa 1972.

Muddy Tires and Broken Rails

"We have succeeded in abandoning most of our unproductive branch lines, so that it is no longer necessary to waste the railroad's resources maintaining track which produced virtually no revenue." Katy President R. N. Whitman, 1972.*

Shortly after the Missouri-Kansas-Texas Railroad filed applications to abandon most of its Northwestern District and all of its Beaver, Meade & Englewood, Katy management sought to streamline its corporate structure by dissolving the Wichita Falls Railway and the Wichita Falls & Northwestern Railway of Texas, two subsidiary companies. The Wichita Falls Railway was Joseph A. Kemp's first railroad project, comprising trackage between Wichita Falls and Henrietta, Texas; it also faced abandonment in 1969. The Wichita Falls & Northwestern of Texas owned the line of road extending from North Yard in Wichita Falls to the south bank of the Red River, nearly 18 miles. The Boards of Directors of these two companies, meeting in Wichita Falls during June 1969, gave their blessings to the proposal. Shortly thereafter, the Interstate Commerce Commission authorized the M-K-T to acquire all assets and franchises of the two former Kemp and Kell lines.[1]

The corporate structure of the M-K-T had undergone a considerably more significant alteration two years previously, when on August 24, 1967, Katy Industries was incorporated in Delaware. A holding company organized to acquire the common stock of the Missouri-Kansas-Texas Railroad, Katy Industries was also designed to provide for expansion and diversification into fields other than transportation. As a result of this diversification plan, in which the railroad company was the central ingredient, Katy's stock rose 153 percent in 1967. One observer attributed this dramatic rise to the faith which investors had in Katy President John W. Barriger. "He has a personal reputation as a surgeon of sick railroads and is one of the dominant intellectual influences of American railroading in the twentieth century," said another. These investors naturally hoped that Katy's reorganization and diversification plan would change it from a weak company into a profitable one.[2]

In 1970, John Barriger left the M-K-T. He was 70 years of age, five years older than Katy's retirement policy usually allowed. His efforts had revived the nearly moribund railroad, and its public image had been renewed. Barriger richly deserved the accolades which he received when he left the Katy after five difficult but nevertheless rewarding years as its chief executive. He was succeeded by Reginald N. Whitman, a former Federal Railroad Administrator for the Department of Transportation and a man who additionally had long service in the operating departments of both the Great Northern and the Alaska Railroad. Whitman's appointment naturally added fuel to merger speculations which involved one of his former employers, the Great Northern, now a part of the Burlington Northern. However, merger talks with the BN ended in 1970, although they were terminated with the assumption that they would be resumed in the future.[3]

President Whitman had the extremely happy task of announcing that, for the first time since 1963, Katy earned a modest profit in 1971. In that year, revenues rose by 6.9 percent, although

*Missouri-Kansas-Texas Railroad, *Annual Report, 1971*, p. 1

213

carloadings were down by 3.6 percent. Whitman cautioned that Katy yet faced grave difficulties, but assured stockholders that the road was building "on a firm base, since during the past five years many of the worst crises have been faced and mastered." The M-K-T, Whitman pointed out, was "no longer a Granger road, depending for its revenue almost entirely upon the wheat harvest." To be sure, Katy's traffic mix had changed markedly. In 1945, petroleum products contributed 23.72 percent of all traffic handled on the road, while wheat traffic amounted to 6.489 percent of the total. Twenty-one years later, wheat was number one both in terms of cars handled and percentage of earned revenue. In 1968, wheat still held first place as a revenue producer but had slipped to second place in terms of total cars handled. In the latter category, wheat dropped to sixth place in 1970 and to tenth place in 1971. This change in traffic mix implied that Katy could indeed afford to divest itself of the 330.99 miles of railroad in western Oklahoma which traditionally had constituted its premier grain-loading lines. Whitman said as much in 1972.[4]

Before permission to abandon most of the Northwestern District and all of the BM&E had been received, a number of reductions in service had been implemented on those lines. The last switch engine assignment on the entire Northwestern District was terminated on December 24, 1970, when the job at Altus was abolished. One year earlier, the telegraph lines between Wichita Falls and Forgan had been retired and removed. Thereafter all communications were conducted by way of a direct phone circuit leased from Southwestern Bell to link all stations with the Denison offices. Three of these stations, Gate, Burkburnett, and Camargo were closed between 1969 and 1971. The building at Burkburnett then was donated to the Burkburnett Study Club and that at Camargo similarly was rescued for posterity, but the Gate depot, although thoroughly vandalized, remained at its usual wind-swept location.[5]

Other reductions in service occurred in December 1970, when Katy established a new schedule of operations on the Northwestern. Using only two crews, it called for a single round trip between Wichita Falls and Forgan each week on the following basis:

By 1972, virtually all veteran station agents on the Northwestern District had retired. When C. H. Gardiner retired at Forgan, he was succeeded by Lloyd H. Freeman who formerly had been a clerk at Denison, Texas on Katy's main line. *Author's photograph*

Sunday—Wichita Falls to Altus
Monday—Altus to Elk City
Tuesday—Elk City to Altus
Wednesday—Altus to Wichita Falls

Crew Number Two

Tuesday—Elk City to Woodward
Wednesday—Woodward to Forgan
Thursday—Forgan to Woodward
Friday—Woodward to Elk City

Through tonnage was exchanged at Elk City. This arrangement was partially the result of an amendment to federal law which reduced from 16 to 14 the number of hours that crews could be worked between rest periods. It also reflected the continued erosion of business on the lines. For instance, Sheppard Air Force Base accounted for 194 cars in 1962 but only 94 cars in 1971.

Mangum shippers still forwarded cotton and drain pipe, and LPG plants at Hocker and Laverne generated a modicum of traffic. An ever-increasing flow of cement was unloaded by one firm on the M-K-T at Woodward, but these cars arrived there via the AT&SF. Unhappily, the milo traffic moving from the BM&E had nearly ended, and wheat had become the Northwestern's single major traffic commodity.[6]

During the 1950s and early 1960s, most of the Northwestern District's veteran employees retired. They had begun working for the railroad when it was opened for traffic or shortly thereafter. The next generation of employees, those who hired on during the 1920s, retired in the late 1960s or in the early 1970s. Many of these men were in station service; and in 1971, nearly every open depot on the line was manned by a veteran.

There was little to do at Vici in later years so the agent there, Earl G. Cramer, took up painting. *Author's photograph*

215

For the last time, on November 30, 1971 P. A. Johnston answered the telephone at Elk City with his traditional greeting—"Katy depot." *Author's photograph*

By 1973, however, all had retired. P. A. Johnston was representative. For the last time, on November 30, 1971, Johnston answered the telephone at the Elk City depot with his traditional greeting, "Katy Depot." In late years, there had been no "extra board," or reservoir of station employees, from which new men could be drawn to fill the remaining positions when vacated. Moreover, employees from other divisions hesitated to accept positions on the Northwestern when its future was in doubt. Thus Katy was forced to improvise in filling these assignments. When Walter W. Roan retired at Vici, a local rancher, Earl G. Cramer, was asked to become agent at that point. Cramer, who had worked at various stations on the M-K-T between 1946 and 1954, accepted the invitation and stayed until the line was abandoned in 1973. When C. H. Gardiner retired at Forgan, he was succeeded by Lloyd H.

Freeman who had been a clerk at Denison.[7]

Snow frequently was a burden on the operation of the Northwestern and the BM&E. The blizzards of 1911, 1937, and 1957 were legendary, but that of February 21-22, 1971, was the worst of all. One day after that storm had passed, a twin-engine plow extra was dispatched from Elk City to clear the line, but was promptly derailed at Leedey; following additional frustrations, the train limped back to Elk City. After lengthy contemplation, Katy officials acknowledged that a snow plow would be necessary to open the road. Unfortunately, Katy owned no such equipment. The problem was finally solved when a make-shift rail-and-sheet-steel plow was welded to the frame of locomotive number 118. This home-made and self-propelled snow plow eventually broke through the drifts at Leedey on March 6. Two weeks later and nearly 30 days

Track scene between Gate and Knowles. Note the cattle guard—few remained anywhere on the line when this view was made in mid-1972. *Author's photograph*

The storm clouds in the background of these views were symbolic of diffcult days on the Northwestern. On August 24, 1972 extra 111 experienced three severe derailments between Forgan and Gate. *Author's photographs*

217

The footboards of locomotives 107 and 109 had been splintered by earlier derailments before the train reached Leedey, Oklahoma on the day after Thanksgivig ,1972
Author's photograph

after the storm, extra 118 reached Keyes—its broken headlight, shattered number plates, and bent hand-rails bearing testimony to earlier but victorious battles with snow-packed cuts.[8]

Another problem in removing snow after the 1971 blizzard was the condition of the track. In years gone by, engineers did not fear making high-speed runs at snow-filled cuts because they had confidence in the track. By 1971, this was hardly the case. In the spring of that year, after the snow had entirely melted, it was possible to stand on the main street crossing at Willow, look in either direction down the track, and not see a single tie. At that location, and nearly everywhere on both the Northwestern and on the BM&E, dirt and matted weeds stretched from the ball of one rail to the ball of the other. Actually it was this impacted condition, rather than ties and spikes, which held much of the track together. All went well if train speeds were low and if trains did not operate immediately after the roadbed had been soaked with moisture.

Oklahoma's 1972 wheat crop surprised the experts and resulted in a 1.54 billion bushel harvest valued at a record $3.4 billion. The vast majority of it, 85 percent, graded number one, and as always, most of it was exported. In May and June, long strings of empty box cars were moved north from Wichita Falls and spotted for loading at the country elevators. In June and July, the process was reversed—loaded cars were moved south. For a couple of weeks, operations on the Northwestern were reminiscent of the "old days." On June 13, there were 23 loads of wheat at Woodward awaiting movement. Two weeks later, there were 118 loads at that point, 53 loads at Fort Supply, and 9 loads at Sharon—all awaiting southbound handling. At Vici, the 530,000-bushel concrete barrel elevator was nearly full and loading every empty car that Katy could supply. It was the same at every other station as the harvest peaked. For several days, two trains leapfrogged tonnage from long sidings at Fort Supply, Woodward, and Leedey, where cars from other

218

trains had been reduced due to heavy southbound grades. Then, after the accumulated tonnage all had been moved, the Northwestern returned to its usual routine of one train each way per week.[9]

On the BM&E, wheat was almost the only commodity shipped in 1972. Except for one car of fertilizer from Straight and 21 cars of milo shipped from Mouser and Eva, all outbound business consisted of wheat. However, it contributed a not inconsiderable 740 carloadings for 1972; Floris and Hough were the leading wheat-loading stations. There were only 32 inbound loads to BM&E stations during the year. Of these, 13 were fertilizer and 11 were lumber. Beaver was the most important station for inbound shipments, receiving 14 carloads. At most stations on the Beaver Road, revenues for 1972 were less than those of 1971. For example, cars handled to and from Hooker and its allied stations (Baker, Mouser, Straight, Hough, and Muncy) totaled only 244 in 1972 as compared to 431 a year earlier.[10]

To handle all this traffic in 1972, it was necessary to call the BM&E crew only 60 times. Some of these calls represented no more than a Forgan-Beaver turn, but the train went as far as Hooker on 48 occasions. However, it was necessary to send the crew as far as the end-of-track at Keyes only seven times; five of these trips were made in July and August. Prior to this, it had appeared that the road would be abandoned at the end of June; as most of this traffic was handled on the eastern end of the line, little maintenance was performed west of Hooker and none at all beyond Hough. Furthermore, crop failures had been forecast, and thus no business was anticipated. As a result, weeds grew hip-high along the track east of Straight and equally as high between the rails west of that point. Before the coming of diesel power, enterprising BM&E employees had devised a way of using live steam from locomotives to kill bothersome weeds along the right-of-way. Chemicals and oil solutions were later sprayed to accomplish the same task. That form of maintenance was abandoned after 1970, and then weeds took command of the road. When a train was ordered to deliver 10 empty grain boxes for loading at Eva in June, 1972, it had a severe battle with the weeds and succeeded in reaching that station only by "doubling the hills" and by waiting while section men scooped sand on the rails to counteract the slipperiness caused by weeds crushed between the locomotive's drive wheels and the rails.[11]

Beginning in late summer of 1972 and continuing for several months, the area from Al-

During the summer of 1972, for several days at least, two trains leapfrogged heavy tonnage in wheat from sidings at Fort Supply, Woodward, and Leedey. The prints on these two pages show extra 107 returning from Leedey to Woodward for another train of wheat on June 30. The bulkhead flat, incidentally, was a part of every train on the Northwestern District in those times; it carried spare ties, rails, and angle bars. Derailments obviously were expected. *Author's photographs*

tus to Keyes received unusually frequent and heavy rains. The upshot was that the entire operation between those two points fell apart. On August 24, extra 111-96 left Forgan with 49 loads and 3 empties, 4,109 tons; but a few miles east of town, the train stalled while attempting to negotiate a lengthy hill. Engineers ordinarily made "a run" for the hill, but on that day, the track was so soft that such an attempt was impossible. Moreover, the locomotive's wheels crushed weeds which covered the tracks and this made the rails slippery. In sum, traction was at a premium. Thus the crew was forced to "double the hill," proceeding toward Mocane with only one-half of the train. A few miles later, a rail turned over under the heavy load and several cars were badly derailed. Since there was additional tonnage to

move at Gate and Laverne, the crew decided to take the four cars behind the engines which had not derailed and proceed. Less than one-half mile beyond that derailment, these last four cars also jumped the track. With their entire train stalled or derailed behind them, the crew boarded the diesels and headed east, but before reaching Gate, the hind unit derailed. It was the last straw; the crew gave up in desperation and returned to its terminal by automobile. This series of incidents involving only one train unhappily was merely a harbinger of things to come. On November 2, BM&E extra 109 left Forgan with a train of empties and went as far as Hooker. The following day, it took several of these cars to Mouser and Hough, but not until 14 days and several derailments later did that same train return with loads.

On June 2, 1972 the wheat rush on the BM&E clearly had not yet begun. Extra 107 is
shown here east of Baker. *Author's photograph*

Conductor Lester W. Barnett closes a switch at Hooker before boarding the caboose for
a long, dusty ride to Forgan. June 2, 1972. *Author's photograph*

In a few weeks the wheat in the foreground will be moved to market via the BM&E/Katy route. Turpin; June 2, 1972. *Author's photograph*

In years gone by Keyes had been an extremely important loading point on the BM&E. By 1972 that era had passed. *Author's photograph*

BM&E westbound extra 109 near Baker. November 2, 1972. *Author's photograph*

BM&E eastbound extra 107 at Hooker. June 2, 1972. *Author's photograph*

Midway, Oklahoma on the BM&E. *Author's photograph*

The stark quality of the Southern High Plains is evident here as extra 111 leaves Keyes. The time is 7:00 a.m.; the date, July 26, 1972. *Author's photograph*

BM&E trains like this one on July 26, 1972 would leave from Keyes only four more times before abandonment. *Author's photograph*

Since abandonment of the BM&E was anticipated prior to the wheat harvest of 1972, no weed control was practiced. Thus when extra 112 attempted to take empty cars to elevators west of Hooker on June 28, it was forced to chop its way through weeds that had grown pilot high. *Author's photograph*

Extra 112 rumbled out of Hovey Cut into the Goff Creek bottoms late in the afternoon of June 28. Note the shovel behind the grab-irons of the locomotive. In a few minutes extra 112 would stall in the deep weeds on the upgrade west of Goff Creek. That shovel and others would then be employed by section men who scooped sand onto the rails in an attempt to improve traction. It was a frustrating day for veteran BM&E employees who remembered the better conditions of yesteryear. *Author's photograph*

Then several additional derailments plagued the train on its trip east of Hooker. Amazingly, not until December 18 were all the cars which extra 109 had taken from Forgan on November 2 returned as loads to the M-K-T.[12]

Conditions did not improve. On the day after Thanksgiving, 1972, extra 107-109 slowly rumbled out of Leedey with about 50 cars of wheat from the Panhandle. It was a dark, damp, snowy day. The long train of red box cars was brushed with a coating of snow which did not blow off; the train simply did not move fast enough for that. Every flanged wheel had muddy

tires and the footboards of both locomotives were splintered from earlier angry derailments. South of Leedey, another such incident occurred, and it was several days before the train eventually reached its terminal. This road between Leedey and Hammon would cause continual bottlenecks until the last train had passed over it. Rain and snow continued, and one Katy spokesman grimly noted that "every time you call a train out there you have a derailment." He did not overstate the case. One train left Woodward three days before Christmas, but experienced four major derailments between there and Hammon. Meanwhile,

Section foreman Bill Furr and the BM&E train crew contemplated a means of getting the lead trucks of locomotive #109 back on the rails at milepost 51. November 3, 1972. *Author's photograph*

In the last days of the BM&E agony, it took two days to get a train from Forgan west to Hooker. After an all day ordeal extra 109 tied up at Hooker as the sun set on November 2, 1972. *Author's photograph*

228

When sand reserves on BM&E locomotives were depleted away from the Forgan terminal, it fell to the section men to resupply them. On June 29, 1972, they were forced to do that at Eva. *Author's photograph*

George Balch, manager of the Woodward Co-operative Elevator, a facility located on the M-K-T, complained that he had ordered 80 cars to move grain from his elevator, but Katy had not been able to provide them due to the several derailments north of Elk City. Other elevators were similarly distressed. Katy tried to service them but the track failed. On January 3, 1973, one train derailed at Leedey, and the next day another train derailed south of Elk City. On January 10, a Katy official announced that three separate derailments were blocking the line between Wichita Falls and Woodward. The road's total collapse, long forecast, had occurred. The I.C.C. had originally given Katy permission to abandon all of the BM&E and the Northwestern District above Altus, effective June 30, 1972. Later it had granted a 60-day extension; then the Katy itself postponed the abandonment until January 15, 1973. As they struggled to move traffic over the railroad in the winter of 1972-1973, Katy officials must have questioned those decisions.[13]

Before the Interstate Commerce Commission handed down its decision permitting abandonment of the Northwestern District north of Altus and the entire BM&E, worried residents of western

Even the crossing gate guarding the CRI&P at Baker had seen better days by the summer of 1972. *Author's photograph*

Hooker, June 28, 1972. *Author's photograph*

Hough, June 28, 1972. *Author's photograph*

230

Oklahoma had begun to consider means by which rail service over these lines could be continued. Some considered that Katy had misrepresented its financial condition and therefore assumed that the regulatory agency would reprimand the railroad and demand that adequate service be maintained. Others better understood Katy's economic embarrassment and were not surprised when the I.C.C. permitted abandonment. One of these, Charles G. Huddleston, an Enid lawyer, had forcefully represented the Oklahoma Farm Bureau and other interests during all the legal proceedings. He had labored especially in defense of the wheat farmers who he said would lose $1 million per year if the lines were scrapped. Huddleston felt that the hearing examiner was fair and,

In July, 1972 the BM&E right-ofway east of Eva looked like this. *Author's photograph*

Midway, June 28, 1972. *Author's photograph*

231

On July 26, 1972 BM&E extra 111 grew in length as loaded cars of wheat were added at nearly every elevator. Top, Muncy; bottom, east of Hovey; right, Mouser. *Author's photographs*

although disappointed, fully anticipated the Commission's judgment. While he appealed the decision, Huddleston concomitantly labored for an alternate means of saving the railroad. As early as November 1970, he convinced the Oklahoma Farm Bureau to take a strong stand for retention of the lines. Then, with the backing of the Farm Bureau, he began the process of drafting a plan designed to save the trackage—a plan which he hoped would be considered by the next session of the Oklahoma legislature. The proposal was drawn narrowly to apply only to the lines in question, and fashioned from previous legislation which had created toll roads under the Oklahoma Turnpike Authority.[14]

Huddleston met with western Oklahoma legislators soon after the 1971 session began. Within this group, there was bipartisan support for his proposal. Subsequently, on March 29, 1971, Representative Jack M. Harrison (D-May) introduced House Bill 1483, "An Act Relating to the Oklahoma Railroad Maintenance Authority." Within a few days, the bill emerged from the House Commerce Committee with a "do-pass" endorsement; the full body of the House concurred on April 6 with a vote of 96-0. The Senate followed suit on June 4 and the bill was signed into law by the governor on June 19, 1971. In early 1972, the Oklahoma Supreme Court determined that the bill met constitutional requirements.[15]

The Oklahoma Railroad Maintenance Authority (ORMA) was empowered to acquire, maintain, and operate the Katy lines from the Oklahoma-Texas line near Devol to the end-of-track at Keyes. Included was the railroad from the Red River to Altus, not a part of the 1969 abandonment application, but a piece of track which some thought the Katy would be pleased to sell. Management of the Authority was vested in a board of five members to be appointed by the governor, but subject to confirmation by the Senate. The ORMA was authorized to accept state or federal grants and contributions from any source. However, the Authority was not funded through the legislation which created it.[16]

There were no votes cast against the bill creating the ORMA in either house of the Oklahoma legislature. Nevertheless, the bill encountered heavy opposition. Forces from the Tulsa vicinity did not favor retention of this particular railroad, for its traffic tended to originate or terminate in Texas commercial centers or at Gulf ports. These elements hoped that wheat especially could be diverted from the Panhandle and western Oklahoma to the new Kerr-McClelland Arkansas River Waterway at nearby Catoosa. Motor carriers, too, opposed the creation of the ORMA, for abandonment of the railroad would encourage greater truck traffic. Teachers feared that the loss of ad valorem taxes would damage the economic viability of affected school districts, but this

Members of the Oklahoma Railroad Maintenance Authority. Left to right: James McManus, Brandon Frost, Governor David Hall, Julius W. Cox, Roy L. Craig, and R. L. Patton. *Julius W. Cox collection*

As the ORMA labored to save the Katy lines in western Oklahoma, trains like this one at Laverne in August, 1972 continued to move tonnage. *Author's photograph*

problem was resolved by including a section in the legislation which provided for "payments in lieu of taxes." Finally, the majority leader of the Oklahoma Senate did not favor the plan. However, the bill did not call for the expenditure of any state funds. This fact, more than any other, predisposed legislators from all sections of the state to vote for a measure that favored only the agricultural and commercial interests of a thinly populated rural area. Thus the proponents of the measure eventually prevailed.[17]

In October 1971, Governor David Hall announced his appointments to the ORMA. Julius W. Cox, a former member of the legislature and former highway commissioner from Boise City was named Chairman. Roy L. Craig of Leedey was chosen as Vice Chairman, while James McManus of Frederick was named Secretary-Treasurer. Other members included Brandon Frost from Woodward and R. L. Patton of Mangum. All were active members in the Democratic Party, and all were businessmen or farmers. Each member represented a particular geographic portion of the line which the ORMA hoped to acquire. The appointees uniformly considered it a civic duty to further the interests of western Oklahoma and the Panhandle, and each saw the Oklahoma Railroad Maintenance Authority as a means of doing this. At their first meeting, members of the Authority appointed the energetic Charles G. Huddleston, an active Republican, as

General Counsel. Another man well known within his profession, H. E. Bailey, was appointed Chief Engineer. Members of the Authority, the General Counsel, and the Chief Engineer all served without remuneration, although certain expenses were paid.[18]

On April 5, 1972, the I.C.C. extended the abandonment date from June 30 to August 30. This allowed the ORMA additional time to seek funding for the acquisition of the lines. At a meeting in Woodward on May 12, Julius Cox and the members of the Authority discussed with interested farmers, businessmen, and local governmental officials the idea of obtaining sufficient pledges to warrant the issuance of revenue bonds. It was hoped that $1 million could be raised in pledges, for they believed that this amount would be sufficient to purchase the track, right-of-way, and facilities from Katy and still leave a small surplus. Cox argued that it was imperative to acquire the property at the earliest possible moment; then the ORMA could work to obtain federal funds to upgrade the trackage to acceptable operating standards. Most participants, however, contended that they could not make pledges before seeing a report on the feasibility of retaining rail service. Late in June, the ORMA released a "Preliminary Feasibility Report," an evaluation written by an outside agency. The authors of this study concluded that there was "a short and long term need for the rail service provided by the MKT lines,"

Northbound extra 112 had a short train of mixed freight on this day in July, 1972. South of Leedey. *Author's photograph*

The Katy line passed through picturesque rolling country between Leedey and Trail.
Author's photographs

and that a short line railroad operation over this trackage could become a profit-making venture.[19]

Armed with hearty optimism and the new feasibility report, members of the ORMA journeyed to Washington, where they met with the entire Oklahoma Congressional delegation and where they hoped to secure a $4 million loan and a grant which could be used to repair and upgrade the M-K-T lines. The Authority members advised the Oklahoma Congressional delegation that the Katy railroad was as important to western Oklahoma as the Arkansas River Navigation Project was to the eastern part of the state. The argument was convincing; the Oklahoma delegation told the Authority members that it was solidly committed to doing all within its power to bring about federal assistance. To this end, Senator Henry Bellmon (R-Oklahoma) introduced a bill entitled the Rural Railroad Assistance Act of 1972, under which the Department of Transportation (DOT) would have been permitted to make loans and loan guarantees to state and local public bodies for the establishment or re-establishment of rail service in rural areas. The measure eventually passed the Senate but died for lack of action in the House.[20]

As the August 30 deadline approached, the ORMA still did not have the money necessary to purchase the Katy lines, but it continued to explore new possibilities. Then the railroad, still moving the large 1972 wheat crop, consented to postpone its abandonment until January 15, 1973. Meanwhile, Charles Huddleston was not optimistic but neither was he pessimistic. On the first day of September, he contended there was still "a good possibility" that the Katy properties could be purchased, and he revealed that the ORMA had "one very live prospect which would like to operate a short line operation on it." One month later a Texas industrial group met with the Authority and expressed an interest in purchasing or leasing the trackage.[21]

A new problem for the Authority developed when its members learned that the M-K-T wanted more money for the lines than had been expected. Katy contended that the salvage value had increased dramatically since the abandonment petition had been filed in 1969. Moreover, the company now had a purchase offer from a Missouri salvage firm which would pay the railroad considerably more than $700,000 and, additionally, would ship the scrap to market over the Katy — thereby giving the railroad another $300,000. Julius Cox estimated that the property could still be purchased by the ORMA for $1.2 million. He reminded legislators at an Elk City meeting that "once the railroad leaves it will never come back." The lawmakers were advised that it would take another $6.5 million to upgrade the line; but Brandon Frost, ORMA member, contended that "if we can acquire the road, we have the thing whipped." Frost predicted that general federal legislation soon would provide for the kinds of loans and guarantees needed by the Authority. Meanwhile, other members agreed the road could struggle along in the same fashion as had typified Katy operations. They noted that even if the road under the ORMA should fail, the scrap value would cover most of the original investment obligations. Chief Engineer H. E. Bailey opined that it "would be a black day for Oklahoma if we lose this railroad." Bailey predicted that heavy trucks would destroy between 300 and 400 miles of cheaply constructed asphalt highway every year if these railroad lines were dismantled and their traffic diverted to roadways. In short, said Bailey, "the highway damage would probably be three or four times greater than the cost of repairing the damage to the rail lines."[22]

Western Oklahoma legislators took the railroad problem to the governor in late November. They asked that the 1973 state budget include $1.2 million to purchase the Katy trackage and, following the suggestion given to the ORMA members by Senator Bellmon, argued that the funding should come from the $20 million expected under the federal revenue-sharing program. On-line newspapers counseled their readers to pressure the governor and the legislators for action on the railroad proposition. Even the *Wichita Falls* [Texas] *Times* hoped that "citizens in western Oklahoma who see the railroad as a lifeline to the wheat market will succeed in their nearly impossible task."[23]

Governor Hall was sympathetic with the desires of rural western Oklahomans to save the Katy lines, but advised that he felt the cities and counties through which the railroad passed should share approximately twenty percent of the total cost of purchasing the line. Hall agreed that the state might then make up the final eighty percent. On December 6, 1972, the governor was advised that municipal and county officials from the affected area had pledged $180,000 to

$200,000 from their anticipated federal revenue-sharing funds to buy the lines. ORMA's Vice-Chairman Roy Craig, then identified three separate firms which had discussed the possibility of operating the railroad on a lease from the Authority. At year's end, however, the Authority had no firm financial commitment from the governor.[24]

Late in 1972, legislators from western Oklahoma and members of the ORMA also explored the possibility of interesting the Oklahoma Highway Department in purchasing the railroad. The Highway Department expressed such an interest after learning that acquisition of the trackage would include 3,700 acres of deeded land and 1,400 acres of track easement. Highway officials indicated that some of the real estate might be desirable for roadway purposes if the rail line failed. This brought an angry blast from groups having a vested interest in roadway programs. Nevertheless, Senator Herschal Crow (D-Altus) introduced a bill which would have empowered the Highway Department to lend money to the ORMA for the purpose of purchasing the M-K-T lines in western Oklahoma. In response, Katy extended its deadline to January 19, but advised that there would be no further extensions.[25]

Julius Cox announced on January 13 that an operator of a short line railroad in one of the southern states had notified him that he would sign an agreement to operate the Katy lines and would invest a minimum of $3 million in repairs if the state would first acquire the trackage and lease it back. However, the legislation which would have allowed the use of Highway Department funds encountered severe opposition, and Senator Crow had to admit that the time factor and various pressures were unfavorable to his proposal. Senator Gene Stipe (D-McAlester), Chairman of the Senate Roads and Highways Committee and a resident of eastern Oklahoma, contended that the rail line should be purchased with revenue-sharing funds and not by way of a loan from the Highway Department. However, Governor Hall favored the use of a loan from the Highway Department. The legislative and executive branches were thus at loggerheads on January 19 when Dewey Enterprises of Bartlesville, Oklahoma, signed an option to purchase for salvage the trackage from Altus to Keyes.[26]

Meanwhile, BM&E trains had run their last

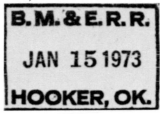

BM&E agency service at Hooker ended on January 15, 1973. *Author's collection*

miles. On New Year's Day, 1973, T. J. "Jim" Robb, Jr. opened the throttle of engine number 98 and the last westbound BM&E train left Forgan. In tow were five empty grain boxes which were delivered to the large Riffe-Gilmore elevator at Hough. Three days later, these cars plus five others had been loaded and were returned to Forgan. Appropriately, the BM&E's very last train operated over the road from Forgan to Beaver, its original trackage. On January 10, the crew—conductor L. W. Barnett, engineer T. J. Robb, Jr., and brakeman L. E. Smith—was called for this last run. Shortly after dawn they took an electrical transformer to Beaver. When engine 98 returned with its short train of two empty flat cars and ground to a halt in front of the Forgan depot at 12:35 p.m., railroad services on the Butter, Milk & Eggs ended forever.[27]

Elsewhere, several crews labored to clear the derailments between Altus and Woodward. At the same time agents were notified that the Northwestern District north of Altus was subject to an

The last westbound train on the BM&E left Forgan on New Year's Day, 1973. *Author's collection*

239

When extra 98 returned from Beaver with its short train of two empty flat cars and ground to a halt in front of the Forgan depot on January 10, 1973, service on the Butter, Milk & Eggs ended forever. *Author's photograph*

embargo effective January 15. The agents also were notified that their jobs would be abolished on that date. Then, on January 12 at 8:00 a.m., a clean-up train left Forgan without fanfare of any kind. It consisted of locomotive number 98, three empty flat cars and one box car which had been loaded with company equipment from Forgan; it arrived in Woodward ten hours later. The crew of this train—conductor Lorton E. Pierce, brakeman Adrian G. Adams, and engineer John B. Murphy, all of Altus—collectively represented more than 100 years service on the Northwestern District. The same crew eventually handled the clean-up train all the way to Wichita Falls.[28]

The final operations from Woodward were postponed, however, when it was discovered that there were three loads of feed at Elk City for consignees at May and Laverne. These cars were isolated due to derailments between Elk City and Woodward and thus were rerouted to Woodward via the CRI&P and the AT&SF. At the same time, the M-K-T implemented I.C.C. Service Order No. 80 which allowed it to divert all loads and all foreign equipment to connecting carriers. On January 13, no less than 29 loads and 40 empties were delivered to the AT&SF at Woodward; shortly after noon, these cars were wheeled out of town by a Santa Fe local. The feed was finally received on January 18 and peddled to the elevators at May and Laverne. Two days later, the empties were gathered and returned to Woodward. Several members of the Cimarron Valley Historical Society were allowed to ride the train on its trip from Laverne, but the Katy otherwise successfully eschewed publicity. Few residents knew of the train's final passing, although one farm woman took a picture as the train passed her home, and Wesley P. Altland, a retired Katy agent, sadly viewed its passage at Fort Supply.

240

The last train in Beaver County left Forgan on January 12, 1973. Here it is heading into the morning sun at Mocane. *Author's photograph*

Katy conductor Lorton O. Pierce signs the train register at Forgan for the last time. *Author's photograph*

Missouri-Kansas-Texas R. R. Co.

TRAIN ORDER No. 30   January 12 1973

To C+E Eng 98

At Forgan

Eng 98 run Extra Forgan to Woodward
This order is cancelled at 7:00 PM
                DWC

Made Com Time 7 34 a M Freeman Opr.

The last train order copied at Forgan.
Author's collection

Otherwise, the train went unnoticed.[29]

One day earlier, a southbound train reached Altus, and a northbound train reached Woodward. The line was cleared of derailments and ready for the clean-up train in charge of Trainmaster Albert Dowdy. All stations had been closed, and when the train left Woodward at 7:35 a.m. on January 24, it operated without train orders under Rule 93. After the train gathered company equipment at Sharon, Vici, and Camargo, it had grown to 16 cars. Aboard the train

or following it in automobiles and trucks were the Northwestern District's bridge and building gang, the rip-track gang from Wichita Falls, the Altus-based extra gang, an Assistant Roadmaster, and two section crews. At Leedey, a photograph was made of the entire group, and then the train rolled on. A few minutes later at milepost 167 near the Dewey-Custer County line, both locomotives and one box car were badly derailed. Twenty-four hours later the train was moving again; but on the next day, another derailment took place near Mangum. This one was minor in nature, and the train limped on toward Altus in

Forgan agent Lloyd H. Freeman hands orders to the crew of the last Katy train. Left to right: Freeman, brakeman A. G. Adams, conductor L. O. Pierce, and engineer John B. Murphy. *Author's photograph*

Katy conductor Pierce and BM&E engineer Robb say farewell prior to the departure of the last train from Forgan. *Author's photograph*

The last train from Forgan creeps slowly along a time worn track laid 61 years earlier by WF&NW engineers who sought the easiest grades through the hill country. *Author's photograph*

243

Members of the Cimarron Valley Historical Society, the author, and the train crew all posed for a photograph before the clean-up train left Laverne. *Lawrence Gibbs photograph*

Locomotive #98 at Laverne prior to the departure of the last train from that point. January 20, 1973. *Lawrence Gibbs photograph*

The clean-up train near historic Fort Supply. *Author's photograph*

Engineer John B. Murphy obligingly posed the train on the lengthy single-deck trestle over Wolf Creek east of Fort Supply. *Lawrence Gibbs photograph*

The last train from Laverne near Fort Supply. Above, *Author's photograph.* Below, *Lawrence Gibbs photograph*

Last train from Laverne after its arrival at Guest Yard, Woodward. January 20, 1973. *Author's photograph*

A long track going back. The receding right-of-way rolls up behind the caboose of the last train. Near May. *Lawrence Gibbs photograph*

Conductor L. O. Pierce signals "highball" and a few minutes later rail service at Camargo ended forever. January 24, 1973. *Author's photograph*

Clean-up train at Leedey. *Author's photograph*

View from locomotive #98, looking back along the clean-up train as it moved along between Trail and Leedey. *Author's photograph*

Get off the track! On the day after clean-up run—and thereafter—stray steers like this one could wander the Katy right-of-way without fear. *Author's photograph*

The train crew, section men, extra gangs, and others who accompanied the last train posed at Leedey for this group portrait. January 24, 1973. *Author's photograph*

Within minutes after the group portrait was made at Leedey, the clean-up train derailed at milepost 67. *Author's photograph*

After the last train had passed Mangum a phantom operator moved the depot's train order signal to the "stop" position—prohibiting movement of all but ghost trains in either direction on the Northwestern District above Altus. *Author's photograph*

the waning sun. The last miles were observed by a reporter for the *Altus Times-Democrat* and by television newsmen.[30]

At 6:30 p.m. on Friday, January 26, the beam from engine 98's headlight touched milepost 78 at Welon Yard on the northern outskirts of Altus. Engineer John Murphy closed the throttle, leaned back in his seat, and let the train drift to a stop. Murphy recalled that engine number 98 had handled the last M-K-T train on the Wellington Branch, the last BM&E train, and now the clean-up run all the way from Forgan to Altus. In that train were several box cars bearing

the inscription "Katy Serves the Southwest." After January 26, 1973, that promise was only a mocking reminder of a previous era on the 225.3-mile route of the Northwestern District from Altus to Forgan and on the entire 105-mile route of the BM&E.[31]

Denouement?

"We are trying to save an industry for western Oklahoma." Julius W. Cox, Chairman, Oklahoma Railroad Maintenance Authority, 1973.*

Immediately after the clean-up train arrived in Wichita Falls on January 27, 1973, the M-K-T abolished all train service on the Northwestern District while simultaneously re-establishing service between Wichita Falls and Altus. At the same time, the last switch engine assignment at Wichita Falls was terminated. All switching duties at Wichita Falls subsequently were assigned to the single remaining train crew, which also was assigned to man the Wichita Falls-Altus run.[1]

All employees on the Northwestern District were protected by the "Burlington Agreement" which was imposed by the Interstate Commerce Commission as a condition in granting the abandonment of the Northwestern north of Altus and the entirety of the BM&E. The "Burlington Agreement" provided for wage protection, moving expenses, and the reimbursement of any loss due to the sale of employee homes. The employees who remained in service on the Northwestern District between Wichita Falls and Altus after the abandonment, as well as those who elected to accept positions on other M-K-T operating divisions were also guaranteed wages for four years, equal to those which they had earned in 1972. Personnel who were displaced and did not elect to transfer were considered to have forfeited their rights of protection under the "Burlington Agreement."[2]

Before the abandonment of the Northwestern above Altus, there were eight men in two train crews; after the abandonment, five stayed to man the one remaining job between Wichita Falls and Altus, and the other three accepted positions on other divisions. Two members of the former Wichita Falls switch crew moved to other locations on the M-K-T, and two forfeited their rights. Of the six station agents formerly assigned between Altus and Forgan, two forfeited their rights, and the remaining four accepted other jobs. The Altus-based extra gang was retained at that point, but the Northwestern's bridge and building gang was reassigned at Denison, Texas. Of the 15 affected maintenance of way personnel, 11 initially took jobs elsewhere on the system, but some of these men subsequently left the company rather than move their families to new locations. On the BM&E, all three agents forfeited their rights, as did one member of its former three-man train crew; the BM&E's engineer and conductor both took jobs elsewhere on the Katy System.[3]

Even as the clean-up train was struggling to reach Altus, members of the Oklahoma Railroad Maintenance Authority, members of the Oklahoma legislature, and Governor David Hall were attempting to negotiate some type of agreement with Dewey Enterprises of Bartlesville, Oklahoma, by which the lines could be saved. Surprisingly, on January 29, Dewey Enterprises forfeited its earnest money and thereby defaulted on its option to purchase the lines. Shortly thereafter, however, the L. B. Foster Company of Houston took an option on the 330.99 miles of railroad and it exercised that option on February 8. The Foster Company, a major steel dealer and salvage contractor, paid Katy $1.7 million for the rail, fastenings, and buildings. Under the same con-

*Daily Oklahoman [Oklahoma City], January 16, 1973.

255

Northwestern Oklahoma Railroad

Woodward. Okla. 73801

F. W. Pollock, Jr.
President

P. O. Box 1131
Phone 256-7601

Frank W. Pollock, Jr. *Author's photograph*

tract the Foster Company likewise acquired all property belonging to the railroad between Altus and Keyes except for four minor tracts which had been sold earlier by the Katy to other parties. On the BM&E, a short stretch of track had been sold to the Stafford Elevator at Keyes so that it could obtain rail service from the nearby Santa Fe. At Baker, also on the BM&E, the Rock Island had purchased short trackage to serve the Riffe-Gilmore elevator at that point. The same company also had secured short pieces of industry and team tracks at Mangum on the Northwestern. At Woodward, substantially all of the yard tracks had been sold to a most unusual gentleman.[4]

Frank W. Pollock, Jr., had always wanted to have his own railroad. He satisfied that desire on January 24 by purchasing 3.3 miles of main track and 5 or 6 miles of sidings from the Katy at Woodward. Pollock boasted no prior experience as a railroad operator; previously he had been a manufacturers' representative and a sewing machine salesman. However, he shrewdly calculated that by performing switching duties for former Katy customers he could make a profit. Woodward, he knew, had been one of the few growth stations on the Northwestern District. In 1972, customers there had received a total of 763 carloads, up from 574 in 1971. Total revenues for 1972 had been $457,352, an increase of $27,544 over 1971. Pollock calculated that he would receive switching revenue on every car that he moved between on-line industries and the AT&SF transfer. Moreover, his local short line railroad also would receive line haul revenue on loads moving between the AT&SF transfer and Guest, the former Katy yard in North Woodward. This factor was crucial, as an important cement unloading facility was located at Guest. Thus Pollock formed the Northwestern Oklahoma Railroad on February 23, 1973, for the purpose of ". . . maintaining and operating a railroad for the transportation of freight and passengers . . ." in and around Woodward, Oklahoma, on the former Northwestern District of the M-K-T.[5]

At the same time, Julius W. Cox, Chairman of the Oklahoma Railroad Maintenance Authority continued to explore means by which the rest of the abandoned lines could be resurrected, but he was confronted by numerous difficulties. Cox found that the railroad which the ORMA hoped to acquire now was held not by only one party but rather by two. Actually, the Foster Company had an interest only in the rail and fastenings and, although not a part of the Foster-Katy contract, the land, ties, bridges, fixtures, buildings, and mineral rights all had been secured by Veldo H. Brewer of Holdenville, Oklahoma. Brewer, a respected contractor and civic leader, had dismantled other rail lines but never before had purchased the land and fixtures as he did in this instance. He anticipated, however, that there would be a market for the used ties, the land, the mineral rights, and even some of the buildings. Brewer expected to use the bridge timbers in future construction projects. He viewed the acquisition as a speculative opportunity, but he also saw it as something of a personal adventure. Yet if the ORMA found a way to fund the purchase of Brewer's new holdings, he indicated a willingness to sell. On February 12, he offered the right-of-way, bridges, and depot buildings—sans mineral rights—to the Authority for $500,000, and Cox declared "We're back on the track."[6]

The Chairman of the ORMA also announced that he had located a prospective operator of the Altus-Keyes line in Craig E. Burroughs, the energetic 31-year-old President of both Trans-Action Associates, a transportation management firm based in Joliet, Illinois, and the East Camden and Highland Railroad of Arkansas. Burroughs agreed to lease the line if the state could acquire it, and he proposed a revenue bond issue of between 6 and 12 million dollars to finance the reconstruction of the line. Brewer and the Foster Company gave the ORMA until March 30 to conclude a purchase agreement.[7]

On March 1, the Authority announced plans to mount an $8 million revenue bond sale. Cox stressed that the bond issue did not involve state funds. Rather, such bonds were to be retired from revenues produced by the operation of the railroad. Governor Hall, numerous legislators, and of course all ORMA members were enthusiastic, but there was scattered and powerful opposition in the legislature and elsewhere. One newspaper columnist was delighted when the property ultimately passed to the scrappers rather than to the state: "That averted another headache of the state being in the railroad business." M. L. Hart, a Hobart businessman, was a particularly vocal critic of state intervention in the rail line's abandonment and urged Governor Hall to dissolve the ORMA. Hart complained that the Authority was an "unnecessary expense of public

257

The long pile trestle over the South Canadian River near Camargo in August, 1973. The scrappers had begun their labors. *Author's photographs*

funds." Furthermore, said this critic, "if the Governor wants to enter the railroad business, I suggest he resign his office and get into it."[8]

In March and April, enthusiasm for the acquisition of the line waned as it appeared that the State of Oklahoma would give the project no financial assistance and no more than a modicum of moral support. On March 30, the offer to sell the property lapsed. Fifteen days earlier, the purchase agreement between the L. B. Foster Company and the M-K-T was formally consummated when the Northwestern District from Altus to Forgan was "100 percent retired and sold." The entire Beaver, Meade & Englewood Railroad Company was similarly stricken from Katy's books two weeks later. Even before that, Foster's crews had begun dismantling operations. The rails at Keyes, those which were the last laid by the BM&E in June, 1931, were the first to feel the cutting torch on March 21. Elsewhere Brewer's men began to dismantle the historic trestle over the South Canadian River near Camargo, and the Foster Company concluded a contract to export the rail from the line between Elk City and the South Canadian bridge.[9]

Craig Burroughs, however, remained opti-mistic. He produced another feasibility study which, like earlier ones, demonstrated that the operation of the route as a short line railroad would result in sufficient revenue to redeem the bonds. In due course, Burroughs also interested several investors in the project. On May 10, a writer for the *Daily Oklahoman* went so far as to state that the ORMA was on the verge of concluding a purchase agreement. A joint resolution empowering the ORMA to put up the railroad property as security for the bonds, passed earlier by both houses of the Oklahoma legislature and signed by the governor, was expected to provide the security which investors had long demanded. Unhappily for the Authority, however, the "eastern money men" failed to attend a special meeting held in the Blue Room of the Governor's office. The prospective bond buyers apparently were frightened by the drastically increased purchase price. In 1969, the M-K-T would have sold the entire property at its salvage value of $652,000. In early 1973, it sold the same property for approximately $1.75 million. By May, however, Brewer asked $750,000 for the right-of-way, buildings, and bridges alone, and the Foster Company demanded $2,544,000 for just the rail

By July, 1973 rails had been removed from the former BM&E track west of Hough.
Author's photograph

and fastenings. Foster and Brewer extended the sales offer once more to May 25 and then again to May 29, but neither Burroughs nor the ORMA could locate adequate funds to acquire the property—and the scrappers renewed their dismantling. By June 1, the rail had been removed as far east as Hovey on the BM&E, and another crew was working north of Elk City on the Northwestern.[10]

Elsewhere, elevator operators in the grain producing areas were experiencing great difficulty in obtaining rail cars to ship the remnants of the 1972 crop. Along the former Northwestern District above Altus and on the defunct BM&E the situation was considerably more critical. One grain dealer at Elk City complained, "We have no box cars, but not only that—we have no railroad . . .; trucks are rarely available."[11]

Then, when all hope of saving the line seemed to have vanished, a Georgia firm expressed a serious interest in purchasing revenue bonds from the ORMA. A hastily arranged meeting in Oklahoma City on June 12 brought together representatives of Seaney & Company of Atlanta, members of the ORMA, Craig Burroughs, Veldo Brewer, an official of the L. B. Foster Company, and various bonding advisors. As a result, the bond underwriters, Seaney & Company, agreed to purchase $6 million in ORMA revenue bonds at "up to 7½ percent interest." The Authority subsequently agreed to pay Brewer and the Foster Company a total of $3,319,000 for their interest in the line. After a short deliberation, they accepted the offer. Then the ORMA signed a 30-year contract with Craig Burroughs who agreed to operate the line for the state at an annual rate of $90,000. Burroughs announced that the new company—the Oklahoma Western Railway, the "Panhandle Route" —would have its headquarters at Woodward. The rapidity of these developments startled Julius Cox and the others who had labored so long to save the railroad. Yet Cox and the others did not delude themselves; they had been disappointed before.[12]

Their skepticism was warranted. On August 7, the underwriters for the bond issue, Seaney and Company, reluctantly advised the ORMA that in spite of a generous 15 percent discount rate, the bonds could not be sold due to the current unsettled and apparently deteriorating economic conditions. As Julius Cox later recalled:

"The bond market went all to hell." It was the last straw; Cox and the ORMA admitted defeat. Craig Burroughs likewise gave up; he had lost an estimated $50,000 of his own money in the attempt to resurrect the lines. State Representative Ernest Isch (R-Cheyenne) later tried to find some other means of regaining rail service north of Altus, but he too was unsuccessful.[13]

Julius Cox frequently defined the work of the Oklahoma Railroad Maintenance Authority. Said Cox, "We are trying to save an industry for western Oklahoma." But Cox and the ORMA had faced a constant struggle. There were several reasons for this. First, the efforts to save the railroad never had enjoyed the full support of western Oklahoma residents. The number of farmers, individual elevator operators, shippers, businessmen, and others who had a direct stake in the retention of this rail service was extremely small. Others, indirectly affected, did not clearly perceive the need for retaining this service. Second, the number of people in the affected area likewise was small; they had little "political clout." Residents of the Panhandle, for instance, argued with some validity that the only time the rest of the state acknowledged the existence of the area was at tax time. Third, the possible entry of the state into the railroad transportation business had excited the active opposition of certain groups which discerned in the ORMA a threat to their well-being. This was especially true of the highway and trucking interests. Fourth, legislators, administrators, and even affected shippers who earlier had supported the establishment of the ORMA blanched when it came to providing funds for the acquisition of the railroad. The Authority suffered from an overabundance of fair-weather friends. Fifth, "timing" had been against the ORMA. Julius Cox correctly understood this misfortune: "There is no question in my mind that during the next several years Congress will pass comprehensive legislation designed to save the railroads, but it will be too late for the Katy in western Oklahoma." Finally, and perhaps most important, the notion of the state government buying or operating a railroad as a necessary aspect of providing needed transportation service for its citizens proved to be a mind-boggling idea for those who otherwise voted government aid to highway, airway, and waterway projects with unflinching regularity. Nevertheless, the magnitude of this abandonment and the resulting efforts

Wheat was stored on the ground at Knowles in July, 1973 because there were not enough trucks. *Author's photograph*

After the abandonment of the BM&E, local artists used the former station board at Baker for their own playful purposes. *Author's photograph*

Results of abandonment: wheat piled high on the ground between the elevators at Floris on the BM&E. July, 1973. *Author's photograph*

made by legislators, shippers, agri-businessmen, and farmers to retain rail service for a rural area already poor in transportation devices had attracted regional as well as national attention.[14]

Meanwhile, farmers of western Oklahoma had harvested a bumper wheat crop in 1973 and were receiving record payments for it. During the early summer, long strings of red Katy box cars were spotted for loading at country elevators on the Northwestern between Wichita Falls and Altus and on the Hollis & Eastern from Altus to Hollis. Farther north, along the abandoned lines, wheat was piled high on the ground at Vici, Knowles, Floris and elsewhere as elevators filled to capacity. For the first time since wheat had been sown in the area, there was no railroad to transport it to market. Truckers were busy elsewhere with more lucrative hauls, and the 1973 harvest was only gradually moved out of the producing area by them. Nevertheless, for wheat farmers and for country elevators, it was an unusually profitable year: they could absorb the

Obituary of the Katy at milepost 191 south of Vici. October, 1973. *Author's photograph*

losses from storing wheat on the ground and they could absorb the higher truck rates. As a result, farmers and elevator operators will feel the loss of the railroad more in the future—in a season when the margin is not so large—than they did in 1973.[15]

Before July 1, 1974, scrappers had taken up the rail on the entire BM&E; their work on the Northwestern—nearly completed at that time— would be finished before fall. Other gangs at various locations were engaged in salvaging the reusable ties. Many miles of rail from these lines were exported to foreign countries, to Mexico in particular, while most of the reusable ties were sold to the Sante Fe.[16]

Physical changes of another type had occurred on the remaining Wichita Falls-Altus line. During the summer of 1973, a tornado severely damaged the depot at Frederick and a fire of unknown origin completely consumed the large station at Grandfield. It mattered little; Katy closed these stations and Altus as well when all were combined under a mobile agency arrangement on November 1, 1973.[17]

By 1974, the goals of Kemp and Kell had long since been met. Their railroad had earned them handsome profits and at the same time it had helped to make Wichita Falls the transportation and commercial center of north Texas. Its construction had given birth to new towns; it had served to promote the prosperity of its trade area by performing necessary transportation services; and it had created employment opportunities in a variety of fields. Furthermore, their WF&NW ultimately became an important and profitable feeder system for the new owner—the M-K-T.

The goals of the Beaver Road had been accomplished in like manner. Beaver City had been saved from an untimely demise by its construction, and the road had made significant profits for Jacob Achenbach and his associates. At the same time the BM&E provided the Panhandle with its only east-west rail service. It had effectively tied the area to the rest of Oklahoma and simultaneously provided the most direct route (via connections) to Fort Worth and the Gulf. Unhappily, the BM&E's arrival at Keyes in 1931 corresponded with the arrival in the Panhandle both of the depression and of the Dirty Thirties.

A tornado hit the Katy station at Frederick (above) during the summer of 1973. Agency service there and at Altus (below) was terminated at the end of October, 1973. *Author's photographs*

Frank Pollock purchased an ex-Sacramento Northern locomotive for his railroad at Woodward. July, 1973. *Author's photograph*

Throughout its history the BM&E alternately waxed and waned along with the people which it served. Between 1919 and 1972, the road earned profits in 25 seasons; in the remaining 29 years, it sustained losses. Observers in later years criticized former Katy Presidents Columbus Haile and M. H. Cahill for purchasing the Beaver Road, but they failed to understand the difficult position that confronted the Katy management at that time. In reality, it had no choice; loss of the BM&E traffic to the Rock Island clearly would have prejudiced the economic viability of the entire Northwestern District and ultimately of the Katy itself. As late as 1952, it should be recalled,

V. V. Masterson had characterized the Beaver Road as one of Katy's "valuable feeders."[18]

Nevertheless, only two decades later, in 1973, the BM&E was abandoned along with most of the Katy's Northwestern District. Then only the trackage between Wichita Falls and Altus remained under the Katy banner, and the future for even that remnant was uncertain. Yet an important new shipper, Pittsburgh Plate Glass, was located on the line between Wichita Falls and Burkburnett in the spring of 1973. This new plant reportedly promised to generate 4,500 new carloads of revenue for the line each year. For that matter, general business in Wichita Falls was

Pollock goes over the switch list with brakeman Otto Byrd. *Author's photograph*

The major traffic on the NWO is inbound cement. *Author's photograph*

Pollock also purchased considerable passenger equipment, much to the joy of area rail buffs who have been treated to periodic fan trips. This one, drawn by NWO's newly painted locomotive #1, occurred during July, 1974. *Lawrence Gibbs photograph*

Rebuilding the track between North Yard (Wichita Falls) and the new Pittsburgh Plate
Glass plant south of Burkburnett. July, 1973. *Author's photographs*

Veteran employees on the Northwestern District had reason to rejoice at the sight of track machines and ballast trains. *Author's photographs*

During the summer of 1974, Frank W. Pollock, Jr. made good on that portion of the Northwestern Oklahoma's corporate charter which permitted the transportation of passengers. *Lawrence Gibbs photograph*

up sharply in 1973 and 1974 over 1972. These factors plus an expanding carriage of grain, cement, cotton, and gypsum products on the Wichita Falls-Altus line resulted in the establishment of two round trips weekly on that route. At the same time, Katy happily found it necessary to add another crew to its Wichita Falls board. Long-time Katy employees at that point, employees who recalled the mixed blessings of the past, looked forward to the future with confidence. As evidence in support of their optimism they pointed to the recently raised and ballasted track between Wichita Falls and the new plant south of Burkburnett. They, as well as many others, speculated that the abandonment of the road above Altus eventually will prove to have been a monumental mistake—especially in view of an increasingly severe energy crisis. They hoped, perhaps vainly, that rails might again carry heavy trains along the ghost route between Altus and Keyes. Elsewhere, the Hollis & Eastern (current owner of the former Wellington Branch) and the Northwestern Oklahoma Railroad (current owner of the former Katy trackage at Woodward) both showed promising vitality. Thus there is no denouement for the surviving former Kemp and Kell lines, not in 1974 at least. The curtain has fallen on one act; another has begun.[19]

Endnotes

Farewell To Cow Country

[1]Jonnie R. Morgan, *The History of Wichita Falls* (Wichita Falls, Texas: Nortex Offset Publications, 1971, facsimile reprint of 1931 edition), pp. 29-30; Richard C. Overton, *Gulf to Rockies: The Heritage of the Fort Worth and Denver—Colorado and Southern Railways, 1861-1898* (Austin, Texas: University of Texas Press, 1953), p. 99.

[2]Ibid., pp. 31, 93, 96, 99.

[3]Frank W. Johnson, *A History of Texas and Texans.* Five volumes. Edited by Eugene C. Barker with the assistance of Ernest W. Winkler (Chicago: The American Historical Society, 1914), II, p. 811; Morgan, p. 30.

[4]Overton, pp. 97, 96, 108.

[5]Ibid., pp. 108, 120, 125, 129, 181.

Joseph A. Kemp The Energizer

[1]Frank W. Johnson, *A History of Texas and Texans.* Five volumes. Edited by Eugene C. Barker with the assistance of Ernest W. Winkler (Chicago: The American Historical Society, 1914), II, pp. 811-813; S. G. Reed, *A History of the Texas Railroads and of Transportation Conditions Under Spain and Mexico and the Republic and The State* (Houston: The St. Clair Publishing Co., 1941), p. 390.

[2]Richard C. Overton, Gulf to Rockies: The Heritage of the *Fort Worth and Denver—Colorado and Southern Railways, 1861-1898* (Austin: University of Texas Press, 1953), p. 345; Reed, p. 542; Jonnie R. Morgan, *The History of Wichita Falls* (Wichita Falls, Texas: Nortex Offset Publications, 1971, facsimile reprint of 1931 edition), p. 67; Johnson, IV, p. 1964.

[3]Morgan, pp. 53-55; *The National Cyclopedia of American Biography.* 52 volumes (New York: James T. White and Co., 1941), XXIX, pp. 467-468; Johnson, IV, pp. 1964-1966; *Wichita Falls Daily Times,* March 6, 1960; *Wichita Falls Record-News,* November 17, 1930.

[4]Reed, p. 390; V. V. Masterson, *The Katy Railroad and the Last Frontier* (Norman: University of Oklahoma Press, 1952), p. 263.

[5]Reed, p. 390; Morgan, p. 67; Masterson, p. 263.

[6]Overton, p. 336; Reed, p. 384; Overton, p. 340.

[7]Masterson, p. 264; Reed, p. 390; Memorandum written by K. L. Fleming, Manager of Bond Department, Knaught, Nachod & Kuhne, New York, 1915.**

Enter Frank Kell

[1]F. Hol Wagner, Jr., *The Colorado Road: History, Motive Power and Equipment of the Colorado and Southern and Fort Worth and Denver Railways* (Denver: Intermountain Chapter, National Railway Historical Society, 1970), pp. 193, 21; Richard C. Overton, *Burlington Route: A History of the Burlington Lines* (New York: Alfred A. Knopf, 1965), p. 273.

**WF&NW File, Baker Library, Harvard University.

[2]Frank W. Johnson, *A History of Texas and Texans.* Five volumes. Edited by Eugene C. Barker with the assistance of Ernest W. Winkler (Chicago: The American Historical Society, 1914), II, pp. 811-813.

[3]Ibid.; *Wichita Falls Daily Times,* May 12, 1957; Tom Truly, "Frank Kell, Top West Texan," *West Texas Today* (January 1936), pp. 18, 289; Jonnie R. Morgan, *The History of Wichita Falls* (Wichita Falls, Texas: Nortex Offset Publications, 1971, facsimile reprint of 1931 edition), p. 70; *Wichita Falls Times,* May 12, 1957.

[4]Truly, p. 18; Frank Kell, November 11, 1906, to Martin A. Knapp, Chairman of the Interstate Commerce Commission, Files of the Operating Division, I.C.C., 1887-1906 (No. 106119), National Archives; Martin A. Knapp, December 31, 1906, to Frank Kell, with enclosed memorandum, Files of the Operating Division, I.C.C., 1887-1906 (No. 106119), National Archives.

[5]L. J. Storey, Member of the Railroad Commission of Texas, April 29, 1902, to the Interstate Commerce Commission, Files of the Operating Division, I.C.C., 1887-1906 (No. 58271), National Archives; Ira G. Clark, *Then Came the Railroads: The Century from Steam to Diesel in the Southwest* (Norman: University of Oklahoma Press, 1958), p. 249.

The Kemp and Kell Roads

[1]S. G. Reed, *A History of the Texas Railroads and of Transportation Conditions Under Spain and Mexico and the Republic and the State* (Houston: The St. Clair Publishing Co., 1941), p. 390; V. V. Masterson, *The Katy Railroad and the Last Frontier* (Norman Oklahoma University Press, 1952), p. 263; Jonnie R. Morgan, *The History of Wichita Falls* (Wichita Falls, Texas: Nortex Offset Publications, 1971, facsmile reprint of 1931 edition), p. 67.

[2]Reed, p. 542; *MK&T Lines Corporate History,* n.p., n.d., pp. 43-44, 82; U.S., Interstate Commerce Commission, *Valuation Reports,* Volume 34, (Washington D.C.: Government Printing Office, 1931), p. 599.

[3]Memorandum written by K. L. Fleming, Manager of the Bond Department, Knaught, Nachod & Kuhne, New York, 1915 **; *Wichita Falls Daily Times,* June 15, 1947.

[4]Morgan, pp. 37-38; Clyde L. Jackson and Grace Jackson, *Quanah Parker, Last Chief of the Comanches: A Study in Southwestern Frontier History* (New York: Exposition Press, 1963), p. 145.

[5]Minnie King Benton, *Boomtown: A Portrait of Burkburnett* (Quanah, Texas: Nortex Offset Publications, 1972), p. 38; J. W. Williams, *The Big Ranch Country* (Wichita Falls, Texas: Terry Brothers Printers, 1954), pp. 144, 198, 203.

[6]*Wichita Falls Daily Times,* June 19, 1932; Benton, pp. 6, 39.

[7]Williams, p. 203; Benton, pp. 5, 30.

[8]Benton, p. 31; *Wichita Falls Daily Times,* June 15, 1947.

[9]Benton, p. 6; *MK&T Lines Corporate History,* p. 82; *Poor's Manual of the Railroads of the United States,* 1907, p. 1730, referred to hereafter as *Poor's Manual.*

[10]*Wichita Falls Times,* June 13, 1967; Louis J. Wortham, *History of Texas From Wilderness to Commonwealth.* Five volumes (Fort Worth: Wortham-Molyneaux Co., 1924), IV, pp. 249-251.

[11]*Wichita Falls Daily Times,* June 1, 1907, June 7, 1907; Benton, pp. 7, 39; *Burkburnett* [Texas] *6666 Star,* September 11, 1907.

[12]Reed, p. 391; Morgan, p. 67; *Wichita Falls Daily Times,* December 10, 1907.

[13]I.C.C., *Valuation Reports,* Volume 34, pp. 494, 562, 559-560.

[14]Benton, p. 7.

[15]*Poor's Manual,* 1907, p. 1730; ibid., 1908, p. 631.

[16]Wortham, IV, pp. 294-296.

[17]J. A. Kemp, October 5, 1906, to Commissioner of Indian Affairs, Records of

---

** WF&NW File, Baker Library, Harvard University.

the Bureau of Indian Affairs, Letters Received, 1881-1907 (88598-1906), National Archives, hereafter referred to as BIA, Letters Received; U.S. Department of the Interior, *Report of the Commissioner of Indian Affairs for the Year Ending 30 June 1903*. Two Parts (Washington: Government Printing Office, 1904), I, pp. 67-75; ibid., 1904, I, pp. 91-92.

[18]C. P. Larabee, Acting Commissioner of Indian Affairs, July 24, 1907, to the Secretary of the Interior, BIA, Letters Received (63336-1907).

[19]John Embry, U.S. Attorney at Guthrie, June 24, 1927, to J. P. Blackmon, Kiowa Agent, BIA, Letters Received (59236-1907); J. P. Blackmon, Kiowa Agent, June 24, 1907, to Commissioner of Indian Affairs, BIA, Letters Received (59236-1907; Acting Commissioner of Indian Affairs, July 8, 1907, to J. P. Blackmon, BIA, Letters Received (60910-1907); Phillip Taylor, July 9, 1907, to the President, BIA, Letters Received (63336-1907).

[20]J. P. Blackmon, Kiowa Agent, July 10, 1907, to Commissioner of Indian Affairs, BIA, Letters Received (62368-1907); John Embry, U.S. Attorney at Guthrie, June 24, 1907, to J. P. Blackmon, Kiowa Agent, BIA, Letters Received (59236-1907).

[21]J. P. Blackmon, Kiowa Agent, July 17, 1907, to Commissioner of Indian Affairs, BIA, Letters Received (63842-1907); John Embry, U.S. Attorney at Guthrie, July 23, 1907, to the Attorney General, BIA, Letters Received (64482-1907); J. P. Blackmon, Kiowa Agent, July 23, 1907, to Commissioner of Indian Affairs, BIA, Letters Received (65449-1907); *Wichita Falls Daily Times*, August 17, 1907.

[22]An undated and uncredited clipping in the "Mr. and Mrs. Frank Kell File," *Wichita Falls Times* Library, Wichita Falls, Texas; Jackson and Jackson, p. 146; Benton, p. 34; J. P. Blackmon, Kiowa Agent, November 28, 1908, to Commissioner of Indian Affairs, BIA, Letters Received (83374-07-305); *The Official Guide of the Railways* (September 1907), p. 917; ibid., (January 1908), p. 903; ibid., (December 1908), p. 860; George Shirk, *Oklahoma Place Names* (Norman: Oklahoma University Press, 1965), p. 74.

[23]*Wichita Falls Daily Times*, May 17, 1907, May 27, 1907.

[24]*Poor's Manual*, 1908, p. 631; *Wichita Falls Daily Times*, November 16, 1907.

Truly Northwestern

[1]*The Official Railway Equipment Register*, Vol. XXIV (June 1908), p. 434.

[2]C. P. Parks, former WF&NW and M-K-T conductor, Altus, Oklahoma, personal interview with the author, November 17, 1972; V. V. Masterson, *The Katy Railroad and the Last Frontier* (Norman: University of Oklahoma Press, 1952), p. 279.

[3]*Wichita Falls & Northwestern Railway, Trust Deed to the First Trust and Savings Bank, Trustees. Securing $2,300,000 First Mortgage Five Per Cent Gold Bonds dated 1 January 1909*, p. 1**; U.S. Interstate Commerce Commission, *Valuation Reports*, Volume 34 (Washington, D.C.: Government Printing Office, 1931), pp. 658-659; *Poor's Manual of the Railroads of the United States*, 1914, p. 1301, referred to hereafter as *Poor's Manual*.

[4]Ibid., 1911, p. 1194; Preston George and Sylvan R. Wood, "The Railroads of Oklahoma," *Bulletin No. 60*, Railway and Locomotive Historical Society (1943), pp. 69, 38.

[5]Ibid., p. 43; O. P. Sturm, "Review of the Past Year's Development," *Sturm's Oklahoma Magazine*, Vol. IX (January 1910), p. 31.

[6]Walter G. McComas, "Altus, A Growing City of Western Oklahoma," *Sturm's Oklahoma Magazine*, Vol. VI (July 1908), pp. 81-82.

[7]Altus, Roswell & El Paso Railway Company, incorporation papers (file number 1116).***

[8]Altus, Wichita Falls & Hollis Railway Company of Oklahoma, incorporation papers file number 5560).***

[9]S. G. Reed, *A History of the Texas Railroads and of Transportation Conditions under Spain and Mexico and the Republic and the State* (Houston: The St. Clair Publishing Co., 1941), p. 542.

[10]*Indenture of Trust, Wichita Falls & Northwestern Railway Company to First Trust and Savings Bank and Emile K. Boisot, Trustees.* Securing $900,000 First Lien Collateral Trust Five Percent Bonds, January 1, 1910, p. 1**; U.S. Interstate Commerce Commission, *Valuation Reports,* Volume 34 (Washington, D.C.: Government Printing Office, 1931), pp. 571, 665-666, 659.

[11]George H. Shirk, *Oklahoma Place Names* (Norman: University of Oklahoma Press, 1965), p. 67; *Duke, Oklahoma: The Newest City in the Newest State* (Altus, Oklahoma: n.p., n.d.), pp. 7-8; Eugene Thomas, "Cities Worth Knowing, No. Thirty-One: Duke, Oklahoma," *The Consolidator,* Vol. 5 (July 1950), pp. 4, 26.

[12]I.C.C., *Valuation Reports,* Volume 34 (Washington, D.C.: 1931), p. 497.

[13]Wichita Falls & Northwestern Railway. *Annual Report,* 1910, p. 1; *MK&T Lines Corporate History,* n.p., n.d., p. 43; C. P. Parks, interview, November 17, 1972.

To the Panhandle—And Beyond?

[1]George H. Shirk, *Oklahoma Place Names* (Norman: University of Oklahoma Press, 1965), pp. 22, 39, 116; Byron Clancy, "History of Carter, Oklahoma," *Prairie Lore,* Vol. 5 (October 1968), p. 76; Wichita Falls & Northwestern Railway, *Annual Report,* 1910, p. 1.**

[2]Preston George and Sylvan R. Wood, "The Railroads of Oklahoma," *Bulletin No. 60,* Railway & Locomotive Historical Society (1943), p. 43; Francis Elgin Herring, 1860-1938 (obituary), *The Chronicles of Oklahoma,* Vol. XVI (December 1938), p. 507; Walter G. McComas, "Elk City, Leading Market of Western Oklahoma," *Sturm's Oklahoma Magazine,* Vol. VI (April 1908), p. 83.

[3]*Poor's Manual of the Railroads of the United States,* 1911, p. 1195, referred to hereafter as *Poor's Manual;* Nat M. Taylor, *A Brief History of Roger Mills County,* privately printed, n.d., pp. 7-8; Mrs. E. B. Savage, pioneer resident of Hammon, Oklahoma, personal interview with the author, November 15, 1972; *Poor's Manual,* 1912, p. 1257.

[4]Taylor, p. 7; Oklahoma & Northwestern Rail Road Company, incorporation papers (file number 5295A) ***; Taylor, p. 7; Beaver Valley & North Western Railroad Company, incorporation papers (file number 9576A) ***; Oklahoma Northwestern Railway Company, incorporation papers (file number 8960). ***

[5]J. A. Kemp, October 1, 1910, to the National City Bank of Chicago. **

[6]George and Wood, p. 38.

[7]Wichita Falls & Northwestern Railway Company, incorporation papers (file number 8084A, also files 8727 and 9667) ***; George and Wood, p. 15.

[8]*First and Refunding Mortgage, The Wichita Falls & Northwestern Railway Company to United States Mortgage & Trust Company* [of New York] *and Calvert Brewer, Trustees,* August 29, 1911, pp. 2, 12, 25-26, 29-33, 120 **; *Poor's Manual,* 1914, p. 1301; ibid., 1912, p. 1258; ibid., 1913, p. 1078.

[9]U.S. Interstate Commerce Commission, *Valuation Reports,* Volume 34 (Washington, D.C.: Government Printing Office, 1931), pp. 658-659.

[10]George and Wood, p. 15; *A History of Beaver County,* Two Volumes (Beaver, Oklahoma: Beaver County Historical Society, 1971), II, p. 128.

[11]Sue Hocker Ward, resident of Camargo, Oklahoma, personal interview with the author, November 14, 1972; Shirk, p. 35; Camargo Townsite Ledger, First State Bank, Camargo, Oklahoma, p. 17; Abstract of Title Number 1081, Dewey County, Oklahoma, First State Bank, Camargo, Oklahoma.

[12]M. H. Farris, resident of Elk City, Oklahoma, personal interview with the author,

---

**WF&NW File, Baker Library, Harvard University.

***Oklahoma Secretary of State's office, Oklahoma City.

November 16, 1972; John Leonard, resident of Camargo, Oklahoma, personal interview with the author, November 14, 1972; George T. Wheritt, former farmer of Camargo, Oklahoma, personal interview with the author, November 14, 1972.

[13]Shirk, p. 208; L. C. Rodgers, former WF&NW and M-K-T locomotive engineer, Wichita Falls, Texas, January 22, 1973, and March 8, 1973, to the author.

[14]A History of Beaver County, II, pp. 88-89, 128; Walter P. Smith, resident of Laverne, Oklahoma, September 6, 1972 to the author; Mrs. Anna S. Connet, pioneer resident of Laverne, Oklahoma, September 2, 1972 and November 8, 1972, to the author.

[15]George T. Wherritt, interview, November 14, 1972; Walter R. Smith, September 6, 1972, to the author; Mrs. E. B. Savage, interview, November 15, 1972; Mrs Anna S. Connet, November 8, 1972, to the author.

[16]Mrs. Gertie Balfour, February 14, 1911, to Mrs. Nancy Jane Balfour, a letter held by Mrs. Pearl Rogers, Laverne, Oklahoma; Camargo [Oklahoma] Comet, April 12, 1912.

[17]Walter R. Smith, September 6, 1972, to the author; Leon H. Sapp, M-K-T Trainmaster, Denison, February 15, 1973, to the author. The information on engine number 24 is from records held by the Mechanical Department, M-K-T, Denison, Texas.

[18]"Woodward, Wonder City of the West," The Wide West, Vol. 4 (November 1911), pp. 18-19; George and Wood, p. 38.

[19]Unidentified memorandum regarding WF&NW, February 19, 1911**; M-K-T, D-616 Woodward County [Oklahoma] Deed No. 14, George W. Patterson and Martha S. Patterson to the WF&NW, August 9, 1911, Land Department, M-K-T, Dallas; Before the Interstate Commerce Commission, Finance Dockets 7624 and 7680, Brief for the Missouri-Kansas-Texas Railroad Company, September 10, 1929, p. 9 †; Shirk, pp. 146, 182.

[20]A History of Beaver County, I, p. 302; Earl Kerns, farmer, Gate, Oklahoma, personal interview with the author, October 19, 1972.

[21]A History of Beaver County, II, p. 153; Mrs. Amy Patton, pioneer resident of Gate, Oklahoma, personal interview with the author, October 20, 1972; A History of Beaver County, I, p. 54.

[22]Ibid., II, p. 153.

[23]Ibid., I, p. 170; ibid., II, pp. 200-213.

[24]Ibid., pp. 149, 201, 238; Shirk, pp. 182, 146; George and Wood, p. 15; Beaver [Oklahoma] Herald-Democrat, November 7, 1929.

[25]Time; The Weekly Newsmagazine, Vol. XVIII (July 13, 1931), p. 37; Frances Murray Huston, Financing an Empire: History of Banking in Illinois. Four volumes (Chicago: S. J. Clarke Publishing Co., 1926), III, 5-9, 73-74; A History of Beaver County, II, pp. 128-130; ibid., I, p. 166; William Salomon, February 1, 1913, to Messrs. Estabrook & Company. **

Settling and Civilizing

[1]First and Refunding Mortgage, The Wichita Falls & Northwestern Railway Company to the United States Mortgage and Trust Company and Calvert Brewer, Trustees, August 29, 1911, pp. 29-33 **; Before the Interstate Commerce Commission, Finance Docket Nos. 7624 and 7680, Brief of the Missouri-Kansas-Texas Railroad Company, September 10, 1929, pp. 8-11. †

[2]John W. Morris, Oklahoma Geography (Oklahoma City: Harlow Publishing Co., 1954), p. 39.

[3]Forgan [Oklahoma] Enterprise, February 27, 1913; Harlow's Weekly, Vol. 3 (August 9, 1913), p. 10; James Marshall, Santa Fe: The Railroad That Built an Empire (New York: Random House, 1945), pp. 430-431.

**WF&NW File, Baker Library, Harvard University.

†Legal Department, M-K-T, Dallas.

[4]M. H. Farris, resident of Elk City, Oklahoma, personal interview with the author, November 16, 1972; John Leonard, resident of Camargo, Oklahoma, personal interview with the author, November 14, 1972; O. P. Sturm, "Review of the Past Year's Developments" *Sturm's Oklahoma Magazine,* Vol. IX (January 1910), p. 31; Cecil R. Chesser, *Across the Lonely Years: A History of Jackson County* (Altus, Oklahoma: Altus Printing Co., 1971), p. 149; *A History of Beaver County,* Two volumes (Beaver, Oklahoma: Beaver County Historical Society, 1970), I, p. 116; *Harlow's Weekly,* Vol. I (November 16, 1912), p. 10.

[5]U.S. Interstate Commerce Commission, *Valuation Reports,* Volume 34 (Washington, D.C.: Government Printing Office, 1931), pp. 652-653, 669.

[6]U.S. Department of Commerce, Bureau of Census, "Year of Maximum Population by Counties of the United States," Map G. E.—50, No. 37 (Washington, D.C.: Government Printing Office, 1971).

[7]Mrs. Marshall Word, former resident of Hammon, Oklahoma, July 18, 1972, to the author; State of Oklahoma, Banking Department, Chapter No. 914' to First State Bank of Camargo, September 28, 1911; Mrs. Gertie Balfour, February 14, 1912, to Mrs. Mary Jane Balfour, a letter held by Mrs. Pearl Rogers, Laverne, Oklahoma; *Camargo* [Oklahoma] *Comet,* April 12, 1912, November 20, 1914.

[8]Mrs. Amy Patton, pioneer resident of Gate, Oklahoma, personal interview with the author, October 20, 1972; Walter R. Smith, resident of Laverne, Oklahoma, personal interview with the author, November 9, 1972; *Beaver* [Oklahoma] *Herald-Democrat,* November 7, 1929; *A History of Beaver County,* I, p. 54.

[9]Mrs. E. B. Savage, pioneer resident of Hammon, Oklahoma, personal interview with the author, November 15, 1972; *Beaver* [Oklahoma] *Herald-Democrat,* November 7, 1929; *A History of Beaver County,* II, pp. 203, 236; ibid., I, pp. 54, 560, 304.

[10]Ibid., pp. 121, 150, 161, 414, 276, 54, 358.

[11]Ibid., p. 303.

[12]*Forgan* [Oklahoma] *Enterprise,* August 7, 1913.

The Wichita Falls & Northwestern Railway

[1]John W. Morris, *Oklahoma Geography* (Oklahoma City: Harlow Publishing Co., 1954), pp. 11, 19, 39; U.S. Interstate Commerce Commission, *Valuation Reports,* Volume 34 (Washington, D.C.: Government Printing Office, 1931), pp. 654-655.

[2]Ibid.

[3]Ibid.; ibid., p. 332.

[4]Ibid., p. 655, 302-303; *Wichita Falls Times,* November 13, 1967.

[5]*Poor's Manual of the Railroads of the United States,* 1907, p. 1730, referred to hereafter as *Poor's Manual;* ibid., 1912, p. 1257; Sylvan R. Wood, "Locomotives of the Katy: Missouri-Kansas-Texas Lines," *Bulletin No. 63,* Railway and Locomotive Historical Society (January 1944), pp. 102-103.

[6]*The Official Guide of the Railways* (September 1907), p. 917, referred to hereafter as *Official Guide;* ibid., (December 1908), p. 860; ibid., (February 1911), p. 615; ibid., (January 1912), p. 603.

[7]Leo A. McKee and Alfred L. Lewis, eds, and compilers, *Railroad Post Office History* (Pleasantville, New York: Mobile Post Office Society, 1972), p. 61; *The Official Railway Equipment Register,* Vol. XXIV (June 1908), p. 434.

[8]Mrs. E. B. Savage, pioneer resident of Hammon, Oklahoma, personal interview with the author, November 15, 1972; C. P. Parks, former WF&NW and M-K-T conductor, Altus, Oklahoma, personal interview with the author, November 17, 1972.

[9]*Elk City* [Oklahoma] *Daily News,* November 30, 1971; Mrs. E. B. Savage, interview, November 15, 1972; *Elk City* [Oklahoma] *Daily News,* April 11, 1970.

[10]Walter R. Smith, resident of Laverne, Oklahoma, November 9, 1972, to the author;

**WF&NW File, Baker Library, Harvard University.

*Legal Department, M-K-T, Dallas.

Victor E. Harlow, *Oklahoma: Its Origin and Development* (Oklahoma City: Harlow Publishing Co., 1934), p. 331.

¹¹*A History of Beaver County.* Two volumes (Beaver, Oklahoma: Beaver County Historical Society, 1970), I, p. 53; Walter R. Smith, November 9, 1972, to the author.

¹²*A History of Beaver County,* II, pp. 206, 237; *Forgan* [Oklahoma] *Enterprise,* August 7, 1913; *Poor's Manual,* 1909, p. 615; ibid., 1913, p. 1077.

¹³WF&NW Freight Bill No. 343, Camargo, April 4, 1913‡; WF&NW Freight Bill No. 57, Camargo, May 5, 1913 ‡; *A History of Beaver County,* II, pp. 201-202.

¹⁴J. W. Williams, *The Big Ranch Country* (Wichita Falls, Texas: Terry Brothers Printers, 1954), p. 204; Minnie King Benton, *Boomtown: A Portrait of Burkburnett* (Quanah, Texas: Nortex Offset Publications, 1972), pp. 11, 16; M. H. Farris, resident of Elk City, Oklahoma, personal interview with the author, November 17, 1972; Walter R. Smith, resident of Laverne, Oklahoma, personal interview with the author, November 9, 1972.

¹⁵Mrs. E. B. Savage, interview, November 15, 1972; *Forgan* [Oklahoma] *Enterprise,* August 7, 1913; *A History of Beaver County,* II, p. 201; *Camargo* [Oklahoma] *Comet,* November 20, 1914; WF&NW Dispatcher's Sheet for Saturday, August 18, 1917. ‡

¹⁶Memorandum on WF&NW Railway Company, First and Refunding Mortgages. Knaught, Nachod & Kuhne, New York, 1915, p. 2 **; *A History of Beaver County,* I, p. 409; *Poor's Manual,* 1910, p. 615; ibid., 1913, p. 1077.

¹⁷Ibid., 1909, p. 615; ibid., 1910, p. 1196; ibid., 1911, p. 1194; ibid., 1912, p. 1258; ibid., 1913, pp. 1077-1078; U.S. Interstate Commerce Commission, *Valuation Reports,* Volume 34 (Washington, D.C.: Government Printing Office, 1931), p. 644.

Katy and Hard Times

¹Preston George and Sylvan R. Wood, "The Railways of Oklahoma," *Bulletin No. 60,* Railway and Locomotive Historical Society (January 1943), pp. 42, 38, 40; *Harlow's Weekly,* Vol. 5 (March 14, 1914), p. 14; AFE W-480-2-0. ††

²V. V. Masterson, *The Katy Railroad and the Last Frontier* (Norman: University of Oklahoma Press, 1952), pp. 278-279; *The American Review of Reviews,* Vol. 40 (November 1909), pp. 528-529; Donovan L. Hofsommer. "A History of the Iowa Central Railway," (unpublished M.A. thesis, University of Northern Iowa, 1966), pp. 163-201; Frank P. Donovan, Jr., *Mileposts on the Prairie: The Story of the Minneapolis & St. Louis Railway* (New York: Simmons-Boardman, 1950), pp. 123-135.

³Masterson, pp. 278-279; *Poor's Manual of the Railroads of the United States,* 1912, p. 1257, referred to hereafter as *Poor's Manual;* Missouri, Kansas & Texas Railway Company, *Report to the Stockholders for the Year Ending June 30, 1912,* pp. 12-14; *The Official Guide of the Railways* (January 1912), p. 603; ibid., (May 1913), p. 1098; ibid., (November 1914), p. 1088; *Poor's Manual,* 1916, p. 1787.

⁴U.S. Interstate Commerce Commission, *Valuation Reports,* Volume 34 (Washington, D.C.: Government Printing Office, 1931), p. 657; *Poor's Manual,* 1916, pp. 1786-1787.

⁵Masterson, p. 282; *Poor's Manual,* 1916, pp. 1783-1784; ibid., 1920, p. 1908.

⁶J. A. Kemp, May 28, 1914, to K. L. Fleming, Jr. **; J. A. Kemp, April 6, 1915, to K. L. Fleming, Jr. **; K. L. Fleming, Jr., December 9, 1915, to Charles H. Engel, with accompanying memorandum. **

⁷Report on the WF&NW Ry. Co. First & Refunding Mortgage Gold Bonds, Wm. Morris Imbrie & Company, July 26, 1916, p. 7. **

⁸*Poor's Manual,* 1920, pp. 1918-1919, 1924; Elisha Walker, July 3, 1917, to Holders of First and Refunding Mortgage 5% Gold Bonds of the WF&NW Ry. Co. **

---

‡Author's collection.

**WF&NW File, Baker Library, Harvard University.

††Valuation Engineer's office, M-K-T, Denison, Texas.

[9]*Poor's Manual,* 1920, p. 1918.

[10]Masterson, pp. 282-283; *Missouri, Kansas & Texas: A Story of the MK&T Railway and the Plan for Reorganization,* The National City of New York, 1921, pp. 6-7, Library of Congress; S. G. Reed, *A History of the Texas Railroads and of Transportation Conditions Under Spain and Mexico and the Republic and the State* (Houston: St. Clair Publishing Co., 1941), pp. 391-392.

[11]I.C.C. *Finance Reports,* Volume 76, pp. 97-100; *Poor's Manual,* 1923, pp. 1972-1973; Masterson, p. 284; The National City Bank of Chicago, March 26, 1923, to Holders of WF&NW 1st Lien Collateral Trust 5% Gold Bonds **; RJB (no other identification), February 14, 1922, to Herbert B. Shonk **; AFE R-75-1-T. ††

Bottles of Bourbon, Barrels of Oil

[1]L. C. Rodgers, former WF&NW and M-K-T locomotive engineer, Wichita Falls, January 22, 1973, to the author.

[2]Carl Coke Rister, *Oil! Titan of the Southwest* (Norman: University of Oklahoma Press, 1949), pp. 108-115.

[3]Minnie King Benton, *Boomtown: A Portrait of Burkburnett* (Quanah, Texas: Nortex Offset Publications, 1972), pp. 9-10; *Burkburnett* [Texas] *Star,* December 14, 1917.

[4]Ibid., January 3, 1919; J. W. Williams, *The Big Ranch Country* (Wichita Falls, Texas: Terry Brothers Printers, 1954), p. 205.

[5]Ibid.; Rister, p. 16; Boyce House, *Oil Boom: The Story of Spindletop, Burkburnett, Mexia, Smackover, Desdemonda, and Ranger* (Caldwell, Idaho: Caxton Printers, 1941), p. 91; Rister, p. 16; House, p. 66.

[6]Ibid.; Williams, p. 205; House, p. 57; *Burkburnett* [Texas] *Star,* October 24, 1925; Benton, p. 41.

[7]*The Official Guide of the Railways* (February 1919), p. 259; House, pp. 53, 68; C. A. Warner, *Texas Oil and Gas Since 1543* (Houston: Gulf Publishing Co., 1939), p. 237; L. C. Rodgers, January 22, 1973, to the author; C. P. Parks, former WF&NW and M-K-T conductor, Altus, Oklahoma, personal interview with the author, November 17, 1972.

[8]*The Official Guide of the Railways* (July 1919), p. 562; ibid., (March 1923), p. 611; ibid., (December 1929), p. 740; ibid., (February 1922), p. 602; C. P. Parks, interview, November 17, 1972.

[9]Ibid.; House, p. 51.

[10]Ibid., p. 47; Rister, p. 118; Benton, p. 16.

[11]Information from various AFE files dealing with Burkburnett station buildings ††; Benton, p. 17.

[12]Wichita Falls & Northwestern Ry. of Texas, Station Maps, Burkburnett, Texas (milepost 12-18), August 21, 1921 (revised).††

[13]L. C. Rodgers, January 22, 1972, to the author; C. P. Parks, interview, November 17, 1972.

[14]Charles Evans, "Mangum and Greer County Proven Oil Territory," *Harlow's Weekly,* Vol. 16 (April 23, 1919), pp. 7-9; Ira G. Clark, *Then Came Railroads: The Century from Steam to Diesel in the Southwest* (Norman: University of Oklahoma Press, 1958), p. 249; Rister, p. 115, 118; Jonnie R. Morgan, *The History of Wichita Falls* (Wichita Falls, Texas: Nortex Offset Publications, 1971, facsimile reprint of 1931 edition), pp. 99-102; Benton, pp. 49, 56.

[15]*The Commonweal,* Vol. XXXII (September 13, 1940), p. 429; *The New Republic,* Vol. 103 (August 19, 1940), p. 240; *Newsweek,* Vol. 16 (September 9, 1940), p. 62; *Time: The Weekly News Magazine,* Vol. 36 (August 26, 1940), p. 48; Benton, p. 21.

**WF&NW File, Baker Library, Harvard University.
††Valuation Engineer's office, M-K-T, Denison, Texas.

The Beaver, Meade & Englewood Railroad

[1]George Rainey, *No Man's Land: The Historic Story of a Landed Orphan* (Guthrie, Oklahoma: Co-operative Publishing Co., 1937), pp. 85-88, 122.

[2]Victor, E. Harlow, *Oklahoma: Its Origin and Development* (Oklahoma City: Harlow Publishing Co., 1934), p. 256; Carl Coke Rister, *No Man's Land* (Norman: University of Oklahoma Press, 1948), pp. 157, 164, 171; Preston George and Sylvan R. Wood, "The Railroads of Oklahoma," *Bulletin No. 60,* Railway and Locomotive Historical Society (1943), p. 43.

[3]Rainey, pp. 145-147; Rister, p. 47.

[4]*A History of Beaver County,* Two volumes (Beaver, Oklahoma: Beaver County Historical Society, 1970), I, pp. 54, 184, 414.

[5]*The Atchison, Topeka & Santa Fe Railway, Excerpts from the Presidents's Annual Reports to the Stockholders With Special Reference to the Construction History of System Lines,* 1873-1916, known internally as *Santa Fe Splinters,* 34 Volumes, n.p., n.d., Vol. I, p. 80; *Chronological Development of the Atchison, Topeka & Santa Fe System,* mimeographed, n.d., Sheets 5, 22; *J. M. Meade's History of the Santa Fe,* blueprint (1918), p. 172. All items cited in this footnote are available through the Valuation Engineer's office, AT&SF, Topeka.

[6]Oklahoma and Northwestern Rail Road Company, incorporation papers (file number 5295A) ***; Rister, p. 226; Beaver Valley & North Western Railroad Company, incorporation papers (file number 9576A) ***; David F. Myrick, *New Mexico's Railroads: An Historical Survey* (Golden, Colorado: Colorado Railroad Museum, 1970), pp. 131, 135-136.

[7]Rainey, p. 226; *A History of Beaver County,* II, p. 128.

[8]Beaver, Mead & Englewood Railroad Company, incorporation papers (file number 9735). ***

[9]George and Wood, p. 15; Rainey, p. 227.

[10]Ibid.; George and Wood, p. 15; Rister, p. 172.

[11]George and Wood, p. 16; Rister, p. 172.

[12]*Harlow's Weekly,* Vol. I (October 5, 1912), p. 9; *Hardtner* [Kansas] *Press,* December 3, 1915.

[13]Jacob A. Achenbach, *History and the Life of Jacob A. Achenbach,* n.p., n.d. (1910?), pp. 1, 6, 7.

[14]Kiowa, Hardtner & Pacific Railroad, Various contracts and papers, KH&P file, Wunsch & Wunsch Law Offices, Kingman, Kansas; *Kiowa* [Kansas] *News-Review,* June 10, 1910, July 15, 1910.

[15]Ibid., April 8, 1935; *Hardtner* [Kansas] *Press,* December 2, 1937; Beaver, Meade & Englewood Railroad, "Consist of Rail in Main Track," May 6, 1969, Chief Engineer's office, M-K-T, Denison, Texas; George and Wood, pp. 15-16, 43; *Kiowa* [Kansas] *News-Review,* April 8, 1935.

[16]*Journal of the Illinois State Historical Society,* Vol. 24 (July 1931), p. 364; U.S. Interstate Commerce Commission, *Valuation Reports,* Volume 103 (Washington, D.C.: Government Printing Office, 1926), p. 631; *Hardtner* [Kansas] *Press,* July 7, 1916; Leonard J. Achenbach, a grandson of Jacob A. Achenbach and a farmer of near Hardtner, Kansas, personal interview with the author, July 19, 1972.

[17]I. C. C., *Valuation Reports,* Volume 24, pp. 630-632; *Hardtner* [Kansas] *Press,* July 7, 1916.

[18]*Harlow's Weekly,* Vol. 3 (August 9, 1913), p. 10; *Chronological Development of the Atchison, Topeka & Santa Fe Railway,* Mimeographed, n.d., Sheet 7, Valuation Engineer's office, AT&SF, Topeka; Alva, Buffalo & Colorado Railway Company, incorporation papers (file number 16193) ***; Buffalo Northwestern Railway Company,

---

††Valuation Engineer's office, M-K-T, Denison, Texas.

***Oklahoma Secretary of State's office, Oklahoma City.

incorporation papers (file number 18559) ***; *Railway Age Gazette,* Vol. 63 (November 23, 1917), p. 963; *Chronological Development . . . Santa Fe Railway,* Sheet 18; *Harlow's Weekly,* Vol. 9 (August 7, 1915), p. 140.

[19]*Hardtner* [Kansas] *Press,* July 7, 1916.

[20]Ibid., September 25, 1919.

[21]*The Official Guide of the Railways,* various issues 1918-1924; George W. Crosby, former BM&E locomotive engineer, Forgan, Oklahoma, personal interview with the author, November 11, 1972.

[22]*Poor's Manual of the Railroads of the United States,* 1920, p. 2121; ibid., 1926, p. 1631; Beaver, Meade & Englewood, Beaver Station and Right-of-Way map, September 2, 1931 ††; *The Official Guide of the Railways* (May 1921), p. 1123; *Poor's Manual,* 1922, p. 2098.

BM&E West: 1924-1927

[1]*Poor's Manual of the Railroads of the United States,* 1920, p. 2121; ibid., 1921, p. 2088; ibid., 1922, p. 2098, referred to hereafter as *Poor's Manual; Moody's Manual of Investments, America and Foreign: Railroad Securities,* 1924, p. 1730, hereafter referred to as *Moody's Manual;* ibid., 1926, p. 827; *Hardtner* [Kansas] *Press,* July 13, 1922.

[2]Carl Coke Rister, *No Man's Land* (Norman: University of Oklahoma Press, 1948), pp. 174-175; B. F. Markland, "Wheat in the Panhandle of Oklahoma," *My Oklahoma,* Vol. 2 (August 5, 1938), p. 11.

[3]U.S. Interstate Commerce Commission, *Finance Reports,* Volume 86 (Washington, D.C.: Government Printing Office, 1924), pp. 286-288.

[4]Ibid., pp. 288-289; AFE W-480-2-0 ††; *Hardtner* [Kansas] *Press,* July 13, 1922, November 8, 1923; I.C.C., *Finance Reports,* Volume 86, p. 286.

[5]*Hooker* [Oklahoma] *Advance,* April 11, 1924, April 18, 1924, BM&E, Right-of-Way and Track Maps, Beaver to Hooker. ††

[6]Beaver, Meade & Englewood Railroad, amended incorporation papers (file number 45156)***; Panhandle Construction Company, incorporation papers (file number 45154) ***; Panhandle Townsite Company, incorporation papers (file number 45192). ***

[7]I. C. C., *Finance Reports,* Volume 90, pp. 296-297; Beaver, Meade & Englewood Railroad, V.O.3. Report by the I.C.C. Examiners for the Period 6-30-18 to 12-31-27, pp. 11, 47, †† referred to hereafter as V.O.3. Report; *Hardtner* [Kansas] *Press,* May 13, 1920; *Hooker* [Oklahoma] *Advance,* May 16, 1924, and July 11, 1924; *Hardtner* [Kansas] *Press,* July 3, 1924.

[8]*A History of Beaver County,* Two volumes (Beaver, Oklahoma: Beaver County Historical Society, 1970), II, pp. 118-119, 134; *Hooker* [Oklahoma] *Advance,* December 26, 1924; BM&E, Right-of-Way and Truck Maps, Beaver to Hooker. ††

[9]George H. Shirk, *Oklahoma Place Names* (Norman: Oklahoma University Press, 1965), p. 128; *A History of Beaver County,* II, p. 256; *Hooker* [Oklahoma] *Advance,* November 28, 1924, December 5, 1924.

[10]*Moody's Manual,* 1926, p. 837; *Hooker* [Oklahoma] *Advance,* April 29, 1926; I.C.C., *Finance Reports,* Volume 111, pp. 137-146.

[11]*Hooker* [Oklahoma] *Advance,* April 2, 1925; V.O.3. Report, p. 33; I.C.C., *Finance Reports,* Volume 99, p. 183; ibid., Volume 117, p. 183.

[12]V.O.3. Report, pp. 34-45.

[13]*Hooker* [Oklahoma] *Advance,* September 2, 1926; Shirk, p. 15.

[14]V.O.3. Report, p. 48; George L. Risen, merchant, Hooker, Oklahoma, personal interview with the author, October 20, 1972; *Hooker* [Oklahoma] *Advance,* March 24,

---

††Valuation Engineer's office, M-K-T, Denison, Texas.
***Oklahoma Secretary of State's office, Oklahoma City.

1927, August 2, 1951; *A History of Beaver County*, I, p. 575; Guy Winn, farmer of near Hardtner, Kansas, and a member of the Achenbach family by marriage, personal interview with the author, May 4, 1973.

[15]*Hooker* [Oklahoma] *Advance*, October 28, 1926, January 13, 1927.

[16]Ibid., March 10, 1927, March 17, 1927; A. D. Brawner, former CRI&P agent at Hooker, Oklahoma, personal interview with the author, November 3, 1972; V.O.3. Report, p. 6.

[17]*Hooker* [Oklahoma] *Advance*, April 7, 1927, May 12, 1927, September 15, 1927, October 27, 1927, November 17, 1927, October 27, 1927.

[18]BM&E, Right-of-Way and Track Maps, Beaver to Hooker ††; BM&E, "Summary of Bridges," Chief Engineer's office, M-K-T, Denison, Texas; V.O.3. Report, p. 11.

[19]*The Official Guide of the Railways*, various issues, 1925-1927; Locomotive number 229, a 4-6-0, was acquired by the Panhandle Construction Company and transferred to the BM&E on May 17, 1928, V.O.3. Report, pp. 3, 9; *Poor's Manual*, 1927, p. 1667; ibid., 1928, p. 1656; George W. Crosby, former BM&E locomotive engineer, Forgan, Oklahoma, personal interview with the author, November 10, 1972; Hugh H. Parks, former BM&E section foreman, Hooker, Oklahoma, personal interview with the author, June 27, 1972.

[20]V.O.3. Report, pp. 4, 31-33, 47-48; *Moody's Manual*, 1928, p. 150.

[21]*Beaver* [Oklahoma] *Herald-Democrat*, November 7, 1929; *A History of Beaver County*, II, p. 133.

Panhandle Odyssey

[1]John W. Morris, *Oklahoma Geography* (Oklahoma City: Harlow Publishing Co., 1954), p. 39.

[2]U.S. Interstate Commerce Commission, *Finance Reports*, Volume 138 (Washington, D.C.: Government Printing Office, 1928), pp. 279-284.

[3]*Hooker* [Oklahoma] *Advance*, March 22, 1928.

[4]Ibid., March 29, 1928.

[5]*Beaver* [Oklahoma]*Herald-Democrat*, September 15, 1927; *Hooker* [Oklahoma] *Advance*, October 27, 1927; BM&E, Right-of-Way and Track Maps, Hooker to Keyes. ††

[6]*Hooker* [Oklahoma] *Advance*, April 5, 1928, May 3, 1928, May 10, 1928, May 24, 1928, July 5, 1928, July 19, 1928.

[7]Deed Record, Texas County (Oklahoma), Volume 159, p. 99, Texas County Court House, Guymon, Oklahoma; George H. Shirk, *Oklahoma Place Names* (Norman: University of Oklahoma Press, 1965), p. 145; Warranty Deed, Edward Eden to Panhandle Townsite Company, June 16, 1928, Abstract No. 16034, Guaranty Abstract Company, Guymon, Oklahoma; Shirk, p. 106; Deed Record, Texas County (Oklahoma), Volume 180, p. 28.

[8]*Hooker* [Oklahoma] *Advance*, May 10, 1928; BM&E, Right-of-Way maps, Hooker to Keyes ††; BM&E, AFE Register Book, p. 2. ††

[9]Vance Johnson, *Heaven's Tableland: The Dust Bowl Story* (New York: Farrar Strauss & Co., 1947), pp. 109-119, 147, 113; *Moody's Manual of Investments, America and Foreign: Railroad Securities*, 1930, p. 156, referred to hereafter as *Moody's Manual*.

[10]Texas County (Oklahoma) District Court, Case No. 4283, "Petition," BM&E. Plaintiffs vs. R. F. Baker, et. al., Defendants, November 27, 1929; Texas County (Oklahoma) District Court, Case No. 4283, "Journal Entry of Judgement," BM&E, Plaintiff, vs. R. F. Baker, et. al., Defendants, November 27, 1929; Cases Determined by the Supreme Court of Oklahoma, *Oklahoma Reports*, Vol. CLXVII (Oklahoma City: Harlow Publishing Co., 1934), pp. 568-573.

[11]*Wichita Eagle*, January 25, 1930; *Hooker* [Oklahoma] *Advance*, February 26, 1931.

---

††Valuation Engineer's office, M-K-T, Denison, Texas.

[12]A typed history of the Chicago, Rock Island & Pacific Railroad, Volume J, p. J-9, Public Relations Office, CRI&P, Chicago; *Rock Island Magazine*, (July 1929), p. 6; *Hooker* [Oklahoma] *Advance*, August 1, 1929.

[13]*Chronological Development of the Atchison, Topeka & Santa Fe Railway System*, mimeographed, n.d., p. 17, Valuation Engineer's office, AT&SF, Topeka; *Daily Oklahoman*, October 3, 1925; *Chronological Development . . . Santa Fe Railway*, pp. 19-21; The Atchison, Topeka & Santa Fe Railway, *Excerpts From The President's Annual Report to Stockholders with Special Reference to the Construction History of System Lines*, 1873-1916, known internally as *Santa Fe Splinters*, 34 volumes, Vol. II, pp. 33-35, Valuation Engineer's office, AT&SF, Topeka; Preston George and Sylvan R. Wood, "The Railroads of Oklahoma," *Bulletin No. 60*, Railway & Locomotive Historical Society, (1943), p. 39; James Marshall, *Santa Fe: The Railroad That Built an Empire* (New York: Random House, 1945), pp. 440-443; For a very fine treatment of railroad development in Cimarron County, Oklahoma, see Charles Brooks Lewis, "The Development of Cimarron County," (unpublished Master's Thesis, University of Oklahoma, Norman, 1939), pp. 70-90.

[14]*The Official Guide of the Railways* (February 1928), p. 1336; ibid., (September 1928), p. 1290; ibid., (December 1929), p. 1322.

[15]T. J. Robb, Jr., former BM&E locmotive engineer, Forgan, Oklahoma, personal interview with the author, August 25, 1972; W. H. Wells, former BM&E cashier at Hooker, Oklahoma, personal interview with the author, June 1, 1972.

[16]Ibid.; George Burdge, municipal official, Hooker, Oklahoma, personal interview, with the author, October 20, 1972.

[17]W. H. Wells, interview, June 1, 1972; T. J. Robb, Jr., interview, January 11, 1973.

[18]Sylvan R. Wood, "Locomotives of the Katy: Missouri-Kansas-Texas Lines," *Bulletin No. 63*, Railway & Locomotive Historical Society (January 1944), pp. 62-63, 66, 73-74; T. J. Robb, Jr., interview, August 25, 1972; George H. Crosby, former BM&E locomotive engineer, Forgan, Oklahoma, personal interview with the author, November 10, 1972.

[19]I.C.C., *Finance Reports*, Volume 150, pp. 345-348; *Hooker* [Oklahoma] *Advance*, February 20, 1930, May 29, 1930; *Moody's Manual*, 1937, p. 829; Beaver, Meade & Englewood Railroad Company, amended incorporation papers (file number 67086).***

[20]BM&E, Right of Way and Track Maps, Hooker to Keys ††; BM&E, "Summary of Bridges," Chief Engineer's office, M-K-T, Denison, Texas.

[21]*Railway Age*, Vol. 90 (January 3, 1931), p. 62; BM&E, Ledger No. 1, AFE 30-34 ††; BM&E, Right-of-Way and Track Maps, Hooker to Keyes ††

[22]*Railway Age*, Vol. 90 (January 3, 1931), p. 62; *Hooker* [Oklahoma] *Advance*, March 12, 1931; BM&E, Ledger No. 1, AFE 31-34 ††; H. E. Knight, former BM&E agent at Keyes, Oklahoma, personal interview with the author, January 14, 1973.

[23]BM&E, Right-of-Way and Track Maps, Hooker to Keyes ††; Shirk, pp. 208, 75.

[24]*The Official Guide of the Railways*, (December 1930), p. 1322; ibid., (July 1931), p. 1322; *Moody's Manual*, 1930, p. 156.

The "Orphan" No More

[1]*Kiowa* [Kansas] *News-Review*, July 15, 1910.

[2]*Daily Oklahoman*, June 28, 1936; Mrs. Walter Ferguson, "This Farmer's Railroad Brought a Rich Harvest." *The American Magazine*, Vol. CXIV (July 1932), p. 64; Preston George and Sylvan R. Wood, "The Railroads of Oklahoma," *Bulletin No. 60*, Railway & Locomotive Historical Society (1943), p. 40.

[3]Ferguson, p. 65; Leonard J. Achenbach, grandson of Jacob A. Achenbach and

---

***Oklahoma Secretary of State's office, Oklahoma City.
††Valuation Engineer's office, M-K-T, Denison, Texas.

farmer of near Hardtner, Kansas, personal interview with the author, July 19, 1972; Memo written by President C. N. Whitehead, October 11, 1926, in BM&E file, Legal Department, M-K-T, Dallas, referred to hereafter as Katy file.

[4]C. J. Turpin, November 3, 1928, to President C. Haile, BM&E file, CRI&P Legal Department, Chicago, referred to hereafter as RI file; C. Haile, November 5, 1928, to C. J. Turpin, RI file; C. Haile, March 6, 1927, to C.J. Turpin, RI file; C. J. Turpin, March 8, 1929, to C. Haile, RI file; C. Haile, April 27, 1929, to C. J. Turpin, RI file; C. Haile, April 27, 1929 (Western Union telegram), to C. J. Turpin, RI file.

[5]Resolution of CRI&P Board, April 3, 1929, RI file; Sales Agreement and Explanatory Memorandum, April 25, 1929, RI file; U.S. Interstate Commerce Commission, *Finance Reports,* Volume 158 (Washington, D.C.: Government Printing Office, 1930), p. 220; C. Haile, May 17, 1929 to J. M. Bryson, Katy file.

[6]*Hooker* [Oklahoma] *Advance,* May 23, 1929, June 13, 1929, June 20, 1929.

[7]Ibid.; ibid., July 4, 1929.

[8]Memorandum of the M-K-T Board of Directors, June 19, 1929, Katy file; I.C.C., *Finance Reports,* Volume 158, p. 220.

[9]*Hooker* [Oklahoma] *Advance,* February 20, 1930; "Cost of Rehabilitating BM&E Railroad; Program for 1929," RI file; W. H. Wells, former BM&E cashier at Hooker, Oklahoma, personal interview with the author, June 1, 1972; I.C.C., *Finance Reports,* Volume 158, p. 220.

[10]Before the Interstate Commerce Commission, Finance Docket Nos. 7624 and 7680, *Brief of Applicant, the Chicago, Rock Island & Pacific Railway Company,* September 12, 1929, pp. 3, 14, 22, 24, 26, 39, 42, 55, referred to hereafter as *Rock Island Brief.*†

[11]Before the Interstate Commerce Commission, Finance Docket Nos. 7624 and 7680, *Brief for the Missouri-Kansas-Texas Railroad Company,* September 10, 1929, pp. 10-12, 15-16. †

[12]Ibid., pp. 22, 29, 32, 34, 37, 40-41, 61.

[13]Before the Interstate Commerce Commission, Finance Docket Nos. 7624 and 7680, *Brief of the Intervenors, the Hooker, Oklahoma, Chamber of Commerce and the towns of Mangum, Frederick, Altus, Leedey, Elk City, Forgan, Woodward, Vici, Laverne, and Guymon,* September 10, 1929, pp. 16, 29. †

[14]I.C.C., *Finance Reports,* Volume 158, pp. 231-233.

[15]*Hooker* [Oklahoma] *Advance,* November 28, 1929; Clifford W. Ferguson, November 28, 1929, to Charles S. Burg, Katy file; *Hooker* [Oklahoma] *Advance,* December 12, 1929; Clifford W. Ferguson, November 28, 1929, to Charles S. Burg, Katy file; *Hooker* [Oklahoma] *Advance,* February 20, 1930.

[16]Ibid.; ibid., February 27, 1930; Lease Agreement, Rock Island Improvement Company and Panhandle Construction Company, et al., June 1, 1930, Katy file; Mark M. Hennelly, General Counsel Missouri Pacific Railroad, St. Louis, August 3, 1972, citing records in his department, to the author; *Daily Oklahoman,* June 28, 1936.

[17]Clifford W. Ferguson, October 15, 1930, to Charles S. Burg, Katy file; *Time,* Vol. XVIII (July 13, 1931), pp. 37-38; Memorandum to BM&E security holders, undated (1931), Katy file.

[18]Sales Agreement between the owners of the Beaver, Meade & Englewood Railroad and the Missouri-Kansas-Texas Railroad, February 26, 1931, p. 16, Katy file; *Hardtner* [Kansas] *Press,* March 12, 1931; *The Traffic World,* Volume XLVII (March 14, 1931, p. 646; I.C.C., *Finance Reports,* Volume 170, pp. 556-558; *The M-K-T Annual Report to the Stockholders for* 1931 reported the cost of acquiring the BM&E road equipment at $2.5 million, p. 15; *Hooker* [Oklahoma] *Advance,* March 12, 1931, March 19, 1931.

[19]Ibid., July 2, 1931; *The Official Guide of the Railways* (January 1932), p. 742; *Hooked* [Oklahoma] *Advance,* July 2, 1931.

---

†Legal Department, M-K-T, Dallas.

[1]Walter R. Smith, resident of Laverne, Oklahoma, personal interview with the author, November 9, 1972.

[2]WF&NW, Station Map of Wichita Falls, Texas ††; L. C. Rodgers, former WF&NW and M-K-T locomotive engineer, Wichita Falls, March 8, 1973, to the author.

[3]*The Official Guide of the Railways,* (February 1922), p. 602, hereafter referred to as *Official Guide;* ibid., (September 1923), p. 632; ibid., (December 1929), p. 740.

[4]L. C. Rodgers, March 8, 1973, to the author; *Laverne* [Oklahoma] *Leader-Tribune,* September 22, 1966.

[5]Minnie King Benton, resident of Burkburnett, Texas, personal interview with the author, December 2, 1972; Mrs. Marshall Word, former resident of Hammon, Oklahoma, July 18, 1972, to the author; *A History of Beaver County,* Two volumes (Beaver, Oklahoma: Beaver County Historical Society, 1970), I, p. 486; *Laverne* [Oklahoma] *Leader-Tribune,* November 9, 1972; Sue Hocker Ward, resident of Camargo, Oklahoma, personal interview with the author, November 14, 1972; Ralph Barby, rancher of near Knowles, Oklahoma, personal interview with the author, November 3, 1972.

[6]P. O. Parks, former WF&NW and M-K-T conductor, Woodward, Oklahoma, personal interview with the author, November 19, 1972; W. P. Altland, former M-K-T station agent, Woodward, Oklahoma, personal interview with the author, November, 14, 1971; Walter R. Smith, interview, November 9, 1972; W. P. Altland, interview, November 24, 1972.

[7]*Beaver* [Oklahoma] *Herald-Democrat,* November 7, 1929; Cliff Kay, former M-K-T station agent, now of Ponca City, Oklahoma, July 20, 1972, to the author; E. B. Parks, former M-K-T station agent, Mangum, Oklahoma, personal interview with the author, November 15, 1972; Dan B. Cullen, former WF&NW and M-K-T conductor, Sharon, Oklahoma, personal interview with the author, November 19, 1971; E. B. Parks, interview, November 15, 1972; R. Walthen Medley, an official of the Medley Distilling Company, Owensboro, Kentucky, November 28, 1972 and December 12, 1972, to the author.

[8]Cliff Kay, July 20, 1972, to the author; L. C. Rodgers, March 8, 1973, to the author.

[9]MK&T, Time Table, July 28, 1912, p. 3; Dan B. Cullen, interview, November 19, 1971; P. A. Johnston, former M-K-T station agent, Elk City, Oklahoma, personal interview with the author, October 15, 1971; *A History of Beaver County,* II, pp. 149, 238.

[10]Cliff Kay, July 20, 1972, to the author; *Official Guide* (June 1936), p. 662; ibid., (June 1941), p. 674.

[11]P. A. Johnston, interview, October 15, 1971; M-K-T, Inspection Trip by the Members of the Boards of Directors of the Missouri-Kansas-Texas Railroad Company and its Subsidiaries, May 1939, pamphlet, Bureau of Economics Library, Association of American Railroads, Washington, referred to hereafter as Inspection Trip; W. P. Altland, interview, November 19, 1971.

[12]K. E. Bailey, former M-K-T agent, Altus, Oklahoma, personal interview with the author, November 24, 1971; Mrs. Earl Kerns, farm wife, Gate, Oklahoma, personal interview with the author, October 19, 1972; Allen D. Wherritt, retired farmer, Camargo, Oklahoma, personal interview with the author, November 14, 1972.

[13]Minnie King Benton, *Boomtown: A Portrait of Burkburnett* (Quanah, Texas: Nortex Offset Publications, 1972), p. 60; William D. Dennis, Sales Manager, M-K-T, Wichita Falls, personal interview with the author, December 1, 1972; E. B. Parks, interview, November 15, 1972.

[14]Benton, p. 8; WF&NW, Station Map of Burkburnett, Texas ††; C. A. Warner, *Texas Oil and Gas Since 1534* (Houston: Gulf Publishing Company, 1939), pp. 252-253; P. A. Johnston, December 4, 1972, to the author; M-K-T, Side Track Record, sheet 132 ††; L. C. Rodgers, January 22, 1973, to the author; P. O. Parks, interview, June 30, 1972.

[15]*A History of Beaver County,* I, p. 303; *Beaver* [Oklahoma] *Herald-Democrat,*

††Valuation Engineer's office, M-K-T, Denison, Texas.

November 7, 1929; *The M-K-T Employes' Magazine* (June 1945), p. 28.

[16]*A History of Beaver County,* I, p. 346; ibid., II, p. 237; ibid., I, pp. 30-32; Ralph Barby, interview, November 2, 1972.

[17]W. P. Altland, interview, November 19, 1971; C. W. Dowdy, former WF&NW and M-K-T locomotive engineer, Mangum, Oklahoma, personal interview with the author, November 15, 1972; P. O. Parks, interview, November 4, 1972.

[18]Jacob C. Holmes, proprietor, Holmes Livestock Co., Laverne, Oklahoma, personal interview with the author, August 24, 1972; Cliff Kay, interview, June 20, 1972; *A History of Beaver County,* II, pp. 132, 135.

[19]Ibid., pp. 205, 562, 132, 156; *Beaver* [Oklahoma] *Herald-Democrat,* November 7, 1929; Benton, p. 45; P. A. Johnston, December 4, 1972, to the author; W. P. Altland, interview, November 19, 1971; E. B. Parks, interview, November 15, 1972; Cliff Kay, interview, June 20, 1972; Pearl Rogers, resident of Laverne, Oklahoma, personal interview with the author, August 25, 1972; M-K-T, Inspection Trip.

[20]Ibid.; P. A. Johnston, December 4, 1972, to the author; Dan B. Cullen, interview, November 19, 1971; W. P. Altland, interview, November 19, 1971; P. O. Parks, interview, June 30, 1972.

[21]M-K-T, Inspection Report.

[22]C. P. Parks, former WF&NW and M-K-T conductor, Altus, Oklahoma, personal interview with the author, November 17, 1972; V. L. Alsup, farmer and rancher of near Duke, Oklahoma, personal interview with the author, November 16, 1972; E. B. Parks, interview, November 15, 1972.

[23]W. P. Altland, interview, November 24, 1972; E. B. Parks, interview, November 15, 1972; WF&NW, Station Map of Wellington, Texas ††; F. Hol Wagner, Jr., *The Colorado Road: History, Motive Power and Equipment of the Colorado & Southern and Fort Worth & Denver Railways* (Denver: Intermountain Chapter, National Railway Historical Society, 1970), p. 195.

[24]M-K-T, Carload Business Received and Forwarded From and To Stations on the Wellington Branch for the Five Year Perod 1938 to 1942, Inclusive, Wellington Branch File. †

[25]WF&NW, Station Map of Wichita Falls, Texas ††; Sylvan R. Wood, "Locomotives of the Katy: Missouri-Kansas-Texas Lines," *Bulletin No. 63,* Railway & Locomotive Historical Society (January 1944), pp. 72, 102; WF&NW, Dispatcher's Sheet, August 18, 1917, collection of Albert Dowdy, Wichita Falls.

[26]C. W. Dowdy, interview, November 15, 1972; Wood, p. 102; M-K-T, Northwestern District Time Table No. 21 (February 4, 1945), pp. 3, 7.

[27]*M-K-T Employes' Magazine* (November 1945), p. 19; *Railway Age,* Vol. 89 (October 11, 1930), p. 757; ibid., Vol. 92 (January 2, 1932), p. 52; M-K-T, *Miscellaneous Statistics,* Seventh Edition (July 1, 1972), p. 32; Dan N. Bascot, "An Analysis of Missouri-Kansas-Texas," mimeographed, n.p., (December 21, 1931), pp. 23-24†; *Business Week,* (July 15, 1944), pp. 63-64.

[28]Ibid.; Willard V. Anderson, "Katy Serves the Southwest," *Trains,* Vol. 9 (April 1949), pp. 16-25.

For Better or For Worse

[1]*Hooker* [Oklahoma] *Advance,* July 2, 1931; *M-K-T Employees' Magazine,* Vol. 19 (August 1931), pp. 6-7; BM&E, Right-of-Way maps. ††

[2]*M-K-T Employees' Magazine,* Vol. 19 (August 1931); pp. 6-7; *The Official Guide of the Railways* (July 1931), p. 1322, referred to hereafter as *Official Guide; Hooker* [Oklahoma] *Advance,* September 10, 1931.

[3]*Hooker* [Oklahoma] *Advance,* July 16, 1931, July 2, 1931; *Hardtner* [Kansas]

---

†Legal Department, M-K-T, Dallas.

††Valuation Engineer's office, M-K-T, Den ison, Texas.

Press, July 2, 1931; *M-K-T Employees' Magazine,* Vol. 19 (August 1931), pp. 6-7; Byron Bates, former M-K-T locomotive engineer, Elk City, Oklahoma, personal interview with the author, November 16, 1972.

[4]W. H. Wells, former BM&E cashier, Hooker, Oklahoma, personal interview with the author, June 1, 1972.

[5]*M-K-T Employees' Magazine,* Vol. 19 (August 1931), p. 7; *Hooker* [Oklahoma] *Advance,* July 16, 1931.

[6]Before the Interstate Commerce Commission, Finance Docket Nos. 7624 and 7680, *Brief for Missouri-Kansas-Texas Railroad Company,* September 10, 1929, pp. 55-56. †

[7]*Hooker* [Oklahoma] *Advance,* March 12, 1931; *A History of Beaver County,* Two volumes (Beaver, Oklahoma: Beaver County Historical Society, 1970), I, p. 528; *Railway Age,* Vol 92 (January 2, 1932), p. 30; David F. Myrick, *New Mexico's Railroads: An Historical Survey* (Golden, Colorado: Colorado Railroad Museum, 1970), p. 135; *Hooker* [Oklahoma] *Advance,* October 20, 1932; BM&E AFE B-41-2-0. ††

[8]Carl Coke Rister, *No Man's Land* (Norman: University of Oklahoma Press, 1948), p. 191; W. H. Wells, interview, June 1, 1972; Vance Johnson, *Heaven's Tableland: The Dust Bowl Story* (New York: Farrar, Strauss & Co., 1947), p. 147; Charles Brooks Lewis, "The Development of Cimarron County" (unpublished M.A. thesis, University of Oklahoma, 1939), p. 66; Johnson, pp. 149-150; Lewis, p. 67.

[9]*M-K-T Employees' Magazine,* Vol. 19 (August 1931), pp. 4, 6, 48; E. B. Parks, former M-K-T station agent, Mangum, Oklahoma, personal interview with the author, November 15, 1972; Johnson, p. 150; *Hooker* [Oklahoma] *Advance,* November 3, 1932.

[10]*Alva* [Oklahoma] *Review,* April 11, 1895; *Hooker* [Oklahoma] *Advance,* Pictorial Edition, n.d. (1928); BM&E, Right-of-Way maps ††; Johnson, pp. 169-170; Rister, pp. 181-183; Johnson, p. 173; *A History of Beaver County,* I, p. 314.

[11]John W. Morris, *Oklahoma Geography* (Oklahoma City: Harlow Publishing Co., 1954), p. 39; Lewis, pp. 67-68; Johnson, pp. 185-189; Rister, pp. 182-185.

[12]Mrs. Ruby Risen, former CRI&P station agent at Baker, Oklahoma, November 15, 1972, to the author; Caroline A. Henderson, "Letters From the Dust Bowl," *The Atlantic Monthly,* Vol. 157 (May 1936), pp. 540-549; Hugh H. Parks, former BM&E section foreman, Hooker, Oklahoma, personal interview with the author, June 27, 1972.

[13]Henderson, pp. 541, 547.

[14]Johnson, pp. 195, 206-207, 214, 216, 256; Rister, p. 185.

[15]George W. Crosby, former BM&E locomotive engineer, Forgan, Oklahoma, personal interview with the author, November 10, 1972.

[16]Ibid.; Hugh H. Parks, interview, January 12, 1973; E. B. Parks, interview, November 15, 1972.

[17]BM&E, Employes' Time Table No. 24, May 14, 1939; Byron Bates, interview, November 10, 1972; Hugh H. Parks, interview, June 27, 1972.

[18]*Hooker* [Oklahoma] *Advance,* March 26, 1931; George W. Crosby, interview, November 10, 1972.

[19]*Official Guide* (July 1935), p. 659; George W. Crosby, interview, November 10, 1972; Mrs. Ruby Risen, November 15, 1972, to the author.

[20]Rister, p. 187; Johnson, p. 274; Morris, pp. 149-150; U. S. Department of Commerce, Bureau of the Census, "Year of Maximum Population by Counties of the United States," Map G.E.—50, No. 37 (Washington, D.C.: Government Printing Office, 1971); Rister, p. 191.

[21]*M-K-T Employees' Magazine,* Vol. 19 (August 1931), p. 6; Sylvan R. Wood, "Locomotives of the Katy: Missouri-Kansas-Texas Lines," *Bulletin No. 63,* Railway & Locomotive Historical Society (January 1944), pp. 62-63, 66, 73, 74; T. J. Robb, Jr., former BM&E locomotive engineer, Forgan, Oklahoma, personal interview with the author, January 12, 1973.

[22]*Official Guide* (October 1932), p. 704; ibid., (February 1933), p. 676; BM&E, Right-of-Way maps ††; Lester W. Barnett, former BM&E conductor, Forgan, Oklahoma, personal interview with the author, June 27, 1972; CRI&P station map, Baker, Oklahoma,

---

†Legal Department, M-K-T, Dallas.

††Valuation Engineer's office, M-K-T, Denison, Texas.

January 10, 1936 ††; Lawrence E. Smith, former BM&E brakeman, Forgan, Oklahoma, personal interview with the author, June 27, 1972.

[23]George W. Crosby, interview, November 10, 1972; Albert Dowdy, M-K-T Trainmaster, Wichita Falls, personal interview with the author, March 31, 1973; Elsie W. Walters, former BM&E station agent, Keyes, Oklahoma, personal interview with the author, July 26, 1972; T. J. Robb, Jr., interview, July 26, 1972.

[24]BM&E, Right-of-Way maps ††; A. D. Brawner, former CRI&P agent at Hooker, Oklahoma, personal interview with the author, November 3, 1972; *Hooker* [Oklahoma] *Advance,* March 16, 1944, March 23, 1944; George W. Crosby, interview, November 10, 1972.

[25]*A History of Beaver County,* II, p. 569; George W. Crosby, interview, November 10, 1972; T. J. Robb, Jr., interview, July 26, 1972; *Hooker* [Oklahoma] *Advance,* January 20, 1944; George W. Crosby, interview, November 10, 1972.

[26]BM&E, Right-of-Way and Station maps, Beaver, Oklahoma ††; A. D. Brawner, interview, November 3, 1972; Lester W. Barnett, interview, June 27, 1972.

[27]A. D. Brawner, interview, November 3, 1972; C. W. Dowdy, former M-K-T locomotive engineer, Mangum, Oklahoma, personal interview with the author, November 15, 1972.

[28]BM&E, Employes' Time Table No. 24, May 14, 1949; Hugh H. Parks, interview, January 12, 1973; George W. Crosby, interview, November 10, 1970.

[29]BM&E, Conductor's Train Book, T. J. Robb, Jr., Conductor, July-October, 1944, passim; *M-K-T Employees' Magazine* (November 1943), p. 289.

[30]Compilation of data taken from *Moody's Manual of Investments, American and Foreign: Railroad Securities for the years 1931-1951;* Karl R. Ziebarth, M-K-T Treasurer, Dallas, March 15, 1973, to the author.

Of Men and Events

[1]Personal Record File Numbers, Superintendent of Rule's office, M-K-T, Denison, Texas.

[2]Minnie King Benton, resident of Burkburnett, Texas, personal interview with the author, December 1, 1972; C. P. Parks, former WF&NW and M-K-T conductor, Altus, Oklahoma, personal interview with the author, November 17, 1972; L. C. Rodgers, former WF&NW and M-K-T locomotive engineer, Wichita Falls, January 22, 1973, to the author.

[3]Ibid.; Stanley W. Bradley, "The Railroad Boomer," *The Bulletin,* National Railway Historical Society, Vol. 37 (1972), pp. 20-21; C. W. Dowdy, former WF&NW and M-K-T locomotive engineer, Mangum, Oklahoma, personal interview with the author, November 15, 1972; C. P. Parks, interview, November 17, 1972.

[4]Walter P. Smith, resident of Laverne, Oklahoma, November 9, 1972, to the author; Clifton Kay, former M-K-T station agent, now of Ponca City, Oklahoma, July 20, 1972, to the author; *Elk City* [Oklahoma] *Daily News,* November 30, 1971; *Woodward* [Oklahoma] *Press,* January 26, 1972.

[5]L. C. Rodgers, January 22, 1972, to the author; C. P. Parks, interview, November 17, 1972; Dan B. Cullen, former WF&NW and M-K-T conductor, Sharon, Oklahoma, personal interview with the author, November 19, 1971; P. O. Parks, former WF&NW and M-K-T conductor, Woodward, Oklahoma, personal interview with the author, June 30, 1972; Payroll Records, Superintendent of Rules office, M-K-T, Denison, Texas.

[6]C. W. Dowdy, interview, November 15, 1972; Byron Bates, former M-K-T locomotive engineer, Elk City, Oklahoma, personal interview with the author, November 16, 1972.

[7]Personal Record File 1908, M-K-T, Denison, Texas, hereafter referred to as PR; PR 1976; PR 580; PR 1887; PR 1922; PR 582.

[8]F. P. Blount, April 30, 1935 to Glen Grace, PR 1887; PR 1908; E. B. Parks,

††Valuation Engineer's office, M-K-T, Denison, Texas.

former M-K-T station agent, Mangum, Oklahoma, personal interview with the author, November 15, 1972; Wesley P. Altland, former M-K-T station agent, Woodward, Oklahoma, personal interview with the author, November 24, 1972; PR 1908; PR 1887.

[9]Clifton Kay, July 20, 1972, to the author.

[10]Ibid.; Pearl Rogers, resident of Laverne, Oklahoma, personal interview with the author, August 25, 1972; PR 1976; PR 1982; C. W. Dowdy, interview, November 15, 1972.

[11]P. O. Parks, interview, June 30, 1972; Pearl Rogers, interview, August 25, 1972.

[12]Walter P. Smith, September 6, 1972, to the author; Mrs. Jacob C. Holmes, resident of Laverne, Oklahoma, personal interview with the author, August 24, 1972; *Enid* [Oklahoma] *Morning News,* July 30, 1972.

[13]PR 1166; Bertie L. Denton, former M-K-T station agent, Carter, Oklahoma, April 8, 1973, to the author.

[14]U.S. Railroad Administration, *Agreement Between the MK&T MK&TofT, and the WF&NW and the Brotherhood of Locomotive Fireman and Enginemen,* (October 1, 1918), p. 3; *U. S. Railroad Administration, Agreement between the MK&T, MK&TofT, and the WF&NW and the Brotherhood of Locomotive Engineers,* (October 1, 1918), p. 3; Enginemen's Rate of Pay Machine Codes. All items cited here were made available through the Manager of Personnel's office, M-K-T, Dallas.

[15]*Agreement Between the MK&T (and affiliates) and the MK&T Association of Metal Craft and Car Department Employees,* (October 16, 1922), pp. 22, 26-30; Rates of Pay, information supplied on March 9, 1973 by Fred R. Carroll, Manager of Personnel, M-K-T, Dallas; *Agreement Between the MK&T (and affiliates) and the Order of Railroad Telegraphers,* March 16, 1922), pp. 43-45. See also endnote number 14.

[16]*M-K-T Employees' Magazine* (April 1943), p. 13; L. C. Rodgers, March 8, 1973, to the author; *Wichita Falls Times,* May 10, 1970; Albert Dowdy, M-K-T Trainmaster, Wichita Falls, personal interview with the author, December 2, 1972; M-K-T Southern Division Bulletin No. 12 (February 2, 1973).

[17]AFE W-438-1A-0 ††; L. C. Rodgers, January 22, 1973, to the author; *A History of Beaver County,* Two volumes (Beaver, Oklahoma: Beaver County Historical Society, 1970), II, p. 217; Clifton Kay, July 20, 1972, to the author; Mrs. Earl Kerns, farm wife, Gate, Oklahoma, personal interview with the author, October 19, 1972.

[18]*Forgan* [Oklahoma] *Enterprise,* August 7, 1913; L. C. Rodgers, January 22, 1973, to the author; C. W. Dowdy, interview, November 15, 1972.

[19]W. P. Altland, interview, November 19, 1971; L. O. Pierce, M-K-T conductor, Altus, Oklahoma, personal interview with the author, January 24, 1973; on caboose cooking, see William F. Knapke with Freeman Hubbard, *The Railroad Caboose:Its 100 Year History, Legend and Lore* (San Marino, California: Golden West Books, 1968), pp. 51-78.

[20]C. W. Dowdy, interview, November 15, 1972; L. C. Rodgers, January 22, 1973, to the author; *A History of Beaver County,* II, p. 569; W. P. Altland, interview, November 19, 1971; Dan B. Cullen, December 20, 1971, to the author.

[21]WF&NW Dispatcher's Sheet, August 18, 1917 ‡; F. W. Grace, June 7, 1921, to C. E. Schaff, Chief Engineer's office, M-K-T, Denison, Texas; WF&NW, Station Map of Burkburnett, Texas ††; Mrs. Marshall Word, former resident of Hammon, Oklahoma, July 18, 1972, to the author; U.S. Army Corps of Engineers, Tulsa District, *Fort Supply Lake—Oklahoma,* pamphlet (May 1972); U.S. Army Corps of Engineers, Tulsa District, *Optima Dam and Lake—Oklahoma,* pamphlet (June 1972).

[22]M-K-T, Right-of-Way map, Bridge 183.0 over South Canadian River, Camargo, Oklahoma, Chief Engineer's office, M-K-T, Denison, Texas; Transcript of Record, Bridge No. 183, provided by John H. Hughes, Chief Engineer, M-K-T, Denison, Texas.

[23]Ibid.; M-K-T, Southern Division Time Table No. 1 (September 29, 1968), p. 13.

---

‡Author's collection.
††Valuation Engineer's office, M-K-T, Denison, Texas.

Deramus and Damnation

[1]P. A. Johnston, former M-K-T station agent, Elk City, Oklahoma, personal interview with the author, October 15, 1971; *The Official Guide of the Railways* (July 1950), p. 708, referred to hereafter as *Official Guide.*

[2]Sylvan R. Wood, "Locomotives of the Katy: Missouri-Kansas-Texas Lines," *Bulletin No. 63,* Railway & Locomotive Historical Society (January 1944), pp. 67-68, 70, 72.

[3]Willard V. Anderson, "Katy Serves the Southwest," *Trains,* Vol. 9 (April 1949), p. 22; K. H. Hanger, "Diesels Can Operate Over Old Light Rail," *Railway Age,* Vol. 133 (October 6, 1952), pp. 98-99; Between August, 1950 and the end of steam power on the Northwestern District, the following locomotives were serviced at the Forgan engine facility: 429, 492, 494, 508, 511, 516, 521, 526, 535, 538, 539, 542, 555, 559, 594, 596, and 608. Missouri-Kansas-Texas Locomotive Inspection Reports, Form 1056, Forgan, Oklahoma file, August 4, 1950 through February 9, 1952 ‡; V. V. Masterson, *The Katy Railroad and the Last Frontier* (Norman: University of Oklahoma Press, 1952), p. 289; M-K-T, Station Map of Wichita Falls, Texas ††.

[4]*Railway Age,* Vol. 92 (January 2, 1932), p. 69; Wood, p. 44; U. S. Postal Transportation Service, Eleventh Division, *Schedules of Mail Routes No. 361* (March 15, 1954), p. 110.

[5]Mrs. Allen D. Wherritt, resident of Camargo, Oklahoma, personal interview with the author, November 14, 1972; P. A. Johnston, interview, October 15, 1971; Dan B. Cullen, former WF&NW and M-K-T conductor, Sharon, Oklahoma, personal interview with the author, November 19, 1971; *Official Guide* (May 1954), p. 714; ibid., (July 1957), pp. 718-719; Corporation Commission of the State of Oklahoma, *Fiftieth Annual Report for the Year Ending June 30, 1957* (Oklahoma City: State Printer, 1957), p. 378; Before the Interstate Commerce Commission, Finance Docket No. 25613, "Return to Questionnaire," mimeographed, (April 21, 1969), p. 6.†

[6]Masterson, p. 289.

[7]U.S. Interstate Commerce Commission, *Finance Reports,* Volume 124 (Washington, D.C.: Government Printing Office, 1927), pp. 401-407; Floyd W. Mundy, ed., *Mundy's Earning Power of Railroads,* 28th Edition (New York: Jas H. Oliphant & Co., 1933), pp. 449-454; *Railway Age,* Vol. 142 (January 21, 1957), pp. 15, 39.

[8]*Who's Who in America, 1972-1973,* 37th Edition, Two volumes (Chicago: Marquis Who's Who, Inc., 1972), I, p. 790; *Railway Age,* Vol. 142 (April 29, 1957), p. 9; David P. Morgan, "Is There a Cure for What Ails Katy?" *Trains,* Vol. 20 (August 1960), p. 24; *Railway Age,* Vol. 144 (January 6, 1958), p. 27; Morgan, p. 18.

[9]Morgan, pp. 18-25.

[10]*Moody's Transportation Manual,* 1969, p. 270, referred to hereafter as *Moody's Manual; Who's Who in America, 1972-1973,* I, p. 790; *Railway Age,* Vol. 144 (January 1958), p. 27; Morgan, p. 25.

[11]*Railroad Magazine,* Vol. 74 (June 1963), p. 58; Morgan, p. 21; M-K-T, Roster of Diesel Motive Power, 1971, Superintendent of Rules' office, M-K-T, Denison, Texas.

[12]Various Correspondence and Documents, Wellington Branch file, referred to hereafter as WBF †; D. V. Fraser, April 28, 1953, to H. M. Warden, et al., WBF; H. M. Warden, et al., May 9, 1953, to D. V. Fraser; Various Correspondence and Documents, WBF; H. Gifford Till, August 24, 1955, to D. V. Fraser, WBF; D. V. Fraser, March 26, 1956, to C. T. Williams, WBF.

[13]D. V. Fraser, June 11, 1956, to W. R. Howell, WBF; Various Documents, WBF; W. R. Howell, December 10, 1956, to Harold D. McCoy, WBF.

[14]Wesley P. Altland, former M-K-T station agent, Woodward, Oklahoma, personal interview with the author, November 24, 1972; Before the Interstate Commerce Commission, Finance Docket Nos. 19590, 19591, and 19592, "Amendments to Consolidated

---

‡Author's collection.
†Legal Department, M-K-T, Dallas.
††Valuation Engineer's office, M-K-T, Denison, Texas.

Questionnaire," mimeographed (May 31, 1957) †; Interstate Commerce Commission, "Decision and Order," Finance Docket No. 19592, Missouri-Kansas-Texas Railroad Company—Abandoment—Wellington Branch, mimeographed, February 17, 1958, p. 6. †

[15]Ibid., pp. 7, 15, 12; Claude Brown, banker, Duke, Oklahoma, personal interview with the author, November 16, 1972.

[16]Earl G. Cramer, former M-K-T station agent, Vici, Oklahoma, personal interview with the author, October 28, 1971; T. A. Judy, rancher of near Mocane, Oklahoma, November 12, 1972, to the author; Jacob E. Holmes, proprietor, Holmes Livestock Co., Laverne, Oklahoma, personal interview with the author, August 24, 1972; C. M. Hester, July 14, 1959, to F. J. Heiling, Miscellaneous File, M-K-T Station, Laverne, Oklahoma, referred to hereafter as MF; C. M. Hester, October 12, 1965, to L. R. Deaver, MF; W. W. Renfro, October 20, 1965, to C. M. Hester, MF; AFE 13068-6-0 and various station maps ††; D. A. Fuhrig, May 10, 1972, to all agents, MF.

[17]*Railway Age,* Vol. 126 (February 12, 1949), p. 367; Minnie King Benton, *Boomtown: A Portrait of Burkburnett* (Quanah: Nortex Offset Publications, 1972), pp. 54-55; Sales Records, Sales Manager's office, M-K-T, Wichita Falls, Texas.

[18]*Elk City* [Oklahoma] *Daily News,* November 30, 1971; Sales Records, Sales Manager's office, M-K-T, Wichita Falls.

[19]Guy W. Howell, Jr., an official of the Sun Oil Company, December 8, 1972, to the author; Interstate Commerce Commission, Car Service Order No. 957 (December 15, 1965).†

[20]Station revenue statistics were prepared by the M-K-T Legal Department in preparation for the abortive 1964 abandonment application. †

[21]M-K-T, Northwestern Division Employes' Time Table No. 26-A (June 18, 1950) pp. 1-4; Before the Interstate Commerce Commission, Finance Docket No. 25613, "Return to Questionnaire," mimeographed (April 21, 1969), p. 6 †; M-K-T, Southern Division Time Table No. 1, (September 29, 1968), p. 13; M-K-T, Southern Division Superintendent's Bulletins, various.

[22]I.C.C., Service Order No. 957 (December 15, 1969) †; William A. Thie, General Counsel, M-K-T, personal interview with the author, March 23, 1973.

[23]David P. Morgan, "Can Mr. B. Save Miss Katy?," *Trains,* Vol. 26 (August 1966), pp. 24-26; Nancy Ford, "Can Barriger Revive the Katy?," *Modern Railroads,* Vol. 20 (October 1965), pp. 68-77; *Parsons* [Kansas] *Sun,* November 15, 1966; Katy Industries, Incorporated, *Annual Report,* 1968, p. 7.

[24]"John W. Barriger," *Railroad Magazine,* Vol. 74 (June 1963), pp. 34-36; *Who's Who in America, 1972-1973,* pp. 166-167; *New York Times,* April 6, 1969; William A. Thie, interview, March 23, 1973; M-K-T, Annual Report, 1965, p. 20; *Wichita Falls Times,* May 6, 1965, June 2, 1966, June 22, 1965; M-K-T, *Annual Report,* 1965, p. 5; Albert Dowdy, M-K-T Trainmaster, Wichita Falls, personal interview with the author, December 2, 1972.

[25]M-K-T, *Annual Report,* 1965, p. 10; ibid., 1966, p. 6; ibid., 1967, p. 7; *Parsons* [Kansas] *Sun,* September 16, 1967; Sales Records, Sales Manager's office, M-K-T, Wichita Falls. The statistics are for the crop year, i.e., beginning with the shipment of the first car in one season and extending to the shipment of the first car of the next; M-K-T, various tariffs for the dates indicated; Sales Records, Sales Manager's office, M-K-T, Wichita Falls; M-K-T, *Annual Report,* 1966, p. 12; M-K-T, Southern Division Time Table No. 1 (September 29, 1968), p. 19; *Woodward* [Oklahoma] *Daily Press,* January 26, 1972.

[26]Sales Records, Sales Manager's office, M-K-T, Wichita Falls; *A History of Beaver County,* Two Volumes (Beaver, Oklahoma: Beaver County Historical Society, 1970), II, p. 237; Earl Kerns, farmer, Gate, Oklahoma, personal interview with the author, October 19. 1972; E. B. Parks, former M-K-T station agent, Mangum, Oklahoma, personal interview with the author, November 15, 1972; L. Sam Fisher, grain dealer, Woodward, Oklahoma, April 9, 1973, to the author; Robert F. Axtell, operator of Axtell Mining Co., Gate, Oklahoma, personal interview with the author, November 9, 1972.

---

†Legal Department, M-K-T, Dallas.

[27]Ford, p. 75; *Wichita Falls Times,* May 25, 1967, June 13-16, 1967; *Laverne* [Oklahoma] *Leader-Tribune,* September 15, 1966, September 22, 1966, October 6, 1966; M-K-T, *Annual Report,* 1967, p. 1; John W. Barriger, former M-K-T President, St. Louis, February 9, 1973, to the author.

[28]Byron Bates, former M-K-T locomotive engineer, Elk City, Oklahoma, personal interview with the author, November 16, 1972; John W. Barriger, February 7, 1973, to the author; Frank P. Donovan, *Mileposts on the Prairie: The Story of the Minneapolis & St. Louis Railway* (New York: Simmons-Boardman, 1950), pp. 187-198.

From Branch Line to Short Line

[1]Claude Brown, banker and former H&E official, Duke, Oklahoma, personal interview with the author, November 16, 1972; Interstate Commerce Commission, Decision and Order, Finance Docket No. 19592, Missouri-Kansas-Texas Railroad—Abandonment —Wellington Branch, mimeographed (February 17, 1958), referred to hereafter as M-K-T Decision and Order. †

[2]Stuart L. Schokk, "Ground-Water Irrigation in the Duke Area, Jackson and Greer Counties, Oklahoma" *Mineral Report No. 18,* Oklahoma Geological Survey (Norman: Oklahoma Geological Survey, 1948), mimeographed, p. 6; Eugene Thomas, "Cities Worth Knowing, No. Thirty-One; Duke, Oklahoma," *The Consolidator,* Vol. 5 (July, 1950), pp. 4, 26.

[3]Claude Brown, interview, November 16, 1972; M-K-T, Decision and Order, pp. 6, 3.

[4]Ibid., pp. 14, 3; *Wichita Falls Times, Features Magazine,* June 28, 1959, p. 13; E. S. Stephens, former H&E President, Fort Smith Arkansas, personal interview with the author, February 6, 1973; Certificate of Incorporation, Patent, and Articles of Organization, Hollis & Eastern Railroad (October 15, 1958). ***

[5]Hollis & Eastern, Board of Directors' Minute Book, November 28, 1958. Entries are made by date and not by page number. Referred to hereafter as MB. Available at the general offices of Republic Housing Corporation, Dallas; Interstate Commerce Commission, Decision and Order, Finance Docket Nos. 20440 and 20441, Hollis & Eastern Railroad Company—Acquisition and Operation, Etc.—Jackson and Harmon Counties, Oklahoma, mimeographed (February 3, 1959), p. 1, referred to hereafter as H&E Decision and Order †; ibid., pp. 2, 3, 6.

[6]Ibid., pp. 4-5.

[7]Journal Entry No. 1 of February, 1959, a part of the MB; MB, February 24, 1958, May 20, 1959.

[8]MB, February 16, 1959; Quitclaim Deed, February 10, 1959, M-K-T to H&E, a part of the MB; Journal Entry No. 3 and No. 4 for February, 1959, a part of the MB; Bill of Sale and Agreement, February 16, 1959, M-K-T and H&E, a part of the MB; Journal Entry No. 6 of February, 1959, a part of the MB; *Deed Record,* Volume 148, Collingsworth County (Wellington, Texas), pp. 1-12.

[9]Construction Contract, H&E and S. E. Evans, Incorporated, March 13, 1959, a part of the MB; *Wichita Falls Times, Features Magazine,* June 28, 1959, p. 13; MB, November 10, 1960.

[10]Howard Cotner, member, H&E board of directors, Altus, Oklahoma, personal interview with the author, June 21, 1973; MB, January 12, 1961, January 11, 1962, October 15, 1963, December 7, 1964, October 28, 1964.

[11]Sales Records, Sales Manager's office, M-K-T, Wichita Falls; MB, March 9, 1965, April 15, 1965, May 14, 1965.

[12]MB, August 15, 1963, October 17, 1964, May 12, 1964.

[13]Ibid., June 18, 1964, December 16, 1965, September 9, 1965; V. L. Alsup, farmer

---

†Legal Department, M-K-T, Dallas.
***Oklahoma Secretary of State's office, Oklahoma City.

and rancher of near Duke, Oklahoma, personal interview with the author, November 16. 1972.

[14]Compilation of data taken from MB entries, 1966.

[15]E. S. Stephens, interview, February 6, 1973.

[16]Ibid.; *Duke* [Oklahoma] *Times*, September 16, 1971.

[17]*Annual Report of the Hollis & Eastern Railroad to the Interstate Commerce Commission for the Year Ending December 31, 1971*, p. 2; Charles Onan, H&E General Manager, Duke, Oklahoma, personal interview with the author, November 16, 1972.

[18]Ibid.; John L. Rodda, H&E Administrative Manager, Duke, Oklahoma, personal interview with the author, November 30, 1972.

[19]Ibid.

[20]*Des Moines Register,* January 6, 1973, March 21, 1973.

[21]*Wichita Falls Times, Features Magazine,* June 28, 1959 p. 13; *Duke* [Oklahoma] *Times,* September 16, 1971.

An Early Autumn

[1]L. W. Barnett, September 21, 1968, to C. W. Robbins (wire), Message File, M-K-T station, Forgan, Oklahoma ‡; Before the Interstate Commerce Commission, Finance Docket Nos. 25613 and 25614, "Prepared Testimony of John H. Hughes," mimeographed (undated, 1969), pp. 15-17, hereafter referred to as Testimony of John H. Hughes. †

[2]*Moody's Manual of Investments, American and Foreign: Railroad Securities, 1951,* p. 689, hereafter referred to as *Moody's Manual;* K. H. Hanger, "Diesels Can Operate Over Old Light Rail," *Railway Age,* Vol. 133 (October 6, 1952), pp. 98-99; AFE B-98-20 and AFE B-18-1-0 ††; C. H. Gardiner, former BM&E agent, Forgan, Oklahoma, personal interview with the author, November 19, 1971.

[3]BM&E, Employes' Time Table No. 26 (May 1, 1950); ibid., No. 27 (October 14 1956); BM&E, General Order No. 1 (January 1, 1966); ibid., No. 2 (February 20, 1969); ibid. (February 20, 1970); ibid. (March 26, 1958); AFE B-118-1-0 ††; M-K-T, Southern Superintendent's Bulletin No. 4 (January 14, 1971).

[4]*Moody's Manual,* 1954, p. 479; ibid., 1955, p. 120; ibid., 1957, p. 816; *Railway Age,* Vol. 142 (April 29, 1957), p. 9; Prepared Testimony of John H. Hughes, p. 16; D. Keith Guthrie, August 25, 1958, to Richard S. Prosser: a personal letter loaned to the author.

[5]John T. Griffin, President of Griffin Grocery Company, Muskogee, Oklahoma, October 12, and October 26, 1972, to the author; An unidentified newspaper clipping in the Griffin Grocery Company files, Muskogee, Oklahoma; *The Chronicles of Oklahoma,* Vol. XXVII (Spring 1949), pp. 120-122.

[6]W. H. Wells, former BM&E cashier at Hooker, Oklahoma, personal interview with the author, June 1, 1972; T. J. Robb, Jr., former BM&E locomotive engineer, Forgan, Oklahoma, personal interview with the author, January 11, 1973; George W. Crosby, former BM&E locomotive engineer, Forgan, Oklahoma, personal interview with the author, November 10, 1972; Personal Record File 217, BM&E station, Hooker, Oklahoma, referred to hereafter as PR.

[7]For a glimpse of a railroading as seen by employees see Richard Reinhardt, ed., *Workin' on the Railroad: Reminiscences from the Age of Steam* (Palo Alto, California: American West Publishing Company, 1970); Stanley W. Bradley, "The Railroad Boomer," *The Bulletin,* National Railway Historical Society, Vol. 37 (1972), pp. 20-21; George W. Crosby, interview, November 10, 1972; PR 131-6; Charles H. Gardiner, interview, November 19, 1971.

---

†Legal Department, M-K-T, Dallas.
††Valuation Engineer's office, M-K-T, Denison, Texas.

[8]*A History of Beaver County,* Two volumes (Beaver, Oklahoma: Beaver County Historical Society, 1970), I, pp. 459-460; PR 119-2; W. H. Wells, May 1, 1972, to the author; Byron Bates, former M-K-T locomotive engineer, Elk City, Oklahoma, personal interview with the author, November 16, 1972; BM&E, Superintendent's Bulletin No. 1 (January 10, 1966); BM&E, Employes' Time Table No. 27 (October 14, 1956); *Hooker* [Oklahoma] *Advance,* March 24, 1932.

[9]C. W. Dowdy, former M-K-T locomotive engineer, Mangum, Oklahoma, personal interview with the author, November 15, 1972; PR 123; PR 138; *M-K-T Employes' Magazine* (November 1943), p. 24; Elsie L. Walters, former BM&E station agent, Keyes, Oklahoma, personal interview with the author, July 26, 1972; F. W. Topinka, former BM&E station agent, Hooker, Oklahoma, personal interview with the author, November 19, 1971.

[10]George W. Crosby, interview, November 10, 1972; PR 116; PR 102.

[11]T. J. Robb, Jr., interview, June 29, 1972; W. H. Wells, interview, June 1, 1972; PR 217; PR 119-2; PR 141; PR 123; PR 124; *Railway Age,* Vol 125 (August 28, 1948), pp. 440; A. W. Riley, former Order of Railroad Telegraphers representative, Muskogee, Oklahoma, October 14, 1972, to the author; "Agreement Between Beaver, Meade & Englewood Railroad Company and its Employees Represented by Transportation-Communication Employees Union, No. DP-403," (November 14, 1967); "Agreement Between the Beaver, Meade & Englewood Railroad Company and Section Foremen and Section Laborers Represented by Brotherhood of Maintenance of Way Employees, No. DP-92 Revised" (October 2, 1950).

[12]*Moody's Manual,* 1960, p. 328; ibid., 1961, p. 55; ibid., 1963, p. 279; ibid., 1965, p. 128.

[13]John W. Morris, *Oklahoma Geography* (Oklahoma City: Harlow Publishing Co., 1954), pp. 149-150; *Who's Who in America, 1972-1973,* 37th Edition, Two volumes (Chicago: Marquis Who's Who, Inc., 1972), I, p. 790; Moody's Manual, 1965, p. 128; William A. Thie, General Counsel, M-K-T, Dallas, personal interview with the author, March 23, 1973; Nancy Ford, "Can Barriger Revive the Katy?," *Modern Railroads,* Vol. 20 (October 1965), pp. 68-77; *Parsons* [Kansas] *Sun,* November 15, 1966; William A. Thie, interview, March 23, 1973; M-K-T, *Annual Report,* 1965, pp. 5, 20.

[14]Public Service Assessment and Tax Rolls, County Assessor's Office and County Treasurer's Office, Cimmaron and Texas Counties (Oklahoma), for the years indicated.

[15]AFE B-118-1-D ††; M-K-T, *Miscellaneous Statistics,* Seventh Edition (Denison, Texas: M-K-T, 1972), p. 30; BM&E, various tariffs for the dates indicated.

[16]Sales Records, Sales Manager's office, M-K-T, Wichita Falls.

[17]BM&E, Private Track Agreement, Contract B-623 (April 19, 1968) ††; Sales Records, Sales Manager's office, M-K-T, Wichita Falls; BM&E, Private Track Agreement, Contract B-565 (November 4, 1964) ††; Sales Records, Sales Manager's office, M-K-T, Wichita Falls; Interstate Commerce Commission Car Service Order No. 957 (December 15, 1964). †

[18]R. B. George, December 24, 1964, to all agents †; B. R. Bishop, March 11, 1968, to F. W. Topinka, et. al. †; Sales Records, Sales Manager's office, M-K-T, Wichita Falls; J. M. McLaughlin, official of the Mobil Oil Company, Oklahoma City, December 4, 1972, to the author.

[19]Sales Records, Sales Manager's office, M-K-T, Wichita Falls; *Moody's Manual,* 1965, p. 128; ibid., 1967, p. 261; ibid., 1969, p. 282; ibid., 1971, p. 43.

Decision for Euthanasia

[1]*Wichita Falls Times,* May 6, 1965, June 22, 1965, June 21, 1966.

[2]*Denison* [Texas] *Herald,* July 8, 1968; *The Official Guide of the Railways* (December 1958), p. 647; ibid., (June 1959), pp. 623-625; *Wichita Falls Times,* November 13, 1967; M-K-T, Southern Division Superintendent's General Order No. 2 (January

---

††Valuation Engineer's office, M-K-T, Denison, Texas.

1, 1970); *Wichita Falls Times,* October 31, 1969.

[3]John W. Barriger, former M-K-T President, St. Louis, February 9, 1973, to the author; U. S. Interstate Commerce Commission, *Finance Reports,* Volume 338 (Washington D.C.: Government Printing Office, 1972), p. 730.

[4]Before the Interstate Commerce Commission, Finance Docket Nos. 25613 and 25614, "Prepared Testimony of John W. Barriger," mimeographed (undated, 1969), pp. 16, 5-6, 18. †

[5]Before the Interstate Commerce Commission, Finance Docket Nos. 25613 and 25614, "Prepared Testimony of John H. Hughes," mimeographed (undated, 1969), pp. 7-9, 13-17, 22-23. †

[6]Before the Interstate Commerce Commission, Finance Docket Nos. 25613 and 25614, *Brief of the Applicants* (August 3, 1970), p. 56, referred to hereafter as *Katy Brief* †; Before the Interstate Commerce Commission, Finance Docket Nos. 25613 and 25614, "Prepared Testimony of Billy R. Bishop" (undated, 1969), p. 9 †; *Katy Brief,* pp. 58, 60-61, 48.

[7]Ibid., pp. 16, 6, 13, 17; *Moody's Transportation Manual,* 1963, p. 279; ibid., 1965, p. 128; ibid., 1967, p. 261; ibid., 1969, p. 282; ibid., 1971, p. 54.

[8]*Katy Brief,* pp. 48, 5-6, 21, 7, 16.

[9]Before the Interstate Commerce Commission, Finance Docket Nos. 25613 and 25614, *Brief of Protestants, Oklahoma Corporation Commission,* et al. (July 27, 1970), pp. 97, 127, referred to hereafter as *Protestants Brief* †; Southern Pacific and the Texas & Pacific: John W. Barringer, March 25, 1969, to the presidents of the Southern Pacific and the Texas and Pacific, Abandonment File, Northwestern District, referred to hereafter as Katy File † ; John W. Barringer, July 9, 1969 to Jervis Langdon, Jr., Katy File; Jervis Langdon, Jr., July 22, 1969, to John W. Barriger, Katy File; *Protestants Brief,* P. 87.

[10]Ibid., pp. 106, 36, 39, 15, 38, 64.

[11]Ibid., pp. 54, 87-95, 59, 61.

[12]Ibid., pp. 84, 58, 85, 52, 73.

[13]Ibid., pp. 123, 99, 26, 33, 127, 106.

[14]I.C.C., *Finance Reports,* Volume 338, pp. 730-731, 737-739, 728.

[15]Ibid., pp. 741-742.

[16]Ibid., pp. 731, 743-748.

[17]Ibid., pp. 751-752; I.C.C., Finance Docket Nos. 25613 and 25614, Order (April 5, 1972) †; M-K-T, Southern Division General Order No. 9 (January 31, 1973).

[18]*Labor,* July 15, 1972; U.S. *Congressional Record,* 92nd Congress, 2nd Session, 1972, Vol. 118 (April 27, 1972), pp. S6808-S6809; ibid., (May 23, 1972), pp. S8206-8207; ibid., (June 30, 1972), p. S10939; ibid., (August 4, 1972), pp. S12721-S12726.

Muddy Tires and Broken Rails

[1]*Wichita Falls Times,* June 20, 1969; *Moody's Transportation Manual,* 1969, pp. 260-270, referred to hereafter as *Moody's Manual.*

[2]Ibid.; *Newsweek,* Vol. LXX (December 25, 1967), p. 59.

[3]*Dallas Times Herald,* December 7, 1970; *Moody's Manual,* 1970, p. 1706.

[4]*Tulsa Daily World,* March 16, 1972; M-K-T, *Annual Report,* 1971, pp. 1-2; ibid., 1945, pp. 42-43; ibid., 1966, p. 6; ibid., 1968, p. 11; ibid., 1971, pp. 1, 18.

[5]*Elk City* [Oklahoma] *Daily News,* November 30, 1971; AFE 14-616-6-0 and AFE N-611-1-T ††; Wesley P. Altland, former M-K-T station agent, Woodward, Oklahoma, December 10, 1971, to the author; M-K-T, Southern Division Superintendent's General Orders, various, 1969-1971; *Wichita Falls Times,* October 7, 1970.

---

†Legal Department, M-K-T, Dallas.
††Valuation Engineer's office, M-K-T, Denison, Texas.

[6]M-K-T, Southern Division Superintendent's Bulletin No. 74 (December 17, 1970); M-K-T, Southern Division Superintendent's Bulletin No. 6 (January 29, 1971); Sales Records, Sales Manager's Office, M-K-T, Wichita Falls.

[7]*Elk City* [Oklahoma] *Daily News,* November 30, 1971; Earl G. Cramer, former M-K-T station agent, Vici, Oklahoma, personal interview with the author, November 19, 1971; Floyd H. Freeman, former M-K-T station agent, Forgan, Oklahoma, personal interview with the author, November 10, 1973.

[8]*A History of Beaver County,* Two volumes (Beaver, Oklahoma: Beaver County Historical Society, 1971), II, p. 569; P. A. Johnston, former M-K-T station agent Elk City, Oklahoma, personal interview with the author, October 15, 1971; M-K-T, Train Register Book, Elk City, Oklahoma.

[9]*Daily Oklahoman,* October 20, 1972, December 13, 1972; M-K-T, 94 Report, Woodward, Oklahoma (June 13, 1972 and June 28, 1972).

[10]BM&E, Waybill Records, Forgan, Hooker, and Keyes for 1972; BM&E, Comparative Statement of Revenue Business Handled, Hooker, 1972.

[11]BM&E, Train Register Books, Forgan, Hooker, and Keyes for 1972; Lester W. Barnett, former BM&E conductor, Forgan, Oklahoma, personal interview with the author, June 27, 1972.

[12]*Sunday Oklahoman,* November 12, 1972; M-K-T, Train Register Book, Forgan; BM&E, Train Register Books, Forgan and Hooker, for 1972.

[13]*Woodward* [Oklahoma] *Daily Press,* January 4, 1973; *Daily Oklahoman,* January 4, 1973, January 5, 1973, January 10, 1973; I.C.C., Finance Docket Nos. 25613 and 25614, Order (February 23, 1972) †; *Daily Oklahoman,* September 2, 1972.

[14]*Daily Oklahoman,* October 22, 1970; Charles G. Huddleston, General Counsel for the Oklahoma Railroad Maintenance Authority, Enid, Oklahoma, personal interview with the author, June 6, 1972.

[15]*Daily Oklahoman,* March 30, 1971, June 5, 1971, June 20, 1971.

[16]*Oklahoma Session Laws, 1971,* Thirty-Third Legislature, 1st Session and Extraordinary Session (St. Paul: West Publishing Co., 1971), pp. 943-947.

[17]Charles G. Huddleston, interview, June 6, 1972.

[18]*Guymon* [Oklahoma] *Daily Herald,* October 28, 1971; *Oklahoma Session Laws, 1971,* p. 944.

[19]I.C.C., Finance Docket Nos. 25613 and 25614, Order (February 23, 1972) †; *Daily Oklahoman,* June 21, 1972; *Preliminary Feasibility Report: A Short Line Railroad in Western Oklahoma* (Norman: Oklahoma Development Foundation, 1972), p. iii.

[20]*Woodward* [Oklahoma] *Daily Press,* June 27, 1972; *Labor,* July 15, 1972; *Congressional Record-Senate,* June 30, 1972, p. S10939; ibid., August 4, 1972, pp. S12721-S12726; *Daily Oklahoman,* August 5, 1972.

[21]Ibid., September 2, 1972; Charles G. Huddleston, interview, September 1, 1972; *Daily Oklahoman,* July 27, 1972, Actober 17, 1972.

[22]*Oklahoma City Times,* November 14, 1972; *Daily Oklahoman,* November 15, 1972; *Oklahoma City Times,* November 15, 1972; *Daily Oklahoman,* November 13, 1972; *Elk City* [Oklahoma] *Daily News,* November 15, 1972.

[23]*Vici* [Oklahoma] *Beacon-News,* November 23, 1972; *Daily Oklahoman,* November 15, 1972; *Wichita Falls Times,* November 6, 1972.

[24]*Altus* [Oklahoma] *Times-Democrat,* November 30, 1972; *Daily Oklahoman,* December 8, 1972.

[25]Ibid.; ibid., January 10, 1973.

[26]Ibid., January 13, 1973, January 20, 1973; *Stillwater* [Oklahoma] *News-Press,* January 24, 1973; *Daily Oklahoman,* January 25, 1973.

[27]BM&E, Train Register Book, Hooker, Oklahoma; BM&E, Train Register Book, Forgan, Oklahoma; ironically, when the last train arrived in Forgan on January 10, 1973, BM&E agents held orders for 72 cars which on-line elevators desired for wheat loading. F. W. Topinka, former BM&E station agent, Hooker, Oklahoma, personal

†Legal Department, M-K-T, Dallas.
††Valuation Engineer's office, M-K-T, Denison, Texas.

interview with the author, January 12, 1973.

[28]M-K-T, Train Register Book, Forgan, Oklahoma; when the last train left Forgan on January 12, 1973, orders had been placed for 66 grain cars by elevators between Forgan and Woodward. Lloyd H. Freeman, former M-K-T station agent, Forgan, Oklahoma, personal interview with the author, January 12, 1973.

[29]Albert Dowdy, M-K-T Trainmaster, Wichita Falls, personal interview with the author, January 13, 1973; M-K-T, Daily Interchange Report of Cars, Form 1116, Woodward, Oklahoma, January 13, 1973; *Stillwater* [Oklahoma] *News-Press,* January 22, 1973.

[30]Albert Dowdy, February 3, 1973, to the author; L. O. Pierce, M-K-T conductor, Altus, Oklahoma, February 1, 1973, to the author.

[31]Ibid.; M-K-T, Southern Division Bulletin No. 9, January 24, 1973; M-K-T, Southern Division General Order No. 9, January 31, 1973.

Denouement?

[1]M-K-T, Southern Division Bulletin No. 9, January 24, 1973.

[2]L. H. Sapp, M-K-T Trainmaster, Denison, Texas, personal interview with the author, May 10, 1973.

[3]M-K-T, Southern Division Superintendent, Seniority Roster for Conductors, Brakemen, Switchmen, Engineers, and Firemen, July 1, 1972; L. H. Sapp, interview, May 10, 1973; T. G. Todd, February 2, 1973, to Trainmen and Enginemen Holding Seniority in Western Subdivision.

[4]*Oklahoma Journal* [Oklahoma City], January 24, 1973; *Daily Oklahoman,* January 30, 1973, January 31, 1973, February 10, 1973; William A. Thie, M-K-T General Counsel, Dallas, personal interview with the author, March 22, 1973.

[5]*Oklahoma City Times,* January 30, 1973; M-K-T, Comparative Statement of Revenue Business Handled, Form 61, Woodward, Oklahoma, December, 1972; Northwestern Oklahoma Railroad Company, incorporation papers (no file number assigned as of May 1, 1973) ***; *Sunday Oklahoman,* February 25, 1973.

[6]*Oklahoma City Times,* February 13, 1973; *Daily Oklahoman,* February 14, 1973; Veldo H. Brewer, contractor, Holdenville, Oklahoma, personal interview with the author, April 11, 1973.

[7]Ibid.; *Oklahoma Journal* [Oklahoma City], February 14, 1973.

[8]*Daily Oklahoman,* February 14, 1973; *Oklahoma City Times,* March 1, 1973; *Medford* [Oklahoma] *Patriot-Star,* January 25, 1973; *Daily Oklahoman,* January 15, 1973, February 5, 1973.

[9]AFE 73-20-6-0 and B-73-1-0 ††; Veldo H. Brewer, interview, May 5, 1973.

[10]*Daily Oklahoman,* May 4, 1973, May 10, 1973, May 11, 1973, May 25, 1973.

[11]*Sunday Oklahoman,* May, 6, 1973.

[12]*Daily Oklahoman,* June 9, 1973, June 12-13, 1973; Veldo H. Brewer, interview, June 15, 1973; Julius W. Cox, Chairman, Oklahoma Railroad Maintenance Authority, Boise City, Oklahoma, personal interview with the author, May 25, 1973, June 1, 1973.

[13]*Daily Oklahoman,* August 8, 1973; Julius W. Cox, interview, July 19, 1973, October 22, 1973; *The Daily Armorite* [Ardmore, Oklahoma], August 23, 1973.

[14]*Daily Oklahoman,* January 16, 1973, January 13, 1973.

[15]George W. Riffe, grain dealer, Baker, Oklahoma, personal interview with the author, July 19, 1973.

[16]Veldo H. Brewer, interview, January 18, 1974, June 26, 1974.

[17]Before the Corporation Commission of the State of Oklahoma, Case No. 24886, Order No. 100117, September 28, 1973 †; *Daily Oklahoman,* July 13, 1973.

[18]Compilation of data from *Poor's Manuals,* 1919-1921, *Moody's Manuals,* 1922-1971, and information supplied by Karl P. Ziebarth, M-K-T Treasurer, Dallas; V. V. Masterson, *The Katy Railroad and the Last Frontier* (Norman: University of Oklahoma

---

**WF&NW File, Baker Library, Harvard University.

***Oklahoma Secretary of State's office, Oklahoma City.

Press, 1952), pp. 285-286.

[19]Leon H. Sapp, interview, January 17, 1974.

---

†Legal Department, M-K-T, Dallas.

Index

Hocker, Mrs. Phil 150

Hocker, Oklahoma 207, 215

Hocker, Phil 37

Hocker, Walter E. 26, 27

Hollis & Eastern Railroad 158, 165, passim 173-186, 261, 270

Hollis Cotton Oil Mill 180

Hollis, Oklahoma 21, 102, 129, 155, 176, 177, 262

Hollister, Oklahoma 15

Holmes, Jacob C. 101, 159

Holmes Livestock Co. 101, 132, 159

Holmes, Mrs. Jacob C. 132

Hooker [Oklahoma] *Advance* 72, 76, 79, 81, 88, 90, 92, 108, 110

Hooker Guarantors 72, 82, 90, 91

Hooker, Oklahoma 62, 71, 72, 75, 79, 82, 84, 86, 87, 108, 110, 115, 189, 220, 227

Hooker Railroad Committee 76

Hopkins, Ed 81

Hopkins, Oklahoma 113, 115

Hopkins, Z. G. 88

Horton, Paul 177

Hossack, William 9

Hough, A. Carey 72, 74, 79, 80, 84

Hough, Oklahoma 80, 81, 84, 86, 92, 109, 115, 201, 202, 208, 220, 221, 239

Houssels, R. S. 15

Houston, Texas 109

Hovey, Oklahoma 85, 107, 113, 126, 260

Hovey's Cut, BM&E 85

Huddleston, Charles G. 231, 233, 235, 238

Huff, C. C. 20, 91, 133

Huff, R. E. 4, 9

Hughes, John H. 187, 206

Huntington, C. P. 49

Hutchinson, Kansas 83, 84, 109

Indian Territory 8

Innis, J. A. 26, 27

Interstate Commerce Commission 8, 37, 71, 73, 79, 82, 88, 153, 158, 173, 198, 203, 209, 213, 229; "Burlington Conditions" 212, 255; "downgrading of service issue" 210; "50-percent formula" 209

Iowa Central Railway 49

Isch, Ernest 261

Jackson County, Oklahoma 19, 20, 37, 173, 176, 177

Jal, New Mexico 159

Jayroe, Jayne Anne 168

Johnson, Vance 81

Johnston-Murray Bridge 150

Johnston, P. A. 130, 145, 216

Jones, Colonel Morgan 3, 7, 37

Judy, T. A. 159

Kaiser Gypsum Co. 153, 155

Kamas, George 208

Kansas 8, 9, 16, 24

Kansas & Oklahoma Railway 49, 71, 72

Kansas City, Mexico & Orient Railroad 19, 50, 94

Kansas City, Missouri 5, 47, 84, 115, 166

Kansas City Southern Railway 88, 151, 153

Kansas City Star 96

Kansas City Union Stockyards 110

Katy Industries 213

Katy Railroad. See MK&T and/or M-K-T.

Kay, Clifton 129

Kell, Frank 7, 9, 11, 15, 16, 17, 19, 23, 24, 25, 26, 27, 31, 34, 35, 37, 41, 50, 53, 55, 56, 59, 62, 263, 270

Kell, Oklahoma Territory 14, 15

Kemp and Kell lines 9, 17, 49

Kemp and Kell Office Building, Wichita Falls 42

Kemp, Joseph A. 2, 3, 7, 9, 11, 13, 17, 19, 23, 24, 25, 26, 31, 35, 37, 41, 50, 51, 53, 55, 56, 59, 203, 213, 263, 270

Kenton, Oklahoma 80

Kerns, Mr. and Mrs. Earl 166

Kerns, Mrs. Earl 97, 137

Kerns, Samuel 31, 71

Kerr-McClelland Arkansas Riverway 233

Keyes, Oklahoma 79, 80, 84, 85, 89, 92, 107, 108, 109, 113, 115, 126, 188, 196, 205, 220, 263, 270

Key, J. D. 39, 100

Kimball Elevator Co. 90

King, Samuel A. 129

Kiowa-Comanche Reservation 11, 13

Kiowa, Hardtner & Pacific Railroad 65, 67, 87, 91

Kiowa, Kansas 65

Kirby's Restaurant, Hollis, Oklahoma 179

Kirkhart, Lois 196

Knaught, F. R. 12

Knaught, Nachod & Kuhne Co. 51

Knight, Dan R. 184

Knight, H. E. 85

Knight, H. L. 108

Knowles, Oklahoma 27, 34, 39, 41, 45, 47, 100, 101, 159, 164, 208, 262

Laird, Dr. 44

La Junta, Colorado 25, 62

LaKemp & Northwestern Railroad 67

LaKemp, Oklahoma 39, 67

Langford, Kenneth R. 177